Theology and the Cartesian Doctrine of Freedom

Other Books of Interest from St. Augustine's Press

Theology and the Cartesian Doctrine of Freedom

Étienne Gilson

St. Augustine's Press
South Bend, Indiana

Manufactured in the United States of America.

1 2 3 4 5 6 25 24 23 22 21 20 19

Library of Congress Cataloging in Publication Data
Gilson, Étienne, 1884–1978.
[Doctrine cartésienne de la liberté et la théologie. English]
Theology and the Cartesian doctrine of freedom / Étienne Gilson; translated by James G. Colbert.
pages cm
Includes bibliographical references and index.
ISBN 978-1-58731-858-0 (hardback)
1. Descartes, René, 1596–1650. 2. Free will and determinism. 3. Philosophy and religion. 4. Theology, Doctrinal – History – 17th century.
5. Jansenists. I. Title.
B1875.G5313 2015
194 – dc23 2015011369

∞ The paper used in this publication meets the minimum requirements of the American National Standard for Information Sciences - Permanence of Paper for Printed Materials, ANSI Z39.48-1984.

St. Augustine's Press
www.staugustine.net

Table of Contents

Translator's Preface

Gilson began his publishing career a little over one hundred years ago with a study of the theological environment in which modern philosophy, that is to say Cartesian philosophy, arose. Behind the theologians who were Descartes' contemporaries stood Augustine, Aquinas, and Scotus, and the rest, as they say, is history. But before Gilson devoted his life to medieval thought, he produced a work that gives us a splendid feel for the French seventeenth-century intellectual world and brings Descartes to life in a way the *Meditations on First Philosophy* or the *Discourse on Method* taken by themselves fail to do. *Theology and the Cartesian doctrine of Freedom* is not Gilson's last word on Descartes. It was followed by his *Discours de la méthode, Texte et Commentaire* in 1925 and *Études sur la rôle de la pensée médiévale dans la formation du système cartésien* in 1930. Gilson also directed Henri Gouhier's doctoral thesis on Descartes' religious thought, which was followed by several other books by Gouhier on Descartes. However, the present book is an arresting view of Descartes' place in the great tradition, I believe, well worthy of attention.

Gilson habitually gives very faithful paraphrases of the authors he presents. Therefore, it seems unnecessary to translate Latin footnotes. The occasional Latin phrases included in the body of the text not only reinforce Gilson's paraphrases but also eloquently remind us of Descartes' Scholastic background.

On the other hand, Gilson's mode of referring to Adam and Tannery's complete works of Descartes is often unhelpful for those who have access to that multi-volume work. I have tried to complete the references and have verified the Latin quotations from the *Meditationes de Prima Philosophia* and the *Principia Philosophiae*. Gilson, incidentally, frequently refers to the *Meditations* by the title of the French version, *Méditations métaphysiques* without indicating thereby that he is referring to the French translation as opposed to the Latin original. The translations of passages from Descartes' letters are mine, but I have checked my versions against those letters and those passages that appear in volume III of *The Philosophical Writings of*

Descartes, Correspondence, translated by John Cottingham, Robert Stoothoff, Dugald Murdoch, and Anthony Kenny.

I have verified all references to St. Thomas, correcting a few typographical errors. Gilson cites *Summa Theologiae* I, 82, 6. Part I, question 82, which has only five articles in the two versions of the *Summa* I have checked, and I have been unable to locate the passages cited as coming from I, 82, 6, elsewhere.

Gilson uses the Wadding edition of Scotus, in some cases getting material from Wadding through secondary sources. Although he faithfully acknowledges this, his practice in citing does not always make the exact origin clear. I have verified references to Scotus (or pseudo-Scotus), and I have indicated references to the Vivès edition in square brackets. Gilson mentions *De Rerum Principio* and *Meteorologia*, or more correctly *Quaestiones Meteorologicae*, which are apocryphal, as he notes in his *Jean Duns Scot*. But of course Descartes, and more importantly his contemporaries, did not know that.

Obviously, references to material published after 1913 or in English are mine.

I would like to thank Professor Walter Redmond for his help in translating material in German.

James G. Colbert

INTRODUCTION

We would like, first of all, to specify briefly the particular goal we have pursued.

The reader should not expect to find unpublished texts of Descartes in this work. After so many research projects whose object was to find those texts and, above all, after the admirable labors of Charles Adam and Paul Tannery, such discoveries are hardly to be expected. We can only hope for chance discoveries of the very rare texts that may have escaped all past researchers.

Still, we have not limited ourselves to the simple study of Descartes' texts as their recent editors present them to us. We believe that the multitude of analyses and syntheses of Cartesian thought, carried out by so great a number of perceptive historians and philosophers, precludes that method's leading to new results. Accordingly, we do not propose to reconstruct Cartesian philosophy or to rediscover the internal structure of his system and its general orientation by enclosing ourselves within its texts. The standpoint we have chosen to adopt is quite different.

We want to attempt with Cartesian philosophy an experiment that has often given excellent results with other philosophical or literary works. We want to discuss what is involved in placing a work back into its environment. Perhaps nothing needs this more than Descartes' philosophy, because there are few philosophies that historians have more obstinately tried to isolate from their existential conditions. It seems that philosophical thought was completely overhauled by Cartesianism, that the *Cogito* marks the frontier separating the age of Scholasticism from the period of modern philosophy in the vast field of the history of ideas. The advent of Descartes would mean a complete break with the philosophy of the past. It is not within the scope of the present work to investigate what shaped this view. However, it is contradicted by the very general law that every product of human thought is closely tied to the environment where it arose and to the conditions in which it developed.

The environment in which Cartesian metaphysics was born and developed was essentially theological. In the sixteenth century, it would have been very difficult to emancipate philosophical thought from the guardianship of theology. Descartes' teachers were theologians by profession. They taught the Scholasticism of St. Thomas, a philosophy where the reason for being of each proposition was in the theological developments to which it contributed. A great many of Descartes' friends and correspondents were theologians. He dedicated the *Meditations on First Philosophy* to certain theologians and expected objections from them. He chose the format of *Principles of Philosophy* with Jesuit schools in mind. In this period, there was still no philosophical audience distinct from the audience of theologians, because the distinction between philosophy and theology had not yet been really achieved. Descartes intended to inaugurate this distinction, but centuries-old habits of thought subsisted, and perhaps his break with the past was less noticeable in his work than in his intentions.

If this is the case, it is conceivable that a new point of view on Descartes' work may be possible, which would consist of searching for clarifications on Cartesian philosophy in the theological environment where that philosophy took shape. In fact, in the last few years, many scholars have perceived that it would be useful to situate themselves in this perspective, as fissures have kept appearing in the closed system of Descartes' doctrine.[1] Our only goal will be to take this standpoint and, by considering a clearly delimited part of Descartes' doctrine, examine it as completely as possible. It may sometimes seem that we have wandered from philosophy into theology, but when Descartes attempts to resolve the dual problems of divine and human freedom, he comes in the wake of numberless theologians whose ponderings on these matters would fill many volumes. He cannot help taking them into account, and the historian of philosophy as such cannot ignore them without being exposed to a number of mistakes.

Our objective might be summed up in these terms: to bring out everything that can explain the structure and development of the Cartesian doc-

1 Cf. the studies by Freudenthal, Hertling, etc. See the introduction to our *Index scolastico-cartésien*. [Translator: Étienne Gilson, *Index scolastico-cartésien*, Paris: F. Alcan, 1912 and Paris: J. Vrin, second edition, 1979.] Jacob Freudenthal, 1839–1907 was a historian of philosophy who wrote on ancient philosophy and Scholasticism but especially on Spinoza; Georg Freiherr von Hertling, 1843–1919, "Descartes' Bezihung zur Scholastik," in vol. II, S*itzungsberichte der Bayerischen Akademie der Wissenschaften Philosophisch-Philologische und Historische Klasse*, 1898.]

trine of freedom within the theological environment in which the doctrine arose. That is the essential goal we pursue, without renouncing the possibility of consideration of different orders when it seems necessary.

We are not deceived about how delicate this sort of research is. If some useful and definitive results can be found among the hypotheses that we formulate, we will be pleased that credit be given to those who were our teachers at the Sorbonne: Lucien Lévy-Bruhl (to whom we owe several of the guiding notions of this project, in addition to the primary conception of our research) and Victor Delbos. Through their advice and their example in scrupulously applying a method to the problems of history of philosophy, they have always been our guides. May their pupil be allowed here to testify to his deepest gratitude.

Part I

Divine Freedom

Chapter One

Descartes at La Flèche The Texts

Among the theological influences that greater impact on Descartes' thought, the most general and least debatable is that of St. Thomas. Throughout the present study, we will assume this influence, and we will not hesitate to invoke the teachings of the *Summa Theologiae* and of its commentators when they seem capable of bringing some elucidation. Accordingly, it is important to resolve a preliminary problem immediately: Did Descartes know St. Thomas's theology and can we believe that he knew it sufficiently for it to exert real influence upon his thought? There can be no doubt about the answer. We know that Descartes studied philosophy in the Jesuit school of La Flèche, where (as he writes to a correspondent) philosophy was taught better than other places in the world.[1] Descartes takes care to tell us that he was a pupil there and informs us that he was not judged inferior to his companions, although several among them were destined to fill the places of their teachers.[2]

Descartes completed the whole cycle of philosophical subjects as it was organized at La Flèche School and devoted the years 1609–1610, 1610–1611, and 1611–1612 to that cycle. Baillet gives no information about his teachers, but we know from other sources that Fr. François Véron was his professor for this period and Fr. Étienne Noël was the *repeater* [Translator: teaching assistant]. The fact that Fr. Véron was Descartes' teacher is certified by the list of teachers at La Flèche preserved in the Gesù Archives in Rome.[3] It would not be useful to study Fr. François

1 Letter to... September 12, 1638, II, p. 378. (References are to volume and page of Descartes, *Oeuvres*, edited by Charles Adam and Paul Tannery, 13 volumes, Paris: L. Cerf, 1897–1910. For *Principia Philosophiae* and the *Passions* the book and chapter will be indicated.)

2 *Discourse on Method*, VI, p. 5. We refer to pupils from the Jesuit novitiate, who took their philosophy courses at La Flèche.

Véron in the hope that his doctrine might let us perceive the first outlines of Cartesian philosophy. For some time it was thought that it might be possible to find the seeds of Cartesianism in Descartes' teacher, but it seems necessary to renounce any such endeavor for two reasons. The first is that a philosophy teacher at a Jesuit school would have been removed from his post at the first sign of any inclination to stray from the straight path of Scholasticism. Descartes' teacher could only teach the doctrines of Aristotle and St. Thomas. The second reason is that even if the circumstances had allowed him to do so, Fr. François Véron was not the man to wander from Scholasticism, and it would be truly difficult to see a precursor of his pupil in this teacher. A celebrated controversialist and apologist, Fr. François Véron had won recognition with several works of apologetics.[4] He was born in Paris in 1578 and entered the Society of Jesus on September 10, 1595. By temperament, Fr. Véron was a militant, aggressive controversialist. He seems to wonderfully embody the spirit of that Scholasticism ardent for disputation, harsh in the struggle of ideas, passionate about argument, and having no greater joy than silencing an

3 This list was first published by A. Georget (*Une découverte qui n'est pas une*, Tours: Ladevèze, 1870) and a second time by Fr. Camille de Rochemonteix, S.J. (*Le Collège Henri IV de La Flèche*, 4 vols., Le Mans: Leguicheux, 1889). Vol. IV is particularly useful to establish the environment in which Descartes lived.

4 The most famous was *Methodus Veroniana qua nimirum ex quibusvis Bibliis cuivis haeretico ministro silentium imponitur*. See Sommervogel's article "Véron."

[Translator: Augustin de Backer, S.J., rediscovered the version of *Biblotheca Scriptorum Societatis Iesu*, published in Rome in 1676. It had successively been re-worked by Pedro de Ribadeneyra, S.J., Philippe Alegambe, S.J., and Nathaniel Southwell, S.J. With his brother Alois de Backer, S.J., Augustin de Backer is co-author and co-editor of the seven-volume *Bibliothèque des écrivains de la Compagnie de Jésus*, first edition, Liège: Grandmont-Donders, 1853–1861. The second edition adds as co-authors and co-editor Carlos Sommervogel, S.J., Liège and Paris: 1869–1876. A. de Backer is listed as the Liège publisher and C. Sommervogel as the Paris publisher. Carlos Sommervogel continued the labor under the title of *Bibliothèque de la Compagnie de Jésus*,

[The lengthy English title of the work by Véron published at Douai: Widow of L. Kellam, 1616 makes Gilson's point crystal clear: *M. le Hucher minister of Amyens in France compelled to fly from the pure word of holy write; strucke dumme; and made to runne away: Vppon the subiect of the B. Sacrament of the altar. By F. Francis Veron of the Society of Iesus, encountring him with the Bible of Geneua only. In the presence of the Duke de Longueuille. VVith a briefe and easie meanes, by which each Catholike may, in like manner, put to flight any minister or sectarie. Sent from Sieur de la Tour one of the sayd Dukes gentlemen, to Sieur de Rotois, gentleman of the Kings game.*]

enemy by arguments put into form and developed in good order. In Fr. Véron's case, the enemy was the Protestant, and if the method Véron employed to combat the Protestant had any influence on Descartes, it was to alienate him from it forever, so much did it bring together in one place all the imaginable defects that Descartes was to reproach in the Scholastic method. Furthermore, the field of scholastic disputes soon became too narrow for Véron's activity. He opened up a broader field by leaving the Society of Jesus during 1620 to occupy the parish of Charenton, where he remained until his death, which occurred December 6, 1649. Despite an interesting biographical essay,[5] Véron's life during this period is not well known. What is reported about him only reveals his concern to put into practice the celebrated method he discovered: to provoke the most prominent Protestant ministers, to compel them to enter into public disputation with him, if necessary to engage them in their churches and in the place of predication, and ultimately, through the rigor of his dialectic, to drive them to confess their errors or take flight — such seems to have been his only concern during the years he spent as pastor of Charenton. As evidence of this feverish activity, Fr. Véron left us some eighty works whose exact enumeration has not yet been made,[6] and whose titles are all summons to battle or bulletins of victories, for example "The Shameful Flight of the Sieur du Moulin." These or the defeat of some ministers are the ordinary subject of his narratives. This was Descartes' teacher: a great debater, ardent polemicist, but without interest in renewing philosophy or in remaking the indestructible work of Aristotle in any part, however minimal. Fr. Noël's personality seems to have been more original. Destined to a brilliant future in the Society of Jesus, this young priest would have been more capable of departing from the paths trod by Aristotle, but nothing lets us think that he dreamed of doing so during the period when he was young and without authority and had no other duty than to faithfully comment on Fr. Véron's course. When later, after an already long career, he

5 *Un curé de Charenton aux dix-septième siècle*, by one of his successors, Fr. Pierre Féret, Paris: J. Gervais, 1881.

6 Sommervogel only gives us the works written by Véron while he belonged to the Society of Jesus. In his 1825 edition of François Véron's *Règle générale de la foi catholique*, Paris-Besançon, Jean Labouderie gives a bibliographical note on the works written by Véron after he left the Society. Fr. de Backer made some additions to this notice in vol. III of his *Bibliotheca Scriptorum Societatis Iesu*, but, Sommervogel remarks, "Neither of them has the last word on the question." A number of Fr. Véron's works are likewise mentioned in Pierre Feret's work cited above.

introduced some new ideas in his *Aphorismi Physici* or his *Sol Flamma*, it was partly under the influence of the movement created by Descartes, so that the influence seems to be exercised less by the teacher on the pupil than by the pupil on the teacher.

Accordingly, we believe there are no grounds to search in the teaching Descartes received at La Flèche for the seed of new ideas that he was to offer. But on the other hand, we certainly can look for the Scholastic concepts that Descartes would never forget, despite his distaste for them. Philosophical studies at La Flèche were distributed over a period of three years.[7] These studies lasted so long only in important schools that had a sufficient number of students. In the Paris Province, only the La Flèche and Clermont schools had three years of philosophy. La Flèche in particular had up to 200 students in philosophy at one point in time. To use Descartes' own words, he completed the whole philosophy program and not an abbreviated program taught in the less important centers. The first year (1609–1610) was devoted to logic and ethics; the second (1610–1611) to physics and mathematics; and the third (1611–1612) to metaphysics.[8] We have reason to think that there was hardly a minute wasted in these three years: two lectures of two hours per day, plus a daily repetition; an oral argument every Saturday and every month a solemn competition in which pupils disputed with their philosophy professors and their companions. All these exercises took place in Latin, and imposed a scholastic discipline on those who engaged in them, whose rigor cannot be exaggerated.[9]

The doctrine of Aristotle and St. Thomas essentially constituted the

7 We will hold to the dates provided by Baillet in what regards Descartes' stay at La Flèche. The hypothesis offered by Adam (XII, pp. 564–65) that would push back Descartes' departure from La Flèche to 1614, is based on considerations that could make it fairly plausible. Moreover, it is clear that Baillet's reliability about dates is very much open to challenge. Still, given that Descartes' own affirmations about the length of his stay at La Flèche (IV, pp. 122, 160–61) are contradictory, it seems more prudent to retain Baillet's dates until there is more evidence to the contrary.

8 Here we reject the order followed by Baillet, who gives the following organization: 1609–1610, logic and ethics; 1610–1611, physics and metaphysics; 1611–1612, mathematics (cf. Baillet, *Vie*, 1, 24, 26, 27). This organization corresponds to the order followed by the Jesuits at the point when Baillet wrote; but the plan of studies had been changed in 1626. From 1606 to 1626, the period that includes Descartes' stay at La Flèche, the program of studies of philosophy was what we have given (cf. Rochemonteix, *Le Collège*, IV, pp. 29 and 32.) The plan of studies completed by Descartes must be reconstructed according to these indications.

9 Rochemonteix, *Le Collège*, IV, p. 22.

content of the teaching thus organized.[10] It was recommended that the teacher should only depart from Aristotle where he taught propositions contrary to faith or different from the more generally accepted opinion. This teaching in no way sought originality and required that the teachers *communiores magisque nunc approbatas philosophorum sententias tueri*. This is why the courses followed St. Thomas's interpretation of Aristotle. The rule of conduct for the good philosophy teacher was to follow Thomas everywhere it was possible, and depart from him only rarely and always with deference. The fidelity of the members of the Society of Jesus to their superiors' instructions, the discipline that reigned in the order, the philosophy textbooks published by them during this period that rigorously comply with the orientations we have indicated, are sure guarantees that these guidelines were followed.[11] Therefore, it is certain that Descartes was subject for three years to a scholastic discipline of a kind that subsequently made it unlikely for him to be ignorant of anything about the essential positions of St. Thomas's philosophy. If we add to this that the religious education properly speaking must have continually recalled Descartes' attention to Scholastic demonstrations of Christian dogmas, we can hardly conceive that he ever escaped from the influence of his teachers, however much he believed he had, and that in no case did he ever completely forget their teaching.

Accordingly, Descartes left La Flèche a skilled disputant, nourished by Scholastic philosophy. Several anecdotes in Baillet, which may be true at least at their core,[12] would incline us to think so, as would the facility with which he intersperses his French with Scholastic Latin.[13] How long he remained in contact with Scholastic philosophy after leaving school is harder to decide. In reading the first part of the *Discourse on Method*, we rather

10 On this point we will limit ourselves to remit the reader to what Rochemonteix writes about the teaching at La Flèche, basing himself principally on the *Ratio Studiorum* of 1586 (cf. *Le Collège*, IV, p. 22 and supporting material). The details that could be added to this exposition would not shed light on Descartes. However, we will observe that to our understanding, literal explanations of Aristotle, as the *Ratio Studiorum* imposes them, must have been rare in class. Courses dictated in this period and half-witted manuscripts abound in libraries, and they contain either complete courses, where commentary occupies the whole space, or summaries of courses, but nothing ever indicates that an explanation of texts ought to be inserted at any place.

11 Regarding the textbooks, see below and also the passages published in the *Index scolastico-cartésien*.

12 Baillet, *Vie*, I, pp. 136, 163.

13 Letter to Clerselier, April 23, 1649, V, p. 357.

get the impression that from the end of his schooling and almost during it, Descartes distanced himself from the useless study that detains itself at merely likely opinions. Also, as soon as his age allowed him, Descartes abandoned entirely the study of letters, by which we understand Scholastic philosophy, to no longer seek from another science what he could find in himself or else in the great book of the world.[14]

However, there are some reasons to believe that this break was neither so rapid nor so complete as it might seem. If only out of prudence, it was necessary for Descartes to assure himself that his doctrines were not going to clash with Church teaching and that his works should not seem to be weapons aimed at the Scholastic philosophy. For this reason alone, Descartes must never have completely stopped reading the Scholastics, at least the most famous and authoritative ones. We know that 25 years after he left La Flèche, he went on a trip taking a *Summa* of St. Thomas,[15] besides the Bible. Moreover, in a letter of 1640, Descartes declares that he has not read Jesuit philosophy for twenty years. If we take this figure to be precise, it would put back the date when Descartes stopped reading the Scholastic philosophers, at least in Jesuit manuals, to 1620. However that may be, it remains certain that his break with St. Thomas was never absolute or definitive. Did Descartes read other Scholastics? It is probable that at La Flèche besides the course of his professor, he must at least have consulted some well-known manuals of his time. The supposition is all the more reasonable if we remember that Jesuits composed most of them, and they must have been given to their pupils. At La Flèche, Descartes knew "the Conimbricenses, Toletus, and Rubius" to whom we must add the Feuillant monk, Eustachius a Sancto Paulo,[16] author of a *Summa* of Philosophy, valuable for its clarity and concision. The first three names are attached to a series of commentaries on the texts of Aristotle, with which the course faithfully fulfilled the program drawn up in the *Ratio Studiorum* of 1586. It gives us a very precise idea of the course Fr. François Véron must have given at La Flèche.

14 *Discourse on Method*, VI, p. 9.

15 "Besides, I am not so lacking in books as you think and I still have a *Summa* of St. Thomas and a Bible that I brought from France." To Mersenne, December 25, 1639, II, p. 630. There is no way to determine whether it was the *Summa contra Gentes* or the *Summa Theologiae*.

16 Letter to Mersenne, September 30, 1640, III, p. 185. See III, pp. 194–196 for the summary bibliography of these authors. [Translator: The Feuillants were a branch of Cistercians.]

Apart from these textbook authors and St. Thomas, it is impossible to affirm that Descartes read or even consulted any Scholastic philosopher. The passages in his *Correspondence* make it difficult to make up one's mind on this point. Let us simply note that Descartes verified the meaning of a Scholastic term in Suárez,[17] that he cited Peter Lombard,[18] Duns Scotus,[19] and Nicholas of Cusa.[20]

The incidental bits of information that Descartes furnishes us about his reading are not very helpful. All that can be affirmed is that the teaching of the Jesuits, of which the period's manuals give us an idea, saturated young Descartes with Scholastic philosophy for three years or at least more than two years. For the detail of the ideas, only a comparison of texts will allow us to establish which Scholastic doctrines were known to Descartes that he wanted to oppose, and also those that, "after having adjusted them to the level of his reason," he simply took up and utilized. Before attempting this test on the Cartesian conception of divine freedom, it is advisable to consider the conception itself in the texts where it is set out.

If we place value on its first appearance, the problem of divine freedom seems to occupy only a secondary place in Cartesian philosophy. In the *Meditations* and the *Principles*, Descartes develops his conception of human freedom unconcernedly. He remains silent about what pertains to divine freedom. A passage on God's creative power now and then barely manages to recall that everything without exception takes its origin from that power.[21] Or again, in a few lines, Descartes very quickly affirms that God produces all things by a single, simple action, always similar to itself, because at the same time, he understands, wills, and produces all things.[22] But nothing lets the reader who is not on the lookout guess that under these few words hides perhaps what is Descartes' newest and quite certainly one of his most fertile metaphysical conceptions. It is difficult to see the reason for this silence or at the very least for this extreme discretion.

We will perhaps be all the more astonished because very early on, the ideas of the philosopher were fixed upon this point. From 1630 in three letters to Mersenne he sets the conceptions out in their boldest and most paradoxical side. He proposes "in his *Physics* to touch upon" a certain number

17 Second response, *Quartae Responsiones*, VII, p. 235.
18 *Méditations Métaphysiques*, IX, p. 230.
19 *Méditations Métaphysiques*, IX, p. 94.
20 *Discourse on Method*, VI, p. 51.
21 *Principia*, I, 24.
22 *Principia*, I, 23.

of metaphysical questions and particularly to demonstrate that the mathematical truths have been created by God and are dependent on him in the same way as other creatures: "It is, indeed, to speak of God as of a Jupiter or Saturn and to submit him to the Styx and destiny, to say that these truths are independent of him."[23] Descartes begs Mersenne to assure and broadcast everywhere that God has established the laws in nature as a king establishes the laws in his kingdom, and he immediately gives the proof that the eternal truths really depend on God who established them. None of these truths, in fact, exceeds the limits and range of our understanding. They are innate in us, therefore contained in our thought and there is none of them that we could not comprehend if our mind gives itself over to considering it. God's greatness is known to us but incomprehensible. This very incomprehensibility of God, by making us better perceive the distance that separates us from him, gives us a more exalted idea of his power, just as a king is more inspiring to his subjects if they know him from a little further off than if they belong to his household. This is why we must judge God's greatness, which is knowable to us but incomprehensible, to be above the eternal truths that are all comprehensible to our minds.[24]

Such an argument seems to provoke a very serious objection. The eternal truths appear immutable to us. If God's will has created them freely, we cannot be sure that the same will is not going to change them, just as when it pleases a king, he can change the laws he has established. However, there is a simple answer to this difficulty. God's will could change the eternal truths, if his will could change; but God's will is immutable and eternal; therefore the truths it has created are immutable and eternal.[25]

Perhaps it will be objected that this solution produces a new problem. If God's will is immutable and cannot change, how are we to admit that on the other hand it is free? But here we must bow before the incomprehensible power of God. Our finite mind cannot understand how the divine will can be at the same time free and still immutable. It remains for us to admit it without explaining it. We can certainly affirm that God can make all that we can understand and that consequently he can make the eternal truths. But it would be absurd to affirm that infinite God could not make something incomprehensible to our finite spirit. Therefore, we will recognize without understanding it that God is at the same time immutable and free. Moreover,

23 Letter to Mersenne, April 15, 1630, I, p. 145.
24 Letter to Mersenne, April 15, 1630, I, p. 145
25 Letter to Mersenne, April 15, 1630, I, p. 146.

Descartes is so sure of his thought on these various points that he wants to write all this in his physics within the next two weeks. However, with his customary caution, Descartes begs Mersenne to take advantage of opportunities to disclose the ideas just expounded, always provided that he do so without naming Descartes. Descartes expects thereby to become aware of objections that will be made and also to arrange a better reception for his ideas.[26]

This desire to see the public become accustomed to his ideas reveals a Descartes whose thought is surer of itself than of its orthodoxy. Moreover, starting with Mersenne's response, he must have felt the beginning of the resistance he foresaw. He offers ever more categorical affirmations against Mersenne's objections. Whether we consider the eternal truths as possibles within God's understanding or as realized actuals, they must be said to be true or possible because God knows them as such rather than that God knows them as such, because they are possible or true.[27] Since Mersenne no doubt distinguished between the eternal truths in relation to God's understanding and their independence in relation to his will, Descartes destroys the possibility of such a distinction at its very root. We cannot say that the eternal truths are prior to God's knowledge or to his will, because will and knowledge are one in God. Just by wanting something God knows it, and it is true for that alone. To express ourselves otherwise is blasphemy and furthermore absurd, because it amounts to affirming that even if God did not exist, these truths would still be true. Rather, God's existence is the first and most eternal of all the truths that can be, and the one from which alone all the others proceed.[28] Descartes bases this new affirmation on the reason he had briefly set out in the previous letter, the difficulty we experience in admitting that the eternal truths, and notably the mathematical truths, were created by God comes from our comprehending these truth with perfect certainty, while God, by contrast, is only imperfectly known. The atheists conclude quite wrongly that, if they are certain, these truths cannot depend on God whose existence they do not comprehend perfectly, while the true conclusion ought to be completely the opposite. Our understanding perceives some truths that it can completely grasp and also a divine power that is

26 Letter to Mersenne, April 15, 1630, I, p. 146

27 "For the eternal truths, I say flatly: *sunt tantum verae aut possibiles quia Deus illas veras aut possibiles cognoscit, non autem contra veras a Deo cognosi quasi independenter ab illo sunt verae.*" Letter to Mersenne, May 6, 1630, I, p. 149.

28 Letter to Mersenne, May 6, 1630, I, p. 150.

incomprehensible; it ought to judge that these truths "are something less than that incomprehensible power and subject to it."[29] Furthermore, the objection that could be drawn from the necessity of the Trinitarian processions of the divine persons, processions where God's free will does not intervene, ought not to be taken into consideration here. The necessity that may exist in the production of the Word in relation to the Father does not conflict with what we have said about divine freedom, and, furthermore, here we have a point of theology, about which Descartes need not be concerned.

Mersenne was not yet satisfied by these responses and no doubt thought that by establishing the eternal truths Descartes had not meant a strict creation of these truths, but simply a disposition of them or their production through a kind of causality different from the efficient cause, for example, the exemplary cause. However that may be, in a last response Descartes clarifies and leaves no escape: To Mersenne who asks: "*In quo genere causae Deus disposuit aeternas veritates?*"[30] Descartes responds that it is *in eodem genere causae* that God created everything, that is to say *ut efficiens et totalis causae.*[31] God created them as efficient cause, strictly and according to the Scholastic definition, *id a quo veritates aeternae sunt aut fiant.* And he created them as total cause, that is, God alone suffices to account for all that these eternal causes contain. By himself, God furnishes the complete explanation of their total being.[32] Therefore it is impossible to admit the solution Mersenne must have proposed: God is considered as knowing the eternal truths or the essences of things from all eternity and creating them by a free decree of his will in the sense that it depends on him alone that this or that essence should be effectively realized. This distinction cannot be admitted because, since God is the efficient and total cause of all things, he is that cause of all that these things contain, therefore the cause of essences as well as of existences. These essences are nothing but the

29 Letter to Mersenne, May 6, 1630, I, p. 150.

30 Letter to Mersenne, Amsterdam, May 27, 1630 (?), I, p. 151.

31 Letter to Mersenne, Amsterdam, May 27, 1630 (?), I, p. 151.

32 Cf. Eustachius a Sancto Paulo, *Summa Philosophiae*, IV, 61: "Quinta [*scilicet*, species efficientis causae] in totalem et partialem, quo spectat alia divisio in sufficientem et non sufficentem; illa dicitur quae sola in suo ordine et genere totum effectum producit, ut equus qui solus traheret currum; haec vero quae cum alia aut pluribus ejusdem generis et ordinis concurrit ad eumdem effectum producendum, quod ut plurimum contingit, quia sola non posset ipsum producere, ut cum plures equi trahunt currum. Tunc unus quisque ex illis censetur causa efficient partialis istius tractionis."

eternal truths, "which I do not conceive as emanating from God like the rays of the sun; but I know that God is the Author of all things, and that these truths are something, and consequently, that he is their Author."[33] Besides, there can be no surprise that this production of eternal truths by God is something incomprehensible, because God is infinite and all-powerful, while our soul is finite and limited. But we can know without comprehending; we can touch him with our thought without taking him in with our thought. If our reasoning leads us to acknowledge that God, who is author of all things, must have created the eternal truths, which are things, then we certainly ought to admit it, although our finite mind cannot comprehend it.

Mersenne still asks: Since these truths are necessary and yet God created them, what necessitated God's having created them? To this Descartes answers: nothing. We ordinarily recognize that God was free to create or not to create the world, and that creatures are not conjoined to the divine essence. The same must be said of the eternal truths, which are creatures like others: "and I say that he was as free to make it untrue that all lines drawn from the center to the circumference are equal as to not create the world."[34]

Lastly Mersenne asks: Therefore what is the nature of the act by which God produces these eternal truths? The reply is that God produced things by an absolutely simple act; simply by having wanted and understood them, he created them.[35]

Moreover, to understand this act, no priority must be attributed to the will, the understanding, or to creation. In God, will, understanding, and creative power make just one thing, not only in the sense that will, understanding, and creative power are not three separate attributes and three really distinct things, but in the sense that among them there is not even a distinction of reason. There is nothing in God that justifies a distinction, however superficial we might make it, between his power, his understanding, and his will.

As for the new theological objection that Mersenne tries to oppose to Descartes' conception, namely that if God created eternal truths, he also created

33 Letter to Mersenne, Amsterdam, May 27, 1630 (?), I, p. 152.

34 Letter to Mersenne, Amsterdam, May 27, 1630 (?), I, p. 152.

35 "I say that *ex hoc ipso quod illas ab aeterno esse voluerit et intellexerit, illas creavit,* or else (if you only want to apply the word *creavit* to the existence of things) *illas disposuit et fecit.* Because, in God it is one and the same to want, to understand, and to create, without one preceding the other, *ne quidem ratione.*" Letter to Mersenne, May 27, 1630 (?), I, pp.152–53.

good and evil and that consequently if God wanted, he could damn all humans indistinctly for eternity, Descartes does not have to respond because the issue is within pure theology. He does not admit the arguments of the libertines who entrench themselves behind the impossibility in which we are placed of avoiding damnation, if God has judged it good to damn us. On the contrary, he believes their reasons are frivolous and absurd. By building on an argument that he doubtless takes from St. Thomas, Descartes alleges that the wish to base these truths on human reasons that are only probable and incapable of demonstrating them is to wrong the truths of faith, which are revealed and consequently known with certitude from their supernatural source.[36]

These passages contain Descartes' whole doctrine on divine freedom, and he will add nothing further to his thought on this point. In the three letters to Mersenne, we find the categorical affirmation of God's creation of the eternal truths and the arguments upon which Descartes bases this affirmation. We see how he is interested in giving rigorous expression to his thought on this subject and what importance he attributes to his position, since he gives it a decisive place among the questions he proposes to touch upon in his physics. However, the *World* had not appeared because Galileo's condemnation frightened Descartes, and Descartes refrains from publishing his opinion during some time. He is silent in the *Discourse on Method* in 1637. Nor does Descartes say more in the *Meditations* in 1641. It is only after unexpected circumstances and to answer a criticism that dealt with another point that Descartes took advantage of the occasion offered him to develop his thought publically in the *Responses to Objections*.

It is not that Descartes felt any hesitation in the intervening period or that he retreated the slightest bit from his first opinion. Eight years after

36 "But because I hold that it is to wrong truths that depend on faith and that cannot be proved by rational demonstration, to want to affirm them through merely human and probable arguments . . ." Letter to Mersenne, May 27, 1630 (?), I, p. 153. Cf. St. Thomas Aquinas, *Summa Theologiae*, part I, question 32, article 1: "Qui autem probare nititur Trinitatem personarum naturali ratione, fidei dupliciter derrogat. Primo quidem quantum ad dignitatem ipsius fidei, quae est ut sit de rebus invisibilibus, quae rationem humanam excedunt; unde apostolus dicit Ad Hebraeos, 11:1 quod *fides est de non apparentibus*; et idem Apostolus dicit I Ad Corinthios 2:6: *Sapientiam loquimur inter perfectos*; *sapientiam vero non hujus saeculi, neque principium hujus saeculi; sed loquimur Dei sapientium in mysterio, quae abscondita est.* Secundo quantum ad utilitatem trahendi alios ad fidem. Cum enim aliquis ad probandum fidem inducit rationes quae non sunt cogentes, cedit in irrisionem infidelium. Credunt enim quod hujusmodo rationibus innitamur, et propter eas credamus."

writing to Mersenne in the terms we reported, we meet it again. The context is to determine whether there would be real space if God had created nothing. Descartes recalls to Mersenne that in his opinion not only would there be no space, but even the eternal truths would not be truths if God has not wished them to be. Furthermore, he recalls having written this to Mersenne previously.[37] Apart from this brief recollection, we must arrive at the *Quintae Responsiones* to see this conception (which Descartes had intended to publish since 1630) openly expounded. In the Fifth Meditation, seeking to determine the essence of material things,[38] Descartes discovers an infinity of ideas about certain things within himself, which, although perhaps they have no real existence outside him, still cannot be considered pure nothing. Although it is within our freedom to think them or not to think them, it still does not depend on us to make them up, because they have their true and immutable natures. If I imagine a triangle, Descartes adds, although perhaps there is no such figure in any corner of the world and it never existed, still there is a certain determined nature or form or essence of this figure, which is immutable and eternal, which I have not invented at all, and which in no way depends upon my mind.[39] Moreover, this seems evident from the fact that I can demonstrate different properties of this triangle, for example that its angles are equal to two right angles, that the largest angle is subtended by the largest side, and a great many others that I know clearly and distinctly belong to it, and that I cannot have made up or invented, since I did not think about them at all the first time I imagined a triangle.

In his objection, Gassendi emphasizes the expression *natura immutabilis et aeterna*, and without wanting to linger on the point, he only insists that it seems hard to witness an immutable and eternal nature thus established outside of the thrice great God.[40]

37 "On the question: to know whether there would be real space just as now, in the case that God had created nothing, although it seems to go beyond the limits of the human mind and that it is not at all reasonable to argue about it any more than about the infinite, still, I believe that it only is beyond the limits of our imagination, like the question of the existence of God and of the human soul, and that our understanding can reach the truth about it, which is, at least in my opinion, that not only would there be no space, but even that those truths that are called eternal like *totum est maius sua parte*, etc., would not be true at all, if God had not established it so, which I believed I already wrote you previously." Letter to Mersenne, May 27, 1638, II, p. 138.

38 *Meditations* (Fifth Meditation), VII, p. 64, lines 6–24.

39 *Meditations*, (Fifth Meditation), VII, p. 64, lines 14–17.

40 Fifth Set of Objections to *Meditations*, VII, p. 319.

Descartes rejects the objection with some vigor. Responding as if he were addressing some Scholastic, he first makes Gassendi note that his objection would be relevant if the passage in question dealt with really existing things instead of simple essences.[41] At least, it would also be necessary that what he is reproached with having posited as immutable should be so in such a way that this immutability did not depend on God. Going behind the simple Scholastic viewpoint here, Descartes employs a comparison that lets us glimpse his real thought. The immutability he has recognized in certain natures, like the nature of the triangle, is a completely conditional immutability subordinated to God's free will; in Scholastic language we would say immutability *ex hypothesi*. Just as the poets imagined that destiny was once created by Jupiter, who then submitted himself to it, so Descartes thinks that the essences of things and all these mathematical truths that can be drawn from them, are not independent of God, but, nevertheless, because God has so willed it and so disposed it, they are immutable and eternal. Furthermore, Gassendi may find this hard or soft; it is enough for Descartes that it is true.[42]

In this reply to Gassendi and also in some other lines of the *Quintae Responsiones*, an attentive mind may discern the conception Descartes had formed of the origins of the eternal truths. After having written that God had created them as Jupiter had created destiny, Descartes would again speak of these true and immutable natures that God had established.[43] Besides, Descartes had wanted Mersenne to make Descartes' later critics see the objections that the earlier critics had made and the replies he had directed to them.[44] There were enough of them for the theologians who examined the *Meditations* and the *Replies* at the same time to raise objections on this point so closely connected with theological speculation. In the *Sextae Objectiones* we meet a two-pronged attack on the Cartesian conception of divine freedom.

41 "Merito sic videtur, si de re existente quaestio esset." *Quintae Responsiones*, VII, p. 380, lines 2–3.

42 ". . . ita, ego non puto essentias rerum mathematicasque illas veritates quae de ipsis cognosci possunt, esse independentes a Deo; sed puto nihilominus, quia Deus sic voluit, quia sic disposuit, ipsas esse immutabiles et aeternas. Quod seu durum, seu molle esse velis, sufficit mihi quod sit verum." *Quintae Responsiones,* VII, p. 380, lines 7–13.

43 "Multae veritates . . . quae . . . merito dicuntur immutabiles et aeternae . . .; et . . . haud dubie sunt conformes verae illi rerum naturae quae a Deo condita est." *Quintae Responsiones*, VII, p. 381.

44 Letter to Mersenne, January 21, 1641, III, p. 282.

The first of the two concerns that engaged Descartes' critics arose from his conception of human freedom, more specifically from his critique of "freedom of indifference." In several texts to which we will have to return, the philosopher had denied that indifference constituted a perfection of freedom and, on the contrary, affirmed that it was a genuine defect; to such an extent that the indifference would disappear each time the soul clearly discovered what it must believe, do or not do. Such positions necessarily would lead to the destruction of divine freedom. What did not belong to human freedom could not belong to divine freedom, because the essences of things are like numbers, immutable and indestructible. Human nature, for example, does not apply to one human more or less than to another human. Likewise, we cannot add anything to an essence any more than to a number without changing the nature of this essence or without changing the nature of the number.[45] Therefore, God's freedom cannot be different by nature from man's, and if indifference is a defect in our freedom, it follows that it is equally a defect in God's. That cannot be maintained, if we reflect that, on the one hand, we must admit as a truth of faith that God has been indifferent from all eternity to creating this world rather than another or to creating just one or several or none; and, on the other hand, we cannot doubt that God has always seen in a very clear intuition what he was to do or not do. It follows from this that a very clear vision and conception of things does not suppress indifference, and, since essences are indivisible, that in God or in us, indifference is part of genuine freedom.[46]

The second concern stems from the replies Descartes offers to the fifth objections and resolutely poses the problem of the eternal truths. How can the geometrical or metaphysical truths, like the truths that Descartes recalls, be immutable and eternal without still being independent of God? Taking up a phrase that would seem to come from the hand of Mersenne, the

45 Eustachius a Sancto Paulo, *Summa Philosophiae*, IV, 34: "Essentiae . . . dicuntur indivisibiles, quod nulla sit natura quae secundum rationem specificam inaequaliter participetur ab individuis, ut patet inductione; verbi gratia, natura humana non est secundum magis vel minus in uno quam in alio homine; quo fit ut non datur unus magis homo quam alter. Deinde etiam, quia nihil quod pertineat ad essentiam addi vel detrahi potest, quin statim mutetur et fiat alia natura seu essentia. Ex quo intelligere est illud quod docet Aristoteles 8 *Metaphysicae* capitulo 3, t. 10: essentias rerum esse numeris similes; sicut enim numerus addita vel sublata, unitate mutat speciem, sic addito vel detracto essentiali aliquo actu essentia seu natura rei mutat speciem."

46 *Sextae Objectiones*, VII, pp. 416–17.

contradictor asks: "In what genus of cause do they depend on him?"[47] Could God therefore, make the nature of the triangle not exist? How could he make from all eternity that it should not be true that two times four is eight, or that the triangle should not have three angles? Consequently, it must be admitted either that these truths depend on our understanding only while it thinks them, or that they depend on existing things, or else that they are independent absolutely speaking, since it does not seem that God could have acted in a fashion that any of these essence should not exist from eternity.[48]

To the first objection that we just reported, Descartes would reply by denying that it is legitimate to assimilate divine freedom to human freedom, and in a letter to Mersenne he immediately disputes that we may reason about God starting from humans.[49] Moreover, he did not at all think that it is *de fide* to hold that God is indifferent and, in fact, Descartes is right to doubt strongly that there is a point of faith here, since no Council has ever defined the proposition in this form. In the eyes of Descartes, this proposition could only be of any importance in the case that a dogmatic definition of indifference had been imposed. According to him, this indifference not only belongs to God's will, but also constitutes its highest perfection. His only ambition is to understand better than St. Thomas and in a manner more worthy of divine omnipotence. As for his contradictor, Descartes responds in the *Sextae Responsiones* and, putting the Scholastic distinctions to work in his turn, opposes the contradictor with a direct argument. The principle of indivisibility of essences does not permit us to affirm that freedom is identical in God and man. When we conclude thus from humans to God, we forget the great Scholastic principle that no attribute can belong *univoce* to God and creatures.[50]

47 "Nam in quo genere causae dependent ab eo?" *Sextae Objectiones*, VII, pp. 417–18. Cf. Letter to Mersenne, Amsterdam, May 27, 1630 (?), I, p. 151: "*In quo genere causae Deus disposuit aeternas veritates*?"

48 *Sextae Objectiones*, VII, pp. 417–18.

49 Letter to Mersenne, April 21, 1641, III, p. 360: "As to my writing that indifference is rather a defect than a perfection of freedom in us, it does not follow that it should be the same in God, and still, I do not know at all that it is *de fide* to believe that God is indifferent..."

50 "Neque hic refert quod essentiae rerum dicantur esse indivisibiles; nam primo nulla essentia potest univoce Deo et creaturae convenire . . ." *Sextae Responsiones*, VII, p. 433. Cf. St. Thomas, *Summa Theologiae*, part I, question 13, article 5: "Respondeo dicendum quod impossibile est aliquid praedicari de Deo et creaturis univoce . . . Et sic cum hoc nomen, *sapiens*, de homine dicitur, quodammodo circumscribit

To the contrary, it would be more logical to conclude that if indifference belongs to divine freedom, that can only be in a completely different sense from what is meant by indifference in human freedom and one that supposes no imperfection in God.

The essence of freedom is completely different in God. We must recognize that it must be accepted that God's will is indifferent from all eternity to anything that has been done or ever will be done. For, there is "no idea that represents the good or the true, that which must be believed, that which must be done or must be omitted, that we may claim was the object of the divine understanding before its nature was constituted as such by the determination of God's will."[51] Therefore, God's freedom is supremely indifferent, because it is impossible to conceive any priority between the divine will and the divine understanding, so that no idea of Good could push God to choose one thing rather than another. It is not just priority in time that is inadmissible, but we cannot admit a priority in natural order or of reasoned reason [translator: *ratio ratiocinata*]. The distinction between the divine will and divine intelligence is a distinction that has no basis in the nature of things and corresponds to absolutely nothing in God. We must observe to what degree Descartes' affirmations, which are expressed here in Scholastic language, are precise and rigorous. He is not content to reject grossly anthropomorphic conceptions that would picture the eternal truths as first conceived by the divine intellect and later accepted by the will. Descartes rejects the conception, to which we will return, of a basically identical will and understanding, but between which a priority of order can be established according to which one or the other is given preeminence; or again a priority of nature according to which we admit that the understanding does or does not condition the will. Descartes refuses any distinction of reasoned reason. That is to say, one that claims to be justified by an appearance, however minimal, of distinction between the understanding and the will of God.[52] For

et comprehendit rem significatam, non autem cum dicitur de Deo; sed relinquit rem significatam ut incomprehensam et excedentem nominis significationem. Unde habet quod non secundum eamdem rationem hoc nomen, *sapiens*, de Deo et de homine dicitur. Et eadem ratio est de aliis. Unde nullum nomen univoce de Deo et creaturis praedicatur."

51 IX, p. 233 and *Sextae Responsiones,* VII, p. 432.

52 *Sextae Responsiones*, VII, p. 432: "Neque hic loquor de prioritate temporis, sed ne quidem prius fuit ordine, vel natura, vel ratione ratiocinata, ut vocant, ita scilicet ut ista boni idea impulerit Deum ad unum potius quam aliud eligendum." Cf: Francisco Suárez, *Disputationes Metaphysicae*, disputation 7, section 1, number 14:

example, God did not want to create the world in time because he saw it would be better than to create it in eternity. He did not want the three angles of a triangle to be equal to two right angles, because he knew it could not be otherwise. On the contrary, because he wanted to create the world in time, it was better that way than if God had created it from eternity. It is because he wanted the angles of a triangle to be necessarily equal to two right angles that this is true now and could not be otherwise, and so on for everything else.[53] Perhaps it will be objected that the merits of the saints are the cause of their obtaining eternal life. But these merits are not the cause in the sense that they determine God to want something or other. They are the cause of the saints' salvation as of an effect of which God from all eternity wished that they should be the cause.[54] From all that, we must conclude that the surest sign of God's omnipotence is the supreme indifference that we discover in him. Is it necessary to observe that matters are completely different for man, who finds the nature of all good and all truth already determined by God? Since his will cannot give itself over to anything else, it is evident that humans embrace the good all the more voluntarily and all the more freely, and they discover the true more clearly. Finally, it is evident that humans are never indifferent except when they do not know what is best, or truest, or at the very least when they do not see with enough evidence to be unable to doubt it. This indifference applies to human freedom in a completely different sense than to divine freedom.[55]

With that, we see the fitting response to the theologians' second misgiving. When we are careful about God's immensity, it becomes evident that absolutely nothing exists that does not depend on him — not only

"... est certum dari praeter distinctionem realem distinctionem rationis. Et est illa, quae formaliter et actualiter non est in rebus quae sic distinctae denominantur, prout in se existunt, sed solum prout substant conceptibus nostris et ab eis denominationem aliquam accipiunt, quomodo distinguimus in Deo unum attributum ab alio, vel relationem identitatis a termino, quando dicimus: Petrum esse idem sibi. Haec autem distinctio duplex distingui solet: una quae non habet fundamentum in re et dicitur *rationis ratiocinantis* . . . alio quae habet fundamentum in re, et a multis vocatur *rationis ratiocinatae*." [Translator: *Disputationes Metaphysicae*, Salamanca: 1597, 2 folio vols. Gilson does not give an edition but might have used the *Disputationes* in vols. 25 and 26 of the 28 volume *Opera Omnia*, Paris: Louis Vivès, 1856–1878. This was reproduced Hildesheim: G. Olms, 1975. The *Disputationes* are available on-line.]

53 *Sextae Responsiones*, VII, p. 432

54 *Sextae Responsiones*, VII, p. 432.

55 *Sextae Responsiones*, VII, pp. 432–33.

nothing in existence, but even no order, no law, no essence of the true and the good. If things were otherwise, God would not have been perfectly indifferent to creating what he has created.[56] If any essence of the good had preceded its preordination, it would have determined God to do the best, whereas to the contrary, because God has decided upon just what is to be done now, these things, in the words of Genesis, *sunt valde bona*.[57] In other words, the reason for their goodness, for what good may be in them, depends on God having made them such. There is no point in seeking by what form of causality this goodness and the other truths, whether mathematical or metaphysical, depend on God. Since those who enumerated the different kinds of causes doubtless did not imagine that there could exist a causality of this nature, there would be nothing surprising about their not having given it a name.[58] However, they did give one. It can be called *efficient*, and we can recognize the same nature in it as what makes the king be author of the law, although the law is no longer something endowed with physical existence but is what is called a moral being. There is no longer any room to seek how God could have been able to make from all eternity two times four be eight, and so forth. There is no doubt whatever that this is unintelligible for us. However, we also understand clearly that there is no kind of being, physical or moral, true or possible, being of existence or being of essence, which does not depend on God. Furthermore, it is easy to institute certain things in such a way that it becomes incomprehensible for us humans that these things should be otherwise than they are. Consequently, it would be unreasonable to doubt a thing that we do clearly comprehend because of another that we do not comprehend and that we do not see that we should comprehend. It is wrong to conclude that the eternal truths depend on the human understanding or on the existence of things other than themselves.

56 *Sextae Responsiones*, VII, p. 435: "Attendenti ad Dei immensitatem, manifestum est nihil omnino esse posse, quod ab ipso non pendeat; non modo nihil subsistens, sed etiam nullum ordinem, nullam legem . . . nullamve rationem veri et boni; alioqui enim ut paulo ante dicebatur, non fuisset plane indifferens ad ea creanda quae creavit." For the meaning of *subsistens* in this passage, cf. Eustachius a Sancto Paulo, *Summa Philosophiae*, IV, 41–42: "Subsistere enim quinque modis praesertim dicitur; primo enim idem est, ac vere et realiter esse."

57 *Sextae Responsiones*, VII, pp. 435–36: "Sed contra, quia se determinavit ad ea qua jam sunt facienda . . ." Clerselier translates inexactly, *Méditations métaphysiques,* IX, p. 235: ". . . because he has decided to make the things that are in the world . . ." [". . . parce qu'il s'est déterminé à faire les choses qui sont au monde . . ."]

58 *Sextae Responsiones*, VII, p. 436.

They depend on God alone, who as sovereign legislator established them from all eternity.[59]

Descartes' correspondence lets us conclude that he never abandoned this point of view. In 1644 he wrote to Mesland that, as difficult as it is to conceive, it must be admitted that it was "free and indifferent for God to make untrue that the three angles of a triangle should equal two right angles, or generally, that contradictions cannot be together."[60] The reason that leads us to admit this is, first, that God's power cannot have limits. Then, there is also the consideration

> . . . that our mind is finite and created to be of such a nature that it can conceive as possible the things that God wanted to be truly possible, but not of such nature that it could also conceive as possible those that God could have made possible but that he, however, wanted to make impossible. The first consideration makes us realize that God cannot have been determined to make it be true that contradictions cannot be together, and that consequently he could have done the contrary. Then, the other consideration assures us that, although it is true, we ought not to strive to comprehend it, because our nature is not capable of it. Although God wanted that some truths should be necessary, that is not to say that he willed them necessarily. It is something completely different to will that they be necessary and to want necessarily or to be necessitated to will.[61]

Perhaps it will be objected that there are certain contradictions that we cannot imagine even for a single instant that God could have made to be true, for example, that creatures would not be dependent upon him. Unquestionably, when we think about contradictions of this sort, we can only judge them "entirely impossible." Also, we must not picture them, if we want to know the immensity of his power, and we must not "conceive any preference or priority between his understanding and his will. The idea we have of God teaches us that there is only a single action in him, completely simple and

59 "Nec proinde putandum est *aeternas veritates pendere ab humano intellecto, vel aliis rebus existentibus,* sed a solo Deo, qui ipsas ab aeterno, ut summus legislator, instituit." *Sextae Responsiones*, VII, p. 436.

60 Letter to Mesland, May 2, 1644, IV, p. 118.

61 Letter to Mesland, May 2, 1644, IV, p. 118.

completely pure, something St. Augustine's words express very well: *Quia vides ea, sunt . . .*[62] for in God *videre* and *velle* are but one and the same thing."[63] Lastly, in his conversation with Burmann[64] and in a letter of July 29, 1648 to Arnauld, Descartes maintains this same point, declaring that everything good or true that can exist depends on God's omnipotence, to such a degree that it cannot be said that it would be impossible for God to make a mountain without a valley or to make two and two be three.[65]

As has been rightly observed,[66] the texts where Descartes affirms his conception of divine freedom are scattered throughout his entire philosophical life. In our philosopher's eyes, this is a fundamental doctrine, one that we would like to connect with the generally accepted theological teaching of his time.

62 St. Augustine, *Confessions*, book XIII, chapter 38.

63 Letter to Mesland, May 2, 1644, IV, p. 119.

64 Conversation with Burman, V, p. 165.

65 Letter to Arnauld, July 29, 1648, V, pp. 223–24: "Mihi, autem non videtur de ulla unquam re esse dicendum, ipsam a Deo fieri non posse; cum enim omnis ratio veri et boni ab ejus omnipotentia dependeat, nequidem dicere ausim, Deum facere non posse ut mons sit sine valle, vel ut unum et duo non sint tria, etc.; sed tantum dico illum talem mentem mihi indidisse, ut a me concipi non possit mons sine valle, vel aggregatum ex uno et duobus quod non sint tria, etc., atque talia implicare contradictionem in meo conceptu."

66 Émile Boutroux, *De Veritatibus Aeternis apud Cartesium*, Paris: G. Bailliere, 1874, (reproduced Kessinger Publishing, n.d.) p. 11.

Chapter Two
Descartes' Adversaries

Descartes' thought on the question of divine freedom, as on many other matters, is set up in opposition to Scholastic philosophy. Where we might be tempted to look for the expression of a line of thought that is developed for its own sake, very often we ought to see the negation of this or that doctrine that was familiar to his contemporaries. In what follows we will see how this is the case with passages in which Descartes sets out his conception of divine freedom. Therefore, if we wish to delve into the meaning of this conception, it is first important to know the adversary whom Descartes intended to oppose on this point.

If we pay attention to the text of the first letter in which Descartes broaches the question, we can hardly establish that he had a particular adversary in mind. He simply seems to be opposed to those who try to remove the domain of eternal truths from God's free choice and to render them independent of the Creator in any way whatsoever. In what does this pretended independence consist? Descartes, who is sharing a simple project of criticism with Mersenne, does not clarify that. In a general way, he rejects the wish to constitute the eternal truths as an order of reality at whose origin creation is not found. In all likelihood, Mersenne himself, in a lost letter, requested Descartes to make his thought on this point more precise. The issue is to discover what is understood by this objectionable independence of the eternal truths. Did Descartes simply want to say that mathematical truths must not be conceived as subsisting from all eternity in God's understanding independently of his will? Or must the term *independence* rather be taken in the strong sense as meaning a priority of eternal truths and essences of things in relation to God's will with his understanding? These two very different viewpoints need to be distinguished here. Whatever Mersenne's additional questions may have been, it is certain that in his answer Descartes seems deliberately to employ *independent* in the strong sense. What he proposes to criticize is the conception of eternal truths that not only removes them from the free decree of the divine will, but, furthermore, considers them as subsisting in themselves, independently of the divine understanding and prior to the knowledge God has of them. The eternal truths are only true or possible because God knows them as true or possible. But God does not recognize them as true as if they were so outside of him. What must not be said is: *Si Deus non esset, nihilominus istae veritates essent verae.*[1]

Can we discover the adversary whose conclusions Descartes is rejecting? We cannot draw any information on this point from the letters to Mersenne. Descartes attacks "the unrefined" or "people," without specifying further. Whether out of prudence or the simple habit of never attacking an author openly, or whether ultimately he is not really thinking of any particular adversary, Descartes does not cite a philosopher to whom the theories he refutes could be connected. At least it would seem that, if he envisages an adversary, it is neither St. Thomas nor some Scholastic philosopher. Within the terms in which the problem is posed, Descartes and Scholasticism agree perfectly on the appropriate solution. In neither of these two philosophies could the supposition have any meaning that there could exist eternal truths, even if God did not exist. Descartes declares this conception absurd. Anyone who reflected on it would not dare to say that the truth of something could subsist independently of God. Likewise, St. Thomas, in establishing the existence of exemplar forms or ideas in God, denies that these ideas or forms could exist outside of God and elsewhere than in the divine understanding. That would be to suppose the absurdity that God does not find within himself all that is necessary for his action and that he is obliged to seek the exemplar forms, the models of what he does, outside his own essence.[2]

This is impossible because God could not seek a goal or rule of action outside of himself; independent essences would still be that, because nothing exists that is not God or a creature of God. On this point, we cannot differentiate between essences and existences. When God gives being to an essence, he does not only create the being but also the essence. Therefore, it is impossible to claim that God only creates existence and not essence, since before receiving existence this essence was nothing. It already existed in

1 Letter to Mersenne, May 6, 1630; I, pp. 149–50.

2 St. Thomas Aquinas, *Quaestiones Disputatae de Veritate*, 3, 1, end of body of article: "Sed quia forma exemplaris vel idea habet quodammodo rationem finis, et ab ea accipit artifex formarum qua agit si sit extra ipsum; non est autem conveniens ponere Deum agere propter finem alium a se, et accipere aliunde unde sit sufficiens ad agendum; ideo non possumus ponere ideas esse extra Deum, sed in mente divina tantum."

some manner in the creator's understanding, but it was not there *qua* creature. It was the creative essence. Therefore, if we consider essences in the divine understanding, they are part of the divine essence. If we consider them *qua* created essences, they are nothing, either as existence or as essence, before being created. Consequently, in no case are they independent of God.[3] This doctrine of St. Thomas is the constant Scholastic doctrine. If the opposite thesis seemed reprehensible to Descartes, it seemed absolutely incompatible with Catholic doctrine to Suárez. We cannot imagine a Catholic teacher admitting that in itself, and without God being its free efficient cause, the essence of a creature could truly be a thing, truly possessing a being that is real and distinct from divine being.[4] If we consider the essences of creatures as actually realized and existing outside the divine essence, it must be recognized with St. Thomas that in this precise sense they are not absolutely anything before having been created by God.[5] Therefore, when Descartes opposes those who say that even if God did not exist, the eternal truths would exist, he is in complete agreement with Suárez and St. Thomas.

Furthermore, we can hardly doubt that Descartes heard this reproach directed against some theologian during the course of his studies at La Flèche. The accusation was both frequent and serious, and adversaries hurled it at each other. For example, Suárez congratulates a theologian for having numbered among Wycliffe's heresies the affirmation that creatures possess a real being, distinct from God's being, from all eternity.[6] Also, we know that the Thomists reproached Duns Scotus for maintaining a doctrine of this kind, an accusation that is manifestly absurd[7] if we ponder what

3 St. Thomas Aquinas, *Quaestiones Disputatae de Potentia*, 3, 5, reply to objection 2: "Ad secundum dicendum, quod ex hoc ipso quod quidditati esse attribuitur, non solum esse, sed ipsa quidditas creari dicitur; quia antequam esse habeat, nihil est; nisi forte in intellectu creantis, ubi non est creatura, sed creatrix essentia."

4 Suárez, *Disputationes Metaphysicae*, disputation 31, section 2, number 3: "Nec potuit in mentem alicujus doctoris catholici venire, quod essentia creaturae ex se et absque efficientia libera Dei sit aliqua vera res, aliquod verum esse reale habens distinctum ab esse Dei."

5 Suárez, *Disputationes Metaphysicae*, disputation 31, section 2, number 1: "Principio statuendum est, essentiam creaturae, seu creaturaram de se et prius quam a Deo fiat, nullum habere in se verum esse reale, in hoc sensu praeciso esse existentiae, essentiam non esse rem aliquam, sed omnino esse nihil." In all these texts, we regard the terms *essence* and *eternal truths* as synonyms. The reason will appear by itself in the continuation of our exposition.

6 Suárez, *Disputationes Metaphysicae*, disputation 31, section 2, number 1.

7 Cajetan, *Commentarium Summae Theologiae*, part I, question 17, article 5.

Scotus teaches about divine freedom. It is true, on Suárez's account, that Scotus directs the same reproach at Henry of Ghent. Henry is accused of writing in different places that the essences of things possess a certain being in themselves *qua* essences, real, eternal, and uncreated being; this being would belong to creatures independently of God and would be prior in them not only to the efficacy of the divine will, but also to the knowledge God has of them.[8] However, if we recur to the texts under attack and in general to the passages where Henry treats the question, we can report that he never maintained anything of the sort. The Augustinian Henry of Ghent[9] distinguishes the essence insofar as it exists in the divine understanding *qua* exemplar from the essence considered as existing when it is produced by divine creation in time.[10] To say of the essence, insofar as contained in the divine understanding, that it is *res* disagrees in nothing with constant Scholastic doctrine. It matters little that essences are considered realities, if these realities are not situated outside of God himself, that is, if we consider them as existing in God's intellect from all eternity. The essences of things are true essences and existences in themselves, although they still only subsist in God. Therefore, according to this doctrine, it follows that God cannot be eliminated without, by that very fact, eliminating the eternal essences of things.[11] Only an inexact interpretation of the texts allows the rejected doctrine to be attributed to Henry of Ghent. The distinction that he establishes between *esse essentiae*, the being possessed by the essence insofar as it is

8 Suarez, *Disputationes Metaphysicae*, disputation 32, section 2, number 2: "Quin potius idem Scotus in allegata distinctione 36, impugat Henricum, eo quod variis locis asseruerit, essentias rerum ex se habere quoddam esse essentiae, quod vocat esse reale aeternum et improductum, conveniens creaturis independenter a Deo, quodque in eis supponitur, non solum ante efficientiam, sed etiam ante scientiam Dei."

9 Henricus or Henry of Ghent or de Gandavo. See Henricus Gandavo, *Summa Quaestionum Ordinarium Theologiae*, Paris: Badius, in folio, 1520. Also *Quodlibeta Magistri Henrici Goethals a Gandavo*, Paris: Badius, in folio, 1519.

10 Henricus, *Summa*, 21, 4, article 9: "Essentia enim, ut dictum est, dicitur res ex respectu ad Deum, inquantum ab ipso exemplata est ab aeterno. Dicitur autem existens, ex respectu ad Deum in quantum ipsa est effectus ejus ex tempore."

11 Henry of Ghent, *Quodlibeta* 8, question 1: "Sed sciendum est quod secundum rationes ideales Deus alia a se intelligit dupliciter. Uno modo secundum quod sunt essentiae vel existentiae quaedam in se. Alio modo secundum quod sunt quaedam operabilia a Deo . . . Unde et Plato hujusmodi ideas in Deo posuit esse ipsas rerum quidditates, dicente Seneca . . . Plenus est iis figuris quas Plato ideas appelat; itaque homines pereunt, ipsa vero humanitas ad quam homo effingitur permanet."

the object of knowledge in an understanding, and the *esse existentiae* that things possess in themselves outside the understanding, forbids him to subscribe to the affirmation that the essences really exist outside of God. Let us add that in his turn Henry reproaches Avicenna with having neglected this distinction and posited things as really existing outside the divine understanding.[12] Whatever may be the case on this last point, it certainly seems that Suárez is right to put in doubt, as a general proposition, that a Catholic theologian could maintain such a doctrine. In the mutual reproaches, we need only see a familiar procedure of Scholastic dialectic. The conceptions of those who do not agree are declared perverse and reprehensible. But the fact remains that in Descartes' first two letters to Mersenne, he seems in his turn to have remembered this very frequent accusation and made it fall upon a doctrine of which he disapproved.

As strange as it may seem after the texts we have just cited, this doctrine is none other than St. Thomas's own. Doubtless, when Descartes rejects the conception of eternal truths and essences independent of God, he is aware that he only repeats in almost the same terms, what Suárez and St. Thomas said before him. But he uses a procedure with respect to them that we have seen the theologians use among themselves. If Suárez and St. Thomas do not expressly maintain the conception of independent eternal truths and essence (which, to the contrary, they formally reject), still it is necessarily deduced from their doctrine. Therefore, we can make them responsible for it and impute it to them. We see the first lines of a completely different conception sketched starting with the 1630 works. The eternal truths would no longer be considered as able to subsist in themselves and independently of the creator, but as subsisting in God's understanding independently of his will. However different these two conceptions may be, we can still believe that Descartes did not distinguish them. He considers them as resting upon a common foundation, and he even sees the second as the natural foundation of the first.

Eternal truths or essences of things come to be seen as realities independent from God and prior to divine knowledge from arbitrarily distinguishing intelligence and will in God. When divine intelligence is considered separately, we are naturally led to attribute content to it. For example, we admit that the essence of things or eternal truths subsist in the divine intelligence from all eternity with the character of necessity that we acknowledge in them. Thereby, the essences are endowed with an existence

12 Henry of Ghent, *Quodlibeta* 8, question 3.

independent of God's will, and we deny that they draw their origin from a creative act. From Descartes' point of view this is to set up the eternal truths as realities independent of God. According to Descartes, God's understanding and his will are just one thing. Consequently, to say that the eternal truths are independent of God's will is to say that they are independent of his understanding. Nothing can be taken away from one without being taken away from the other. However, the *Response to Objections* clearly shows that Descartes does not really confuse the two points of view and that he does not harbor the delusion that Scholasticism had really maintained the doctrine he condemns. In these 1641 works, Descartes no longer seems to envisage the consequences of this distinction from the same standpoint. While in the letters to Mersenne, he changes from one conception to the other without the slightest qualm, in the *Responses to Objections* he seems to take care not to confuse them, when he directs himself to representatives of the pure doctrine of St. Thomas. There, confusing "independence in regard to the divine will" and "independence in regard to God" would doubtless make him liable to be accused of ignorance or bad faith. Accordingly, we will see him limit his critique to the strict terms of Scholastic doctrine. He no longer opposes the conception of independence of the essences of things in regard to the divine intelligence, but only in regard to God's will.

After Mersenne's letters of 1630, certain texts aim especially at this second theory. At that moment, some of Descartes' criticisms already seem intentionally directed against the conception of St. Thomas and of doctors who appeal to Thomas's doctrines on this point. Going by appearances and only reading certain passages of Suárez superficially, we might believe that even on this second point there is perfect agreement between Descartes and his old teachers. As we have seen, both start from the principle that God is the creator of all things, the author of all that exists. It is a doctrine of faith that God alone is a necessary being-of-himself, that nothing has been made without him, and that without his creative power nothing either exists or can possess any real being.[13] From the fact that nothing possessing any reality can exist without being created by God, Descartes concludes that God must create the essences that are realities [translator: essences of real beings]. Such is also Suárez's conception. Without the existence of their first cause,

13 Suárez, *Disputationes Metaphysicae*, disputation 31, section 2, number 3: "Ex ratione probatur ex principiis fidei, qua solus Deus est ens ex se necessarium, et sine illo factum est nihil, et sine effectione ejus, nihil est aut aliquod esse reale in se habet."

the effects that we know could possess no reality. Therefore it is impossible that the essence of things possesses any real existence independently of the Creator's existence.[14] But Descartes goes further. He not only wants the essence to depend on God, he wants God to have created them freely, that they not emanate necessarily from him like the rays of the sun.[15] This is certainly how Suárez understands all creation, and he denies in the same terms that God produces things by natural necessity, by an action that purely and simply flows from him.[16]

Nevertheless, the agreement is only apparent. To get the exact sense of Suárez's doctrine, we must appeal to the distinction of essences into possible and real. A possible essence is not a pure being of reason, that is to say, a being that has no other being than what is conferred to it by human thought, and that only belongs to non-being. The possible essence exists *qua* object of divine knowledge and consequently is capable of real existence. In some measure, it is a being. But it is not an actual being properly speaking, for otherwise it would no longer be a possible. The essence of the creature considered precisely in itself, and before it is realized by creation, has no other actual being than that of its cause.[17] This is precisely the mode of existence that the eternal truths have from all eternity. They possess a certain real

14 Suárez, *Disputationes Metaphysicae*, disputation 31, section 2, number 4: "Item, quia remota existentia et efficientia primae causae nihil omnino manet in effectu, ut ostensum est; ergo, neque essentia manere potest sub aliquo vero esse reali distincto ab esse creatoris."

15 Letter to Mersenne, Amsterdam, May 27, 1630 (?); I, p. 152.

16 Suárez, *Disputationes Metaphysicae*, disputation 30, section 16, number 25: "Nihilominus dicendum est evidenti ratione demonstrari posse, Deum velle res extra se libere, absolute et simpliciter loquendo, et oppositam sententiam, scilicet Deum agere extra se ex necessitate naturae, esse errorem non solum in fide, sed etiam contra rationem naturalem . . . ut nullo modo per intellectum et voluntatem operetur, sed mera actione transeunte ab illo naturaliter dimanante, sicut illuminatio maneat a Sole."

17 Suárez, *Disputationes Metaphysicae*, disputation 31, section 2, number 10: "Ad quartum respondetur, essentiam possibilem creaturae objectum divinae scientiae, non esse ens confictum ab intellectu, sed esse ens revera possible et capax realis existentiae, ideoque non esse ens rationis, sed sub ente reali alioquo modo comprehendi . . . Essentia ergo creaturae, secundum se est ens reale . . . in potentia, non vero . . . in actu, quod est proprie esse ens reale. Quocirca si essentia creaturae praecise ac secundum se sumpta et nondum facta, consideretur ut actu ens, vel ei tribuatur actu esse, sic . . . non est consideranda in se, sed in sua causa, nec habet aliud esse reale ab esse suae causae . . . Dicitur tamen illa natura creabilis vel possibilis, quatenus secundum se realis est et apta ad existendum."

existence, because it is true from all eternity that their essential predicates can be attributed to their essences.[18] But these eternally true truths are not independent of the divine understanding in which they subsist from all eternity.[19]

Such is the thought of St. Thomas, which Suárez appropriates in developing it. The eternal truths are only true from all eternity insofar as they exist objectively in the divine understanding, because they can not exist either subjectively, really in themselves, or objectively, *qua* object of knowledge in an understanding other than God's. For the science by which God knows from all eternity that "Man is a rational animal" to be true science, it is not necessary for man's essence to possess real being in act from all eternity. The being that this essence possesses does not consist of actual, real being, but only of the intrinsic connection that unites the two extreme terms of this proposition by reason of their very nature. This type of connection does not have its basis in an actual being but only in a being of potency, a possible being. Perhaps it will be objected that this science of God does not consist of knowing that a human can be a rational animal but of knowing that he is necessarily a rational animal. It would follow that such a truth supposes not just a possible but rather a necessary being. To this we must reply by simply denying that this consequence is legitimate. The necessity of eternal truths does not consist of the absolute necessity of actually possessing true and real being. They only posses a being that is similar to possibility. The essences of things considered *qua* possible essences only possess conditional necessity: if humans should be created, they will necessarily be rational animals. This necessity is only a certain objective identity of "human" and "animal" that God knows by an absolutely simple vision, although we only know it by composition.[20]

18 Suárez, *Disputationes Metaphysicae*, disputation 31, section 2, number 6: "Praedicata essentialia, ab aeterno vere praedicantur aut praedicari possunt de essentia; omnis autem veritas fundatur in aliquo esse."

19 Cf. St. Thomas, *Summa Theologiae*, part I, question 10, article 3, reply to objection 3.

20 Suárez, *Disputationes Metaphysicae*, disputation 31, section 2, number 8: "Ut autem vera esset scientia, qua Deus ab aeterno cognovit hominem esse animal rationale, non oportuit essentiam hominis habere ex aeternitate aliquod esse reale in actu, quia illud esse, non significat actuale esse et reale, sed solam connexionem intrinsecam talium extremorum; haec autem connexio non fundatur in actuali esse, sed in potentiali. Dices per illam scientiam non cognosci hominem posse esse animal rationale, sed necessario esse animal rationale ergo solum esse potentiale non est sufficiens fundamentum ejus. Respondetur negando absolute consequentiam, quia illa necessitas non est absoluta essendi secundum aliquod esse reale in actu;

When the possible essences are defined in this way, we conceive that they do not have to be created by God as such, since they are not distinguished from him; they have only the aptitude of receiving real being, the non-impossibility of being.[21] The nature of real essences is completely different. An essence becomes real from possible when God confers actual being on it by a decree of his free will. It is only in the second sense that the eternal truths and the essences of things depend on divine creation. Therefore, it is important to distinguish these two viewpoints. When we say *homo est animal*, the copula *est* can have two different senses. It can simply mean that a human really and actually exists and that consequently these two terms, *homo* and *animal*, are united by a real and actual connection. Viewed in this sense, the proposition *Homo est animal* depends on the divine will, because it depends on God, the supreme efficient cause, whether humans exist or do not exist. Therefore, it depends on God whether humans are really and actually animals. But the word *est* can be given another sense. It would no longer signify real existence or the attribution of actual reality to the two terms. The proposition would then be taken in a purely hypothetical and possible sense. When we say that humans are animals, abstracting from the creation of humans in time, we simply want to say that human nature is such that it is impossible to create humans without creating them animal. Consequently, just as the following conditional proposition is eternally true, "If a human exists, he is an animal," or "If he runs, he moves," similarly, this proposition is eternally true, "Humans are animals," and also this other, "Running is movement." Viewed in this sense, similar propositions do not have an efficient cause because every efficient cause brings about the conferral of actual existence, which, by hypothesis, these propositions do not possess.[22] Therefore, as true and real essences, the eternal truths are created

sed quod hoc, est possibilitas tantum. Includit tamen necessitatem conditionalem, quia nimirum, si homo producendus est, necessario futurus est animal rationale, quae necessitas nil aliud est, quam identitas quaedam objectiva hominis et animalis, quam identitatem Deus simplicissime cognoscit; nos autem per compositionem, quam signficat verbum *est*."

21 Suárez, *Disputationes Met*aphysicae, disputation 31, section 2, number 2.

22 Suárez, *Disputationes Metaphysicae,* disputation 31, section 12, number 44: "Haec vero controversia . . . tota consistit in varia significatione illius copulae, *est*, per quam conjuguntur extrema in his enuntiationibus [*scilicet* propositiones aeternae veritatis]. Duobus enim modis accipi potest. Primo ut significet actualem et realem conjunctionem extremorum in re ipsa existentem, ita ut cum dicitur, *homo est animal*, significetur re ipsa ita esse. Secundo, solum significet praedicatum esse de ratione subjecti, sive extrema existant, sive non. In priori sensu veritas proposi-

by God. Insofar as they are possible essences, by their very nature these truths are removed from any creation. Now we see in what sense Suárez took the term *essence* when he presented essences as created by God. The essences were considered not as possibles but as actually existing. The distinction also lets us comprehend certain passages in Suárez that explain why Descartes feels no remorse in deducing this affirmation from Suárez's doctrine: If God did not exist, the eternal truths would no be less true for that. Even while subordinating the existence of these eternal truths to that of God, Suárez can say that even if no efficient cause created humans, the proposition "Humans are animal," would still remain true and necessary *ex hypothesi* in the divine understanding.[23]

In the end, this is exactly the doctrine that Descartes opposes when he explicitly specifies that God's free will creates all essences, all eternal truths, whether real or possible. *Sunt tantum verae aut possibiles quia Deus illas veras aut possibiles cognoscit.*[24] By deliberately using this Scholastic language, he closes down all the issues and leaves no room for distinction.

This unusual attitude on a point where all the doctors agreed, except for some difference of detail, involves Descartes in many difficulties. Perhaps the most outstanding is the incompatibility between the character of necessity acknowledged in the eternal truths and the fact of their free creation by God.

tionum pendet sine dubio ab existentia extremorum, quia juxta illam significationem verbum *est*, non absolvitur a tempore, seu (quod idem est) significat realem et actualem durationem, quae nulla est, ablata existentia extremorum . . . Et in hoc eodem sensu optime probant rationes proxime factae, veritatem harum enuntiationum pendere a causa efficiente, a qua pendent existentia extremorum . . . At vero in alio sensu propositiones sunt verae etiamsi extrema non existant; et in eodem sunt, necessariae ac perpetuae veritatis, quia cum copula est, in dicto sensu non signficet existentiam, non attribuit extremis actualem realitatem in se ipsis, et ideo ad suam veritatem non requirit existentiam, seu realitatem actualem . . . Atque hinc etiam fit, ut hae connexiones in hoc sensu, non habeant causam efficientem, quia omnis efficientia quia omnis efficientia terminatur ad actualem existentiam, a qua dictae propositiones in hoc sensu abstrahunt."

23 Suárez, *Disputationes Metaphysicae*, disputation 31, section 12, number 45: "Quod potest declari ratione facta de propositione conditionali, cujus veritas non pendet ex causa efficiente, vel potente efficere, et ideo aeque reperitur in rebus impossibilibus ac in possibilibus: aeque enim vera est haec conditionalis, si lapis est animal, est sensibilis, ac ista, si homo est animal, est sensibilis; ergo etiam haec propositio: omne animal est sensibile, per se non pendet ex causa quae posit efficere animal. Unde, si per impossibile, nulla esset talis causa, nihilominus illa enunciatio vera esset, sicut haec est vera: chymera est chymera, vel similis."

24 Letter to Mersenne, May 6, 1630; I, p. 149.

The definition of triangle or the truths that can be deduced from it are only necessary truths if they necessarily flow from the very nature of the terms combined and from an intrinsically necessary connection of the essences. The eternal truths are not true because God knows them as true, but rather God knows them as true because they are true. If it were otherwise, we could not explain why God knows the truth of these propositions as necessary. Their truth would come from God himself and would only exist through the intermediary of his will. By getting their origin from a free will, these truths would be contingent; they would not be necessary truths. Therefore God must know them as necessary.[25] We must even go further. In regard to these propositions, the divine intellect only acts to know them without having created them; it behaves like a pure faculty of knowing, not as a faculty of doing. In its purely speculative function, the understanding supposes the truth of its object; it does not create it. Therefore, these eternal truths, which are considered as possible or even as actually realized, are eternally true not only insofar as they exist in the divine intellect but even in themselves in abstraction from this intellect.[26] Let us first observe that Suárez does not contradict his previous affirmations by this last one. He does not say that these truths are true *extra intellectum divinum* nor that even if God did not exist, these truths would still be true. When it is settled that they cannot subsist eternally other than in God's understanding, it remains that it is not their eternal existence there that grounds their truth. The *esse verae* precedes and grounds the *esse cognitae* in them, and it is not because God knows them that they are true, it is because they are true in themselves that God knows them. Since the necessity of their truth imposes them upon the divine knowledge, it is logically prior to the knowledge God has of it.

This last affirmation, expressed in the same terms employed by Suárez, is what Descartes intends to oppose in the letters of 1630. "As for the eternal

25 Suárez, *Disputationes Metaphysicae*, disputation 31, section 12, number 40: "Rursus neque illae enuntiationes sunt verae quia cognoscuntur a Deo, sed potius ideo cognoscuntur, quia verae sunt; aliqui nulla redi posset ratio, cur Deus necessario cognosceret illas esse veras, nam si ab ipso Deo proveniret earum veritas, id fieret media voluntate Dei; unde non ex necessitate proveniret, sed voluntarie."

26 Suárez, *Disputationes Metaphysicae*, disputation 31, section 12, number 40: "Item, quia respectu harum enunciationum comparatur intellectus divinus ut mere speculativus, non ut operativus; intellectus autem speculativus supponit veritatem sui objecti, non facit, igitur hujusmodi enunciationes, quae dicuntur esse in primo, imo etiam quae sunt in secundo modo dicendi per se, habent perpetuam veritatem, non solum ut sunt in divino intellectu, sed etiam secundum se ac praescindendo ab illo."

truths, I say again that *sunt tantum verae . . . quia Deus illas veras . . . cognoscit, non autem contra veras a Deo cognosci quasi independenter ab illo sunt verae*. If men understood the meaning of their words rightly, they could never say without blasphemy that something's truth precedes the knowledge God has of it."[27] Descartes refutes the reasoning upon which this affirmation is based in very precise terms. Suárez said: If the eternal truths do not appear to God as necessaries, they depend on his will and are consequently contingents. Therefore, these truths must have their necessity only from themselves. Descartes responds that this is to conclude illegitimately from the fact that these truths are necessary in regards to humans to their being necessary in regard to God. The eternal truths are necessary in the sense that they are imposed upon our understanding, but that in no way implies that they have their necessity of themselves. They can be necessaries in relation to us and contingents in relation to God, who has freely created them, all the while imposing them on us as necessary. This necessity is manifested sufficiently in our not being able to represent certain contradictions in our mind without judging them completely impossible. However, from this it does not follow that they are also impossible in regard to God: "Again, to say that God wanted certain truths to be necessary, is not to say that he necessarily wanted them, because it is completely different to want them to be necessary and to want them necessarily or for there to be the necessity of wanting them."[28]

However, the new doctrine might meet another objection. Descartes seems to have anticipated the objection without anxiety, since he disposes of the means to dispatch it. Let us concede that God freely created some truths that become necessary for us and that he imposed them on us as a king imposes his laws upon the subjects in his kingdom. It continues to be the case that these laws, contingent in relation to God, always remain contingent in regard to him. The eternal truths may have been created necessary, but God, who created them freely, cannot be bound by the necessity that he conferred upon them. Therefore, he always remains free to create other truths, different from these or even contradictory to them, upon which, if he pleases, he might confer the same character of necessity that he imposes on our mind. These truths, contingent in relation to God and necessary in relation to us, remain contingent in their very root. Perpetually capable of revision by him who created them, they only possess apparent necessity.

27 Letter to Mersenne, May 6, 1630; I, p. 149.
28 Letter to Mesland, May 2, 1644; IV, p. 118–19.

To this objection Descartes opposes the affirmation of God's immutability: "You will be told that if God had established these truths, he could change them as a King does his laws. To this it must be replied that, yes, if his will can change. — But I understand them as eternal and immutable. — And I myself understand the same of God."[29] Thus, the eternal truths that God wanted to be necessary will always be so for us by reason of his creative will that gave them being. By appealing to this attribute of God, Descartes borrows from Scholasticism the weapons he will turn against it. For St. Thomas, God is pure act, and his nature includes nothing that is in potency. Everything that changes is in potency in some respect; therefore no change can be attributed to God, and the divine nature is necessarily immutable. The same consideration forces itself upon us necessarily if we consider God's perfection in itself. Every change must make that which changes achieve something that it had not achieved before. God, who includes within himself the fullness of all perfection by reason of his infinity, cannot achieve any object that has previously eluded him. Furthermore, this is why certain ancients, compelled by the truth, recognized that the first principle of things is unmoved. We must conclude that God is immutable by reason of his simplicity and his infinite perfection,[30] and therefore the same thing must be affirmed concerning his will. A will is said to change when it begins to want what it did not want previously, or when it stops wanting what it did want previously. The possibility of such changes supposes a prior change, whether in knowledge or in the substance that is said to will. Since the will always tends to want the good, it can begin to want a new object for two different reasons. First, because something that was not good for the will begins to be good. For example, it begins to be good to sit near the fire when the first cold weather comes, although it was not good previously. But such change supposes a change in the substance that wills, and since we have just seen that God's substance is immutable, it follows that the divine will cannot change for a reason of this kind. The will can also change by reason of a prior change in the knowledge of the being that wills, if it begins to perceive

29 Letter to Mersenne, April 15, 1630; I, p. 145. Cf. *Quintae Responsioness*, VII, p. 380.

30 Saint Thomas, *Summa Theologiae*, part I, question 9, article 1: "Deus, cum sit primum ens omnino simplex et per essentiam infinitus est simpliciter immutabilis." [Translator: This is certainly the sense of article 1, question 9, first part, but I have not found the sentence quoted; the closest thing to it is ". . . in Deo nulla est compositio, sed est omnino simplex. Unde manifestum est quod Deus moveri non potest."]

that a thing is good for it, whereas previously it did not know that. But God's knowledge is immutable. Indeed, his knowledge is not different from his substance. Since we have proved that this substance is immutable, it follows that his knowledge is equally immutable.[31] Therefore, since God's knowledge is immutable, his substance cannot change. Since the only two possible motives of changes are excluded, it turns out that the divine will is immutable, absolutely speaking.[32]

Descartes retains only the conclusion of this deduction by St. Thomas, without supporting it by any of the arguments that justify it in Scholasticism and without offering a single argument that establishes it from his own viewpoint. This negligence may appear all the more surprising in that divine immutability was to be proposed by Descartes as one of the essential pillars of his philosophy, and that he was to seek in this attribute not only the general guarantee of the stability of the laws of nature but also the immediate metaphysical basis of some of the most important of these laws. In Descartes' eyes, it is a perfection in God to be immutable in himself and it is also a perfection to act in a constant immutable fashion.[33] From there we can deduce certain laws about which we have already spoken: that God who has created the universe with motion and rest must conserve it at present with as much motion and rest as he put in creating the world; also, that left to itself everything remains in the state in which it was: what is square does not change its figure by itself, and what is at rest does not begin to move of itself any more than what is in motion will tend to stop of itself.[34] Every particle of matter tends to move in a straight line,[35] and consequently,

31 St. Thomas, *Summa Theologiae*, part I, question 14, article 15: "Respondeo dicendum quod cum scientia Dei sit ejus substantia . . . sicut substantia ejus est omnino immutabilis . . . ita oportet scientiam ejus omnino invariable esse."

32 St. Thomas, *Summa Theologiae*, part I, question 19, article 7: "Cum enim voluntas sit boni, aliquis de novo dupliciter potest incipere aliquid velle. Uno modo sic, quod de novo incipiat sibi illud esse bonum, Quod non est absque mutatione ejus: sicut adveniente frigore, incipit esse bonus sedere ad ignem, quod prius non erat. Alio modo sic, quod de novo cognoscat illud esse sibi bonum, cum prius hoc ignorasset: ad hoc enim consiliamur, ut sciamus quid nobis sit bonum. Ostensum est autem supra . . . quam ejus scientia est omnino immutabilis. Unde oportet voluntatem ejus omnino esse immutabilem."

33 *Principia*, II, 36: "Intelligimus etiam perfectionem esse in Deo, non solum quod in seipso sit immutabilis, sed etiam quod modo quam maxime constanti et immutabili operetur."

34 *Principia*, II, 37.

35 *Principia*, II, 39.

movement is propagated by collision. From the beginning God created the world full of bodies and of a matter, each particle of which tends to move in a straight line. Therefore, from the first moment of creation these parts of matter must have begun to push each other and to communicate their motion to each other. This is why, since the action by which God conserves the world is the same as that by which he created, he conserves the motion in the particles of matter that he gave them and also the property that their motion has of passing from one to another according to their different collisions. Therefore, the perpetual mutations of things, far from contradicting God's immutability, prove it.[36]

So, Descartes was intensely interested in that question. It must be noted that from 1630 on, he knew how much help the consideration of divine immutability could be to him in physics, since *The World* appealed to it a very long time before *The Principles*. Moreover, it is all the more astonishing how little Descartes worries about legitimating divine immutability, as he relies on the consideration of this attribute to ground the necessity of the eternal truths. In Scholasticism, on the contrary, it is the necessity of the eternal truths or essences of things that grounds, for one thing, the immutability of God's will. We have just seen that the immutable knowledge of Good that God has entails the immutability of his will. If, by contrast, we suppose that the object of divine knowledge is subordinate to God's will that gives it being, the rule of the divine will, which assures its immutability, disappears. Nothing guarantees its stability: *Tam substantia Dei, quam ejus scientia est omnino immutabilis. Unde oportet voluntatem ejus omnino esse immutabilem.*[37] If the will's immutability comes from the immutability of knowledge in God, and if the immutability of his knowledge comes from the necessity with which the eternal truths impose themselves upon it, does it not become odd to appeal to divine immutability to ground the necessity of the eternal truths? Evidently, there was a gap to fill, or rather there would have been a metaphysical assertion there to justify, if Descartes had cultivated metaphysics for itself and if he had taken as his essential goal to construct a rigorous, deeper metaphysics. But he gladly made do with what was

36 *Principia*, II, 42: "Sicque haec ipsa creaturarum continua mutatio immutabilitatis Dei est argumentum." Cf. St. Thomas, *Summa Theologiae*, part I, question 19, article 7: "Respondeo dicendum quod voluntas Dei est omnino immutabilis. Sed circa hoc considerandum est quod aliud est mutare voluntatem, et aliud est velle aliquarum rerum mutationem. Potest enim aliquis eadem voluntate immobiliter permanente velle quod nunc fiat hoc, et postea fiat contrarium."

37 St. Thomas, *Summa Theologiae*, part I, question 19, article 7, end of body of article.

strictly necessary in this order of questions. The affirmation of divine utility seemed useful to him to show the agreement of his physics with theology. Descartes affirms it, but he is not concerned with grounding it, although in that very moment he deprives himself of what Scholasticism considered its principal grounds. No doubt if he had been pressed on this point, he would have made divine immutability one of those attributes that we find necessarily included in God's nature, because it is evident that the possibility of change implies some imperfection. But it certainly seems that for him the evidence of this affirmation is reduced to remembering a Scholastic demonstration that he suppresses without replacing.

We again can observe how little concern Descartes experiences about going into this point more deeply in the brief indication he adds regarding the harmony between God's freedom and his immutability. There too, he remits to the solutions of Scholasticism. It is true that the resolution he takes of never questioning the conclusions of theology suffices to legitimate his attitude. In the face of this purely theological problem, Descartes entrenches himself behind our reason's insufficiency to scrutinize the mysteries of God's omnipotence. God's will is immutable: "But his will is free. — Yes, but his power is incomprehensible and generally, we can certainly assure that God can do everything that we can comprehend, but not that he cannot do what we cannot comprehend."[38] Scholasticism more boldly proposes a justification of this relation as the solution of this problem. It consists of presenting God's freedom as being exercised in a single act and by that very fact evades any necessity coming from prior decisions, as, furthermore, any possibility of change. Immutability would only be a constraint for a will whose decisions were spaced through time. In this case, a prior immutable decision would radically suppress the freedom of all subsequent decisions. But it does not work this way with God, for whom time is nothing and whose will is exercised in eternity. This will, which knows neither past nor future but is a perpetual and immobile present in a single, eternal act, cannot be considered as binding itself by its own immutability. In this way, immutability and freedom are reconciled in God.[39] Descartes, more prudent, admits this compatibility, without seeming to give an explanation. He simply adopts the conclusions that theology has reached on these various points and, feeling protected on that flank, feels no need to develop them further.

Neglecting these secondary questions, Descartes brings all his effort to

38 Letter to Mersenne, April 15, 1630; I, p. 145.

39 Suárez, *Disputationes Metaphysicae*, disputation 30, section 16, number 32.

bear on what constitutes the foundation itself, the real root of the doctrine he combats. He is not content to deny a dangerous conclusion. He wants to deny the premises from which it has been deduced. From this attempt to destroy St. Thomas's doctrine on the eternal truths at its point of departure arises what is rightly considered one of the essential elements of Descartes' metaphysics: the affirmation of the absolute unity of what we call the divine attributes in the Cartesian concept of God's freedom. What allows St. Thomas and Suárez to make the eternal truths independent of the divine will is the distinction they introduce in God between understanding and will. By the very fact of denying this distinction's legitimacy, Descartes blocks those who make the eternal truths independent of the divine understanding and submit the eternal truths to God's will. Only two theses are left standing: absolutely speaking, the eternal truths are independent of God's existence; or God produces the eternal truths like other creatures. Since the first proposition is untenable, we must necessarily come to the second.

At first sight it does not seem that Descartes could have justly reproached Scholasticism with introducing a distinction between understanding and will in God. In the eyes of St. Thomas, simplicity and absence of any composition is one of the principal divine attributes. We can even say it is the principal one in the sense that the true nature of the others cannot be understood if we do not first know simplicity. In the *Summa*, the question *De Simplicitate Dei* comes immediately after the question: *De Deo*: *an sit*. God is not a body. He is not composed of matter and form or of essence and existence, or of genus and difference, or of subject and accident.[40] Besides, the affirmation of divine simplicity naturally follows the proofs that establish God's existence. God has been demonstrated to be the First: first mover, first cause, first being. Unity is found before plurality. Plurality is found in every composite. Therefore, by the very fact that he is before all things, God must be free of all composition. Consequently, God is simple.[41] Among the different aspects through which we can view this simplicity, let us particularly consider the following: God is not composed of substance and accident. God is being itself. That which is being itself cannot participate in anything that is not its essence, for, although that which is may participate in another thing, there is however nothing simpler or more formal

40 St. Thomas, *Summa Theologiae*, part I, question 3 throughout.

41 St. Thomas Aquinas, *Summa contra Gentes*, book I, chapter 18, end: "Ante multitudinem oportet invenire unitatem. In omni autem composito est multitudo. Igitur oportet id, quod est ante omnia, scilicet Deum, omni compositione carere."

than being. Therefore, the divine substance, which is being itself, cannot possess anything that does not belong to its substance, and consequently such a substance cannot have accidents.[42] In other words, since the accident is not the subject's essence, every being in which some accident is found is not all that its essence comprises. God is all that he comprises in himself, since he is his very essence, and therefore he does not include any accident in himself.[43] The minor premise is proved as follows. In all that is not its own essence some composition is necessarily found. We find its essence first of all, and if there were nothing in this thing outside of its essence, everything this thing is would be its essence. It would be its own essence itself. Therefore, if a thing is not its essence, it is necessary that there is something in it outside of its essence and, consequently, that it is composed. So it is that in composites the essence is considered a part, like humanity in a human. We have seen, however, that there is no composition in God, and therefore God is his essence.[44]

Because God is his essence itself, and he does not include accidents, it follows that nothing that we want to attribute to him can be said to be other than his essence. Such is the case of the divine understanding. The act of understanding is to the understanding what being is to essence. We have just proved that divine being is its essence; accordingly, the act by which God understands is his understanding. It is furthermore necessary that the divine understanding be God's essence without constituting an accident in God; therefore, the act by which God understands is not other than his essence.[45] It necessarily follows from that God's will is also nothing but his essence.

42 St. Thomas, *Summa contra Gentes*, book I, chapter 23, paragraph begins *Ipsum enim esse . . .*: "Divina autem substantia est ipsum esse; ergo nihil habet quod non sit de sua substantia; nullum ergo accidens ei inesse potest."

43 St. Thomas, *Summa contra Gentes*, book I, chapter 23, paragraph begins *Amplius*: "Cuicumque inest aliquod accidens non est quidquid habet in se; quia accidens non est de essentia subjecti. Sed Deus est quidquid in se habet. In Deo igitur nullum est accidens."

44 St. Thomas, *Summa contra Gentes*, book I, chapter 21, paragraph begins *In omni enim* "Si igitur aliquid non est sua essentia, oportet aliquid in eo esse praeter ejus essentiam; et sic oportet in eo esse compositionem . . . Ostensum est autem in Deo nullam esse compositionem. Deus igitur est sua essentia."

45 St. Thomas, *Summa contra Gentes*, book I, chapter 45, paragraph begins *Praeterea* "Intelligere comparatur ad intellectum, sicut esse ad essentiam. Sed esse divinum est ejus essentia, ut supra probatum est. Ergo intelligere divinum est ejus intellectus. Intellectus autem divinus est Dei essentia; alias esset accidens Deo. Oportet igitur quod intelligere divinum sit ejus esssentia."

From God's possessing intelligence, it follows that he possesses will: since the proper object of the will is the good apprehended by the understanding, insofar as it is thus apprehended, the good as such must be wanted. It is an understanding that apprehends whatever is apprehended; consequently, the understanding that apprehends the good must, as such, necessarily be a willing. Moreover, we recognize that God, who is perfect intelligence, apprehends simultaneously being and the reason of the good; therefore he apprehends the good by his understanding and consequently is endowed with a will.[46] Thus God possesses a will insofar as he possesses an understanding. His understanding is his essence, as we have proved; therefore the same goes for his will, and consequently God's will is his very essence.[47] From all that has been said, it is evident that most of the actions that are attributed to God like understanding, willing, producing things, and other actions of this kind, are not distinct things in him. Each of these actions is nothing else in God but his very being, which is *unum et idem*.[48] It does not seem that Descartes could ask for more or oppose Scholasticism on this point.

However, let us consider the texts above a little more closely. Although the tenor of their conclusions agrees with Descartes' thought, we can already point out the seeds of a conflict that we will see develop and take shape. St. Thomas clearly affirms the real identity of understanding and will in God.[49] Still, does that mean that it is not legitimate to introduce some distinction between these attributes from any point of view? Let us first observe that there is no contradiction between the simplicity of the divine essence and

46 St. Thomas, *Summa contra Gentes*, book I, chapter 72, paragraph begins *Ex hoc enim* "Necesse est igitur quod intelligens bonum, inquantum hujusmodi, sit volens. Deus autem intelligit bonum; cum enim sit perfecte intelligens . . . intelligit ens simul cum ratione boni. Est igitur volens."

47 St. Thomas, *Summa contra Gentes*, book I, chapter 73, beginning of chapter: "Ex hoc autem apparet quod sua voluntas non est aliud quam sua essentia. Deo enim convenit esse volentem, in quantum est intelligens, ut ostensum est. Est autem intelligens per essentiam suam; ergo et volens. Est igitur voluntas Dei ipsa ejus essentia."

48 St. Thomas, *Summa contra Gentes*, book II, chapter 10, last paragraph: "Patet etiam, ex praedictis, quod multitudo actionum quae Deo attribuuntur, ut intelligere, velle, producere res, et similia non sunt diversae res, cum quaelibet harum actionum in Deo sit ipsum ejus esse, quod est unum et idem."

49 St. Thomas, *De Veritate*, 23, 6, body of article, mid-paragraph: "Quamvis in nobis sit aliud intellectus et voluntas secundum rem . . . in Deo autem est idem secundum rem intellectus et voluntas."

the plurality of divine names. We attribute all the perfections we discover in things to God as their equivocal cause. Just as the hot and the dry, which are distinct qualities in fires, are attributed to the sun as constituting a single virtue in it that is nothing other than its essence, we attribute to God all the perfections that we see belonging to creatures according to their diverse forms, as being a single virtue in him that is nothing but his essence. In the unity and simplicity of his being, God includes much more than any perfection that is found in the multitude of beings. The need to attribute several names to God comes from that. Our natural lights do not permit us to know him other than by going back from his effects to him. That is why the names by which we designate his perfection are necessarily diverse, as the perfections that we find in things are diverse. But if we could comprehend his essence itself, just as it is, and fashion one name that would be proper to him, we would express the perfection with a single name, as is promised to those who see God in his essence: "On that day there will only be one God, and this God will only have one name."[50]

But at the very moment when this doctrine is founded, the doctrine includes the reason that obliges us to limit it. We understand its true meaning if we compare it to St. Thomas's fundamental conception of the knowledge of God by analogy. Our knowledge of God is neither purely univocal nor purely equivocal. We have just seen that all the different perfections that appear in creatures must be attributed to God. But in what sense can we attribute them to him? An effect inferior to its cause cannot have either the same name or the same essence as the cause. Yet, it is necessary that there be some resemblance between this cause and its effect. For, since each thing acts according as it is in act, it belongs to the nature of the agent to produce something like itself. It follows from this that the form of the effect is found in reality in the cause that is superior to it, but in a mode that is not a little different. By reason of this, the name of *equivocal cause* is given to this cause. The sun causes heat in inferior bodies by acting insofar as it is in act; therefore, the heat engendered by the sun must have some resemblance to the active virtue by which the sun produces it. We say that the sun is hot, although the nature of this heat is different in the sun and in the bodies where the sun introduces it. We can say of the sun that it possesses a certain resemblance to all things in which it produces its effect, although, on the other hand, it differs from all these things in that the heat that it produces is

50 St. Thomas, *Summa contra Gentes*, book I, chapter 31. [End of chapter. Aquinas is quoting the prophet Zechariah, 14:9.]

different in nature from that which it possesses itself. It is the same in God, who gives things all their perfections, so that he resembles all things in a certain way, although at the same time he is different from them.[51]

What we have just said is poorly expressed. It is not God who resembles humans. Rather it is humans who resemble God. A thing is said to be similar to another when it possesses its form or quality. Therefore, since what is in God perfectly is found in things imperfectly and by participation, we must say that what provides the matter for the resemblance belongs properly to God and not to the creature. The creature has something of God. That is why it can rightly be called similar to God. But the reverse is not true. God receives nothing from creatures, and God cannot be said to resemble them, any more than we would say that someone resembles his portrait, but on the contrary that the portrait resembles him. This lets us see the names we can attribute to God. Since every perfection of the creature is found in God, but in a higher degree, all the names that designate an absolute perfection, without defect, can be attributed to God, such as the names *goodness*, *wisdom*, *being*, and others of the same kind. But these names can be attributed to God and creatures at completely the same time. For them to correspond to God alone, the names must be made to express the perfection that they describe in a supereminent degree: for example *sovereign good, first being*, etc. Still, it must be said that such names involve no imperfection as to the object they designate, but as to the mode according to which they designate it. It must be recognized that every name involves some imperfection. We name things according to how we understand them, and our knowledge, which starts from sensible things, does not rise above this order of things where matter and form are always distinct. In that order, what possesses the form is subsistent but composed, while the form is simple but does not subsist, is not *quod est* but *quo est*. In this sense, insofar as they involve some imperfection, there are no names that are properly applied to God. Therefore, we must make a distinction. The names that attribute perfection to God can be affirmed and denied at the same time, affirmed because of what they signify, denied because of the manner in which they signify it. We can say: *God is good*, because God is Goodness. We cannot say *God is good*, because God does not possess in himself goodness as a distinct perfection that, united to other perfections of the same kind, composes his essence. As to what is to be expressed by the words *the supereminent mode according to which these perfections are in God*, we cannot even imagine it. We can only

51 St. Thomas Aquinas, *Summa contra Gentes*, book I, chapter 36.

express this supereminence of God negatively, as when we call him eternal or infinite, or relative to other beings, and when we say that he is the first cause, or the sovereign good. We cannot grasp that which God is but that which he is not and the relations he has with things.[52]

If the knowledge we can have of God is either negative or relative, it follows that the perfections that are attributed to God and to creatures cannot be attributed either in a perfectly univocal or perfectly equivocal manner. The attribution cannot be univocal, since we have seen that the perfections are not found in the same mode in God and in the creature, in the one who gives them and the one who receives them. The attribution cannot be purely equivocal because, in spite of everything, there is a certain relation of likeness between things and God.[53] It follows that the attribution is analogous, that is to say, it expresses a relation of proportion, precisely the relation that unites the perfections created and dispersed in creatures by God who is their author.[54] Therefore, we can legitimately claim certain knowledge of God when we start by attributing to him the names by which we designate the effects whose cause he is. Next, although all these names designate just one and the same thing, they are still not identical. We have seen that different things have some likeness with God through the different forms. Our understanding is led to the knowledge of God by the diverse natures or perfections of creatures, and therefore acquires his likeness in some degree. Consequently, what our understanding thinks is not false or empty. It makes several different concepts about a being that is one. Still, however simple the divine nature is, by its nature it is such that certain things can resemble it through different forms. The names we employ designate the likeness of God that we find in the perfections of things and not the unity of God himself. Therefore, they are not synonyms.[55] Provided that our understanding

52 St. Thomas Aquinas, *Summa contra Gentes*, book I, chapter 30, end of chapter: "Modus autem supereminentiae, quo in Deo dictae perfectiones inveniuntur, per nomina a nobis imposita significari non potest nisi vel per negationem, sicut quum dicimus Deum *aeternum* vel etiam per relationem ipsius ad alia, ut cum dicitur *prima causa* vel *summum bonum*. Non enim de Deo capere possumus quid est, sed quid non est et qualiter alia se habeant ad ipsum."

53 St. Thomas Aquinas, *Summa contra Gentes*, book I, chapter 33, paragraph begins *Amplius* . . .: "Ubi est pura aequivocatio, nulla similitudo in rebus illis attenditur, sed solum unitas nominis. Rerum autem ad Deum est aliquis modus similitudines, ut ex supra patet. Reliquitur ergo quod non dicantur de Deo secundum puram aequivocationem."

54 St. Thomas Aquinas, *Summa contra Gentes*, book I, chapter 34.

55 St. Thomas Aquinas, *Summa contra Gentes*, book I, chapter 35.

does not give the object it understands the mode according to which it understands it, that is, provided that in each of our propositions dealing with God's nature we relate the diversity the proposition implies to our understanding and the unity the proposition designates to its object, these propositions cannot be considered empty and without meaning.[56]

The conclusion has considerable importance. Theology becomes possible by it, since we will have relative but true knowledge of God. St. Thomas opens up the possibility of speaking of God other than in a vacuum and the possibility that, by working back from created things to God, our finite mind can know about his perfection. In this way, discovering two perfections in human nature, understanding and will, we truly attribute them to God as belonging to him in a supereminent mode. Among all the perfections that we see in things, the highest is what certain beings posses, that of having an intelligence. The superiority of this perfection comes from the fact that by it, whoever who possesses it is in some manner all things and contains all the other perfections of the universe. Therefore, God, who lacks no perfection, also possesses that one.[57] The same holds concerning the will. But remarkably, St. Thomas attributes the will to God by a completely different path from the one he follows for the understanding. Instead of ascending directly from the will, a perfection of creatures, to God who is its author, he attributes the will to God by the intermediary of the understanding. God possesses intelligence because it constitutes a perfection, and because he possesses intelligence, he is endowed with will. Although understanding and will are two equally infinite perfections in God and although they coincide with his essence in the last analysis, they do not appear as having an identical reason [*ratio*] of perfection. We cannot posit the understanding without positing the will: *voluntas enim intellectum consequitur*.[58] Just as a natural thing is in act thanks to its forms, so also the understanding understands in act by the intelligible form. Each thing is in a relation to its natural form in such a way that, when the thing does not possess

56 St. Thomas Aquinas, *Summa contra Gentes*, book I, chapter 36.

57 St. Thomas Aquinas, *Summa contra Gentes*, book I, chapter 44, Paragraph begins *Adhuc* [The words in italics are from *De Anima* 8: 431 b, 21.] "Deo nulla perfectio deest, quae in aliquo genere entium inveniatur, ut supra ostensum est; nec ex hoc aliqua compositio in eo consequitur, ut etiam ex superioribus patet. Inter perfectiones autem rerum potissima est quod aliquid sit intellectivum; nam per hoc ipsum *est quodammodo omnia*, habens in se omnium perfectiones. Deus igitur est intelligens."

58 St. Thomas Aquinas, *Summa Theologiae*, part I, question 19, article 1, near beginning.

the form, it tends toward it, and when it possesses it, it rests in it. From that it follows that the intellectual nature maintains the same relation with the good that it apprehends thanks to its intelligible form. It must tend toward it or rest in it, and in both cases it makes an act of will. Therefore, since everything endowed with understanding is also endowed with will, God, who possesses the first, also must possess the second.[59] But, at the same time as this relationship shows the intimate union of understanding and will, it brings to light the difference that distinguishes them. Will is one of the species of appetite, and the appetite is *inclinatio quaedam consequens formam*.[60] The natural form of a natural thing entails a natural appetite. A sensitive appetite corresponds to the sensible form. The will corresponds to the intelligible form. It is the nature of this apprehended form that determines the nature of the appetite. Therefore, St. Thomas not only distinguishes between the divine perfections with a distinction of reason, but he even attributes a special role to certain of the perfections as well as a nature that in some measure is proper to them. This is a distinction of reason founded on the nature of the thing. Moreover, we see this clearly if we follow the conclusions to which Suárez comes through a legitimate development of the principles that St. Thomas posits here. If the nature of the appetite is determined by the mode according to which the being endowed with appetite apprehends forms, it follows that what constitutes the degree of perfection or the specific nature of a being is not its will but its cognitive faculty. The appetite alone does not allow its peculiar degree and essential perfection to be determined, because it receives its denomination from the cognitive faculty to which it is joined. If we ignore the mode of knowledge of a being, we cannot conceive the degree of perfection of its nature distinctly. Since it is the nature of the understanding that delineates the nature of willing, the will of a being considered in itself supposes its nature already constituted by the understanding upon which it depends. This is why St. Thomas says that the appetite does not suffice to determine the special degree or order of being. Therefore, while admitting that the will belongs to God's essence as much as the understanding, and that there is no real difference between them, God's will and his understanding still must be distinguished with a distinction of reason. By itself and by its sovereign perfection, the knowledge that the divine understanding possesses includes in its formal reason what constitutes the

59 St. Thomas Aquinas, *Summa Theologiae*, part I, question 19, article 1, near end of body of article: "Et oportet in Deo esse voluntatem, cum sit in eo intellectus."

60 St. Thomas Aquinas, *Summa Theologiae*, part I, question 87, article 4, body of article.

very essence of God in what is proper to it and, so to speak, specific. Regarding the will, however, we cannot say anything other than that it simply belongs to the essence or general reason of perfection, although, on the other hand, the divine understanding is so perfect that the will does not flow from it by way of consequence, but the understanding formally entails it in itself.[61]

If, moreover, we assume the viewpoint of things' relation to divine perfection, a viewpoint that St. Thomas explicitly recognizes as legitimate, we will again be led to establish a distinction of reason between God's understanding and his will. In a spiritual substance, the understanding and the will are based on the different relations the substance can have with things.[62] A first relation consists of things being in the spiritual substance itself, in a certain fashion, not according to their proper being but according to their proper form. For example, the form of the stone, but not the stone itself, is found in the soul insofar as the soul can apprehend the intelligible forms by its faculty of knowing. The will, by contrast, is based on the relation that the spiritual substance maintains with the being of things considered insofar as they exist in themselves.[63] Accordingly, our human reason cannot help establishing a certain distinction in God between understanding and will. From this viewpoint of the relation that the divine essence maintains with

61 Suárez, *Disputationes Metaphysicae*, disputation 30, section 16, numbers 13–14: "Unde, sicut supra dicebamus, intelligere divinum esse quasi ultimum essentiale constitutivum divinae naturae in tali gradu, et excellentia illius gradus, ita nunc dicendum videtur illud intelligere per essentiam tale esse, ut ex vi suae rationis essentialis sit non tantum intelligere, sed etiam velle, quamvis nos per praecisos et inadaequatos conceptus illud dividamus. Et sane hae posteriores rationes efficaciter concludunt, actum volendi esse de essentia et quidditate divinae naturae aeque ac sciendi actum, neque in re posse veram differentiam excogitari. At secundum nostrum modum, concipiendi est aliquale discrimen; nam ipsum scire tale est, ut absque illo non intelligatur illa natura distincte, ut constituta in proprio gradu et perfectione essentiali, et cum illo sufficienter intelligatur formaliter constituta in illo gradu in excellentia ejus. Velle autem non intelligitur ut sic constituens naturam; nam jam praeintelligitur constituta, ipsum tale autem velle intelligitur ut quid consequens. Vel certe intelligtur esse quale exstitit [*sic*, existit?] ipsum intelligere. Propter quod dixit Divus Thomas (I, 70, 30) appetitum non constituere specialem gradum seu ordinem entium."

62 St. Thomas Aquinas, *De Veritate*, 23, 1, second sentence of body of article: "Cognitio et voluntas radicantur in substantia spirituali super diversas habitudines ejus ad res."

63 St. Thomas Aquinas, *De Veritate*, 23, 1, body of article. "Voluntas autem . . . fundatur super habitudinem qua substantia spiritualis refertur ad res ut habens ordinem aliquem ad eas in se ipsis existentes."

things, Suárez deduces the same conclusion with still more precision. Absolutely speaking, for Suárez as for St. Thomas, the divine attributes are God's essence itself; all the divine attributes are included in the essence of each of them.[64] In this sense, we can say without error or absurdity that God's justice as justice is his mercy, that God is merciful by his justice, and that he punishes by his mercy. If we speak of the divine attributes as they are in themselves and outside our faculty of knowing, these propositions are absolutely true. But if we speak of these attributes insofar as they can be distinctly and explicitly known by us, then these propositions become false, because our understanding uses inadequate concepts to grasp a reality that is indivisible in itself. Something that is completely one in itself cannot fall under any of our concepts according to its total and adequate essence. In this case and in this sense, we cannot attribute to one of our concepts what we attribute to the other, because then we do not designate by one concept the same thing viewed in the same relation as by another. So, speaking strictly, a proposition like the following "God is merciful by his justice" is a false proposition.[65]

Furthermore, this distinction that our human reason is forced to establish has its foundation in God's nature, which is absolutely one. Although divine perfection is absolutely one in itself, it does not always operate according to its total and adequate essence. As an example, let us consider sunlight. It remains the same insofar as it eminently contains heat, dryness, and all its other effects. Yet, when it heats, it does not act according to its adequate perfection, and it cannot be said to act *qua* it eminently contains dryness and the other qualities. These other qualities are only accidents in relation to heat. Thus, light can be said to heat in that it eminently contains heat. If we establish a distinction of reason within light among the virtues light has of producing heat, dryness, and so forth, we will say truly that light heats by the virtue it has of producing heat and not by its other virtues. All these words and concepts do not designate light in itself but only considered in its inadequate relations with effects and insofar as it virtually contains them. What we say about God must be understood so. None of the effects God produces outside himself is adequate to his creative power. We say with complete truth that God created humans by the idea of human and not by the idea of horse. Not that these ideas are really distinct in God, but because the idea of human in God is the real cause of humans and is only the cause

64 Suárez, *Disputationes Metaphysicae*, disputation 30, section 6, number 10.
65 Suárez, *Disputationes Metaphysicae*, disputation 30, section 6, number 13.

of horse by accident. We express this relation of divine power with its accidents by these propositions: God is merciful by his mercy and he punishes by his justice. These propositions are true because none of these effects is adequate to God's power.[66]

We understand this still better if we consider the effects God produces not outside but within himself. The theologians say with complete truth that the Son proceeds from the Father by the intelligence and the Holy Spirit by the will. It would be false to say that the Holy Spirit proceeds from the intelligence of the Father and the Son from his will. There is only one and the same essence of the understanding and the will in God the Father. Yet, it is not this total and adequate essence that is the principle of the other two divine persons. God the Father is the principle of the Son insofar as he is intelligence and of the Holy Spirit insofar as he is love. The intelligence and love are the two adequate origins of these two processions. By the terms *understanding* and *will*, we want to designate these attributes of God precisely *qua* inadequate to his total essence. Therefore, the origin of the Son cannot be attributed to the will of the Father without error, or the origin of the Holy Spirit to his intelligence. This is what is frequently expressed when we say that the divine attributes are not actually distinct but they are virtually distinct, and that each attribute is the principle according to which God does or produces some thing insofar as it is virtually distinct from the other attributes. We cannot attribute formally and *per se* to one attribute of God what is proper to another insofar as they are virtually distinguished.[67] In saying that God's attributes are virtually distinct, we mean nothing other than that they virtually contain distinct effects and that, in the unity and simplicity of their nature, they contain what is distinct in other things, or that

66 Suárez, *Disputationes Metaphysicae*, disputation 30, section 6, number 14: "Licet perfectio divina in se una omnino sit, non tamen operatur semper secundum adaequatam suam rationem . . . Quod in effectibus ad extra est clarum, quia nullus effectus est adaequatus virtuti divinae, et ideo vere dicimus Deum creare hominem per ideam hominis, non vero per ideam equi, non quia in re distinctae sint hae ideae, sed quia licet sit unum eminens exemplar ita repraesentans singula, ac si esset uniuscujusque proprium, tamen per se non agit unumquodque, nisi quatenus repraesentat illud, quod autem repraesentet alia, est quasi per accidens ad talem effectum."

67 Suárez, *Disputationes Metaphysicae*, disputation 30, section 6, number 15: "Et hoc idem est, quod aliis verbis dici solet, has scilicet virtutes seu attributa, licet non actualiter, virtualiter esse distincta, et unum attributum esse principium vel rationem operandi seu, producendi aliquid, prout virtute distinguitur ab alio; et ideo non posse formaliter et per se attribui uni quod est proprium alterius, ut virtute ab alio distinguitur."

they are the virtues and the essences in which is found that from which or by which different effects are produced. Consequently, although this virtual distinction only implies the eminence of the divine essence and not a real distinction between its attributes, it still constitutes a foundation that authorizes the distinctions that we introduce into God's productive virtue. The distinctions are made according to the relations considered properly and in themselves that his productive virtue maintains with different effects or terms.[68] This is precisely what another Scholastic, Eustachius a Sancto Paulo, expresses more succinctly when he writes: *Altera est [distinctio] rationis ratiocinatae, quae fit ab intellectu pro varia occasione in rebus ipsis inventa, quomodo in lumine distinguitur vis calefactiva ab exsiccativa, et Theologi distinguunt divina attributa, tum ex divina essentia, cum a se invicem.*[69] This distinction of the divine attributes is not a simple distinction of reason-reasoning [translator: *rationis ratiocinantis*], which would have no foundation in the attributes themselves. It is a distinction of reason-reasoned [translator: *rationis ratiocinatae*] that is to say, a distinction of reason *cum fundamento in re.*

It is easy to recognize what Descartes is combating in this doctrine, when he refuses to allow the least distinction, even of reason, between the divine attributes: "For, in God, willing, understanding, and creating are one and the same without one preceding the other, *ne quidem in ratione*."[70] By *distinction of reason*, we must understand distinction of reason-reasoned. Descartes can only admit that a distinction of reason-reasoning exists, that is, one without foundation in things, since we cannot think anything that does not rest on some foundation.[71] This is what he explicitly understands in the passage where he denies that there can be any distinction in God between the idea of good and God's will, in whatsoever way we want to take

68 Suárez, *Disputationes Metaphysicae*, disputation 30, section 6, number 15: "Unde licet haec virtualis distinctio in re non sit distinctio sed eminentia, est tamen fundamentum respectu nostri distincte concipiendi illam virtutem secundum proprias, et per se habitudines ad distinctos effectus seu terminos, et ideo est etiam sufficiens fundamentum diversarum locuctionum, ut declaratum est."

69 Eustachius a Sancto Paulo, *Summa Philosophiae*, IV, 83.

70 Letter to Mersenne, May 27, 1630 (?); I, p. 153.

71 Letter to . . . 1645 or 1646, IV, p. 349: "Sed ad confusionem evitandum . . . illam [distinctionem] voco distinctionem Rationis (nempe rationis Ratiocinatae) et quia nullam agnosco rationis Ratiocinantis, hoc est, quae non habeat fundamentum in rebus (neque enim quicquam possumus cogitare absque fundamento) idcirco in illo articulo, verbum Ratiocinatae non addo."

it: *ordine vel natura, vel ratione ratiocinata.*[72] At the same time we see that there is no possible doubt about the name of the adversary whom our philosopher opposes. Descartes denies that essences considered as real or even possible can subsist independently of the divine will and the knowledge that God has of them. He makes them absolutely immutable despite that judgment. Lastly, he seeks the root of the doctrine he condemns in any distinction between God's understanding and his will, even a purely abstract distinction. With these three things, Descartes unequivocally adopts a position against Scholastic teaching. His adversary is none other than St. Thomas on this point, so crucial in its theological, metaphysical, and scientific consequences.

72 *Sextae Responsiones*, VII, p. 432.

Chapter Three

Final Causes and the Idea of Infinity

Why did Descartes adopt this attitude? Why did he insist on rejecting in such formal terms a distinction that seems unimportant by the very fact that it does not get to the heart of matters? We will understand him better by seeing what consequences Scholasticism draws from the distinction of reason-reasoned that it introduces between God's understanding and his will. Descartes sees these consequences clearly and condemns them in the *Sextae Responsiones*. If the understanding is distinguished from the will in God, we are led to admit that his freedom is not a freedom of indifference, that the determinations of his will are guided by the indications of his understanding, which reveals the good and the true to him. Precisely this last conclusion is what Descartes attempts to destroy. He wants us to consider the divine will as indifferent from all time to everything that has been or ever will be done, because no good or no truth can be imagined whose idea is found in God's understanding without the good or truth having been created by his will.[1] If we take God's immensity seriously, we still see clearly that absolutely nothing can exist that does not get its origin from him: not only any actually existing thing but even any order, any law, any essence of true and good. Were it otherwise, God would not have been completely indifferent in creating what he did create. For, if any essence of true and good had preceded God's preordaining everything, it would have determined him to make what is best, while, on the contrary, because he wanted to do what he did, that is now what is best.[2] Let us successively consider why Descartes does not allow that there should be a Good or a Truth in God's understanding prior to the free decision of his will.

On the issue of God being totally free to create or not the world, Descartes and St. Thomas could only come to identical conclusions. Orthodoxy required that both affirm this freedom. Descartes is so far from being disposed to deny it that he rather intends to give a more exact idea,

1 *Sextae Responsiones*, VII, pp. 431–432.
2 *Sextae Responsiones*, VII, pp. 435–436.

one more worthy of divine omnipotence than is usually provided. He explicitly affirms that creatures are not conjoined to the essence of God. Likewise, St. Thomas teaches that God has no necessity of willing things. The idea of Good is the proper object of the will. Moreover, what the divine understanding apprehends first, by itself, and as its principal object, is the divine essence. Therefore, the divine essence is the archetypal good, the first and immediate object of God's will.[3] God directly wills his own essence and his own good, and he wills all other things in relation to them with a mediate and secondary will. God's being and goodness are his reason for willing other things. In everything he wills, he wills his being and goodness, as the sight sees light in every color. It is impossible that God should fail to will something with an actual will; for otherwise, he would have goodness only in potency, something impossible because his will is just one thing with his being. Therefore, God necessarily wills his own being and his own goodness.[4] But by willing himself, God wills other things at the same time. We cannot love and will a thing for itself without desiring its perfection. What we love in itself, we always want to see higher and better; we want to see it multiplied as much as possible. God wills and loves his own essence for itself, which, if it cannot be multiplied in itself, still can be multiplied in many things that can participate in its likeness. Therefore, God wants the multiplicity of things by the very fact that he wills and loves his essence and his perfections. Furthermore, whoever loves a thing in itself and for itself consequently loves all that in which it is found. When sweetness is loved for itself, all that is sweet is loved. But God wills and loves his being in itself and for itself. Therefore, he wills all other beings that only exist by likeness and participation in his being. From this it follows that by the fact that God loves himself and wills himself, he wills and loves other things.[5]

But can we say that God wills things with a necessary will? We might think so at first glance. Because if God necessarily wills his own existence and his own good and, furthermore, if God wills all things by the very fact that he wills his own good, it seems to follow that God wills everything

3 St. Thomas, *Summa contra Gentes*, book I, chapter 74, beginning: "Ex hoc autem ulterius apparet quod principale divinae voluntatis volitum est ejus essentia. Bonum enim intellectum est objectum voluntatis . . . Id autem quod a Deo principaliter intelligitur est divina essentia . . . Divina igitur essentia est id de quo principaliter est divina voluntas."

4 St. Thomas, Summa *contra Gentes*, book I, chapter 80.

5 St. Thomas, *Summa contra Gentes*, book I, chapter 75.

necessarily. But the opposite appears true upon closer examination.[6] God only wills other things in relation to his own goodness considered as an end. The will is only led necessarily to want what is required for an end in the case where the end cannot be achieved without it. For example, if a physician wants to cure a patient, there is no necessity for him to give the patient certain remedies without which it is still possible for him to cure the patient. Divine goodness can exist in itself without anything else existing, because there is nothing whose existence could add the least perfection to it. Therefore, God is under no necessity to will things by the fact that he necessarily wills his own good.[7]

We may confirm this even better from another point of view. We have just said that the will tends toward an object according to the relation this object maintains with the end that the will sets itself. Therefore, if the means stands to the end in such a proportion that necessarily the end may not be obtained without it, we will not will the end without necessarily willing the means. The necessity will be that much stricter as it is less possible for the will under consideration to deviate from the rule of wisdom. For example, we cannot want to continue to live without wanting to consume food. But this is not similar to the case we find in God's production of beings. Nothing that divine power produces is equal to its cause. No creature is perfectly like God. Consequently, no creature is adequate to God in whom it finds its end. However high and noble the resemblance of a creature may be in relation to God, however closely it is linked to the divine essence, it always remains possible that a different creature should represent the supreme goodness of God in a perfect and exalted way. So, the dispositions God may make in regard to creatures are not imposed on him necessarily by the love he has for his own goodness. Neither is any necessity imposed on him in regard to creation considered as a whole. Divine Goodness is perfect in itself independently of every creature. It would be just as perfect if nothing else existed because according to the Psalm: "Thou art my God, for though hast no need of my goods." Divine goodness is not an end that can be perfected and completed by what is related to it. Rather, it perfects and finishes what is ordered to it as its end. Therefore it is evident that God necessarily wills all that belongs to his own essence

6 St. Thomas, *Summa contra Gentes*, book I, chapter 81 at *Si autem*, beginning of chapter.

7 St. Thomas, *Summa contra Gentes*, book I, chapter 81 at *Est enim*, second paragraph.

and, by contrast, does not will necessarily anything that is related to creatures.[8]

We cannot indicate any necessarily determining cause to the act of the will by which God wants things. Properly, God's will has no cause. By nature, understanding is such that, if principle and conclusion are understood separately, grasping the principle causes the knowledge we have of the conclusion. But if the understanding discovered the conclusion in the principle itself, by apprehending both in a simple intuition, the knowledge of the conclusion would not be produced in this understanding by grasping the principle, because nothing is its own cause. Nevertheless, the understanding would comprehend that the principle is the cause of the conclusion. The same goes for the will. In the will, the end plays the same role in relation to the means that principles play in the understanding in relation to conclusions. Therefore, for someone who wills the end and means by separate acts, his willing the end causes his willing the means. But if he wills end and means in a single act, his will has no cause because nothing stands as its own cause to itself. Yet, it will be said quite rightly that God wanted to order the means in view of the end. Just as he knows all things by a single act in his very essence, he also wills all things by a single act in his own goodness. Also, just as the knowledge that God has of the cause is not the cause of the knowledge he has of the effect, although he knows the effect as comprised in its cause, so his willing the end does not cause his willing the means, although he wills that the means should be ordered in view of the end. God wills that one thing should be because of another, but he does not will the first thing because of the second.[9]

8 St. Thomas, *De Veritate*, 23, 4, near end of body of article: "Unde patet quod non est necessitas divinae voluntatis ex amore quem habet ad suam bonitatem, quod velit hoc vel illud circa creaturam; nec inest ei aliqua necessitas respectu totius creaturae; eo quod divina bonitas in se perfecta est, etiamsi nulla creatura existeret, quia bonorum nostrorum non eget, ut in Psalmo XV dicitur. Non enim divina bonitas est talis finis qui efficiuntur et perficiuntur ea quae ad ipsum ordinatur. Unde Avicenna dicit (libro VIII; *Metaphysicae*, capitulo VIII, a medio) quod solius actio Dei est pure liberalis, quia nihil sibi accrescit ex his quae vult vel operatur circa creaturam. Patet igitur ex dictis, quod quidquid Deus vult in seipso, de necessitate vult; quidquid autem vult circa creaturam, non de necessitate vult." [Translator: Aquinas and Gilson refer to Psalm 15:2 in The Septuagint-Vulgate enumeration, 16:2 in the Hebrew and more usual enumeration. The New King James version has "You are my Lord. My goodness is nothing apart from you."]

9 St. Thomas, *Summa Theologiae*, part I, question 19, article 5 end of body of article. "Unde sicut in Deo intelligere causam non est causa intelligendi effectus, sed ipse

Still, does this mean that the divine will has no reasons for acting? On the contrary, the divine will has no cause, but it is legitimate to indicate a reason for it. This reason for willing is its goodness. The end is the reason for willing what is related to it. God wills his goodness *qua* end and everything else as subordinated to this end. Therefore, his goodness is the reason for which he wills everything that is not himself,[10] and whatever the intermediate steps through which it is necessary to pass in order to account for things, we must always come to his goodness to furnish their ultimate explanation. So God wills that humans be endowed with reason, because this is necessary for there to be humans. God wills that there should be humans, because it is necessary for the completion of the universe. Finally, he wills that the universe should be good and completed for it to participate in his own goodness. We thereby see that of all the reasons that can be offered to God's will, just one imposes absolute necessity on this will. This is the case in which God wills himself. In all the other cases, the reason for the divine will is only a reason of hypothetical necessity, or of utility, or of suitability. (Examples of these are, respectively: if humans are, they can only be rational; for the universe to be good, it must contain humans; and certain particular goods are appropriate for the ornamentation of the universe.)

But at the same time we see that, though these reasons are not compelling, they are nonetheless real reasons. God, the free creator of all things, acts in view of an end and through means suited to this end. The proof is in the fact that the universe is not arranged by chance, but that it is manifestly ordered with a view to good. To act in view of an end is to act by understanding and will. For something to be perfectly arranged with a view to an end, three conditions are required: the knowledge of this end, the knowledge of the necessary means to attain it, and the knowledge of the necessary proportion between the end and the means. This is to say that in creating the world God acts by his understanding and his will.[11] Moreover, we cannot

intelligit effectus in causa, ita velle finem, non est ei causa volendi ea quae sunt ad finem, sed tamen vult ea quae sunt ad finem ordinari ad finem. Vult ergo hoc esse propter hoc, sed non propter hoc vult hoc." Cf. also *Summa contra Gentes*, book I, chapter 87.

10 St. Thomas, *Summa contra Gentes*, book I, chapter 86.

11 St. Thomas, *Summa contra Gentes,* book II, chapter 23, sixth paragraph, toward middle of chapter: "Deum agere propter finem ex hoc manifestum esse potest quod universum non est a casu, sed ad aliquod bonum ordinatur... Primum autem agens propter finem oportet esse agens per intellectum et voluntatem; . . . Ad hoc enim quod aliquid directe in finem debitum ordinetur, requiritur cognitio ipsius finis et

mean anything else when we simply say: "God's will is good," or "God's will is just." In us, rectitude of the will is really distinct from the will itself, since our will can be righteous or not be righteous. In God we have to distinguish them at least by a distinction of reason and according to our way of conceiving.

Accordingly, it would be an error to believe that the essence of justice depends on God's will alone.[12] Justice consists of a certain rectitude. Therefore, the nature of justice immediately depends upon that thing in which this rule resides according to which the equality and rectitude of justice are established in things. This rule cannot be the will. The will is of such a nature that it cannot play the role of the first rule. It is a right rule itself, because it is directed by understanding and reason, not only in us, but also in God.[13] The only difference resides in our understanding and will really being distinct; our will and its rectitude are likewise really distinct from each other. In God, on the contrary, understanding and will are really identical, while the will and its rectitude are distinguished only by reason. Consequently, the first rule upon which all justice depends is the wisdom of the divine understanding, which establishes all things in the suitable proportion required by their mutual relations and the relation they have to their cause. To say that justice depends on nothing other than the simple will of God is to say that the will does not proceed according to the order of his wisdom, and that is to speak blasphemy.[14]

Consequently, the reason that must be sought for the action of God's will and its directive guide is God's understanding. In God, as in us, *bonum . . . apprehensum est objectum voluntatis*.[15] Just as every voluntary agent

ejus quod est ad finem et debitae proportionis inter utrumque; quod solum intelligentis est. Cum igitur Deus sit primum agens, non agit per necessitatem naturae, sed per intellectum et voluntatem."

12 St. Thomas, *De Veritate*, 23, 7, at second part of *Sed Contra* . . . " . . . justitia est rectitudo voluntatis. Sed rectitudo voluntatis est aliud a voluntate; in nobis quidem secundum rem, cum voluntas nostra possit esse recta et non recta; in Deo autem saltem ratione, sive secundum modum intelligendi. Ergo ratio justitiae non dependet solum ex divina voluntate."

13 St. Thomas, *De Veritate*, 23, 7, about a third of the way through the short body of the article: "Voluntas autem non habet rationem primae regulae, sed est regula recta: dirigitur enim per rationem et intellectum, non solum in nobis, sed in Deo . . ."

14 St. Thomas, *De Veritate*, 23, 7, end of the body of the article: "Et ideo primum ex quo pendet ratio omnis justitiae, est sapientia divini intellectus . . . Dicere autem quod ex simplici voluntate dependeat justitia, est dicere quod divina voluntas non procedat secundum ordine sapientiae, quod est blasphemum."

15 St. Thomas. *Summa contra Gentes*, book II, chapter 24, beginning of chapter.

produces its effect by reason of its understanding, God produces all things into being by reason of the wisdom of his understanding.[16] As St. Thomas explicitly observes, this is what bursts forth in the whole work of creation, where we see manifestly that God always acts with a view to an end. This is what Descartes denies. If we pass from Scholastic metaphysics to Scholastic philosophy of nature, we immediately understand why Descartes always refuses to acknowledge the existence of a subsistent Good in God's understanding, independent of his will. To acknowledge that the divine will models itself in its action upon the divine understanding that knows the good and that without this understanding the will would in some manner be blind, is, by that very fact, to say that God's will always has an end. These ends are the real reasons for which the world is arranged in one way rather than another. Without diminishing himself in any way, God could refrain from willing the world. But if he wills the world, he can only will it in the way that most resembles his perfection; and the good that he has willed to introduce in the world explains the order that we find in it. Therefore, the world can only be understood by trying to find the reasons by which it is thus disposed, by looking for the ends that God proposed in creating the world. Consideration of these ends is indispensable for the metaphysician. The latter sees that beings without intelligence or even knowledge (like natural bodies) tend toward an end. He concludes from that they could not act always in the same way and so as to achieve the best, if they were not determined by an intelligent, knowing being, just as the arrow is directed by the archer. This being, who directs all things and to whom the metaphysician is necessarily led, is God.[17] However, the consideration of the ends of God is no less useful for the natural philosopher. It will explain the *why* of all things. Firstly, it will explain to us how effects are produced in the universe by determined causes. If a cause does not lead to a determined effect, all effects are indifferent to it, and consequently it will not produce one rather than another. It will be impossible for such a cause to act. Therefore, every agent leads to a determined effect because it acts with a view to an end. If things were otherwise, nothing would be produced, no cause would act.[18] Likewise, it cannot be doubted that all the particular dispositions that we observe in

16 St. Thomas, *Summa contra Gentes*, book II, chapter 24, end of second paragraph, beginning *Item*: "Omne igitur agens voluntarium producit effectum secundum rationem sui intellectus: Deus autem agit per voluntatem ut ostensum est. Igitur per sapientiam sui intelllectus res in esse producit."

17 St. Thomas, *Summa Theologiae* part I, question 2, article 3.

18 St. Thomas, *Summa contra Gentes* book III, chapter 2 at *Si agens non tenderet*.

creatures can be explained by the wise preordination of the divine understanding. An order that is always or frequenly observed in things cannot be considered fortuitious. In the works of nature, we see very often or always that everything is established with a view to what is best. The leaves of plants are disposed so as to produce fruits, and the organs of animals to assure their preservation. How is this to be explained, if we do not admit the intervention of an end that has arranged everything according to the principle of what is best?[19] What more satisfactory explanation of all things can be given than to show the particular ends to which God has arranged them? Scholastic natural philosophers devoted themselves to this, and in conformity with the principles posed by St. Thomas, they worked to find the reasons of the order we observe in things. More than once in the course of physics at La Flèche Descartes must have encountered this sort of explanation. The *Commentary on De Anima* by the Conimbricenses contains a fairly large number of them, which are generally taken from the Fathers of the church or older apologists: eyes are placed under the brows as if to shelter them under high rocks that overhang them. Situated at the top of the head they see more and further. Were they situated lower like ears, mouth or nostrils, they would not have been as useful. Sentinels who are placed upon heights can see enemy troops far away and prevent them from occupying the city or surprising their general's army. To avoid incursions of bandits, watchmen are posted on the walls, towers, tops of rocks, and every high place from which they can observe what happens on the plain. The sailor who believes he is approaching land goes up to the mast top, climbs to the highest point of the highest spar, and from there greets the land that his companions still do not see. Perhaps it will be said that, if the eyes had to be placed as high as possible, it was a mistake not to have put them on the very top of the head as they are on beetles. But on that arrangement, the brows would not protect the eyes. The problem consisted of placing the eyes as high as possible while retaining sufficient protection for them. Too high, they do not see further; too low they are exposed to many dangers. Nature provided for

19 St. Thomas, *Summa contra Gentes*, book III, chapter 3 towards the end of the chapter: "Quod provenit ex alicujus agentis actione praeter intentionem ipsius, dicitur a casu vel fortuna accidere. Videmus autem in operibus naturae vel semper vel frequentius quod melius est; sicut in plantis folia sic esse disposita ut producant fructus, et partes animalium sic disponi ut animal salvari posit. Si ergo haec eveniunt praeter intentionem naturalis agentis, hoc erit accidens a casu vel fortuna. Sed hoc est impossibile; nam ea quae accidunt semper vel frequenter non sunt casualia nec fortuita, sed quae accidunt in paucioribus."

this by placing them under the brows and further protecting them by lids whose rapid movement lets images of things pass and prevents everything that can harm our eyes from reaching them. As for the shape of the eyes, it is easy to understand why it is round. First, because what has a spherical shape moves more rapidly in all directions than what has another shape; next, because if the eyes were not round, they could not perceive surfaces larger than their own. Mathematicians demonstrate that we see objects according to straight lines perpendicular to the eye's surface, which converge toward its center. If the eye were a flat surface, it would only receive the perpendiculars of surfaces equal to its own, and consequently would not see any surface larger than it.[20] If we observe the inner structure of the eye instead of its placement and outer form, we will have no fewer motives to be amazed, so cleverly arranged are the innumerable parts that compose it and so cleverly adapted to the functions they must fulfill.[21] It is not just in humans but also in the whole universe that we can explain everything by the adaptation of means to their ends. Considered in itself, the circular movement that the heavens have carried out since their origin in the distant past would not be explained.[22] But we comprehend its reason when we see that the heavenly bodies in their breathtaking movement, insofar as they transmit their influence on the sublunary world, represent and imitate, according to their nature, the superabundant goodness and beneficent action by which the first cause is communicated to all creatures. That is the end assigned to the movement of the heavens. It endeavors to achieve that end by provoking the growth and decline of all sublunary bodies, by producing the distinction of spring, summer, autumn, and winter; by making so many things come forth from the fertile womb of nature; and finally by preparing the matter necessary for the generation of humans, to which all the others are disposed as to their end and the greatest good to which everything is subordinated.[23] This kindness of God, who looks out for all humans, particularly involves the just whom Divine Providence has predestined to the life of beatitude and who fulfill what they must undergo on earth amid sighs and tears, or

20 Conimbricenses, *Commentary on De Anima*, 2, 7, 6, 1.

21 Conimbricenses, *Commentary on De Anima*, 2, 7, 6, 3: "Ex dictis jam facile quivis intelliget maxime idoneam esse ad visus functionem oculorum fabricam, cum tam singulari artificio coagmentata sit, et tot musculis, tot tunicis, tot humoribus, et tam assiduo spirituum defluxu ad id munus praestandum abundet."

22 Conimbricenses, *Commentary on De Coelo*, 1, 2, 3, 1 at *Tertium*.

23 St. Thomas, *Summa contra Gentes*, book III, chapter 22, especially toward end of chapter, *Quia vero per eadem res*.

wait for the number of years and generations to be brought to completion when they will receive eternal life and the happiness of the elect.[24] Therefore, it is evident that the movement of the heavens is not useless, and that what we have just said can account for it.[25]

Starting from a simple distinction of reason-reasoned between God's understanding and will, we arrive at the consequence of a finalistic conception of physics. This conception is what Descartes absolutely wants to avoid, and we have just seen him denying all its antecedents in order to be more certain of destroying it. Whether there is or not a distinction of reason between God's understanding and will, whether knowledge of the Good in that understanding does or does not precede the determinations of the will, these are metaphysical questions that do not interest Descartes for their own sake. They can be denied without the doctrine set out in the *Meditations* being affected in the slightest. They do not have the least importance in what concerns the *Cogito*, the proofs of God's existence, the doctrine of clear and distinct ideas, or the real distinction of body and soul. The real significance must be sought elsewhere and is indicated to us by the consequences related to physics that flow from it in Scholastic philosophy.

If we refuse to admit the distinction of the divine will and understanding, there is no longer grounds to linger over the discussions in which Scholasticism explains the determinations of God's will, when God judges better or more suitable to take a determination in one way rather than in another. Descartes clarifies his thought with an example. Aristotle claims that the world exists from all eternity because God, although acting through his understanding and his will, is still determined by natural necessity to judge and to will what he must do. God, because he is the first mover, moves the world by natural necessity; therefore the world exists from all eternity. Such at least, is how the Scholastic professors interpret Aristotle's thought on this point. For Suárez, however, the demonstration is not convincing. It is not proven that God wanted to create the world from all eternity by affirming that God is necessitated to want and to judge so about it. What would be necessary to prove first is that God necessarily judged it better to create the world from eternity than to create it in time. It may be that God judged it

24 St. Thomas, *De Potentia*, 5, 5, body of the article in general.

25 Conimbricenses. *Commentary on De Coelo*, 1, 2, 3, 3: "Patet ergo ex dictis coelum nequaquam frustra, sed gratia finis, ejusque praestantissimi moveri, talique motu perfectionem consequi; cum naturalium agentium magnum sit ornamentum sese communicare aliis et secundum causalitatis similitudinem, divinam participare bonitatem."

better or more suitable to create it in time than from eternity, in which case he would have created it in time.[26]

According to Descartes, this is the wrong way to approach the question. We are not to wonder whether God judged more suitable or better to create the world in time than to create it in eternity. We should not waste time on all the arguments that have been accumulated about knowing whether, given that the world was created in time as faith teaches, God could have created it from eternity if he had judged that better.[27] All these arguments suppose an idea of Good in God prior to the decisions of his will. This supposition is false and unworthy of God. The previous propositions must be reversed. God does not want what is good. Rather what God wants is good. If God wanted to create the world in time, it is not because he saw that it would be better than if he created it from eternity. On the contrary, because God wanted to create the world in time, it is better than if it had been created from eternity.[28] It is easy to see that, at this moment and beyond the particular example Descartes chooses., he rejects the entire finalistic conception that Scholasticism had taught.

In truth, an intermediate position was open to him: not to deny absolutely that God had created the world according to the principle of the better and with the concern to achieve certain ends, but to consider that the disproportion between the divine understanding and ours is such that the discovery of these ends is completely impossible for us. That would have freed him more easily from the useless and fatal burden of finalistic

26 Suárez, *Disputationes Metaphysicae*, disputation 30, question 16, number 53: "Sed juxta hanc interpretationem enervatur discursus Aristotelis, quo probat mundi aeternitatem: hanc enim colligit ex eo quod primus motor necessitate naturae movet. At si solum credidisset agere ex necessitate naturae praedicto modo, responderi facile posset ipsius discursui: quod licet Deus necessario voluerit creare mundum, illa tamen necessitate voluit illum creare in tempore, non in aeternitate, qui fortasse id naturaliter apprehendit ut melius et convenientius. Debuisset autem Aristoteles probare necessario judicasse Deum, esse convenientius mundum ex aeternitate creare."

27 See this point in the little work by St. Thomas Aquinas, *De Aeternitate Mundi contra Murmurantes*. [Translator: Notably end of section 1: ". . . omnes consentiunt, in hoc scilicet quod Deus potuit facere aliquid quod semper fuit, considerando potentiam istius infinitam."]

28 *Sextae Responsiones*, VII, p. 432: ". . . ita scilicet ut ista boni idea impulerit Deum ad unum potius quam ad aliud eligendum. Nempe, exempli causa, non ideo voluit mundum creare in tempore, quia vidit melius sic fore, quam si creasset ab aeterno; . . . Sed contra, quia voluit mundum creare in tempore, ideo sic melius est, quam si creatus fuisset ab aeterno."

explanations. In fact, Descartes certainly justifies the rejection of final causes in the *Meditations* and the *Principles* in this way. We know that our nature is weak and limited, that the nature of God, by contrast, is immense, incomprehensible, and infinite. That is enough to make us comprehend that God can produce an infinity of effects whose causes we ignore, and that we cannot seek to determine God's ends without temerity, and that is why the whole genus of causes that have been called final causes can have no place in true physics. We ought to reject them if only for this reason alone.[29] This reason that Descartes provides is not added on for purposes of the controversy, without deep connections to the rest of the system. We will see its basis and the source of its true value in Descartes' eyes. Nevertheless, it is only secondary, and the main advantage it offers is to raise fewer difficulties. But the passage that we just quoted seems to invite us to believe that the real reason for the rejection of final causes must not be sought there; *ob hanc unicam rationem*, Descartes writes, meaning, if we understand him correctly, "supposing that there were no others." However, Descartes reveals these other possible reasons to us in the most explicit fashion in his conversation with Burmann.

The first reason is that even if knowledge of final causes were possible, it would be of no use for physics. Knowing something's end does not introduce us to the knowledge of the thing itself, and its nature remains no less hidden from us. We know why it is. We are still ignorant of what it is, and yet what matters to us over anything else is to know that. Aristotle's worst defect is that he always argues about things starting from the consideration of their end. Moreover, let us set aside the ends God himself may have revealed to us and speak purely as philosophers. By talking of God's ends, do we not commit the gravest error? We conceive God as human, very powerful and greater than the rest, but in the last analysis as a human who sets this or that end for himself and tends toward it through this or that means. This is a most unworthy notion of God.[30] It is not enough to declare the quest for

29 *Meditations* (Fourth Meditation); VII, p. 55 [Heffernan, p. 154]: "Cum enim jam sciam naturam meam esse valde infirmam et limitatam, Dei autem naturam esse immensam, incomprehensibilem, infinitam, ex hoc satis etiam scio innumerabilia illum posse quorum causas ignorem; atque ob hanc unicam rationem totum illud causarum genus, quod a fine peti solet, in rebus Physicis nullum usum habere existimo; non enim absque temeritate me puto posse investigare fines Dei." See also *Principia*, I, 28.

30 Conversation with Burman, April 16, 1648; V, p. 158: "Bene hoc est observandum nos nunquam debere argumentari a fine. Nam primo: cognitio finis non inducit nos

God's ends is imprudent, but rather we must go further and declare it impossible, since it is absurd in its foundation. Descartes does not simply advise us to abstain from a difficult and risky search. He counsels against seeking what does not exist. Properly, the search for God's ends is a search without object. Descartes does not want us to be concerned with final causes because, by reason of the peculiar notion he has formed of God's freedom, he believes he is in a position to demonstrate that God never acts with a view to an end. Or rather, it is because Descartes wants to demolish the very foundation of the finalistic concept of nature that he finds himself obliged to go back to God and profoundly modify the notion of God's freedom that Scholasticism has constructed.[31]

Furthermore, there can be no doubt that Descartes reveals his true thought to Burmann on this point. It is worth noting that from 1630 on Descartes includes his feeling about God's freedom in his letters to Mersenne: "But I will not refrain from touching upon some metaphysical questions in my physics and particularly this one…" . . ." From this period onward, the denial of finality in the divine will is the foundation of physics for Descartes, and he writes in the same letter that without the knowledge of God and his true nature, he could never have discovered the foundations of this science.[32] Through that we discover what sense and what scope should be attributed to the Cartesian notion of divine freedom. In Descartes' eyes, the doctrine is first of all the indispensable basis of a physics of efficient causes. He refuses to admit even a distinction of reason between God's

in cognitionem ipsius rei, sed ejus natura nihilominus latet. Et hoc Aristotelis maximum est vitium quod semper a fine argumentatur. Secundo, omnes Dei fines nos latent et temerarium est in eos involare velle. Non loquor autem hic de revelatis, sed qua philosophus eos solum considero. Sed nos hic maxime erramus. Concipimus Deum tanquam magnum aliquem hominem, qui hoc et hoc sibi proponit, et eo his et his mediis tendit, quod certe Deo maxime indignum."

31 This is why we do not believe it is necessary to recur to the distinction proposed by Boutroux between absolute contradiction and relative contradiction in order to explain Descartes' thought. The distinction supposes that a difference remains, however slight it may be, between God's understanding and his will, by which there is still a place for finality (See Boutroux, *De Veritatibus Aeternis apud Cartesium*, pp. 21–22). It is not necessary to consider them as inseparable and *arctissime cohaerentes*, which, even while combining them, is still to distinguish them, but we must say: *unum et idem sunt*. From this it would follow, not that God seeks certain ends, although they are unfathomable for us (Boutroux, pp. 30, 36, and 70), but that God does not seek ends.

32 Letter to Mersenne, April 15, 1630; I, pp. 143–144.

understanding and his will, because the distinction leads one to think that God's will acts according to the good that his understanding apprehends and thereby justifies a finalistic explanation of things. In the *Meditations*, in accordance with the goal he set for himself in publishing it, Descartes poses the metaphysical principles from which unprejudiced minds would be led to admit the true physics without realizing it.[33] If the world was produced in the order of efficient causes and not in the order of finality, it is the order of efficient causes, not the order of final causes that real physics should set out to discover. That is why Descartes never tires of repeating that God created all things as an efficient cause produces its effect. Notably, this is the sense of the comparison he presents between God creating the truths and a king who freely decrees laws in his realm. Again, it is what he wants to make Mersenne understand, when he writes to him that God created things *ut efficiens et totalis causa*.[34] In the *Sextae Responsiones* he returns to the first comparison, specifying it in the sense we have indicated: God created things as efficient cause *eadem ratione qua Rex est legis effector*.[35] In his replies to Gassendi, insisting on the inscrutability of God's ends and on the point that none of them is more easily accessible to us than the others, Descartes explicitly specifies that we must give up guessing about them and substitute the consideration of efficient causes for that of final causes, which alone are capable of making us know the grandeur and perfection of the supreme artisan.[36] Descartes knows that by transforming the notion of creative act that is commonly held, he will no less radically transform the usual conception of what a genuine explanation of the created world must be. The knowledge we have of God's nature and our certitude that he created the world as an efficient cause produces its effect, immediately permits us to deduce what the most perfect science, the only genuine explanation of creation must be: an explanation of effects by their causes.[37] Thus, the quest for final

33 On this point we are inspired by an unpublished course on Descartes delivered by Levy-Bruhl during 1905–1906. Charles Adam arrived at the same conclusion by a completely different route, and we wholeheartedly subscribe to what he has written, *Vie et Oeuvres de Descartes*; XII, pp. 304–307.

34 Letter to Mersenne, Amsterdam, May 27, 1630 (?); I, p. 152.

35 *Sextae Responsiones*, VII, p. 436.

36 *Quintae Responsiones*, VII, pp. 374–375: "Quaecumque deinde affers pro causa finali, ad efficientem sunt referenda; ita ex usu partium in plantis, in animalibus, etc., effectorem Deum mirari, et ex inspectione operum cognoscere ac glorificare opificem, par est, non autem quo fine quidque fecerit divinare."

37 *Principia*, I, 24: "Jam vero quis Deus solus omnium quae sunt aut esse possunt vera est causa, perspicuum est optimam philosophandi viam nos secuturos, si ex

causes becomes not only rash and dangerous, but also even chimerical and groundless. Through his conception of divine freedom and his refusal to distinguish the understanding from the will in God, Descartes believes he has overthrown the structure of Aristotelian natural science and destroyed finality even in God's will, that is to say in its very root.

Parallel to this critique of final causes and often confused with it, Descartes conducts another. This critique is supposed to free the divine will from the apprehension of the true and its submission to the eternal truths. When Scholasticism retains a slight distinction between the understanding of God and his will, it is not only in order to authorize the affirmation that God's will directs itself by the apprehension of the good grasped by the understanding. It also makes room for the possibility of certain eternal truths that subsist in God's understanding independently of his will. The philosophers, including Descartes, affirm that things' essences depend on God in just the same way as existences, but they understand this dependence in quite different senses. To say with the Scholastics that things' essences depend on God is to deny these essences any reality outside of the divine understanding that conceives them. To say in the Cartesian sense that essences depend on God is to make some realities depend on God's understanding and also his will. If we distinguish will from understanding in God, we necessarily limit the freedom of the will. We cannot consider the understanding separately without giving it content and at the same time removing the content from the free choice of the will. We will certainly say that God can do absolutely everything he wants, that he is supremely free, and that his omnipotence has no limits. This signifies that there are no other limits than those that the divine understanding imposes upon it. This is why St. Thomas finds himself naturally led to wonder whether these are not impossibilities even in regard to God's will and to resolve the question affirmatively. Even in regard to God, there are some *impossibilia secundum se*. We know that God's will is the will for the good that his understanding apprehends. What his understanding cannot apprehend cannot be the object of his will. Therefore, it will suffice to determine what cannot fall under God's understanding to determine *ipso facto* what he cannot will and what escapes his will. If we exclude the case of error, which cannot occur in the divine understanding, we see that the understanding is unable to apprehend only what is contradictory, because the contradictory is self-destructive and therefore

ispsius Dei cognitione rerum ab eo creatarum explicationem deducere conemur, ut ita scientiam perfectissimam, quae est effectum per causas, acquiramus."

impossible of itself. And since it cannot be the object of the divine understanding, it also cannot be the object of the divine will.[38]

That whatever is contradictory is intrinsically impossible cannot be doubted. An essence whose definition implies contradiction would be nothing; it would belong to non-being, since it is impossible that a thing should be and not be at the same time. To admit that an essence is at once itself and its contrary is to want to posit simultaneously being and non-being for this essence, to affirm a reality at the same time as to deny it, to suppress the essence whose definition one claims to posit. Therefore, the essence becomes a pure nothing, incapable of furnishing an object of the understanding and consequently for God's will.[39] From that it follows that the essences of things as the divine understanding conceives them are realities in whose nature the divine will can change nothing. If God cannot wish at the same time that a thing should be and not be, neither can he will at the same time that a thing should be and that one of this thing's essential and constituent principles should not be. It is contradictory to posit an essence that lacks any one of its essential principles, since to suppress one of the principles without which the essence is not itself, is properly to suppress the essence. So, God cannot apprehend the human essence other than as rational and endowed with a soul. Nothing forces God to create humans, but supposing that he wants to create them, he cannot create them lacking soul and reason.[40] Humans will be rational or will not be.

38 St. Thomas, *Summa contra Gentes*, book I, chapter 84, at paragraph beginning *Amplius* . . . : "Voluntas non est nisi alicujus boni intellecti: illud igitur quod non cadit in intellectu non potest cadere in voluntate. Sed ea quae sunt secundum se impossibilia non cadunt in intellectu, cum sibi ipsis repugnant, nisi forte per errorem non intelligentis rerum proprietatem, quod de Deo dici non potest. In divinam ergo voluntatem non possunt cadere quae secundum se sunt impossibilia."

39 St. Thomas, *Summa contra Gentes*, book I, chapter 84, at *Item, sicut* . . . last third of paragraph: "... ". . . rationi entis inquantum hujusmodi repugnat quod aliquid sit simul ens et non ens. Non potest igitur Deus velle quod affirmatio et negatio sint simul verae: hoc autem includitur in omni per se impossibili quod ad seipsum repugnantiam habet inquantum contradictionem implicat. Voluntas igitur Dei non potest per se esse impossibilium." Cf. St. Thomas, *Summa contra Gentes*, book II, chapter 25, last sentence of the second paragraph beginning *Primo quidem*: "Hoc igitur Deus non potest ut faciat simul unum et idem esse et non esse: quod est contradictoria esse simul."

40 St. Thomas, *Summa contra Gentes,* book II, chapter 25 about halfway through chapter at *Amplius ad*...: "Ad remotionem cujuslibet principii essentialis sequitur remotio ipsius rei: si igitur Deus non potest facere rem simul esse et non esse, nec etiam potest facere quod rei desit aliquid suorum principiorum essentialium ipsa remanente, sicut quod homo non habeat animam."

St. Thomas establishes eternal truths and the principles of the sciences as natures independent of God's will. The eternal truths are nothing but the formal principles upon which the essences of things depend. It is an eternal truth that the triangle contains three angles whose sum is equal to two right angles, because the very essence of the triangle necessarily implies the truth of this proposition. To deny that and, at the same time, to want to posit the existence of this figure is to want it to be and at the same time not to be. Likewise, to deny that what is said of the genus can be said of the species, or that the radii of a circle are equal is to deny the essences of genus and circle. Therefore, the eternal truths are independent of God's will, because they are implied in the essences of things that themselves are independent of his will.[41] All propositions of this kind impose themselves on God's will as immovable truths, and that is precisely why we can call them necessary. They are not true precisely because God knows them as such, but, on the contrary, God recognizes them as true, because they are true. Therefore, their necessity imposes itself upon his understanding as upon his will.

These consequences flow naturally from the distinction made by Scholastic philosophers between God's understanding and his will. However, Descartes remains consistent with himself by refusing both to recognize this distinction and by making the eternal truths independent of God's will. Along with the Scholastics, he recognizes that the essences of things and the eternal truths are the same. On this point he makes no reservation.[42] But instead of considering that these essences of creatures subsist in God's understanding independently of his will, he makes them free creations of divine omnipotence, which is at the same time intelligence and will, without any possible legitimate distinction. This is why, taking up St. Thomas's own examples, which are standard in Scholasticism, Descartes flatly opposes St. Thomas's conception of the nature of eternal truths. He first takes the example of the circle. God "was as free to make it untrue that all the lines drawn from the

41 St. Thomas, *Summa contra Gentes*, book II, chapter 25, paragraph following passage in note 40 beginning *Praeterea.* "Cum principia quarumdam scientiarum ut Logicae, Geometriae et Arithmeticae, sumantur ex solis principiis formalibus rerum ex quibus essentia rei dependet, sequitur quod contraria horum principiorum Deus facere non possit sicut quod genus non sit praedicabile de specie, vel quod lineae ductae a centro ad circumferentiam non sit aequales aut quod triangulus rectilineus non habeat tres angulos aequales duobus rectis."

42 Letter to Mersenne, May 27, 1630 (?); I, p. 152: "… now this essence is nothing but these eternal truths…" . . ." Cf. *Quintae Responsiones*, VII, p. 380, lines 7–10.

center to the circumference were equal as to not create the world."[43] Some years later, in regard to the question posed by Mersenne about whether real space would exist in the case where God had created nothing, Descartes takes as his example a logical proposition analogous to the one St. Thomas used about genus and species. "These eternal truths, such as *Totum est majus sua parte*, etc., would not be true if God had not so established them."[44] Lastly, in *Sextae Responsiones*, Descartes recalls St. Thomas's last example to contradict its conclusion: "nec voluit [Deus] tres angulos trianguli necessario aequales esse duobus rectis, quia cognovit aliter fieri non posse… [Sed] quia voluit tres angulos trianguli necessario aequales esse duobus rectis, idcirco jam hoc verum est et fieri aliter non potest atque ita de reliquis."[45] In short, God creates all these truths, whatever they are, like other creatures. This is why Descartes sometimes seems to place a restriction of their being given the title of eternal truths. It is quite natural that Scholastic philosophers should consider these truths eternal. Apprehended from all eternity by the divine understanding, they participate in the eternity of this same understanding.[46] If there were not eternal understanding, then there would be no eternal truths, but as the divine understanding is eternal, the truths it apprehends turn out to be necessarily eternal.[47] In Descartes' eyes, by contrast, nothing guarantees the eternity of such truths. They may be eternal because God may have created them from all eternity. It also may be that they had a beginning long ago, in the event that God created them in time, as is generally admitted about the world. Descartes always raises a doubt in this regard. Without settling the question, he simply calls them, "these truths that are labeled eternal."[48]

43 Letter to Mersenne, Amsterdam, May 27, 1630 (?); I, p. 152.

44 Letter to Mersenne, May 27, 1638; II, p. 138.

45 *Sextae Responsiones*, VII, p. 432. Cf. Letter to Mesland, May 2, 1644; IV, pp. 118–119. Moreover, Descartes also attacks another example that St. Thomas takes from the consideration of numbers: "Ratio circuli et *duo et tria esse quinque*, habent aeternitatem in mente divina," writes St. Thomas, *Summa Theologiae*, part I, question 16, article 7 reply to objection 1. See Letter to Arnauld, July 29, 1648; V, p. 224, lines 2–9. And *Sextae Responsiones*, VII, 436, lines 12–14.

46 "Secundum hoc igitur vera et necessaria sunt aeterna, quia sunt in intellectu aeterno qui est intellectus divinus solus." St. Thomas, *Summa Theologiae*, part I, question 10, article 3, reply to objection 3.

47 St. Thomas, *Summa Theologiae*, part I, question 16, article 7. "Unde si nullus intellectus esset aeternus, nulla veritas esset aeterna. Sed quia solus intellectus divinus est aeternus, in ipso solo veritas aeternitatem habet."

48 Letter to Mersenne, May 27, 1638; II, p. 138. Cf. "That the mathematical truths, which you label eternal…" Letter to Mersenne, April 15, 1630; I, 145.

What, then, was Descartes' intention in insisting so strongly on submitting the eternal truths to God's free will? First of all, we must observe that almost all the passages in which Descartes affirms the creation of these truths end in the same conclusion: by admitting the opposite, we ignore the infinite, incomprehensible power of God. We do not formally deny divine omnipotence in words, but, by failing to correctly know its nature, we limit it by making it bow to the essences of things and to the eternal truths. The reason for this error resides in the disproportion between God, who is infinite, and our finite understanding. Through a natural tendency of the mind, we spontaneously acknowledge more reality in what we comprehend than in what we do not comprehend. Everything whose nature is finite is knowable to us in itself and in certain cases perfectly known. For example, this is the case of mathematical truths. Our understanding, which comprehends them in the most clear and distinct way, is naturally led to attribute an absolute necessity of being and a maximal reality to them. Since they are necessary for the understanding, our understanding immediately considers them necessary in themselves, but things are completely different in what concerns the idea of God. God is certainly known to us. We discover the idea in our soul of a being that cannot be bounded by any limits, and therefore we have a very real and very true idea of the infinite. In a certain sense, even God's infinite perfections appear to us with more evidence then anything else, because, by their simplicity and their infinity, they satisfy our intellect better than corporeal things.[49] Yet, the idea that is knowable for us remains incomprehensible to us by reason of the infinity of its object. We know that God exists; we do not comprehend God. We touch him with our thought; we do not embrace him within our thought. By its nature, the infinite cannot be comprehended by a finite mind.[50] Therefore, we comprehend mathematical truths, while we do not comprehend God's essence, and this is why we are inclined to attribute a lesser reality to this essence. It is not at all surprising that once embarked on this road, some can even go into atheism. Without going to that extreme, we still comprehend that the philosophers have attributed to mathematical truths that they embrace within their thought an existence at least as necessary as God's, whose essence escapes the finite mind in all directions. But we must reverse the implicit reasoning that shapes common opinion and deduce a completely opposed conclusion about the difference that we note between these ideas. Since we comprehend

49 *Principia*, I, 19; and Letter to Mersenne, January 21, 1641; III, p. 284.
50 Letter to Mersenne, May 27, 1630; I, p. 152.

mathematical truths perfectly, they are finite in nature.[51] Since we are denied the comprehension of God, he is infinite. Therefore, we must judge that "since God is a cause whose power surpasses the limits of human understanding, and the necessity of these eternal truths does not exceed our knowledge, these truths are something lesser and subject to this incomprehensible power."[52] It only remains for us to submit the finite to the infinite and the mathematical truths to God.

We have, then, clarified the sense of Cartesian thought on this matter. In the refusal to situate eternal truths above God or simply on his level, we must first of all see the refusal to confuse the two orders of infinite and finite or to put them on the same plane. Descartes believes that it was of the greatest importance that these two orders remain strictly distinct and that above all, we, who belong to the finite order, do not seek to penetrate into the realm of the infinite. To exclude the eternal truths from the divine creation is to admit, in Descartes' phrase, that they are necessarily bound to God's essence itself. The conclusion is strictly valid, because we must acknowledge with Scholasticism that whatever is not God is God's creature, and whatever is not God's creature is God.[53] No distinction of whatever type we might make can invalidate this conclusion. For, not only nothing that is God is really distinct from God himself, but also it must be further said that everything that is in God is God.[54] Consequently, if God does not create eternal truths, they are God. Since we perfectly comprehend mathematical truths, it necessarily follows that we comprehend God himself. The mathematical truths are perfectly known. We comprehend them in the strong sense of the term, that is to say, they are completely grasped by our understanding and they do not go beyond it in any way. How can one not see the

51 Letter to Carcavi, June 11, 1649; V, pp. 367–368: "Moneo inquam e contra plane repugnare si quod comprehendam, ut id quod comprehendo sit infinitum; idea enim infiniti ut sit vera, nullo modo debet comprehendi, quoniam ipsa comprehensibilitas in ratione formali infiniti continetur."

52 Letter to Mersenne, May 6, 1630; I, p. 150.

53 Suárez, *Disputationes Metaphysicae*, disputation 31, section 2, number 3: "Unde recte dicunt sancti Patres, quidquid a Deo factum non est, vel Deum esse vel nihil esse. Justinus in *Expositione Fidei*; Cyrilli libro 1 *In Joannem*, capitulo 6; Augustinus libro 1 *De Trinitate* capitulo 6." Cf. Descartes: *Third Objections and Replies*; VII, 188. "In hac idea [Dei] tam immense potentia continetur, ut intelligamus repugnare, si Deus existat, aliquid aliud praeter ipsum existere, nisi quod ab ipso sit creatum."

54 Conversation with Burman; V, p. 166: "Quicquid in Deo est, non est realiter diversum a Deo ipso, imo est ipse Deus."

consequences that are going to flow necessarily from such a position? Encouraged by the mathematical truths that we introduce directly into the divine understanding, we will be inclined to believe, even knowing our finite nature, that we can apprehend something of the infinite and master it in certain regards. We open discussions on the nature and properties of the infinite, on the problems posed by the relations of the parts of the infinite with the whole. This is a dangerous presumption for genuine physics, precisely one from which Descartes proposes to liberate us. But to get that outcome it is necessary to clear the ground of the false precedent of mathematical truths. It was necessary to show humans that that comprehension of necessary truths does not in the slightest lead to the comprehension of the infinite. This is why Descartes strives to prove that mathematical truths are created by God's free will. As creatures, they are not longer part of the divine essence and no longer drag our understanding into a realm that ought to remain forbidden to it.

The first benefit Descartes reaps from this attitude is a valuable confirmation of the reasons that inspired the rejection of final causes and their exclusion from genuine physics. In the Fourth Meditation and in the *Principles*, when Descartes bases himself on God's incomprehensibility in order to forbid us to look for God's ends and to get the basis of the physics of efficient cause, he does not recur to a mere expedient. In his eyes, this is really one of the metaphysical foundations of true physics. God's infinity forbids humans, finite creatures, to share in the activity of creation. Evidently this argument is neither the deepest nor the most decisive of those to which Descartes appeals. He leaves notably unresolved the question of knowing whether God really proposed ends in his action. But it is no longer an extraneous, added element: supposing that these ends exist, God's nature is such that they must necessarily escape us.[55]

In the same way, physics is freed from a whole series of futile questions that had encumbered it until then. Since by its very nature the infinite escapes our grasp, we must be content to acknowledge it without seeking to explain it.[56] This reservation renders the establishment of the science much easier. By refusing to tackle the disputes in which the learned waste part of the time, it aborts them beforehand. We know we are finite. That suffices to turn us away from problems whose solution would suppose the

55 Letter to Chanut, June 6, 1647; V, p. 55; and *Principia*, I, 28

56 Letter to Mersenne, January 28, 1641; III, p. 293; and letter to Mersenne, May 27, 1638; II, p. 138.

comprehension of the infinite.[57] What more precisely are these questions about the infinite from which Descartes seeks to be delivered? They are the topics of Scholastic discussions by which one of his contemporaries, Scipion du Pleix, although explicitly following Aristotle's doctrine, declares himself similarly overwhelmed.[58] Descartes was not the only one to mark the strange contradiction of a finite mind pursuing the explanation of the infinite, the idea of which "is as vain, light, and fickle thing as the concept of our soul itself, which, by participating in divinity that is infinite, really has, as it were, infinite shooting pains, showing the effects of its origin; however, returning to itself, it stops them; or if it follows them indiscriminately, it loses its way afterwards."[59] But during this period not everyone demonstrated similar prudence in this sort of discussion, and in 1630 Fr. Mersenne sent a sample of them to Descartes. By a coincidence that is not accidental, Descartes links his response on this point to the first declaration he made to Mersenne regarding the dependence of the eternal truths upon God. Mersenne had asked how the concept of an infinite line could be justified. Such a line would have to include an infinite number of feet and an infinite number of yards. A yard equals three feet, so we would have to recognize that the infinite number of feet would be three times greater than the infinite number of yards. To this Descartes answers: *Concedo totum*. This infinite is evidently considered as if it were finite, and the proposed multiplication by three would not be appropriate in the case of a genuine infinite. By contrast, if we want to consider this infinite as a genuine infinite, the question would not admit an answer, given that it would stop being infinite if we could comprehend it.[60] This attitude of caution should be adopted whenever discussions of the infinite come up. Therefore, there is nothing to answer to those who ask "whether half a given infinite line is itself infinite," or

57 *Principia*, I, 26: "Ita nullis unquam fatigabimur disputationibus de infinito. Nam sane cum simus finiti absurdum esset nos aliquid de ipso determinare, atque sic illud quasi finire ac comprendere conari."

58 Scipion du Pleix, *Corps de Philosophie*, vol. I, *Physique*, pp. 173–174, 1627, edition: "Others imagined still other distinctions to support disastrous absurdities that are brandished in the schools. But for me, without detaining myself in such useless controversies, believing that nothing is truly infinite but God alone . . ."

59 Scipion du Pleix, *Corps de Philosophie*, vol. I, *Physique*, p. 175.

60 Letter to Mersenne, April 15, 1630; I, pp. 146–147. [Translator: Mersenne's question apparently was about *pieds* and *toises*. The *toise* was a pre-revolutionary measure equal to six *pieds* or feet. Although Gilson's paraphrase correctly says there should be six times as many *pieds* as *toises*, it mistakenly says there are six *toises* in a *pied*.]

"whether the infinite number is even or odd," and other questions of the same sort *quia de iis nulli videntur debere cogitare, nisi quia mentem suam finitam esse arbitrantur.*[61] Let us leave the questions about the infinite to those minds that think themselves infinite.

But at the same time, as Descartes frees himself from useless controversies, does he not attract new difficulties? The physics he wanted to set out in *Principia* was a substitute for the *World* that would never see the light of day. It was an explanation of the universe, not of this or that phenomenon. Was it possible to speak about the world without engaging the question of knowing whether it was finite or infinite? Here again, it may seem that for Descartes the solution of the problem was completely settled. Since he professed to be incompetent in matters of the infinite, it only remained to leave the matter in suspense, and he avoids a useless conflict with Scholastic philosophy \. Perhaps that is what Descartes would have done, if the definition of nature had not come between him and Scholasticism. For Descartes, matter is extension: length, breadth, and depth. It is impossible for us to suppose that there is any void in this matter, because we cannot represent the void as having three dimensions, that is, being extended and material.[62] Descartes' definition of matter is at the very foundation of his system, and he could not yield on this point.[63] The issue is to know whether the concept of a finite world is compatible with this definition of matter by extension. It is evident that it is not. Let us imagine the world to be finite. What will there be beyond the limits? Everywhere we set the limits of the world in our imagination, we immediately conceive other spaces beyond these limits, which are themselves extended and consequently material. In other words, we can only limit matter by other portions of matter, which amounts to saying that we cannot limit it.[64]

We might, of course, take refuge in the hypothesis of the imaginary spaces that Scholasticism supposes. We would distinguish between real space and the space our imagination places at the surface of our limited world.[65] But this imaginary space, which will be conceived only as the void,

61 *Principia*, I, 26.

62 *Principia*, II, 16. Letter to Chanut, June 6, 1647; V, pp. 51–52.

63 VI, p. 36, line 5; Ccf. *Principia*, II, 4.

64 *Principia*, II, 21. Letter to Chanut, June 6, 1647; VI, pp. 51–52.

65 Toletus, *Physica*, text 49, question 8: "Locus alius est verus, alius imaginarius. Imaginarius quidem est, ut extra coelum spatium illud imaginarium, quod ibi quisque imaginari potest. Et vacuum etiam hic in mundo, si esset, imaginarius esset locus, imaginarium videlicet spatium; posset etiam imaginari superficies vacua."

must be rejected for the same reason. How, asks Descartes, can we maintain that those spaces that we conceive at the surface of the real world [translator, i.e. the physical universe] are not real themselves? Do they not also have their three dimensions? If they are extended in length, breadth, and depth, are they not the real matter that pushes back the limits of the world beyond that point that has been set for them?[66]

There remains the hypothesis of the infinite world. This hypothesis offers the advantage of extolling God's greatness to the utmost. But in return, it raises multiple, serious problems. The first, and not negligible one, is that such a doctrine goes against Scholasticism on a point in which philosophy and theology seem equally interested. The doctrine of the world's infinity was not clearly heretical, but it was held to be dangerous and not easily reconciled with strict orthodoxy. Descartes did not feel very secure on this flank. Cardinal Cusa, whose authority he invokes to prove that an orthodox Catholic can teach the infinity of the world, did not constitute a sufficient guarantee for him, because Cusa's credit was quite restricted, and it is doubtful that he ever taught this doctrine. What is found in his work is rather the sketch of what Descartes himself will mention quite explicitly, namely that the world is neither finite nor infinite, but ought to be considered as intermediary between finite and infinite. Was Descartes perhaps led into error on this point through a false report? Did Descartes perhaps also read *Docta Ignoratia* quickly, as it seems he read many books, and was he misled by passages that seemed to imply this doctrine? In any case, strictly speaking, Cusa does not hold it. When he applies to the world the neo-Platonic comparison of the infinite sphere whose center is everywhere and circumference nowhere, he affirms that the center of the world is God himself and that no other circumference ought to be sought than this same God who supports and contains it.[67] But Cusa is very far from affirming the infinity of the world strictly speaking, and the pantheism that has been attributed to him clashes with passages that reveal an irreducible dualism in his doctrine. When we apply the creator's attributes to his creatures, according to Cusa, they must be contracted and restricted to the measure of these creatures, since the creatures have only been produced in the order of the infinite and constitute authentic reductions of God. Accordingly, God is perfectly One

66 Letter to Chanut, June 6, 1647; V, p. 52.

67 Nicholas De Cusa, *De Docta Ignorantia*, 2, 12: "Unde erit machina mundi quasi habens ibique centrum, et nullibi circumferentiam: quoniam circumferentia et centrum Deus est, qui est ubique et nullibi."

and Infinite. The universe too is one and infinite, but with a unity termed by plurality, and an infinity contracted, as it were, by the finite.[68] The universe is infinite, because given any finite thing whatever, we can always imagine another that surpasses it in perfection or quantity. We can imagine nothing of the kind in regard to the universe, because although the divine power could always create a greater universe than any given universe, still since matter is not extensible to infinity in act, there can be no greater universe than the present one. Since it is not terminated by anything (for being the greatest possible one, another limiting it cannot be imagined), this universe is really endless, that is to say infinite.[69] We see how far such a doctrine is from authorizing Descartes to hold the thesis that the world is actually and positively infinite.

Moreover, precisely in the event that Descartes had admitted the infinity of the world, controversies would have been forced upon him that he wanted to avoid. A traditional Scholastic line of argument consisted in confronting those who held the infinity of the world with *aporias* that entangled them.[70] It is impossible for God himself to produce an actual infinite, not because he lacks the power to do so, but because it is something contradictory and impossible in itself, given the absurd consequences that follow upon such a supposition. We would then be driven to admit that something greater than the infinite can exist or that the part is equal to the whole, consequences whose falsehood demonstrates the falsehood of the principle from which they flow. Let us suppose that God has produced the infinite and, for example, that an infinite number of stones exist. Since divine power cannot be exhausted, God could create still more stones and increase the number, with the result that there would exist a number higher than infinity. Or on the

68 Cusa, *De Docta Ignorantia*, 2, 4: ". . . quare quamvis sit maxime unum [*scilicet*, universum] est tamen illa ejus unitas per pluralitatem contracta, sit infinitas per finitatem..." . . ."

69 Cusa, *De Docta Ignorantia* 2, 1 (p. 24): Universum vero cum omnia complectatur quae Deus non sunt, non potest esse negative infinitum, licet sit sine termino, et ita privative infinitum; et hac consideratione, nec finitum, nec infinitum est... . . . Quare licet in respectu infinitae Dei potentiae quae est interminabilis, universum posset esse majus; tamen resistente possibilitate essendi aut materia, quae in infinitum non est actu extensibilis, universum majus esse nequit, et ita interminatum, cum actu majus eo dabile non sit ad quod terminetur, et sit privative infinitum." Cf. *De Docta Ignorantia*, 2, 8 (p. 33) at *Unde quamvis*, and 2, 11 (p. 38) at *Cum igitur*.

70 Scholasticism generally treated the issue under the heading of the following general question: "Possitne infinitum actu divina virtute produci an non?" For philosophers who hold the affirmative, see Conimbricenses, *Physica*, 3, 8, 2, 1.

contrary, let us subtract one hundred stones from this infinite number. If we say that the remainder is still infinite, it follows that the total number of stones removed plus those that remain is not greater than this remainder, since nothing can be greater than the infinite. And that is completely absurd.[71] No less absurd is the supposition of two lines that are infinite by one or the other of their extremities. Since these lines are finite on one end and infinite on the other, we could make one of them bigger than the other without adding anything to it, simply by tugging on the first at the finite end and thus making it pass beyond the other.[72] Lastly, the idea of an actually infinite body is a contradictory one. By definition, a physical body can be moved. The property is intrinsic to its nature. It must be able to change places whether in a straight line, like heavy and light bodies, or in a circle, like the heavenly spheres. An infinite body would not be susceptible to any of these movements. It could not be moved in a straight line because a body of infinite masses would occupy the whole place by being extended on all sides, and consequently no space would remain in which it would be moved. Nor could it be moved in a circle, and this can be proved by the principles of geometry. Euclid (book III, proposition 26) established that all straight lines drawn from the center to the circumference are further apart in proportion as the distance from their center to their end is greater. In the hypothesis that this distance is infinite, these straight lines would therefore be separate from each other by an infinite distance. This posited, it is easy to establish our proposition: if an infinite body travels in a circle and if we suppose two straight lines drawn from its center, a moment could come when in consequence of this body's circular movement, one of the two straight lines would occupy the place of the other. This straight line would have traversed an infinite space in a finite time, which is absurd. Therefore, an infinite physical body could not be moved. Since by definition every physical body is mobile, it follows that no infinite body can exist in nature.[73]

71 Eustachius a Sancto Paulo, *Summa Philosophiae*, III, 84–85. Cf. Conimbricenses, *Physica*, 3, 8, 2, 2 at *ad 7, Rat.*

72 Eustachius a Sancto Paulo, *Summa Philosophiae* III, 84–85: "Fieri enim posset ut cum duae lineae essent infinitae ex una parte, ex altera tamen parte finitae, una fieri posset major altera absque ulla additione, sed sola motione seu trajectione unius prae altera." Cf. Conimbriceneses for another impossibility of the same kind, *Physica*, 3, 8, 2, 2, at *6 Rat.*

73 Conimbricenses, *Physica*, 3, 8, 1, 3: "Nam omne corpus physicum naturaliter cieri potest, vel motu recto, ut corpora gravia et levia, vel in orbem, ut sphaerae coelestes: sed corpus infinitum neutro modo valet motum subire: ergo nullum ejusmodi infinitum in natura datur darive potest."

Therefore, for a philosopher who wanted to avoid these tedious quarrels and who, moreover, defined matter as simple extension, neither the hypothesis of a finite world nor that of an infinite world was acceptable. A solution had to be thought out that allowed the disputes about the infinite to be avoided without thereby rendering necessary the unacceptable supposition of a limited world. Descartes thought he had found the solution of this problem by "inventing"[74] the distinction between the infinite and the indefinite. The infinite is that whose reality we can conceive in a positive way as surpassing all limits. Therefore, the infinite is God and God alone,[75] because we can affirm of God alone that his essence is not limited in any sense.[76] The nature of the indefinite is completely different. We will say that a thing is indefinite whenever we have "no reason by which to prove that it has limits."[77] For example, it is impossible for us to imagine an extension so great that we could not conceive another that surpasses the first; we will therefore say that extension, and consequently also nature and the world, is indefinite. Left to itself in the face of this kind of reality, the human intellect would naturally be impelled to deem it infinite. It would push back its limits indefinitely, and seeing that it is impossible for it to reach them, it would endlessly multiply the indefinite by the indefinite. The indefinite indefinitely multiplied by itself is nothing other than the infinite.[78] But we also have the idea of God within us, and this time we no longer simply observe that our definition of this essence does not allow us to assign it limits, but that the divine nature is such that it surpasses these limits on all sides. Our intellect must stop before this infinite reality. What tells us that the limits of the world, which are inconceivable for the human mind, finite as it is, are not fixed necessarily in regard to God's infinite understanding, which comprehends them? Infinite in relation to us, the world can be finite in relation to God. The solution of such a problem evidently surpasses our capabilities,

74 Conversation with Burman; V, p. 167: "Distinctio illa ab auctore primum est inventa."

75 *Principia*, I, 27: ". . . ut nomen infiniti soli Deo reservamus, quia in eo solo omni ex parte, non modo nullos limites agnoscimus, sed etiam positive nullos esse intelligimus."

76 Letter to Chanut, June 6, 1647; VI, p. 51, lines 25–29.

77 Letter to Chanut, June 6, 1647; V, p. 51, line 30.

78 Conversation with Burman; V, 167: "Quod ad nos attinet, nos non possumus unquam in illis [*scilicet*: mundus, numerus, etc.] terminum aliquem invenire, et sic nostri respectu sunt indefinita, quin etiam forsan infinita, nam indefinitum semper et semper multiplicatum ut hic fit, est ipsum infinitum; sic etiam de numero, etc." Cf. Letter to Chanut, June 6, 1647; V, p. 52, line 19.

and the distinction between the indefinite and the infinite expresses our reservation in presence of what our limited understanding does not allow us to embrace.[79] Such an attitude has evident advantages for Descartes. The success of his whole physics is connected to it in the measure in which the new distinction makes it possible to define matter by extension alone, by excusing Descartes from entering into the maze of discussion that grew up in Scholasticism about the possibility of the actual infinite.

Not only was the new distinction going to facilitate the acceptance of Descartes' physics by Scholastic philosophers and theologians in general, but also, it rendered a certain number of particular notions acceptable that might otherwise have encountered violent resistance. First, Descartes shelters himself from an anticipated objection against the doctrine of vortices. In the hypothesis of a finite and limited world, an objection would have been raised about the possible escape of particles of matter constituting Descartes' vortices into unknown, imaginary spaces supposed to be around the universe. By contrast, in the hypothesis of an indefinite world, the objection fails, since by definition matter extends further than any human understanding can conceive. Moreover, to supposing the world is indefinite, we obtain the same advantages as by considering it infinite, and we avoid the objections that this hypothesis could provoke among philosophers and theologians.[80] If extension defines matter, it follows that not only the void, but also the atom become impossible. Extension is infinitely divisible by thought, and there is no material particle so small that divine power could not still subdivide it.[81] This infinite divisibility is still necessary for the movement of bodies to be possible in an absolutely full universe. A body can only move by expelling a body from the place into which the first body penetrates. In its turn the second body expels another and so forth until we come to a last body that penetrates into the place left free by the first, in the precise moment in which the first body left the place. This is the condition and necessary mode of movement in the plenum.[82] It is easy to show that this circular movement implies the infinite divisibility of matter, that is to say, the impossibility of our supposing matter divided into such small parts that we could not imagine it divided into still smaller parts. To achieve its

79 Letter to Chanut, June 6, 1647; V, 52, lines 21–25; and Conversation with Burman; V, p. 167.

80 Letter to Morus, February 5, 1649; V, pp. 274–275.

81 Kurt Lasswitz, *Geschichte de Atomistik von Mittelalter bis Newton*, Hamburg & Leipzig: L. Voss, 1890, vol. II, pp. 58–59 (reproduced Hildesheim: G. Olms, 1963).

82 *Principia*, II, 33.

circular movement, matter must successively fill parts of space that are one smaller than the other in innumerable degrees. Therefore, it is necessary that one of these parts should spread the innumerable particles of which it is made by some tiny amount from each other in order to fill the innumerable different spaces. The indefinite divisibility of matter, therefore, follows necessarily from the fact that there is a whole series of smaller and smaller spaces through which one part of matter must pass for circular movement to be possible.[83]

We say *indefinite* again because it does not follow from the definition of matter than infinity belongs to it, as it does from the definition of God, but simply that our understanding conceives no limit in the divisibility of its parts.[84] Perhaps it will be asked how the indefinite divisibility of parts is possible. Such a division, which is comprehensible from the abstract purely mathematical point of view, seems to become contradictory from the real, physical viewpoint. Natural bodies are not divisible *ad infinitum* because the form of each species of being requires a certain quantity of matter, below which the natural body can no longer exist. Furthermore, we again meet all the objections raised against the possibility of an actually realized infinite.[85] But Descartes' answer is always ready and ends in non-acceptance. "Although we do not understand how that infinite division takes place, we must not doubt that it does, because we perceive that it follows necessarily from the nature of matter, which is very distinctly known to us, and that we perceive as well that this truth is one of those that we cannot understand because our mind is finite."[86]

By turning our understanding toward God's infinite omnipotence, Descartes intends to garner another no less valuable advantage. He hopes to turn the philosophers away from situating themselves in an anthropomorphic viewpoint in order to explain the world. Why do we spontaneously suppose that the universe is limited? Surely, we do not necessarily conceive it as such. Quite the opposite, philosophers happily imagine non-actualized spaces beyond the universe, but they reason as if our understanding can surpass the limits of creation by its own powers, and assign limits to the world without reason or divine revelation requiring it.[87] Our natural tendency to

83 *Principia*, II, 34.
84 Letter to Morus, February 5, 1649; V, p. 274, lines 5–20 and p. 275, lines 7–13,
85 Conimbricenses, *Physica*, 3, 8, 1, 3 at "*4 Assert.*"
86 *Principia*, II, 35. Cf. Letter to Morus, February 5, 1649; V, p. 273, line 26 ff.
87 *Principia*, III, 2.

limit the world is explained by our deep conviction that the universe was entirely created with us in mind. It does not occur to us for an instant that God may have created things that will never be seen or understood by humans and will never be of any use to them. To explain things by the utility that they may have for us is naïve and must have no place in genuine physics. If we can say that God made all things for our use, that can only be in a moral sense and in order to encourage us to thank him.[88] But this goal will also be accomplished if we place ourselves in the standpoint of efficient causality and if we seek to glorify God as the artisan of the world, instead of vainly trying to guess the ends he had proposed for it. Besides, these purely conjectural explanations that piety legitimates in ethics are out of place in physics where only decisive, evident demonstrations are accepted.[89] It is not true to say that all things have been made for us. What is true is that we can find utility in all things by working to understand them and admire the sublime artisan in each of his works. It is also true that Genesis seems to present humans as the chief subject of creation, but Genesis was written from the point of view of humans and with them in mind. It is not concerned with discovering whether, in creating the world, God proposed other ends. Things may have been made by God for us and for completely different ends at the same time, and it is easy to understand that preachers do not insist on the second point, since it is useless for their essential objective, to encourage our love for God.[90]

In this, Descartes directly opposed St Thomas and the teaching he had received at La Flèche. Moreover, Descartes felt that his doctrine did not harmonize well with Genesis. When God declared, after having created earth, sea, and all within them: "Let us make man in our image and likeness," he immediately added, "and let him rule over the fish of the sea, the birds of the air, the animals, the whole earth and the reptiles that crawl upon it." At that moment God creates humans, whom he makes in his image and, after having blessed them, God adds: "Increase and multiply and fill the earth and submit it, and rule over the fish of the sea, the birds of the air, and all the animals that move upon it." Again the Lord says: "Here is what I give you, all the fruit of the earth with its grain for you to take nourishment from

88 *Principia*, III, 3.

89 *Quintae Responsiones*; VII, pp. 374–375. Descartes still tends to indicate that his physics can provide as powerful weapons for apologetics as traditional natural philosophy does. Doubtless Gassendi's objection (Fifth Set of Objections; VII, pp. 308–309) made him reflect on this point.

90 Letter to Chanut, June 6, 1647; V, pp. 53–54.

it,"[91] This conception of humans as rulers of the world would remain that of St. Thomas, in whose eyes everything in the world is ordered in function of the greatest utility for humans. Mixtures or compounds subsist by the qualities of the elements that compose them. Mixed bodies nourish plants. Animals feed on plants. Lastly, humans use all things according to their needs. Nature created humans naked, because they could find things around them with which to cover themselves. Nature gave humans no natural food except milk, because they can find food around themselves. It has created them weaker and slower than certain animals, because they can use the strength and swiftness of those animals. We can say of humans what the Psalmist says of them addressing God directly: "Omnia subjecisti sub pedibus ejus."[92] We see that the whole universe is ordered in relation to humans. The movement of the heavens is established to determine the generation of all things, and all things are engendered for the greatest good of humans. That is to say, consequently, that all things are made to serve them and that they are the real end.[93]

From St. Thomas this doctrine had entered the teaching of the schools, which also possessed it from the Bible and the Fathers. Descartes must have heard it taught in the context of the explanation of *De Coelo*,[94] and doubtless also in magnificent terms in the context of the explanation of the *Physics*, when the question about the ends which God created the world was resolved right in front of him. He learned that the universal end of all nature is humans, as the scriptures, the Fathers, Plato, and Aristotle testify; and that all things have been created with a view to humans.[95] According to Descartes, however,wehowever, we have abundant reasons to suppose that in creating the world God considered another end than just human utility. Taking

91 Genesis 1: 26–30.

92 Psalm 8:8.

93 St. Thomas, *Summa contra Gentes*, book III, chapter 22 end of chapter: "Si igitur motio ipsius coeli ordinatur ad generationem, generatio autem tota ordinatur ad hominem sicut in ultimum finem hujus generationis, manifestum est quod finis motionis coeli ordinatur ad hominem sicut in ultimum finem in genere generabilium et mobilium. Hinc est quod Deuteronomio 4:19 dicitur quod Deus corpora coelestia fecit *in ministerium cuncti gentibus*."

94 Conimbricenses, *De Coelo*, 2. 3.

95 Conimbricenses, *Physica*, 2, 9, 2, 1: "Est etiam totius corporeae naturae universalis finis: Homo...; ...; tum quia Deus spectabilem hunc mundum hominis gratia procreavit, eique singulari beneficio subjecit omnia; tum quia homo jure insitae nobilitatis, et eminentioris formae praerogativa, totam corpoream naturam ad se convocat, sibique arrogat."

another Scholastic doctrine, this time for his own use, Descartes recalls that the real end of God in creating the universe is much less humans than himself, because it is stated of God that *omnia propter ipsum facta sunt*: "It is God alone who is the final cause as well as the efficient cause of the universe."[96] Scholasticism rightly attributes this end to the existence of all things and wrongly attributes another end to them.[97] This means that, in the consideration of the world and its explanation, the true viewpoint is much less human utility than God's greatness. The consequences of such a viewpoint are fundamental for physics. If we consider things, not in relation to human smallness, but in relation to God's greatness, we are no longer tempted to limit the world. Once someone has turned his attention to God's infinite power and infinite goodness, he will no longer be afraid to imagine his work too vast, too beautiful, and too perfect.[98] He will avoid pronouncing himself on what God could have done in the stars and outside this earth. It will not be argued against the notion of indefinite matter that it supposes the existence of an indefinite number of worlds, an absurd supposition, to be rejected according to what is generally held. How can we know whether God's infinite power created a single world or an infinity of them? It is said that the order manifested by things testifies that everything is disposed with a view to a single end, which is God; that all things that come from God are ordered, one in relation to another, and all in relation to God, in such a way that they constitute a necessarily unique system, which is the world.[99] Others recognize that the supposition of a single creator does not necessarily entail recognition of a single world; that, very much the opposite, the hypothesis of several different worlds is in perfect harmony with the idea of a creator endowed with infinite power, but they add that faith, in the absence of any

96 Letter to Chanut, June 6, 1647; V, p 54, line 1.

97 On the point that God is the supreme end of the universe, over us humans, see St. Thomas, *Summa contra Gentes*, book III, chapter 17, chapter title: "Omnia ordinantur in unum finem, qui est Deus,." and Conimbricenses, *Physica*, 2, 9, 2, 1, at *Est praetera*.

98 *Principia*, III, 1.

99 St. Thomas, *Summa Theologiae*, part I, question 47, article 3. "Respondeo dicendum quod ipse ordo in rebus sic a Deo creatis existens unitatem mundi manifestat. Mundus enim iste unus dicitur unitate ordinis, secundum quod quaedam ad alia ordinantur. Quaecumque autem sunt a Deo, ordinem habent ad invicem, et ad ipsum Deum . . . Unde necesse est quod omnia ad unum mundum pertineant. Et ideo illi potuerunt ponere plures mundos, qui causam mundi non posuerunt aliquam sapientiam ordinatem, sed casum, ut Democritus, qui dixit ex concurso atomorum factum esse hunc mundum, et alios infinitos."

demonstration, forbids us to admit the existence of other worlds beside the one in which we live. Scripture and the Apostle teach us that the whole human race has come from one man, and thereby sin entered the world through one man. From that it follows that the whole human race has been engendered in this single world, propagated itself there, and is contained there; unless we say that God created another world that would not contain humans, or that he transported one human to found a colony there, two equally absurd suppositions that lack the slightest plausibility.[100] But all these arguments are always inconclusive. How do we know whether God produced creatures different from us, other lives, other humans, or other beings analogous to humans? How do we know whether God did not create an infinite number of different species of creatures, scattering his omnipotence about in the creation of things? All that escapes us, because God's ends remain hidden. Therefore, we must not abandon ourselves to the illusion that we are the favorite creatures of God and that everything has been created for our use. Rather, let us think that perhaps there exist an infinity of creatures who live in other worlds and are far superior to us.[101]

This habit of relating everything to our own use is precisely what makes us tend to shrink the world and wrap it around ourselves. Anthropomorphism takes on a remarkable form, whose consequence, geocentrism, is extremely dangerous. From the affirmation that the universe is made for our use, to the other affirmation that the earth, the kingdom of mankind, is the center of the universe there is only a step. In any case, those who view the universe merely as the mere dwelling place of humans diminish its true dimension to such an extent that any explanation of phenomena becomes impossible. Also, the principles of physics gain acceptance by our understanding with difficulty because their vast, fertile principles suppose much more extended space and infinitely more numerous beings than our visible universe can show us.[102] Still, if these principles are clear and evident, if the consequences have been deduced from them with mathematical rigor, and if our conclusions are in perfect agreement with the phenomena, it would do God an injury to suppose our knowledge false. It would be to admit that he has created us such that we can still be mistaken even using

100 Conimbricenses, *De Coe*lo, 1, 8, 1, 2.

101 Conversation with Burman; V, p. 168.

102 *Principia*, III, 4. [Translator: It is difficult to retain the ambiguity in Cartesian terminology here. *Le monde, mundus*, is the world in the sense of the physical universe. *La Terre* is planet earth.]

our reason well.[103] We must avoid belittling the work of creation by reducing it to human scale, and with that very step the conclusions of genuine physics will find free access into our mind.

For example, we will not let ourselves be deceived on the subject of the true dimensions of the earth, the sun, and the moon. If we observe that the fixed stars cannot fail to be farther away from the earth or the sun than Saturn, and that nothing impedes our supposing them separated by an indefinite distance, we will easily understand that seen from the fixed stars, the earth will not appear larger than these same fixed stars seen from earth.[104] Certain phenomena force us to recognize this indefinite distance of the fixed stars as something very real. The explanation of the movements of the heavens leads us to suppose them so far away that even Saturn would appear near by comparison. Therefore, it is not enough simply to consider the fixed stars as being placed above Saturn, which is the ordinary opinion,[105] but we will take the liberty of placing them still higher and even as high as we please. If we compare the distance that everyone attributes to them to terrestrial distances to which we are accustomed, it is so great that it does not seem more credible than any distance whatever,. Besides, in regard to the omnipotence of God the creator, any distance is as plausible as any other. Consequently, nothing keeps us from admitting this indefinite distance of the fixed stars, which makes possible the true explanation of the movement of the planets and comets.

In the same way, we will no longer believe, as the Scholastics did, that comets are meteors engendered in the air quite near us and that are found in the region between the earth and the moon.[106] We know now that their parallaxes are not only above the moon, but above Saturn and far beyond. Likewise we will no longer object that if the earth changes place in relation to the sun, and the sun retains the same position in relation to the fixed stars, it is necessary to admit that the earth gets closer and farther away from the fixed stars alternately all along its orbit. Observation does not allow us to affirm that, since the appearance of the stars does not change.

103 *Principia*, III, 43.

104 *Principia*, III, 7–8.

105 Regarding the size of the fixed stars in relation to the earth, Descartes is not opposing Scholasticism but those who believe the witness of our senses without discussion (Conimbricenses, *De Coelo*, 2, 12, 1, 3). By contrast, on the distance of the fixed stars in relation to Saturn, he is addressing the Scholastic philosophers (Conimbricenses, *De Coelo*, 2, 5, 1, 5).

106 Conimbricenses, *Meteora*, 3, 3.

The truth is precisely that the distance that separates us from the fixed stars is such that the circle described by the earth around the sun is only a point by comparison.[107] But we could say the same about its orbit. That can only seem incredible to those who do not know how to consider the greatness of God's work. They judge that the earth is the chief part of the universe. In their eyes it is the home of mankind for whose sake everything has been created.[108] How will they conceive the possibility of these indefinite spaces in relation to which humanity, the earth that carries it, and even the orbit of this earth, will be nothing but a point? Again, by bringing us to bow down before what our finite intellect cannot comprehend, Descartes prepares our minds to recognize as possible the movement of the earth around the sun.

This also reveals to us the close agreement that Descartes establishes between his metaphysics and his physics on the question of freedom in God. If he refuses to submit the divine will to the eternal truths and to the most necessary principles of the sciences, it is because, to his mind, it is impossible to have a high enough idea of God's infinite power. Descartes wishes to concede nothing to the tendency that leads us to deal with God on an almost equal footing, since we quickly lose sight of the degree to which the infinite fullness of divine reality surpasses and transcends us. By trying to penetrate the mystery of God's essence, by seeking to inform about the intelligence and the will in that essence, we enslave it to our finite understanding and we impose our limits on it. As there is no common measure between the infinite and the finite, the ultimate goal of Descartes in the question of the eternal truths is to accustom our intellect to submit itself to the infinite. He pursues a dual objective and hopes for a dual benefit: to limit the field of our research in one direction and to expand it in another direction. He limits it, first by forbidding humans the futile explanation by ends that remain impenetrable for them and also the useless discussions about an infinite that surpasses us in every direction. Next, he expands it when he commits our human understanding to refrain from denying this infinite when it encounters it, under the mere pretext of not being able to understand it, and to lead the human intellect to not reduce the greatness of God's work

107 This image is generally accepted by Scholastic philosophers. Conimbricenses, *De Coelo*, 2, 14, 2, 1: "Terra comparata ad complexum firmamenti proindeque aliorum orbium superiorum [that is to say the crystalline and empyrean, which are above the firmament or sphere of the fixed stars] quoad nostrum aspectum est instar puncti, hoc est, habet insensibilem magnitudinem."

108 *Principia*, III, 29.

to human dimensions. Convinced of our infinite smallness in the face of the creator's infinite power, we will cease to make the world revolve around us and at the same time we will suppress the limits that the concept of a universe adapted to our dimensions and made just for us has imposed on science.

Chapter Four

The Sources: Duns Scotus and Mersenne

To our knowledge, no study has ever been specifically dedicated to the sources of the Cartesian notion of divine freedom. Yet, somehow, it seems to have become customary to consider Duns Scotus as the immediate predecessor on the path Descartes would choose. When we reconstruct this tradition's history, we unquestionably have to trace it back to Secrétan,[1] who, without establishing a direct connection from Duns Scotus to Descartes, still insists on what the two philosophers have in common, the belief that a free act of the absolute will can effectuate the synthesis of contraries and even contradictories. Later, we find the resemblance between Descartes and our medieval philosopher mentioned almost everywhere. To speak only of the most recent writer who has drawn attention to it, Octave Hamelin, in his remarkable lectures on Descartes' system, declares his conformity to the tradition: "As predecessor he had only Plotinus and Duns Scotus, and perhaps he was unaware of them."[2] The matter of Plotinus must be set aside. It would be worthwhile to find out whether Plotinus can be directly or indirectly listed among the predecessors and sources of inspiration of Descartes. As for Duns Scotus, we are going to examine whether there is some basis for this link.

We find the connection again in Wilhelm Kahl's dissertation on the primacy of the will in St. Augustine, Duns Scotus, and Descartes.[3] According to this historian, Descartes' thought on the divine will is extremely close to that of Duns Scotus: both describe it in almost the same manner,[4] without it being possible, however, to demonstrate that Duns Scotus exercised real influence on Descartes.[5] To our mind, that is not the problem. We do not doubt that if Duns Scotus had really held a doctrine of divine freedom as

1 Charles Secrétan, *Philosophie de la liberté*, Paris: L. Hachette, 1849, third edition, vol. 1, lecture IV.

2 Octave Hamelin, *Le système de Descartes*, p. 234.

3 Wilhelm Kahl, *Die Lehre vom primat des Wille bei Augustinus, Duns Scotus und Descartes*, Strassburg: K. J. Trübner, 1886.

4 Kahl, *Die Lehre*, pp. 114–115.

5 Kahl, *Die Lehre*, p. 115, note 3.

close to that of Descartes as is claimed here, knowledge of that doctrine would have reached Descartes. A conception as original and contrary to the Thomist notion of God's freedom would not have failed to have echoes. It would have been reproduced, commented, disputed, and refuted, but it would have been discussed, and Descartes would have known the discussions. A demonstration of resemblance would be a very powerful presumption in favor of influence, but first it would be necessary to demonstrate that there is resemblance. If we examine the texts more closely, the claimed resemblance does not exist.

To establish it, Wilhelm Kahl bases himself on a certain number of passages that, at first glance, seem to weigh in favor of his conception. To begin with, there are passages where Duns Scotus establishes the primacy of our will over our understanding. The will can be considered superior to the understanding in relation to their object. The object of the understanding is the True, that of the will is the Good. According to St. Thomas, Truth, the understanding's object, is nobler than Goodness, because it is closer to supreme perfection. What is supremely perfect is the being that contains all perfections in itself, and as the true is more closely united to being, Truth is more perfect than Goodness. According to Duns Scotus, this argument demands correction. Let us grant that what is closer to absolute perfection is also the most noble; it follows that Goodness is nobler than Truth. What is good of itself and by essence is better than what is good by participation. The good, which is the object of the will, is good by essence and absolutely, and, by contrast, the true is only good by participation in the good. Therefore, the will is superior to the understanding in its relation to their object.[6] Likewise, St. Thomas had deduced another proof of the understanding's primacy from eudaemonology. The good toward which all the efforts of human faculties tend is the truth, according to Aristotle. Human happiness resides in it. The faculty of the soul that allows us to reach this end will have an indisputable superiority over all the others. In us, this faculty is not the will, but the understanding. Therefore, we must conclude the primacy of understanding over will. Without doubt Aristotle's authority has some weight here. But it must be observed that the Philosopher never distinguishes the

6 Duns Scotus, *Reportata Parisensia*, book IV, distinction 49, question 2, number 7, Wadding vol. 11. p. 895 [Vivès. 24, pp. 623–624] quoted in Kahl, *Die Lehre*, p. 92: "Sed accipiendo eamdem majorem concludo oppositum, scilicet quod ratio boni sit nobilior, quia quod est per se et per essentiam bonum est melius quam quod per partipationem bonum; bonum est per essentiam bonum et absolute bonum, verum autem non est bonum nisi partipatione boni."

distinctive principles according to which understanding and will operate. He considers them one, single, identical principle of action and situates himself more often in the standpoint of the understanding only because its act is easier for us to grasp than that of the will. Furthermore, St. Paul's authority, which is important for a Christian, can be set against Aristotle's. For Paul, nothing is superior to charity. If nothing is superior to charity in this earthly life, nothing will be superior in our heavenly country, where we will live eternally. Therefore, if we compare the capacity of these two faculties, will and understanding, we see that, whether here below or in our permanent homeland, the will has the greater capacity because to it belongs charity, which gives the soul the most perfect disposition it could receive. Therefore, the understanding is less perfect than the will.[7]

The third proof in support of the primacy of the will is the most original. It is also the most appealing because it takes us deep into the heart of Duns Scotus's thought through the analysis of the reciprocal causal relation of will and understanding. According to St. Thomas's doctrine, the equivocal efficient cause is nobler than its effect. The act of the understanding through which it apprehends the end is cause of the act of will, since nothing can be willed without being known, and the good clearly known cannot fail to be wanted: "hoc posito ponitur ille et amoto amovetur." Therefore, the understanding is nobler than the will. But according to Duns Scotus, the argument is inclusive. Intellection is not the total cause; it is only the partial cause of volition. The fact that the understanding is the partial cause of the voluntary act does not suffice to establish its superiority. That the intellection is not the total cause of the volition is evident because, since the first intellection is caused by a purely natural cause and consequently is not free, it would introduce this same necessity into all that of which the intellect might afterwards be the cause. A kind of necessary process would be set up, with purely natural necessity, in which the understanding would completely determine the will. It follows from this that if we want to retain the possibility of human freedom, given intellection, we must say that it does not constitute the total cause of the will, but that the will constitutes a cause of higher order in relation to intellection because it is free.

Besides, if the understanding is a partial cause in regard to the will, the will determines the understanding much more evidently. The will also is an equivocal efficient cause, since, as St. Anselm says,[8] the will moves against

7 Kahl, *Die Lehre*, pp. 93–95.
8 St. Anselm, *De Conceptione Virginis*, 6, 4.

the judgment of other powers and moves all the others according to its command. Or, as St. Augustine says,[9] the will uses all the other powers of the soul. But Duns Scotus does not depend on just the argument based on the Doctors' authority. He tries to determine how the understanding is dependent upon the will. We must observe that the act of understanding is placed under the power of the will because the will can turn the understanding away from one intelligible in order to turn it toward others. Otherwise, the understanding could not be turned away from the contemplation of the most perfect of all objects, about which it would have habitual knowledge. The reality is quite different. Let us consider the case in which the understanding apprehends its object perfectly. The will can still be pleased by what is understood or reject it. If the will is pleased by the intellection and assents to it, the understanding is affirmed and confirmed in its act. If the will rejects this intellection, the understanding is weakened and loses its firmness. Moreover, this is easily understood because the soul can act with as much force when it disperses its faculties as when it concentrates them on one single point.[10] When a perfect intellection is found in our intellect, many others are found at the same time that are imperfect and confused, unless the intellection under consideration is actually perfect to the point of leaving no room for any other. Among these confused and imperfect intellections that are frequently found, the will can give its assent to any whatever and, by fixing itself upon that one, confirm and reinforce it to the degree of conferring such intensity on it that from confused and imperfect the intellection becomes clear and perfect. Therefore, the will can command the understanding, even while it apprehends an object perfectly, and turn it toward the object that pleases the will. The opposite is no less certain, and by rejecting the intellection, the will can weaken it and diminish it to the point of definitively turning away from it. Each of us can experience this in ourselves with a sure experience that cannot be rejected.[11] In the last analysis, the demonstration

9 St. Augustine, *De Civitate Dei*, book XIX, chapter 14.

10 Kahl, *Die Lehre*, p. 99 and p. 21, note.

11 Duns Scotus. *Opus Oxoniense*, book II, distinction 42, question 4, number 11, p. 1052 [Vivès XIII, p. 461]; quoted in Kahl, *Die Lehre*, p. 100: "Dico igitur, quod una intellectione in intellectu existente perfecta, possunt ibi esse multae confusae et imperfectae, nisi illa intellectio esset ita perfecta et actualis, quod non pateretur secum aliam; illis ergo confusis et imperfectis ibi existentibus potest voluntas complacere in qualibet earum, etiamsi illa intellectio non fuerit cognita, ut objectum, actualiter: et ex tertia voluntate complacente in aliqua intellectione confirmat illam et intendit. Illa igitur quae fuerit remissa et imperfecta, fit per istam complacentiam

of the will's primacy looks for its strongest foundation in inner experience that each of us can have.

Outside of these three principal proofs offered by Duns Scotus to establish the will's primacy, we find others, certain of which deserve to be noticed. For example, that thing is nobler and more perfect whose corruption is worse. The corruption of the act of the will is worse than the corruption of the act of the understanding, because the former constitutes sin, while the understanding's error is not an evil, at least in the same degree. Ignorance about God is not an evil comparable to hatred of God, if that hatred can be found in the will properly speaking. Therefore, the will is nobler than the understanding. Likewise, certain people argue that a thing is more perfect in the measure in which it depends less on something else in its perfection, because all dependence is a shortcoming. The act of understanding does not depend on the will but, on the contrary, the act of the will depends on the understanding. To this, Duns Scotus responds that what is posterior in the order of generation depends on what is prior, and still is more perfect than what preceded it. Accordingly, the very being of end depends on the means that accomplish it, although the end is more perfect. Therefore, the will's dependence does not necessarily prove its lesser perfection. Lastly, others conclude from the understanding's immateriality its superiority over the will. Intellection, they say, is a movement of the object toward the understanding. By contrast, volition is a movement of the soul toward the object. Therefore, volition is more material, and the act of the will is less noble than the act of the understanding. But, according to Duns Scotus, we logically ought to conclude the opposite, since the act by which the will is moved to want and love the supreme intelligibles is much more perfect than the act by which the understanding apprehends them. We can love God with all our strength and completely embrace him with our love, while it is forever forbidden to us to know him completely. Therefore, considered in itself, the act of the understanding is less perfect than the act of the will.[12]

We see two very important consequences developing from Duns Scotus's system, one of which places him close to St. Bonaventure's mysticism, while the other brings him near Descartes. Like St. Bonaventure and in opposition to St. Thomas, Duns Scotus makes beatitude consist of an act of

perfecta et intensa, et sic potest voluntas imperare cogitationem et convertere ad illam." [Translator: Gilson sometimes refers to the *Opus Oxoniense* by its more formal name as *Ordinatio in Libros Sententiarum*.]

12 Kahl, *Die Lehre*, pp. 102–103.

the will rather than of the understanding. Also against St. Thomas, Duns Scotus liberates the divine will from the rule of the good, to which it had been submitted until then. Let us consider this last consequence in particular.

As we have seen, St. Thomas, reasoning by analogy to the primacy of the understanding that he finds in humans, has established that God's will itself is in strict dependence on his understanding. The divine will is submitted to the rule of the good. God can only will his own good or the good of creatures, and God wills the good because he is the good. Knowledge of the good precedes the creative will's decision. According to St. Thomas, God's will is bound by the rule of his wisdom, and the will is forbidden to transgress that rule. Moreover, St. Thomas seems to have felt that this conception particularly limits divine freedom and, to soften whatever troubling aspects the notion might have in this regard, he adds that the cause that limits God's will is immanent in God himself and that his will does not seek reasons for its determinations outside of God. Opposing this doctrine, Duns Scotus affirms that the divine will's freedom is unlimited, that it is absolute freedom and constitutes the absolutely independent principle of everything there is. Just as the human will is undetermined and spontaneous in its decisions, the divine will must also be so, independently of any external and even internal motive. It is the last and immediate cause of all things, and to try to look farther for a deeper cause of their being is to look for a cause of that which by its very nature cannot have one.[13] What God wants is good, because God wants it, and the free choice of his will is above the knowledge that his understanding can have about good. If God so wills, he can completely overturn the foundations of the natural order or the moral order. He can choose to replace those orders with others that are completely different. The latter could also be absolutely good, provided only that God had decreed it so.[14] In short, the will's primacy suffers no limitation, and Descartes must

13 Duns Scotus, *Opus Oxoniense*, book II, distinction 1, question 2, number 9 [Vivès, vol. XI, p. 65]; quoted in Kahl, *Die Lehre*, p. 105: "Et ideo ista voluntas Dei qua vult hoc et producit pro nunc, est immediate et prima causa, cujus non est aliqua alia causa quaerenda . . . sed tantum quia voluit hoc esse, ideo bonum fuit illud esse, et quaerere hujus propositionis licet contingentis immediate causam, est quaerere causam sive rationem, cujus non est ratio quaerenda."

14 Duns Scotus, *Opus Oxoniense*, book I, distinction 44, *quaestio unica*, number 2 [Vivès X, p. 745]; quoted in Kahl, *Die Lehre*, p. 106: "Ideo sicut potest aliter agere, ita potest aliam legere statuere rectam, quia si statueretur a Deo, recta esset, quia nulla lex est recta, nisi quatenus a voluntate divina acceptatur."

have envisaged the very essence of God's freedom as a power of action with infinite extension.[15]

This association of Duns Scotus with Descartes seems to us to call for the strongest reservations and is open to various objections. It simultaneously ignores the real thinking of both Descartes and Duns Scotus by attributing to the former a theory of the primacy of the will in God that he did not maintain and to the latter a notion of divine power that he did not teach.

It is beyond doubt that Descartes does not establish a primacy of the will over the understanding in God in the sense in which Duns Scotus does. It cannot be said that Descartes subjects understanding to will even in humans. He nowhere poses the classic Scholastic question of knowing which of the two is nobler. Only one famous passage in the Fourth Meditation, to which we will have to return, seems to assign to the will, considered in itself as infinite, an indisputable superiority over our understanding, which by contrast is finite. But it is necessary to put this passage into its context and see, by the totality of the argument in which it is set, what exactly is its sense and scope. It is also necessary to clarify the passage through its sources, some of which are found in the doctrine of St. Thomas, who however always taught the primacy of understanding over will. Moreover, proofs abound that Descartes did not teach the doctrine of the primacy of the will in what concerns humans.[16] His deeply intellectualist critique of freedom of indifference very explicitly rejects that. But the radical distinction that Descartes himself introduces between the essence of human freedom and the essence of divine freedom, seems to invite us to suppose that, if the primacy of the will is not found in humans, it is at least found in God. God can do everything he wills, just because he wills, and it suffices for God to will something for it to be true and good. Like Duns Scotus, Descartes teaches that what God does is good, because God does it and not that God does something because it is good. Like Duns Scotus, he teaches that God can overturn the foundation of the natural order and of the moral order, always allowing for his immutability, and replace them with others that would be equally good, the only condition required being that God wills them. From that, it seems quite evident that, like Duns Scotus, Descartes conceives divine freedom in the form of absolute independence and of a genuine primacy of the will.

15 Kahl, *Die Lehre*, p. 106.

16 Moreover, Kahl explicitly notes this. See *Die Lehre*, pp. 114, 116.

Such an interpretation seems to us to contradict more than one passage in Descartes along with his authentic intentions. Let us first observe that, even limiting ourselves to Descartes' own expressions, it would be strange that his doctrine of divine freedom should be that of the primacy of the will. He tells us: "Willing and knowing is but one thing in God..." . . ." "In God, willing, understanding, and creating are one and the same, without one preceding the other *ne quidem ratione*." Such expressions are very far from being able to be interpreted in the sense of the primacy of the will. On the contrary, they reject and condemn it. How would the will exceed the understanding in God, since it is identified with it and it is the divine understanding itself? As Descartes conceives God, the expression "primacy of the will" can have no meaning in regard to God. Doubtless the illusion comes from some ambiguous expressions that were difficult to avoid in those circumstances. Descartes opposes adversaries who distinguish the understanding from the will in God and want to exclude the essences of the true and the good from his free choice. According to these philosophers, the divine will is in no way involved in the constitution of essences. It accepts them just as it finds them constituted within the divine understanding. It is easy to understand that Descartes, who is eager to erase the distinctions that are introduced into the divine essence, stresses the role that will plays in the creation of the eternal truths. God is not made in our image and likeness. He is infinite and he is one. God does not dispute with himself and does not seek the truth in himself. He is the indivisible source of the truth. The essences of things depend not only on his understanding but also on his will; and since the involvement of the will is what is disputed here, Descartes will necessarily have to insist on the will to make this new point of view understood. Each time the occasion arises, it will be said that God "wills" that the good should be what it is; that he "wills" that the eternal truths should be what they are. However, such expressions have the following sense: at the origin of all good, as at the origin of all truth, there is the divine intellect, and the divine will is likewise found indistinctly from the intellect. We must not seek the affirmation of the primacy of the will in God here. For there to be primacy, there must be priority. When Descartes affirms that the divine will creates the good and the true, he does so precisely to avoid the introduction of any priority between God's understanding and his will. According to Descartes, no priority in any sense whatever could exist between these two divine attributes, which are identified.

Descartes does not teach the doctrine that Duns Scotus maintains about the primacy of the will, and correspondingly Duns Scotus does not teach the doctrine that Descartes holds about the creation of the essence of the good and of the eternal truths by God. This assertion is not new, and none of those who have studied Duns Scotus directly have been deceived about it.[17] Let us return to the examination of the question that particularly interests us: that of a possible connection between Duns Scotus and Descartes. In the first place, it must be granted that Duns Scotus concedes much more freedom to God's creative will than St. Thomas, or rather he insists more readily than St. Thomas on the role of absolute indetermination that must be acknowledged in this will. For both theologians, God's will of itself attends directly only to the supreme good that is his own goodness. Therefore, it attends necessarily only to what is essentially linked to God"s own goodness, like all the divine attributes and the divine processions. Anything that is a creature is only linked to God's goodness by an accidental bond, since creatures add no more to God's goodness than a point adds to a line.[18] Therefore, God is under no necessity to will creatures. Let us now ask whether God could have willed other creatures than he did will. Scotus answers that God could have done so, since no creature is necessarily conjoined to God's essence. God could have willed creatures governed by other moral laws than those to which he submitted them, since these laws and the justice of these laws are not necessarily conjoined to his essence. Just like creatures, the laws according to which God acts in regard to his creatures are within his power. When the law and the justice of the law, according to which a being acts, are in his power in such a way that this law is only just because the being decreed that it should be, he can act contrary to the law without ceasing to act justly. It remains possible for him to decree that a law different from the one according to which he acted until then is just. This is the way in which a king sets laws at his pleasure, according to which he governs his subjects. Therefore, there are certain general laws concerning what it is appropriate to do, which have been

17 See, for example, Fonsegrive, "Duns Scot," in *Grande Encyclopédie*, vol. XV (31 volumes, 1886–1902). See also Émil Claude Armand Pulaski de Redwing, *Essay sure la philosophies de Duns Scot*, Paris, E. Thorn, 1888. Fortunately, Pulaski has worked to counteract this legend. See also the remarkable little book of Fr. Parthenius Minges, *Ist Duns Scotus indeterminist?* Münster: Aschendorff, 1905. Still, we believe it necessary to take up the problem from a slightly different viewpoint.

18 Duns Scotus, *De Rerum Principio*, question 4, article 1, section 3; Wadding, vol. 3, p. 29 [Vivès 4, p. 307]: "Quare cum voluntas Dei non feratur per se nisi ad bonum adaequatum quod est bonitas sua, non fertur ad volendum necessario nisi illa quae suae bonitati essentialiter sunt annexa, qualia sunt omnia divina et sola intrinseca. Omnis autem creatura ad bonitatem Dei accidentalem habet ordinem, quia ex eis bonitati suae nihil accidit, sicut nec punctum additum lineae."

established by the divine will and not by the divine understanding prior to the act of the will. God could choose others. For example, God's understanding proposes a law like this to his will: no one will be saved without grace. If it pleases God's free will, this law will be the just law, and so on for all other laws. Therefore, if we consider God's power called *potentia ordinata*, he can only act in conformity with the laws that he has imposed on himself. But if we consider the absolute power of God, he can act other than in conformity to these laws, although his action remains just, without the slightest contradiction. Therefore, as God could act other than he acts, he could establish a law other than he has established, and this law would still be just. For, if God established the law, it would be just, since every law is just only because God's will accepts it.[19] What is true for the moral order is equally true for the natural order. Supposing that God should will to make things in such a way that they follow a different order from the one he has attributed to them, they would not be disordered on that account, because the natural laws according to which things occur would constitute an order by the mere fact that God willed them so.[20] In short, the natural order as well as the moral order depends on his will. But, how does God's will produce things and what relation does it maintain with the divine understanding in the creative act? Does freedom consist of an absolute indifference whose determinations are only justified by themselves and without it being possible to assign any other reason to them?

This is what Duns Scotus seems to affirm in a well-known passage that is largely responsible for the ambiguity that surrounds his authentic thought.

19 Duns Scotus, *De Rerum Principio*, question 4; Wadding, vol. III, p. 6: "Sed quando in potestate agentis est lex, et rectitudo ejus, ita quod non est recta, nisi quia est ab illo statuta, tunc potest recte agere agendo aliter quam lex illa dictet; quia potest statuere aliam legem rectam, secundum quam agat ordinate . . . Ista possent exemplificari de Principe et subditis, et lege positiva, etc. Sed quando intellectus offert voluntati divinae talem legem, puta quod *omnis glorificandus prius et gratificandus*, si placet voluntati suae quae libera est, recta est lex: et ita de aliis legibus . . . ideo sicut potest aliter agere . . ." [Translator: I have not located this in *De Rerum Principio*. It does, however, appear in *Opus Oxoniense*, book I, distinction 44 *quaestio unica*, number 5; Vivès vol. X, pp. 744–745; or pp. 364–365 in *Ioannis Duns Scoti Opera Omnia*, VI, Vatican City: Typis Polyglottis Vaticanis, 1963.]

20 Duns Scotus, *Opus Oxoniense*, book I, distinction 44, *quaestio unica*, number 4 [Vivès vol. X, p. 746]: ". . . si faceret [*scilicet*, Deus] alio modo res quam ordinatum est eas fieri, non propter hoc inordinate fierent: quia si statueret alias leges secundum quas fierent, eo ipso ordinate fierent." [Translator: The Scotist Commission reads *nunc* before *ordinatum* p. 369.]

Scotus says that if it is asked why the divine will determines in favor of one of two contradictories rather than of the other, his answer is that Aristotle said that it belongs to an illogical mind to ask for demonstrations of everything, because the principles of a demonstration are not the object of demonstration. The same holds true concerning the principle of contingent things, without which we would regress infinitely in the series of contingents, since the contingent does not follow from the necessary by a necessity of nature. The will by which God wants such and such a thing and produces it at a determined time is therefore a finite and immediate cause for which it is not necessary to seek another cause. In fact, there is no reason that would have determined him to will that human nature should exist in such and such a particular individual, just as there is no reason that should have made him will that a determined thing should exist at a determined time and not at another one. Because God willed it to be so, it was good that it was so. To seek the cause of such a proposition, although it is contingent, is to want to discover a cause where there is no place to look for one.[21]

But what exactly does Duns Scotus understand by *cause* and by *reason*? This *causa sive ratio*, which we have no grounds to assign to the divine will, is the total efficient cause. To say that the divine will has neither cause nor reason is not to say that it has no kind of cause or reason, but only that we cannot assign it any cause or reason that allows us to give a sufficient explanation of it and that completely determines it. More precisely, the divine will has no motor cause, and it is the will alone that plays the role of motor cause in the operation by which God produces creatures, since the divine understanding is only an organizing cause, and the divine power is only involved to execute the decrees of the will. The motor cause and the efficient cause constitute just one thing. In the last analysis, God's will is the efficient cause of all things, and this cause is reducible to no other, since the understanding only directs and the power only executes. In this sense, but only in

21 Duns Scotus, *Opus Oxoniense*, book II, distinction 1, question 2, number 9: Wadding, vol. VI, p. 65 [Vivès, vol. XI, p. 65]: "Indisciplinati est quaerere omnium demonstrationum . . . *principiorum enim demonstrationis non est demonstratio*, et eodem modo in contingentibus . . . Et ideo ista voluntas, qua vult hoc et producit pro nunc, est immediate et prima causa, cujus non est aliqua alia causa quaerenda. Sicut enim non est ratio, quare voluit naturam humanam in hoc individuo esse . . . ita non est ratio, quare hoc voluit nunc et non tunc esse, sed tantum quia voluit hoc esse, ideo bonum fuit illud esse, et quaerere hujus propositionis, licit contingentis, immediate causam, est quaerere causam sive rationem, cujus non est ratio quaerenda."

this sense, causes are not to be assigned to the free decrees of God's will, supreme efficient cause of all creatures.[22] Since it is acknowledged that the executing power and the understanding's knowledge do not suffice to produce things, it still is the case that these two divine attributes are partial and secondary causes of things. God's will is the only true efficient cause; it is the pre-eminent cause, and no other is to be sought above it, but it is not the only cause. The power that executes and, above all, the understanding that organizes and directs also contribute to the production of creatures. To admit that the understanding directs, even granting that properly speaking it does not move, is still to attribute to it a role that deserves to be considered.

If we are alert about the consequences that this distinction entails for the rest of the system, we see clearly that it modifies only very slightly the doctrine of St. Thomas that it claims to oppose. If, after saying that there is no other efficient cause than the will, we still acknowledge that the will does not extend to what the understanding cannot grasp, we have changed the words by which we express the relation between the divine attributes, rather than changing the relation generally acknowledged among them. Like St. Thomas, Duns Scotus explicitly acknowledges that God cannot achieve the combination of contradictories. No doubt, God, who contains all the perfections of which creatures can consist, must combine the contraries within himself in an eminent degree. Moreover, this is why he has the capacity of producing them simultaneously by a single act of his will. There is nothing astonishing in the fact that cold and heat alike proceed from him. But matters are completely different with the contradictories. What is contradictory lacks the nature of being, and consequently cannot be produced by God.[23]

22 Duns Scotus, *De Rerum Principio*, question 4, article 2, section 3, number 19; Wadding, vol. 3, p. 21 [Vivès 4, p. 310]: "Item, potentia executiva existente, et intellectu cognoscente rem producendam, non propterea res producitur, nisi imperet voluntas et ad opus potentia applicetur, ut patet in artifice. Unde potentia executiva videtur esse quasi instrumentum; scientia, vel intellectus quasi ordinans; voluntas autem ut movens; sed efficiens et movens idem sunt; potentia autem etsi movet motum exequendo, movetur tamen primo a voluntate: ergo ei debetur principaliter ratio moventis, ergo potissima ratio causalitatis est in voluntate."

23 Duns Scotus, *De Rerum Principio*, 2, 2, 13; Wadding, vol. 3, p. 8 [Vivès 4, p. 282]: "Sed Deus . . . claudit in se omnem rationem perfectionis altiori modo quam sit in creaturis: ergo potest producere quidquid producunt omnes creaturae, et modo altiori, et etiam plura; quia nunquam creaturae hariunt omnes modi essendi qui sunt in Deo; igitur si Deo nullum esse deficit, quod altiori modo non participat, omnia quae habent quocumque modo rationem entis potest producere immediate. Et ista est causa, quare sola contradictoria a Deo non possunt fieri; quia non claudunt ali-

As we have seen, God could overturn the foundations of the natural order. He could have constituted this order on completely different foundations from those he gave to it, but these foundations and this order cannot be self-contradictory. The essences of things escape God's free choice, and it is not within his power to give them a different content from what they have. Even if God wanted, he could not endow fire with intelligence and will, because that is contradictory to its nature.[24]

Just as the divine will cannot transgress the rule of the true, it cannot transgress the rule of the good that the understanding proposes to it either. As we have seen, God's will necessarily turns *ad bonum adaequatum quod est bonitas sua*. God cannot fail to will his own goodness.[25] Besides, in regard to the imperfect goods that God can will or not will, as he pleases, his will still chooses according to the direction of his understanding. It is always understood that nothing moves the divine will. No motor cause, that is to say, efficient cause, can be assigned to it. But, though not moved, it is directed by the understanding. God's will acts according to God's knowledge that guides it, without moving it toward the different ends that can be offered to it.[26] In addition, when Duns Scotus comments on Aristotle's *Physics*, he does not fail to recur to teleological explanations. The earth is the dwelling place of mankind for him, as it is for all his contemporaries, and things on earth are disposed for our use and convenience. This general conception is encountered again in the detail of the explanation that Scotus offers for different natural phenomena. To explain the final cause of wind, Scotus mentions the primary role of assembling clouds. In the second place, the wind

quam rationem entis." See Minges, *Ist Duns Scotus indeterminist?* p. 127, for several references to passages in *Opus Oxoniense*, where Duns Scotus teaches the same doctrine.

24 Duns Scotus, *Opus Oxoniense*, book I, distinction 43, *quaestio unica*; Wadding V, p. 1363 [Vivès X, p. 735, number 6]."... nec sequitur quod ignis manens ignis possit fieri melior si capax intellectus vel voluntatis, quia non potest esse istorum."

25 Duns Scotus, *De Rerum Principio*, 4, 2–3, 22; Wadding III, p. 22 [Vivès IV, p. 312]: "Item finis movet alia; ergo ultimus finis simpliciter movet omnia simpliciter, et a nullo movetur: hoc est Dei bonitas; ergo voluntas a sola bonitate movetur."

26 Duns Scotus, *De Rerum Principio*, 4, 2–3, 22; Wadding, vol. 3, p. 22 [Vivès, IV, p. 312]: "Item, omne movens facit aliquam impressionem in moto, ac per hanc, re vel ratione, arctat mobile: ergo si voluntas divina movetur a creaturis coarctant eam, et sic diminueret de ratione libertatis; sed oportet dicere, quod Deus per omnem modum libertatis producit res, alioquin ab eis dependeret: ergo a nullo divina voluntas movetur. Dicitur tamen, quod voluntas Dei operatur secundum rationem et scientiam, non moventem sed dirigentem, secundum modum nostrum intelligendi."

is meant to carry clouds from one region to another to assure that the land is watered by rain. Lastly, the wind is intended to maintain trees in good health. Just as humans and animals need not only food but also exercise to remain healthy, trees need to have a little exercise, and the wind gives it to them by shaking them.[27] Therefore, Duns Scotus does not hold either that God can simultaneously carry out contradictories, or that his will does not act according to the ends that his understanding proposes to him.

Furthermore, not only does Duns Scotus teach nothing of what Descartes taught regarding divine freedom, but also, in a certain sense, he is further from Descartes in his voluntarism than St. Thomas's intellectualism was. Careful to reserve all of the creative act's efficacy to the will alone and to sharply distinguish the subordinate role that belongs to the understanding from the primary role that the will retains, Duns Scotus emphasizes the distinction of the divine attributes within God much more than St. Thomas had done. Where St. Thomas only admits a simple distinction of reason and even seems to avoid affirming it explicitly, Duns Scotus introduces a formal and to a certain point real distinction. He emphasizes the distinction's reality with an insistence peculiar to him. He does not go so far as to maintain that God's understanding and will are really distinct in the absolute sense of the word, but the distinction generally established between these attributes clearly seems insufficient and does not satisfy him.[28] It is he who situates himself in the standpoint of the emanation of the divine persons to draw the internal distinction of the divine attributes that Suárez will devote himself to criticizing: since the Son proceeds from the divine understanding because he is the Word, and the Holy Spirit proceeds from the divine will because he is Love, there must necessarily be in God himself some distinction between understanding and will.[29] The difference that exists between God's essential perfections is, therefore, not just a difference

27 Duns Scotus, book 2, *Meteorologia*, question 4, article 4, number 7 [Vivès IV, p. 145; Wadding vol. II]: "*De causa finali ventorum.* De causa finali dicitur quod ventus est principaliter et primo propter congregare nubes . . . Secundo movetur ventus propter deferre nubes de una regione in aliam, propter irrigationem terrae, ita quod per conversionem nubis in aquam diversae partes terrae irrigentur propter motum nubis a vento. Tertio potest dici quod est propter salutem arborum: quia sicut homo et alia animalia praeter nutrimentum indigeret quodammodo exercitio, ut melius conserventur in sanitate: ita consimiliter motus arborum est eis per ventum exercitium."

28 Duns Scotus, *Opus Oxoniense*, book I, distinction 8, question 4; Wadding V, p. 759 [Vivès IX, p. 652, number 10]: ". . . ergo, distinctio attributorum, non est tantum rationis sed aliquo modo ex natura rei."

of reason, one stemming merely from the different ways in which we conceive the same formal object. These perfections are also formally different, and the wisdom considered in itself is not identified with the goodness. It is formally different from it. Furthermore, we recognize this about wisdom and goodness as they exist in humans, though we deny that they are distinct in God on the basis that they are infinite. Infinity cannot destroy the formal reason of that to which we attribute it. Infinite goodness is always goodness and not wisdom, and vice versa. Therefore, if we do not want to confuse wisdom and goodness generally, there is even more reason not to confuse them when these attributes are presented to us as infinite. They are not formally identical even then, and they would receive different definitions if we could define infinite attributes. [30] If we ponder the fact that for Descartes the characteristic of divine freedom is the absolute unity of understanding and will and the absence of the slightest distinction between his attributes, we will see that in spirit as in literal expression, Duns Scotus's conception is diametrically opposed to Descartes'. Therefore, one must look for other sources of Descartes' teaching about God's freedom.

Some historians of Descartes tried another avenue whose fortune has been much more modest than that of the previous one, but whose value still should be made clear. We want to discuss the connection that has been indicated between the Cartesian notion of divine freedom and certain passages in Mersenne on the same question.[31] Historically, these connections

29 Duns Scotus, *Opus Oxoniense*, book I, distinction 8, question 4; Wadding V, p. 754 [Vives IX, p. 643, number 7]: "Distinctio attributorum fundamentum est respectu distinctionis emanationum personalium, quia Filius procedit naturaliter nascendo tanquam verbum conceptum in intellectu. Spiritus Sanctus procedit libere spirando, tanquam amor conceptus in voluntate, et non ut Verbum: quod non potest esse nisi esset aliqua distinctio intellectus et voluntatis ad intra."

30 Duns Scotus, *Opus Oxoniense*, book I, distinction 8, question 4, number 5; Wadding V, p. 767 [Vivès IX, pp. 664–665, numbers 17–18]: ". . . inter perfectiones essentiales non est tantum differentia rationis, hoc est diversorum modorum concipiendi idem objectum formale. . . . Sapientia autem in re formaliter non est bonitas in re. Quod probatur, quia si infinita sapientia esset formaliter infinita bonitas, et sapientia in communi esset formaliter bonitas in communi; infinitas enim non destruit formaliter rationem illius cui additur… Est igitur aliqua non identitas formalis sapientiae et bonitatis, inquantum earum essent distincta definitiones si essent definibiles."

31 On this point see, Alfred Espinas, "Pour l'histoire du Cartésianisme," *Revue de métaphysique et de morale*, May, 1906. In this article there is a rather large number of references to different passages in Mersenne, notably to *l'Impiété des Déistes,* pp.

would be of the greatest interest. Mersenne's works to which the connections are drawn appeared at dates that make the hypothesis of their influence on Descartes' thought perfectly plausible. The *Quaestiones Celeberrimae in Genesim*, which was perhaps involved in adopting the doc trine of innate ideas and St. Anselm's argument, appeared in 1623. *L'Impiété des Déistes*, from which the authors of this comparison extract their texts, appeared in 1624. This period sees an intense process of development of Descartes' thought, and though there is no absolute proof that Descartes read these various works, everything makes us suppose he did so. The close friendship that afterwards links Descartes and Mersenne lets us believe that Descartes went through his friend's books with at least a quick reading.

Just as Descartes extends the dogma of creation to everything, even the eternal truths, Mersenne writes in *l'Impiété des Déistes* in 1624: "Morality comes from the relations our actions have with the rule of the will, which rule from our viewpoint is the *dictamen* of reason; but in God, it is his will itself, because he has no other rule, law, or obligation than himself, so that the morality of God's free actions, like his mercy, his charity, and his love for us, is not the product of any law that the divine intellect gives to the will, but of the divine will, which alone is sinless by nature, in as much as only it is his rule and the formal principle of his moral actions."[32] If we examine this text more closely, we see that Mersenne is very far from teaching what Descartes will concerning divine freedom. The only affirmation that might seem common to the two philosophers is that the divine intellect gives no law to God's will, but it is important to see the sense in which Mersenne understands that. He is not dealing with eternal truths like mathematical truths or the essence of things, but simply with moral laws like those concerning grace, matters of which the Scholastics always admitted that God freely disposed. Mersenne adds nothing here to pure Scholastic tradition, in which, despite so much disagreement about the modality of the gift, it is always admitted that grace is a free gift from God, a superabundance of riches granted to humans without it being in the slightest degree owed them and

50, 310, 520, concerning divine freedom. See also Adam, *Vie et oeuvres*; vol. XII, p. 140 and note *a*. [Translator: Marin Mersenne, 1588–1648, was an alumnus of La Flèche, who became a priest, theologian, a Minim Friar, and, of course, confidant of Descartes, and of many other major intellectual figures.]

32 Marin Mersenne, *l'Impiété*, vol. I, p. 49, quoted by Adam, *Vie et oeuvres*; XII, p. 140.

that, had it pleased God, he could have quite legitimately denied it to them. Likewise, the infinite love by which God willed that his divine Son should expiate on the cross the sins of humans and redeem the human race, is a supereminent gift that God freely made us without anything forcing him to do so. Does it follow that Mersenne would go so far as to give God the power of achieving contradictories, of transforming the essences of things, of making possible what is now impossible in itself? The consequence is not at all necessary, and the texts show that Mersenne did not draw it. In spirit and letter, his notion of divine freedom faithfully reproduces St. Thomas's conception, which Descartes is going to oppose. For him, God's omnipotence admits no limit. God can do anything that is possible, understanding by that anything that does not imply contradiction,[33] everything that is possible absolutely speaking. Everything that can receive being is possible, and God can do it. Only non-being is opposed to being, what implies contradiction, that which in itself is contradictory with itself. It necessarily escapes God's power, not by a deficiency in that power itself, but because it is neither doable nor possible in itself. We would express ourselves more appropriately by saying about what implies contradiction, "that cannot be done," than by saying, "God cannot do that."[34]

In what regards Descartes' critique of teleology, Mersenne sometimes seems to be in complete agreement with Descartes when he writes: "The very simple divine act is very perfect," and "All God made, he made with no emotion, because his eternal decree is quite one and quite simple." But Mersenne also adds immediately that we conceive it "through our different images," and that we need different thoughts when we want to understand

33 Mersenne, *Quaestiones Celeberrimae in Genesim*, chapter I, verse 1, article 5, objection 7, p. 331: "Ut vero nullis finibus terminatur omnipotentia, sic quaecumque in se non implicant, seu omnia factiblia complectitur."

34 Mersenne, *Quaestiones Celeberrimae*, chapter I, verse 1, article 5, objection 7, pp. 332–333: ". . . quicquid rationem entis habere potest continetur sub possibilibus absolutis respectu quorum Deus dicitur omnipotens; nihil autem opponitur rationi entis, nisi non ens, quale solum illud est quod implicat in se esse simul, quod divinae potentiae non subditur, non propter defectum divinae potentiae, sed quia non potest habere rationem factibilis neque possibilis.

"Quaecumque igitur contradictionem non implicant, sub illis possibilibus continetur, respectu quorum dicitur Deus omnipotens. Ea vero quae contradictionem implicant sub divina omnipotentia non continentur, quia non possunt habere possibilium rationem. Unde convenientius dicitur ea non posse fieri quam quod Deus ea non possit facere."

it."[35] Might this distinction that has been introduced in God be a simple distinction of *reasoning reason*? We cannot grant that Mersenne modifies Scholastic doctrine even in this way, because he accepts the distinction of *reasoned reason* that is customarily introduced among the divine attributes without offering the least restriction to it.[36] After that, we cannot be deceived about the import of Mersenne's statements concerning the absolute independence of divine freedom. When he writes: "[T]he creature has no need to look for another reason for the actions of his creation than *sit pro ratione voluntas*... . . .,"[37], we understand that the divine will has no reason outside of God that determines it to will, and that in God himself all that is not necessarily linked to his supreme goodness is indifferent to him. But that does not mean that God does not act according to the ends his understanding proposes to him. Mersenne would not allow such a notion to be attributed to him. It would deprive him of one of the most arresting proofs of God's existence, the proof by teleology.

We cannot look at the world without acknowledging that nothing in all that falls under our senses has been made for itself, but that all things have been made with a view to ends that are outside of them. Everything demands an efficient cause as also a final cause; everything postulates a creator that prescribed for each thing the means through which the thing can attain its ends.[38] Mersenne does not tire of describing and enumerating these ends of God, at least the chief among them, with a lack of hesitation that immediately places him far from Descartes and the physics of efficient causes. The sun is the heart of the world, and it is placed in the world as the heart in humans for the greatest good of all its parts. The same goes for the planets and the stars, whose reason for being is found in the influences that they exert on all things. That inanimate bodies are not created for themselves is something that cannot be doubted, since these bodies do not feel or think

35 Mersenne, *l'Impiété*, pp. 271–272.

36 Mersenne, *l'Impiété*, p. 434: "There is no need for me to go on here further, because your Poet does not deserve it, who, if he had remembered the distinction we place between the divine attributes, which is only of reasoned reason, *rationis ratiocinatae*, would not have had the zeal to infer diversity of subsistences between the divine attributes."

37 Mersenne, *l'Impiété*, p. 464.

38 Mersenne, *Quaestiones Celeberrimae*, chapter 1, verse 1, article 30, p. 125: "nihil inter ea quae sub aspectum cadunt, propter se, sed omnia propter aliquem finem extrinsecum facta esse, sicut et omnia sunt ab aliqua causa agente: quae profecto sola rebus singulis media praescribere potuit quibus ad finem sibi praescriptum pervenirent."

and consequently do not feel any pleasure nor do they obtain any comfort from their own existence or that of other bodies. Therefore, it is certain that these bodies are created for the greatest good of a being capable of receiving some help or experiencing some pleasure from them, and this being is the human. Following Scholastic tradition on this point, Mersenne develops his teleology into genuine anthropomorphism. If humans did not exist, the corporeal world would have no reason to exist in Mersenne's eyes.[39] We will not follow Mersenne in the detail of the explanation by which he strives to make evident the wisdom of a supreme orderer who organizes the world for our use. Mersenne's considerations upon astronomical laws; the marvelous order of the seasons; meteorological phenomena that have been conceived for the well-being of plants and consequently of humans; the admirable spectacle that of earth and sea replete with animals, which are so many servants or subjects in our empire; all show abundantly that Mersenne is very far from renouncing the consideration of final causes. The universe presents itself to him from the same angle from which it appeared to all medieval philosophers, as a totality of means coordinated by a supreme wisdom with a view to certain ends. If the consideration of the organic world is not enough to convince the deist or the libertine, Mersenne will confront him with the marvels that the bodies of animals and the human body reveal to us, with their internal and external parts wonderfully ordered by the creator. Their structural ingenuity is such, and they are so elegantly adapted to their functions or their ends, that no wisdom would find anything to change, withdraw, or amend.[40] If we consider the instincts of animals like the spider,[41] or in a general way all the actions that animals carry out with no knowledge of their end or of the means they employ, or of the relation of these means to their end, we will see that they act like authentic clocks whose hands indicate the time without knowing it, simply because they have been constructed by a skillful worker. Therefore, the ends to which these animals

39 Mersenne, *Quaestiones Celeberrimae*, chapter 1, verse 1, article 30, p. 125: ". . . certum est ea propter se non esse, sed ob aliquem qui ex eis voluptatem atque commodum depromat, videlicet ob hominem, qui si a mundo abesset, tota natura corporea frustra esse videretur."

40 Mersenne, *Quaestiones Celeberrimae*, chapter 1, verse 1, article 30, p. 126: ". . . sunt enim [uniuscujusque rei partes] tam exquisito artificio elaboratae, et tam eleganter ad suas functiones atque fines aptatae, ut nulla sapientia vel minimum adjicere, minuere, vel emendare posit; unde sequitur partes illas a sapientissimo quodam excogitatas et ordinatas esse."

41 Mersenne, *Quaestiones Celeberrimae*, chapter 1, verse 1, article 30, p. 129.

tend without knowing it have been conceived by some higher thought, and this thought is none other than God's.[42] As a teleologist and convinced partisan of the absolute necessity of the eternal truths even in regard to God, Mersenne cannot be considered the inspiration or even the predecessor of Descartes in what concerns divine freedom. Rather, we must include Mersenne among the adversaries whom Descartes would soon confront, and the resistance that Descartes encounters from Mersenne in 1630 should be a sufficient proof that Descartes' doctrine of divine freedom was not Mersenne's, even if the texts did not make that clear already.

42 Mersenne, *Quaestiones Celeberrimae* , chapter 1, verse 1, article 30, p. 127: "Quaecumque sunt in mundo suas vires et operationes habent, quae vel operantis, vel alterius commodum, viis adeo congruis tendunt, ut nulla arte possint aptius; atque finem illum, media vel horum cum fine proportionem minime cognoscunt; igitur ab aliqua mente superiori concipi atque dirigi necesse est. Quomodo enim aliud in finem ordinate tendere potest, nisi fuerit aliquis, qui media ad id apta atque necessaria cognoscat et ordinet? Omnes igitur creaturae mentis expertes sunt horologiorum instar, quae quidem ordinate tendunt ad horarum spatia indicanda, sed quia finem hunc non concipiunt, neque se ad illum disponere valent, necessario ab aliquo haec omnia sciente disponi debent."

Chapter Five

The Cartesian Doctrine of Divine Freedom and Oratorian Theology

Let us first make it clear: no source can be given for the Cartesian doctrine of divine freedom, if by the term *source* one intends to indicate a completely finished doctrine, one that Descartes was satisfied to introduce into his system unchanged. This singular notion of God as absolutely one, creating the eternal truths in an order of causality beyond the comprehension of our finite minds, must be considered the product of our philosopher's personal reflections. On this point, Descartes' sense of bringing forth something new was correct. Of all his metaphysical notions, perhaps this is the most original, the one that contains fewer foreign elements and that is best explained by the system's internal requirements. Perhaps this is also why Descartes refrains from making it conspicuous and seems to hide it. Such affirmations were unheard of and odd for the theologians whom Descartes addressed.

It is not that no one ever held something of the sort. Scattered here and there in St. Thomas there are specks of evidence of a doctrine rather like that of Descartes. In *Summa contra Gentes*, St. Thomas summarily condemns those who teach that God acts not according to the rule of his justice, but by his will,[1] alone, in such a way that there would be no other

1 St. Thomas, *Summa contra Gentes*, book I, chapter 87, end: "Per praedicta autem excluditur error quorundam dicentium omnia procedere a Deo secundum simplicem voluntatem; ut de nullo oporteat rationem reddere, nisi quia Deus vult. Quod etiam divinae scripturae contrariatur, quae Deum perhibet, secundum ordinem sapientiae suae omnia fecisse secundum illud Psalmi (103:24): *Omnia in sapientia fecisti.* Et Ecclesiasticus 1:10 dicit quod *Deus effudit sapientiam suam super omnia opera sua.*" — St. Thomas, *Summa contra Gentes*, book II, chapter 29, end: "Sic igitur per praedicta excluditur duplex error: eorum scilicet qui divinam potentiam limitantes, dicebant Deum non posse facere nisi quae facit, quia sic facere debet; et eorum qui dicunt quod omnia sequuntur simplicem voluntatem, absque aliqua alia ratione vel quaerenda in rebus vel assignanda."

St. Thomas does not specify the adversaries to whom he refers. As is well known, the *Summa* is full of passages like this that denounce a doctrine without

reason to give for things than that God wanted them just as we see them. Moreover, Thomas reports that, according to certain people, God could make an affirmation and its negation true at the same time, and he attributes to weighty authorities the opinion according to which God could make the past not to have existed.[2] Therefore, it seems certain that the doctrine taught by St. Thomas had not always been considered the only one possible.

But these are very rare and isolated texts, mere remarks made in passing, which left no trace in philosophical teaching as it was given in secondary schools. We never find a *Course* where such a doctrine is mentioned. It is never developed or disputed, and authors responsible for it are never named. In short, nothing so far authorizes us to think that Descartes discovered the conception of divine freedom that he constructed anywhere except in his own thought. Therefore, a very unusual accident would have to be imagined, and even this accident would explain nothing, because there is no comparison between the rudimentary texts in St. Thomas that we have recalled and such a full, coherent doctrine that deduces the creation of

naming its author. In the present state of research, it is generally difficult to connect a name with these doctrines. In this case, however, we believe that he is dealing with a Muslim sect, the Asharites (disciples of al-Ash'ari of Basra, 880–940). Maimonides must have been the intermediary for St. Thomas's information. On Maimonides as a very important source for St. Thomas, cf. Louis-Germain Levy, *Maïmonide*, Paris: F. Alcan, 1911 (second edition, Paris: Alcan, 1932), pp. 265, ff. On the Asharites see pp. 146, 154.

2 St. Thomas, *De Aeternitate Mundi*, section 2: "Secundo modo dicitur per repugnantiam intellectuum aliquid non posse fieri, sicut non potest fieri ut affirmatio et negatio sint simul vera quamvis Deus hoc possit facere, ut quidam dicunt. Quidam vero dicunt quod nec Deus potest hujusmodi facere, quia hoc nihil est. Tamen manifestum est quod non potest facere ut hoc fiat, quia positio qua ponitur esse destruit seipsam. Si tamen ponatur quod Deus hujusmodi potest facere ut fiat, positio non est haeretica, quamvis, ut credo, sit falsa, sicut quod praeteritum non fuerit includit in se contradictionem. Unde Augustinus in libro *Contra Faustum*: 'Quisquis ita dicit: Si omnipotens est Deus, faciat ut quae facta sunt non fuerint, non videt hoc se dicere: si omnipotens est, faciat ut ea quae vera sunt, eo ipso quod vera sunt, falsa sint.' Et tamen quidam magni pie dixerunt Deum posse facere de praeterito quod non fuerit praeteritum; hoc fuit reputatum haereticum." — We believe that St. Thomas is thinking of St. Peter Damian in this passage (and perhaps of some disciple) who quite precisely maintained that "Deus potest facere de praeterito quod non fuerit praeteritum;" the label *magnus* would be explained because we are dealing with a saint. Cf. Josef-Anton Endres, *Petrus Damiani und die weltliche Wissenschaft* (*Beiträge zur Geschichte der Philosophie des Mittelalters*, volume VIII, tome 3), Münster: Aschendorff, 1910, pp. 24–27.

external truths, on the one hand, and the negation of teleology on the other, from the absolute unity of God.

Yet, it does not follow that theological thought has nothing to teach us concerning the Cartesian doctrine of freedom. That doctrine is the outcome of Descartes' metaphysical reflection and indisputably new in several dimensions; it remains of a piece with the environment in which it was established. Even if it is explained by the need Descartes felt to give his physics metaphysical grounding, it still owes the general spirit that animates it, as well as some of its essential elements, to Renaissance neo-Platonist movement, very intense at this time and which constituted its true historical antecedent that made its elaboration possible. The Cartesian doctrine of divine freedom does not necessarily result from this movement. But it offers Descartes a metaphysical thought oriented in a direction different from Scholasticism and where "true physics" could easily be accommodated.

St. Thomas's is not the only theological influence to which Descartes' thought was subject. Perhaps it is not the deepest. If, as we can observe, Descartes took many particular explanations from it, the spirit of his metaphysics is much more that of a Neo-Platonic theology renewed by the Fathers and especially by St. Augustine. One of the most active centers of this renaissance, which was intensive enough to disturb certain thinkers,[3] was the new congregation of the Oratory that Pierre de Bérulle had just founded. Descartes knew its founder and several of its most famous members intimately enough for us to be able to credit the spirit that animates these Oratorians with a lasting influence on the general orientation of Descartes' metaphysical thinking.

Without making the relations of Descartes and Cardinal de Bérulle go as far back as some have claimed,[4] we can consider certain that they began

3 On this point we have the curious testimony of Silhon, a friend of Descartes who wrote in 1634 (Jean de Silhon, *De l'immortalité de l'âme*, Paris: P. Billaine, 1634, book I, pp. 31–32): "To my understanding, the devotion of our time is tinged with Platonism, and it is inserted into the makeup of the mystical life and of fashionable theology… . . . Let those who make use of it remember that serpents hide under flowers, that arsenic resembles sugar, and that Origen was poisoned by it! Let them not believe that because they spout many of the names that are found in St. Dennis, that they always have the understanding of those thinkers in their minds." These vigorous declarations did not in the slightest keep Silhon's own theology from being rather abundantly tinged with Platonism.

4 Michel Houssaye, *Le Cardinal de Bérulle et le cardinal de Richelieu*, 1625–1629, Paris: Plon, 1875, pp. 539–540; and Espinas, "Pour l'histoire du cartésianisme." On this point we subscribe to Adam's hypothesis of another Descartes, different

no later than 1627. Adrien Baillet's evidence is definite on this point.[5] Cardinal de Bérulle's influence on Descartes from that period forward would have been such that it must be deemed one of the most important factors affecting his philosophical activity and that in some measure de Bérulle is responsible for Descartes' whole philosophy. After the famous lecture in which Descartes attacked the method and theses of the sieur de Chandoux, de Bérulle asked Descartes to expound his philosophical principles to him in a private conversation. The philosopher considered himself very honored, and as a result of this conversation and of the philosophical project that Descartes expounded to him, the Cardinal had no difficulty in understanding the plan's importance. Judging Descartes the right person to carry it out, the Cardinal utilized the authority he had over Descartes to get him to undertake this great enterprise. He even made it an obligation of conscience for which, since God had given Descartes a mental vigor and discernment not granted to others, Descartes would render an exact accounting to God for the use of his talents and would be responsible before the sovereign judge of men for the wrong he would do the human race by depriving it of the fruit of his meditations.[6] De Bérulle thereby seemed to invest Descartes with a sacred mission, divine in a way. To some degree, our philosopher left France to better carry out this mission by working in the silence and leisure of his retirement to accomplish the exalted scheme.[7] The tradition that recognizes Cardinal de Bérulle's influence upon Descartes' philosophical activity is

from the philosopher (Adam, *Vie et ouevres*; XII, p. 94 b), who would have corresponded with Fr. de Bérulle during this period. Regarding Platonism in the Oratory, see Houssaye, p. 384. [Translator: there are two similarly named congregations of secular priests: the Congregation of the Oratory founded by St. Philip Neri, 1515–1595, starting in 1556, and the Society of the Oratory of Jesus and Mary Immaculate founded by Pierre de Bérulle, 1575–1629, named cardinal in August of 1627.]

5 We would even permit ourselves to judge it a bit too definite. In the Baillet's whole subsequent narrative, we certainly ought to see a solid core of truth and an authentic tradition, but we must be wary about details. The opening only tidies up a passage from Pierre Borel, vol. I, p. 217 note. [Translator: Pierre Borel, 1620?–1671 is the author of *Vitae Renati Cartesii, Summi Philosophi Compendium*, Paris: Billaine, 1656.]

6 Adrien Baillet, *Vie de M. Descartes*, Paris: Daniel Horthermels, 1691 (reprinted New York: Garland, 1987), I, p. 165.

7 Baillet, *Vie*, I, p. 165: "Since the impression left by the exhortations of the pious Cardinal was combined with what his natural inclination and reason had long dictated to him, it turned out to be decisive in his thinking."

confirmed by the fact that Descartes chose Cardinal de Bérulle as his spiritual advisor. The tone that Baillet attributes to de Bérulle in the conversation just mentioned would already lead to suppose that, but elsewhere he confirms the fact explicitly. This point is quite important. When we understand what kind of spiritual director the Cardinal was and with what perseverance he discharged his responsibility, there is no doubt that his recommendation and his general theological spirit would have left their mark on the thought of the philosopher who was his penitent. If we believe Baillet, Descartes regarded him as a second Providence,[8] and Descartes had acquired such liking for de Bérulle's direction that after the death of the founder of the Oratory, he appealed to the fathers for spiritual guidance, rather than to the Jesuits who had been his first teachers.[9] The closeness between de Bérulle and Descartes was deep enough for a lasting influence to have been exerted by one upon the other.

This influence would draw Descartes very far from the paths laid down by Scholasticism. Beyond the very valuable encouragement that Descartes could receive from seeing how a theologian resolutely diverged from the pure and simple metaphysics of St. Thomas, within his director's circle, Descartes could find the rudiments of a new metaphysics, free from connection to false sciences and capable of undergoing more complete development subsequently.

De Bérulle abandoned the customary Scholastic mode of exposition as his disciple Guillaume Gibieuf would do at his instigation. In some regards de Bérulle traveled farther on this road than Gibieuf, since the founder of the Oratory is ranged among the few professional theologians who preferred French to Latin. Above all, de Bérulle's method is characterized by the abandonment of Scholastic dialectics. If *Exercitationes Scholasticae* had relatively little space in Gibieuf, they had none at all in de Bérulle. He did not like disputation. His sole response to certain lampoons and pamphlets

8 Baillet, *Vie*, I, p. 193: "Upon his return from Friesland, Monsieur Descartes lost an excellent director and a very sincere friend in the person of Cardinal Pierre de Bérulle, the first Founder and Superior General of the Congregation of Priests of the Oratory,."

9 Baillet, *Vie*, I, p. 194: "Monsieur Descartes always had great veneration for his merit and great deference to his advice. After God, he considered him to be the chief author of his plans and of his withdrawal from his homeland. After his death, he had the satisfaction of finding some of his disciples, I mean Priests of the Oratory, in whose hands he could entrust the direction of his conscience during the whole time of his stay in Holland."

published against forms of prayer recommended by him to some Carmelite sisters was the theology of the Incarnation that justified such forms of prayer in his eyes.[10] His exposition is not at all like a Scholastic treatise concerned primarily with reducing an adversary to silence, emphasizing the number and order of arguments. De Bérulle simply wants to disclose the truth, and since it was disclosed to him in the silence and fervor of prayer, he also wants to lead his readers to prayer in order to overwhelm them, to hurl them to the feet of the Incarnate Word. We should not be surprised at the tiresome repetitions and very real disorder of certain of his works. The truth is one and we cannot return to it often enough in order to contemplate and adore it. What is important is to show the truth rather than to demonstrate it, and to show it in all its aspects, from all sides, in order to multiply motives for our adoration. The point of arrival for the theologians' labor is prayer.

This mode of exposition, so new and so different from the customary Scholastic one, is the mark of a deep change of mentality in de Bérulle. Doubtless, the new theology is aware of Scholasticism and of St. Thomas, De Bérulle cites him frequently and with deference. But, if there is nothing in the letter of the *Discours de l'État et des Grandeurs de Jésus* of which a Scholastic could disapprove, we must observe that certain traditional Scholastic propositions take on particular value and meaning for de Bérulle. He does not simply reproduce Scholasticism; he transposes it. Even when he follows St. Thomas most faithfully, the spirit of the *Summa* does not animate de Bérulle. On each page of the *Discours* we feel that beyond Scholastic discussions and subtlety, the author has re-discovered the great current of thought created by the Fathers of the Church. Moreover, we know that he frequents them assiduously and studies them very closely. Not content to recommend constantly that his disciples read them, he himself practices such reading daily. They are the great formative influence on his thought, and none of his works fails to be nourished by them. Sometimes he translates them without naming them and incorporates them into his text. Sometimes he refers to their authority and cites them explicitly. St. Jerome, St. John Damascene, St. Gregory Nazianzen, and St. Bernard are cited most often. But his favorite teachers, those by whom his mind is most permeated, are St. Paul and St. Augustine.

10 Pierre de Bérulle, *Discours de l'État et des Grandeurs de Jésus*, Paris: Antoine Étienne, 1623, two vols. (Contained in vol. III of *Oeuvres*, Paris: J. P. Migne, 1856; Alexandria, VA, Alexandria Street Press, 2007.) [Translator: Guillaume Gibieuf, 1583–1650, doctor of theology by the Sorbonne March 1612, entered the Oratory May 1612]

Even when he is not mentioned, St. Paul is always present. Clearly, de Bérulle loves Paul's joy quivering with mysticism that long before had seduced St. Augustine.[11] As for the latter, he is really the teacher above all others, and, addressing God, de Bérulle alerts us to that affinity at the start of his discourse: "And at the opening of this work, allow me to direct to you the words of the most humble and wisest, the holiest and most prudent, of the most modest and most religious Doctor that the earth has produced and that you have given to your Church."[12] So, we have St. Thomas plainly relegated to the background, and de Bérulle does not hesitate to say so. St. Thomas is the Prince of the School, but St. Augustine is the "Eagle of Doctors and the great teacher of St. Thomas."[13] De Bérulle also insistently recommends Augustine to the priests of the Oratory as a master and model at the same time. Among the motives for this very special admiration for St. Augustine, de Bérulle first of all gives one that, in his mind, guarantee beyond doubt Augustine's superiority over the Scholastics; beside the gift of enlightening minds, Augustine has the no less valuable one of touching hearts. "He is very speculative and very affective, and while we only find knowledge in the majority of Doctors, in him we find a certain flavor of wisdom that makes us taste what he says and that, by an uncommon privilege, makes the truth pass from the mind to the heart.[14]

Along with St. Augustine there is another no less important influence that will act upon the thought of de Bérulle: that of Plato and especially the neo-Platonists.[15] The extent of St. Augustine's admiration and gratitude for these philosophers is well known; in his judgment, they set him on the road toward the Christian faith that, in essence, is contained in their works. The doctrine of the Word is found in them.[16] They see that God is infinite, unchanging, and always identical to himself.[17] It may even be thought that, had these philosophers lived in our day, they would only have had to change a few things in their doctrine and their expressions to become Christians.[18]

11 St. Augustine, *Confessions*, VII, 21.

12 de Bérulle, *Discours*, column 154.

13 de Bérulle, *Discours*, column 386.

14 Germain Habert, *la Vie du cardinal de Bérulle*, Paris: Camvsat et le Petit, 1646, book III, chapter 2, p. 827,.

15 On this point see L. Grandgeorge, *Saint Augustin et le néo-platonisme*, Paris: Ernest Leroux, 1896, Bibliothéque de l'École des hautes études. Sciences religieuses, (reproduced Frankfurt am Main: Minerva Gmbh, 1967), especially 23–57.

16 St. Augustine, *Confessions*, VII, 9.

17 St. Augustine, *Confessions*, VII, 20.

18 St. Augustine, *De Vera Religione*, chapter 4.

Plato is the most profound philosopher, and what is purest and most luminous in him shone forth in Plotinus who could be called Plato's reincarnation.[19] For de Bérulle, it was a divine grace to read these philosophers. Contrasted with the works of others, full of flaws and lies, their works unceasingly insinuate the knowledge of God and his Word into the mind,.[20] The deep admiration for these philosophers left quite visible traces in Cardinal de Bérulle's doctrine.

De Bérulle finds a word of admiration, at least in passing, for "this great philosopher" Plato,[21] something that is never found in a Scholastic treatise. As for the neo-Platonists themselves, de Bérulle hesitates even less to bestow praise on them for drawing, in his judgment, part of their knowledge from Holy Scripture.[22] Precisely this preponderant influence of neo-Platonism is what establishes the filiation from St. Augustine to de Bérulle and thereafter from de Bérulle to Gibieuf and to Descartes. Certainly, we do not find the same notion of divine freedom in de Bérulle's works that Descartes would hold and, on the contrary, we could point out indicators that are contradictory to some extent. For example, de Bérulle will speak a great deal about God's councils, and he will distinguish God's council from his cabinet. But these are only metaphors. In reality, de Bérulle never poses the question of divine freedom. Therefore, if the founder of the Oratory was the precursor of the Cartesian theory of divine freedom, it can only be indirectly by bringing a neo-Platonist notion of God to the fore, of which Descartes' theory like that of Gibieuf was only the immediate development and prolongation. It seems beyond dispute that de Bérulle was the precursor in this sense. It is easy to see that the conception of God revealed in the *Discours de l'état et des grandeurs de Jésus* contains all the elements from which the new theories of divine freedom will emerge.

De Bérulle takes from the neo-Platonists the famous comparison between God and the sun, in the form in which pseudo-Dionysius presents it, which decisively influenced Gibieuf's thought.[23] This comparison that originated in Plato was generally suspect in Scholasticism because it seems to

19 St, Augustine, *Contra Academicos*, III, 18.

20 St. Augustine, *Confessions*, VIII, 2.

21 de Bérulle, *Discours*, column 178.

22 de Bérulle, *Discours*, column 235: "He [the Word] is the first-born of God, even the Platonists say, having learned it from our holy writings, where we read that he is the first fruit of the divine fruitfulness." Further on, he calls them "the Platonists... . . . our imitators," column 235.

23 On pseudo-Dionysius's influence, see below in this chapter.

introduce necessity into God's production of things, but it became extraordinarily popular at this time. We could almost consider it to be the primary evidence of the development of new ideas. Whenever we find the comparison, we know that re-born neo-Platonism has made some inroad. We find it used by de Bérulle in profusion. Like the prisoner in Plato's *Republic*, he emerges from the cave where we are detained because we are imprisoned in the flesh, to come to contemplate by the light of day "the sun whose sight this ancient philosopher so esteemed and loved and that we find so beautiful," that "is only an image of Jesus, who is a sun in the world of grace and glory." Accordingly, we must detach ourselves from the things of this world and turn unceasingly toward this uncreated splendor to pray to it and adore it. "So, going out from the darkness of earthly things and coming to contemplate the true Sun of the world, the Sun of this sun that enlightens us, the Sun of justice that gives its light to every man coming into the world, we are surprised and smitten with love and admiration at the first brilliance and the first sight of this splendor and obliged to interrupt our discourse, at the entrance of this work and from the thought of such a praiseworthy subject, in order to raise ourselves to God on the grandeurs of his only Son and on the account of this most holy mystery."[24]

Moreover, we find certain comparisons in de Bérulle that have a more exclusively neo-Platonist character. All the comparisons by the philosophers that seem to express God's unity, infinity, or fecundity in a particularly gripping manner are agreeable to him. Before Gibieuf, de Bérulle takes up the image that symbolizes God's single activity by a circle, where the operation goes from himself to himself by himself.[25] The same image serves him to express God's unity in the eternal emanations.[26] Finally, before Pascal, de

24 de Bérulle, *Discours*, column 159. Also in column 159: "In which we are like someone who, coming forth from a cave and profound darkness, placed on a high mountain, saw the sun, not having ever seen it previously..." . . ." Similarly, *Discours*, column 174. See also column 234: "Thus, he is called *Rising* [*Orient*] in the prophets, because he is a sun just like his Father; and a sun emanates from a sun... . . . But by this emanation, he has the singularity that being a sun like his Father, he is a Rising Sun, which his Father is not. And this sun that we see rise and set in our days, is only his shadow and his portrait; while this sun that according to St. John 1:5 gleams in our shadows and rises in our hearts, is the true Rising upon which we must always look."

25 de Bérulle, *Discours*, column 225.

26 de Bérulle, *Discours*, column 323: "... ". . . and you make this work that encloses and contains you, whose center and circumference you are, have no relations but toward you... . ."

Bérulle takes up the comparison between God and an intellectual sphere, "because the Ancients represent God's infinite being to us as an intellectual Sphere that comprises everything and cannot be comprised."[27] According to this image we must say that God "dwells in things by containing them and not being contained by them; that it gives being, existence, and capacity to the world; that it is infinite, immeasurable, and incomprehensible; and that it is this intellectual sphere, whose center is everywhere and whose circumference is nowhere."[28]

As Cardinal de Bérulle conceives him, God is essentially characterized by two attributes that St. Thomas and Scholasticism explicitly recognize but that take on exceptional importance in the vision of the founder of the Oratory and occupy a privileged place in his theology. These two attributes are goodness and unity.[29] By adopting this position, de Bérulle merely conforms to St. Augustine, who conforms to Plotinus.[30] But, of these two attributes, it is unity that seems to characterize the divine essence in what is most intimate. The insistence de Bérulle employs in making this particular attribute stand out is such that the Cardinal adheres to Plotinus and the doctrine of the First-One more than to St. Augustine. In a sense, de Bérulle insists on the point more than St. Augustine,[31] and if we could say that he was the apostle of the Incarnate Word, we could say equally that he was the apostle of divine unity. He is completely filled and inebriated, as it were, with divine unity. Not content with developing two whole discourses especially to this subject,[32] we see him come back to it constantly in the rest of the work: unity is the first property that Philosophers attribute to the created being. It is the first perfection that Christians recognize and adore in the uncreated being. It is what Scripture most frequently represents for the faithful.[33]

27 de Bérulle, *Discours*, column 264.

28 de Bérulle, *Discours*, column 250.

29 de Bérulle, *Discours*, column 192: "And, consequently, we say that since God's unity and God's goodness are the most acknowledged and best known perfections of divinity."

30 On this point see the texts assembled by Grandgeorge, *Saint Augustin et le néo-platonisme*, pp. 81–84.

31 Grandgeorge, *Saint Augustin et le néo-platonisme*, p. 61 for St. Augustine and p. 69 for Plotinus.

32 de Bérulle, *Discours*, III and IV.

33 de Bérulle, *Discours*, column 192. Cf. *Discours*, column 205: "Thus God is eternally alive in the unity of his essence; thus God is powerfully operative in unity of principle; thus God is happily reigning in the unity of his love." *Discours*, columns 270–271: "And it seems to me that I see in the unities that are observed in the fruit-

Therefore, it is true to say that God is the principle of all unity, that he even is unity in his nature and in his essence.[34] But such an affirmation does not exhaust either the knowledge of the divine unity or the knowledge of its effects. Let us first of all note that God's unity is not only manifested in the eternal procession of divine persons. It is also manifested in all the objects of this created world, the mark left by the artisan on his work. Unity "shines in all God's works as if in so many mirrors that announce and represent it to us... . . . Universal Nature has spoken openly and truly of the unity of its God and of its Artisan through the voice of its first and most excellent philosophers,[35] who have all collaborated together both to acknowledge and announce it to the world."[36] Consequently, there is no surprise in this unity of God's work. It simply proves to us that God is One and that creation bears the characters of the perfect unity that belongs to her creator. Besides, since the very action through which God produces the world is absolutely one, it is impossible that the universe should not conserve something of this unity: "Because it is by the unity of his essence, of his power, of his intelligence that the world is produced; and that is why the world bears the image of God's unity like the mark of its artisan."[37]

Furthermore, it is not enough to say that God's creative activity shows his unity. We must also say that creation flows completely naturally from God's unity. In the divine essence, unity and fruitfulness are confused.[38]

fulness of God, in the divine communication by which, when God communicates himself in himself, he comes to be communicated even to man and to be united to man in the honor of the admirable unities that the human mind conceives and adores in his divine being. Because, for a great clarification of this discourse, we can distinguish, as it were, two excellent orders of divine unities, the first of which consists of the unities that are in God's being, and the second consists of the unities that are in God's works... . . . We see that his goodness and his supreme majesty tend by a secret and deep council to reduce everything to unity and to enclose everything, that is to say the creator and the creature, in a admirable circle of unity, and even tend to unite them to the point and to the center of divine unity by the mystery of the incarnation and by the unity of an uncreated and incarnated person all together."

34 de Bérulle, *Discours*, column 192.

35 We take it that this means the neo-Platonists.

36 de Bérulle, *Discours*, column 189. On this point see St. Augustine, *De Vera Religione*, chapter 32.

37 de Bérulle, *Discours*, column 190.

38 de Bérulle, *Discours*, column 190: "And for the same reason, it [the world] owes homage to God, not only because of his Being, which is the First and Supreme Divine Being, but also by reason of his supreme unity, from which the world takes its origin; because God, not only as God, but as unity, is the principle of this unity."

This is what the neo-Platonists, under whose authority de Bérulle unhesitatingly places himself, understood and taught gloriously: "And the Platonists who are the highest of the pagans in knowledge of sublime things, truly divine men among the naturalists and theologians among the philosophers, speak of nothing so divinely as of unity; and in the elements and secrets of their doctrine, they teach their disciples that the divine essence and fruitfulness is in the unity."[39] So the world is a product of God's fruitful unity. We must not be surprised to see de Bérulle frequently present the created universe as an emanation from the creator and God as "a loving source of continual emanations outside himself."[40] Such an expression (one, furthermore, that Gibieuf and Descartes would either amend or reject as seeming to deny all voluntary activity in God and that Scholasticism condemned for the same reason) situates us in the current of new conceptions that are going to appear among de Bérulle's disciples, who will more readily appeal to the exuberant fullness of the divine essence than to the reflexive pursuit of certain goals in order to explain the work of creation.

That, in essence, is the notion of God that Descartes knew since 1625, whether by reading *Discours de l'État et des Grandeurs de Jésus* or else through Cardinal de Bérulle's spiritual direction. The first elaboration of Descartes' metaphysics must have taken place in 1629. We can observe the proximity of the two dates. It is upon leaving Paris at the urging of Cardinal de Bérulle, to fulfill a mission that his spiritual advisor had just entrusted to him, that Descartes constructs the first draft of his system. At this point, Descartes lives in the theological atmosphere that surrounds his confessor Cardinal de Bérulle. It is difficult to determine what exact influence de Bérulle had on the young philosopher's thinking. He certainly encouraged Descartes to liberate himself from Scholastic theology and to conceive the plan of replacing old and overly dialectical proofs of the existence of God with new, more intuitive proofs. Most likely also, de Bérulle gave Descartes confidence in his metaphysical talent and reassured his Christian conscience about the legitimacy of the endeavor he was about to undertake in the *Meditations*. However that may be, Descartes, who withdrew from society to meditate more easily, was newly molded by Cardinal de Bérulle and

39 de Bérulle, *Discours*, column 192.

40 de Bérulle, Discourse, column 191. See likewise: "That God is the origin of minds and by a kind emanation, the most powerful and the most exalted that is found in the world." de Bérulle, *Oeuvres de Piété*, Lyon: C. de la Roche, 1666, 2 parts in one volume, II, p. 74; cf. p. 41. (Reproduced Alexandria, VA, Alexandria Street Press, 2007.)

permeated by the theology that de Bérulle taught to all who approached him. He believed that God is above all an infinite essence and a perfect unity. By that, we understand an absolute unity in the face of which the unity taught by St. Thomas is only a confused multiplicity, and he also believed that the source of God's fruitfulness resides in this unity. From the Founder of the Oratory, Descartes takes the seed from which his conception of divine unity is going to emerge.

Moreover, there are some reasons to think that the sketch of the *Meditations* drafted in 1629 bore the mark of Cardinal de Bérulle's influence in a more obvious way than the later, definitive version. This first metaphysics of Descartes may have been more spontaneous, more alive, and to be clear, more original than the second version. As a result of Descartes' methodic reflections on the metaphysical requirements of the new physics, under the influence of Oratorian theology, it had a freedom of style that the philosopher's thought was never to find again. Between the first and second versions of the *Meditations*, many things were to happen that little by little modified our philosopher's attitude. Plausibly, the most important was the condemnation of Galileo. It has been said that without the condemnation, instead of the large tome formed by the *Meditations*, the *Objections*, and the *Responses*, we would have those few sheets of metaphysics that Descartes initially composed.[41] We are inclined to think so, but we would graft another hypothesis onto this one. Perhaps it is not simply the extension of his metaphysics that Descartes found himself impelled to modify by fear of theological censures, but the content also.

Descartes' fundamental project in both cases was to lay down the metaphysical principles of his physics, but above all it was to gain approval for this physics by getting its foundations accepted. To reach that goal, Descartes had to succeed in proving that the new physics was closely tied to the essential positions of traditional metaphysics; that not only did corpuscular physics and Cartesian mechanics not entitle the scientist to dispense with God and the immortality of the soul, but even that they implied these two questions. It is only when we have gotten through God and through the notion of a soul that is undying because it is pure thought, that we can call ourselves really Cartesians. It was an excellent precaution, but it involved a drawback. If, by adapting traditional Scholastic metaphysical positions to the requirements of the new physics, Descartes finds himself drawn to a very different notion of God from the one generally taught, the

41 On this point, see Adam, *Vie et oeuvres*; XII, p. 179.

cure is worse than the disease. It would be better not to speak about God and let physics go alone than to tie its fate to that of an unacceptable metaphysics. In the interval that separates the two versions of the metaphysics, Descartes becomes more prudent not only by reason of Galileo's condemnation, but also because he more and more eagerly longs for success, and seeing with increasing clarity how much this success depends on the good will of theologians, he also perceives better how difficult it will be to win it.

Descartes leaves nothing undone to succeed in that effort and the *Meditations on First Philosophy* suppose a painstaking labor of adaptation. Above all, it does not seek originality and Descartes defends himself quite sincerely against the charge of having been original. Certainly, when he claims that the *Meditations on First Philosophy* contain nothing that has not been known in every age and accepted by all, he exaggerates deliberately. But he also expresses what he would have keenly hoped his metaphysics was. On this point, his ideal was certainly to arrange old material used by everyone in a new order, to change any thing in generally accepted opinions only in the measure that was absolutely necessary. This is why, while Descartes deviates from Scholasticism as he does in the proofs of God's existence, he still takes the point of departure of his deduction from it. He always starts from ideas that cannot fail to be granted to him, and to be more secure, he goes looking for them in the doctrine of his adversaries. With the notion of objective reality and the Scholastic principle according to which God is the author of all perfections, Descartes constructs a proof of the existence of God. From the universally admitted principle of continuous creation, he makes another proof emerge. He will search for a third proof from St. Anselm's argument that he modifies so as to shelter it from St. Thomas's criticisms. In what concerns the criterion of truth, Descartes is very careful to justify it in the name of universally admitted principles — divine veracity, unreality of evil and of error as such, and the possibility that always remains to us to avoid evil and error if we wish.[42] Everywhere, Descartes stays as close to generally accepted metaphysics as the combined requirements of his physics and his method allow him. This is especially apparent in what he teaches about God's freedom.

If we take into account the fact that the letters to Mersenne in which we first encounter this doctrine are dated in 1629 and thus contemporary to the first version of the *Meditations*, we will understand that Descartes

42 On this point, see part II in the present study.

assigns it a place of honor in his metaphysics. Moreover, let us note that he is quite satisfied about his discovery and that this is one of the first metaphysical notions whose acceptance he strives to obtain. He is still under Cardinal de Bérulle's direct, immediate influence, but the Cardinal will die soon, years will pass, and with them will come prudence. What good is it to clash frontally with the conception of God that had been traditional in Scholasticism since St. Thomas? It is quite certain that fundamentally important consequences for the new physics are linked to God's absolute unity; yet, however felicitous this deduction may be viewed abstractly, it loses a great part of its value for Descartes if it appears capable of jeopardizing the success of physics. A simple artifice permits him to dispense with it. Starting from the consideration of an attribute of God admitted and taught by everyone, we can manage to justify the rejection of final causes as well as the necessity of making a mental bow to problems raised by the idea of infinity. This attribute is divine incomprehensibility. From that point, Descartes' line of conduct is completely laid out. In place of a profound, new metaphysical deduction, he will substitute a simple appeal to traditional theology, and this would explain why perhaps the most original of Descartes' metaphysical notions has no place either in the body of the *Meditations on First Philosophy* or in the *Principles*. Relegated to the discussion of *Objections*, it appears as an accessory doctrine, whose rejection would in no way undermine the solidity of the overall system. Therefore, while Descartes permits himself the satisfaction of presenting it, he assures himself that the fate of his philosophy will not be attached to it. In place of justifying his conclusions by the conception of God that he took from Cardinal de Bérulle, he contents himself with justifying it summarily by appealing to the conception of God that he takes from St. Thomas.

But in 1629 the seeds planted in his mind by the founder of the Oratory are certainly what have just developed. The conclusions to which his *Meditations* lead him are so naturally linked to them that they seem almost to flow by logical coherence, while they are in formal contradiction with the principles his teachers at La Flèche had tried to inculcate. Here is something that confirms the hypothesis of this influence and filiation in a very peculiar way. At the very moment when Descartes elaborates a notion of divine freedom that we know is closely tied to the requirements of his physics, there is a theologian educated like Descartes in the purest doctrine of St. Thomas, who like Descartes turns away from this doctrine under Cardinal de Bérulle's influence. Unlike Descartes, he is not at all worried about what a new physics must be. Starting from the principles posited by de Bérulle, our theologian winds up denying the existence of any finality. Quite different concerns from those of Descartes suffice to lead him to delve into the thesis of God's absolute unity and develop one of the metaphysical consequences it holds.

This theologian is Guillaume Gibieuf, doctor by the Sorbonne, priest and then superior of the Congregation of the Oratory, author of a book devoted to the freedom of God and creatures. Gibieuf began as an impassioned Scholastic. For some time, the Society of Jesus viewed him with some satisfaction as a future recruit. But he opted for the Oratory and was one of the first priests that de Bérulle was able to attract. Gibieuf was then and, despite all his efforts, he would remain until death a controversialist and an unreconstructed dialectician. But if Gibieuf still conserved something of the Scholastic that he had earlier been, he strove constantly to cast off the old man and substitute the love of serene contemplation and mute adoration before the truth for his innate love of disputation. If we believe Gibieuf's biographers, a short time after his entrance into the Oratory, he perceived the vanity of all the science to which he had been passionately devoted, and this inner change occurred under the influence of Fr. de Bérulle. "The pious conversations that the blessed founder held every day with his disciples, with an unction and a sublimity worthy of the first Fathers of the church, touched his heart in such a way that in a short time he became another person. All the vain self-esteem that the human sciences ordinarily produce in the soul: that itch to dispute about everything that Scholastic subtleties inspire in new doctors and that inordinate passion to know that is so natural in studious persons, seemed to him so opposed to the spirit of Jesus Christ that he entered into a holy horror at himself, for having until then regarded as meritorious something for which he felt such great confusion in himself. He became humble, pious, fervent, docile, and mortified."[43] This was Fr Gibieuf's first conversion.

The conversion, however, was far from being total and definitive, and it may be that his director never desired it to be complete. If de Bérulle lamented that a facility for controversy and dialectical talents was difficult to harmonize with the spirit of the Oratory, he could not fail to acknowledge certain qualities that he personally lacked and that, nevertheless, could be very useful in the defense of the nascent order. The reaction against the

43 Charles Edme Cloyseault, *Recueil des vies de quelques prêtres de la congrégation de l'Oratoire*, Paris: Poussielque, 1882, edited by Augustin Marie Pierre Ingold, I, p. 140.

Scholastic spirit that characterized Fr. de Bérulle's theological posture was completely spontaneous and in some measure sentimental. Nothing in the positions he adopted in regard to Scholasticism lets us believe in a reflective attitude and premeditated plan. He preferred St. Augustine to St. Thomas and admitted it frankly. As for the rest, he followed his inspiration and his personal preferences without worrying about anything else. No definite method, no really precise thesis, no carefully elaborated doctrine is found in his works, but only a way of thinking rather incompatible with the Scholastic mentality and beyond that drafts, sketches, and invitations to push analyses further, beginnings of a new metaphysics yet to be established. What de Bérulle offered was much less a method than a spirit; he found himself absolutely incapable of building a system. Scholastic theologians reproached him for that often enough. They claimed to see in his works only mystical verbiage, food for women, and mere fashionable Platonic nonsense. The truth is that de Bérulle was no dialectician. This was a serious gap for a man constantly at odds with a social order in which dialecticians abounded. Someone was needed to substitute for him, and that was Gibieuf, who played the role of philosopher within the fledgling order. He reflected and rationally grounded the new method that de Bérulle somehow applied instinctively. Gibieuf sorted out the philosophical principles that undergirded his superior's theology and brought out the ordered, logically constructed conception of God that was confusedly implicit in de Bérulle's works. This is the essence of the task carried out by Gibieuf in *De Liberate Dei et Creaturae*.[44]

At first glance, if we take notice only of its title, *De Liberate* seems to be one more theology book, a book nourished by the purest Scholastic tradition. Gibieuf takes cover in an impressive army of theologians and continually refers to their authority at the very heart of his book. In reality, this

44 Guillaume Gibieuf, *De Libertate Dei et Creaturae*, libri duo. "In quibus status et actus tam divinae quam creatae libertatis. Motio causae secundae a prima, scientiae mediae necessitas nulla, depravatae libertatis origo, ortus et natura mali, consummatio libertatis et servitutis, aliaque complura explicatur. Juxta doctrinam Divi Augustini, Divi Thomae, Divi Bonaventurae, Scoti, Gandavensis, Durandi, aliorumque veterum theologorum. Auctore Patre Guillelmo Gibieuf congregationis Oratorii Domini Jesu Presbytero, et in sacra theologiae facultate Doctore Sorbonico. A.S.D.N. Urbanum VIII, pontificem maximum, Parisiis, apud Josephum Cottereau, via Jacobea sub signo Prudentiae M. DC. XXX. Cum priv. reg." Since Gibieuf's book has never been reprinted, copies of it are quite rare. Nevertheless it is found in the Bibliothèque Nationale and the Bibiothèque Municipale of la Rochelle. The Sorbonne library possesses an incomplete copy..

profusion of precautions badly conceals his discomfort. If Descartes was uneasy about the fate reserved for his conception of divine freedom, Gibieuf had experienced the same uneasiness in connection with his own conception. If he felt the need to base himself on pseudo-Dionysius, St. Thomas, Duns Scotus, and other important authors, it is because he feared to appear as an innovator and dreaded a clash with the very widespread prejudice that confused novelty with error in theology.[45] But in the very instant in which Gibieuf took his precautions, he betrayed himself. St. Augustine's name, spread out in large letters in the book"s title was a sure warning to the attentive reader that the work was conceived in a new spirit and under the influence of someone other than St. Thomas. The very form of exposition utilized in *De Libertate* is significant and redolent of novelty. The syllogistic form has vanished and the Scholastic method is deliberately set aside. Except for some bits of Scholastic argumentation indispensable to vanquish the enemy with his own weapons, Cardinal de Bérulle"s method prevails throughout. Gibieuf offers long expositions followed by meditations, elevated thoughts, and prayers. But, instead of being completely spontaneous in applying it as his superior was, Gibieuf wants to define it, analyze it, and show the reader its indisputable superiority.

Moreover, the reasons that Gibieuf offers could not be more instructive.[46] The end of all knowledge is God, that is to say a purer and clearer awareness of God's essence and greatness. Knowledge does not reach its goal unless it becomes intelligence, since intelligence is nothing but a clearer, simpler, better-established knowledge, one more deeply rooted in our soul.

When our soul has reached intelligence, the principles seem to develop under our gaze to the point that the soul discovers the conclusions within the principles themselves. Two paths can bring us to this simple, full intelligence. One links terms to terms, syllogisms to syllogisms, and rolls out endless enthymemes. The other proceeds by simple exposition of principles, and by considering what they contain implicitly and covered up, it explains and develops it. What the defined object presents obscurely, because it presents it in one, simple view, the definition brings to light by employing several terms. This second way is more agreeable and more pleasant than the

45 Gibieuf, *De Liberate*, II, 8, p. 335: "Sed quia ut doctrina haec nova aliquibus videbitur, ita metuendum ne sua illa praejudicata novitate minus grata futura sit, juvat eam communire testimoniis authorum omni exceptione majorum."

46 Gibieuf defines the method in the preface to part II, p. 279 ff.

previous one. By taking pleasure in an infinite multitude of arguments and an endless series of deductions, the first method does not let us bring our attention to bear on the principles as often as would be necessary to increase the light in our souls. By doing this, it diminishes and obscures the light in us, because, dragged along by the perpetual deductive descent, we move further and further away from the principles, the only objects of intelligence that give us light.[47] True and certain science is not discursive. It consists of a simple intuition of the truth.[48]

Therefore, we will resolutely set aside the syllogism. We will remember that the syllogism originates in the teaching of the sophists, who cared less for truth than for glory and public favor and used the syllogism to impose any old proposition on their listeners. The syllogism passed from the sophists into the hands of the heretics, who accepted this vile legacy. Are we to calmly accept its use coming to us from them? Can it be that we, who only seek to discover the truth and make it known, use a method whose true goal is not truth but victory? Let us firmly reject this method, and let us make an effort not to embarrass and reduce our readers to silence, but to make the pure light of truth shine before their eyes. Accordingly, Gibieuf is committed to adopting a different attitude from that of Scholastic philosophers, and, from the first lines of his exposition we have the impression of being carried off, far away from St. Thomas. We find pure Bérulle in *De Libertate*, but set in order and arranged logically. The author does more than keep his promise. He has pledged to abstain as much as possible from Scholastic dialectic, and we see that, following his superior's example, he proceeds by way of demonstrations to a series of hymns and reflections lifting us up toward the greatness of God. Placed in their order of sequential implication, before our eyes, the divine attributes develop the consequences that they possess in relation to the nature of freedom. Interrupted only by meditations and prayers, this exposition unfolds starting from principles set down by de Bérulle, and in the same spirit of profound mysticism that had led the Cardinal beyond the spirit of Scholasticism toward St. Augustine and neo-Platonism.

God is free and supremely free, and if something freer than supreme freedom exists, we must say that God is that something. He is that because he is contained by no limit of place or of nature, and because he fills

47 Gibieuf, *De Libertate*, book II, p. 280.

48 Gibieuf, *De Libertate*, book II, p. 284: "Cum ergo vera legitimaque scientia non discursus sit, sed simplex quidam veritatis intuitus..." . . ."

everything by his infinite essence. God is everything that exists or can exist. Better yet, he infinitely surpasses all that is real or possible. He is free because no place can contain him; no creature can oppose him or stop him, determine him, or move him; no image or concept can express him. God is the author of all things, and it would be false to fail to consider him superior to the effects he produces. God has no other relation with what exists, outside of being its author and dispenser. Beyond the act by which his power communicates their being to all things, he is without relation to them.

Again, it must be noted that this relation is not established between the divine power and things, but between things and the divine power that creates them. In short, when we say that God creates everything, we articulate the only possible relation between creature and creator.[49] Accordingly, from the instant when Gibieuf posits the definition of freedom, by denying that God could ever seek anything whatsoever outside himself, he excludes the possibility of teleology in advance

Consequently, every divine attribute that makes us feel the immensity and infinity of God better will make us perceive the nature of his freedom better. Immense and infinite, virtually comprising all creatures in himself, God is freed from all subjection. We do not depend on what we dominate, and he who depends on nothing evidently possesses perfect freedom.[50] Likewise, all creatures without exception are changing: God alone is immutable and independent. Removed from the influence of creatures, undergoing no change, since nothing can act upon him or move him, God is unchangeable by the very fact of his infinite superiority in regard to all things. That is to say, his immutability necessarily entails his freedom.[51]

Among all the divine attributes, there is one that can show us what divine freedom is better than all the others, because it is the very root of that divine freedom: it is the unity and simplicity of God. All creatures are composite in some measure, and in this regard, all creatures are subjected to some necessity, to corruption and ruin, if God does not preserve them. By contrast, God is absolutely one. Better still, he is the One himself: One in whom all contraries are admirably harmonized, One in whom not only is division absent, but there is not even the slightest shadow of division, and,

49 Gibieuf, *De Libertate*, II, 1, 1, p. 289: "Certe Deus extra se nihil respicit operando et largiendo: nec ullus ei respectus ad extra, aliter quam suae communicatione virtutis, inesse potest: et illa quoque absoluta censanda, nec ipsa ad res, sed res ad ipsam referri."

50 Gibieuf, *De Libertate*, II, 1, 4, p. 291.

51 Gibieuf, *De Libertate*, II, 1, 5, pp. 291–292.

whom we cannot suppose to be subjected to anything at all. Because God is the One, he therefore is supreme, perfect freedom.[52]

On this point Gibieuf simply takes the position adopted by Cardinal de Bérulle, making it more precise: the paradigmatic divine attribute is unity, and all the others, notably fruitfulness and freedom flow from this attribute. We have said that God is free because he is infinitely superior to all things and that the superabundance of his essence exempts him from any dependency. If we wished to summarize the nature of this freedom, we could say that God is freed by reason of his amplitude. This amplitude is only found in the One to which it is closely linked, since amplitude and One mutually imply each other. Other names that can be used to characterize freedom simply deny what contradicts it: mutability, limitation, inherence, dependence, composition, and multiplicity. By contrast, amplitude seems to characterize freedom in itself, in its own essence. It determines what it is and not simply what it is not. This amplitude finds its basis in unity, and it takes its origin from unity. The more something is ample, the less it involves potency and the more it approaches pure act. Since passive potency, that is to say, physical or metaphysical matter, is never without some imperfection or without some negation of a more complete perfection, it always constitutes a contradiction and a limitation. Act, on the contrary, is expansion and extension. That which involves no mixture of potency but is pure act must necessarily develop with infinite amplitude. It must be everything in its unity, be at the same time the One and the All and the supreme good, since it includes all goods virtually and eminently, just as the One comprises them. To be the amplitude and to be the All are the same thing. Therefore, God, who is the One, by the fact of his unity, possesses supreme and perfect freedom.

Accordingly, stammering about divine freedom, as humans are able to do, we put forward omnipotence, omniscience, immutability, independence, holiness, and infinity as so many arguments *a posteriori* and reciprocal properties that suppose freedom. But amplitude appears to us as constituting freedom formally and in itself; and, in the end, the unity of the supreme good appears as the proximate ground and the origin of amplitude. Therefore, in the last analysis, the basis and origin of freedom is found in unity.[53]

52 Gibieuf, *De Libertate*, II, 1, 3, p. 291: "Deus autem plane unus est, imo Unum ipsum est, et tale Unum in quo illa mirifice consentiunt quae in seipsis contraria sunt: Unum omnem omnino vel tenuem divisionis umbram eliminans, quod proinde cuiquam subjici omnino repugnat: quae est summa et perfecta libertas."

53 Gibieuf, *De Libertate*, II, 1, 14, pp. 297–298: "Unitas denique [indicat libertatem]; quia libertas nihil est nisi Amplitudo, quam ubique sectantur insani amatores sae-

Except for some analytic precision, so far we have not seen Gibieuf add anything to the doctrine taught by Cardinal de Bérulle. But a new problem that the founder of the Oratory had not explicitly discussed will make Gibieuf push the investigation further. This new notion plays the same role in Gibieuf's doctrine that the physics of efficient causes played in Descartes', and it will lead our theologian from the affirmation of God's infinity deduced from his unity to the rejection of all teleology. Gibieuf's book is part of a controversy. It is the work through which the Oratory takes a position in the ongoing struggle about the doctrine of grace. In its general directions and in its smallest details, *De Libertate* reveals the constant concern to pursue and eliminate a dangerous adversary, Molinism. In order to be certain of achieving this end, Gibieuf links the conception of divine nature that he takes from the Cardinal and the solution to the problem of human freedom that he plans to oppose to Molina"s solution. Without entering into the details of a doctrine to which we will have to return, we must briefly recall the essential elements of Molinism.

The doctrine was created in the concern to harmonize human freedom and divine predestination. According to the partisans of Molinism or, as Gibieuf prefers to say, middle science [translator: *scientia media*], God can will with an absolute and efficacious will and without any violation of human freedom that we should carry out certain voluntary actions. But this relates to the fact that before issuing his decree, God knows in what circumstances humans will be disposed to freely carry out these acts. It is only after having foreseen that in certain conditions and at a certain instant humans will accept the divine impulse and will respond to grace, that God decides to decree the act that he wants us to carry out. If we set aside everything that this notion of grace entails concerning human freedom, it is easy to see that it implies a certain conception of divine freedom, and

culi, ac nullibi nisi in Uno reperiunt; quia inquam, libertas nihil est nisi Amplitudo quae in Unitate, in qua Unitas, quae Unitati conjunctissima. Et reliqua quidem nomina, removent a libertate quae illi repugnant: mutabilitatem, limitationem, inhaerentiam, admirationem, dependentiam, compositionem, ac multiplicitatem. Amplitudo autem significare aliquo modo videtur id quod ipsa est. At Amplitudo illa in Unitate fundamentum habet, et ab unitate dicit originem... . . . Sic ergo de divina libertate balbutientes hominum more asserimus Omnipotentiam, Omniscientiam, Immutabilitatem, Independentiam, Sanctitatem, Infinitatem, et caeteras plerasque superexcellentissimas divinae majestatis perfectiones, quasi quaedam argumenta a posteriori et proprietates reciprocas, divinam indicare libertatem: Amplitudinem autem summi Boni esse ipsam formaliter libertatem: Unitatem tandem ejusdem summi et primi Boni esse illius fundamentum proximum et originem."

Gibieuf wants to get rid of precisely this conception. Just as Descartes thinks that he has to suppress any shadow of teleology even in God himself in order to reject final causes, so Gibieuf believes he has to go back to divine freedom to suppress Molina's teaching radically and, as it were, make it wither at its very root.

What is this singular God whom the defenders of middle science imagine? What strange notion of his power has been fabricated? If somebody undertakes to build a tower, he will have to evaluate its costs to see if he is in a position to assume them. Likewise, if a king wants to go to war against another king, he wonders whether his ten thousand men will permit him to bear the assault of twenty thousand who oppose him. It means that this person and this king are not all-powerful. If they possess, on the one hand, inexhaustible wealth and, on the other hand, infinite power, they would not be worried about looking ahead at this point. Confident in their strengths, they would calmly undertake their projects without first devoting themselves to diligent examination. The defenders of middle science want to bind God to this completely human prudence and this burdensome worry. God is spoken of as if he were not all-powerful and could come up against some obstacle in the fulfillment of his plans. It seems to be feared that God might not succeed in the difficult undertaking of inclining the human will where he wishes, while safeguarding our freedom. In the last analysis, it is admitted that something goes beyond God's power and that he is not truly all-powerful.[54]

Therefore, we would be badly mistaken to suppose that in God this diligent reflection and this examination would precede his actions. That is to speak of him as a human and not as the true God. Whatever the state in which God finds us, he can obtain our consent to his grace, whether he leaves us in the same state and inclines our will or makes us instantly pass to a more perfect state. In these different operations God uses no science other than that by which he comprehends himself and by which he comprehends the creature in his omnipotence. Those who oblige God to study the human heart exhaustively and to compel him to the consideration of this or that circumstance, wish to subject omnipotence to the condition of human feebleness, as if God himself had to count his resources before undertaking a war or the construction of his tower. But, who are we to pretend to limit God's power? Whom do we believe he resembles? Is he dependent, like a creature, so that we try to constrain him to reason like the children of men,

54 Gibieuf, *De Libertate*, I, 23, 7.

to discuss, to search for the means by which he will be able to accomplish his will? Let us not speak of him as if he had made us share in his councils.[55] We cannot penetrate his knowledge and he has not uncovered the ways of his wisdom to us. Let us bow before him without seeking to comprehend him, because we would lower him to our human condition. Let us judge more worthily of God and let us respect his omnipotent will, which is not compelled to any deliberation or subject to any end.[56]

By declaring that God's action is independent of any pursuit of final causes, Gibieuf renders Molina's doctrine impossible. He has no trouble finding a legitimate ground for the thesis in the definition of freedom he initially posed: Freedom consists of amplitude that itself is based in unity. That being that possesses supreme immensity and is not encompassed by any limit is immensely free. We know that God is that sovereign immensity and that, since he is everything, he cannot go outside himself when acting. In short, we know that he does not depend on any principle and is not subject to any end. In his action, God only responds to the appeal to his own goodness. Action flows from being, and if this action, exempt from any limit and from any subjection, is that of an infinite essence that is diffused and communicated without being exhausted, by definition it is found to be the supreme freedom. Therefore, God's freedom is an effusion and a communication of himself. In such an action, God is neither constrained nor even inclined to an end, which is self-evident. To acknowledge it, it is enough to take notice of the distinction that must always be made between God and the works of God.

God is the beginning and the end of his works, which are creatures, but he cannot be that in regard to himself. God is not his own principle. He has no principle. Nor, properly speaking, is he his end, because the principle and the end of a thing are confused by reason of the rule that everything spontaneously returns toward its principle.[57] With much greater reason, finite creatures cannot play the role of ends for God, and it is important not to picture the creator taking counsel, making deliberations, or anything of the sort. God

55 Gibieuf, *De Libertate*, I, 23, 9: "Quis enim adjuvit spiritum Domini, aut quis consiliarius ejus fuit et ostendit illi? Cum quo iniit consilium et instruxit ejum et docuit eum semitam justitiae et erudivit eum scientia et viam prudentiae ostendit illi?" Cf. Descartes, Letter to Elizabeth, September 15, 1645; IV, p. 232: "and entering into presumptuous impertinence, some want to be part of God's council and with him take charge of conducting the world..." . . ." Cf. likewise, *Principia*, I, 28.

56 Gibieuf, *De Libertate*, I, 23, 9.

57 Again, this concept is taken from Cardinal de Bérulle, who himself takes it from Plotinus.

does not have ends that he proposes to himself and towards which he tends or for whose realization he must put together specific means. The visible world has not been chosen by God after a deliberation of the kind that is generally attributed to him, nor, moreover, after any other deliberation. By the mere fact of his existence and of the superabundance of his essence and his goodness, God acts the way of the rich man scattering his treasures. He does not act with his eyes fixed on an end, nor does he pursue a goal that would be external to him. On the contrary, it is creatures that spring from him as their principle that necessarily tend to return toward him as their end.[58]

In order to definitively establish this bold concept of divine freedom, Gibieuf ultimately has to place it under the patronage of theologians of indisputable authority, and the title of his work reaches out for their agreement. On this point, despite most laudably ingenious efforts, Gibieuf ultimately falls short. If we set aside three chapters he devotes to showing that his theory exactly amounts to St. Thomas's, something that no one will believe,[59] he naturally only finds the philosophers from whom it sprung, that is to say, pseudo-Dionysius or even Proclus and Iamblicus to validate his notion of divine freedom. Moreover, Gibieuf takes sides and, encouraged by the example of Cardinal de Bérulle as well as of St. Augustine, he places himself decidedly under the patronage of the neo-Platonists.[60] Pseudo-Dionysius seems to have

58 Gibieuf, *De Libertate*, II, 4, 4, p. 316: "Quod autem a fine ad agendum non determinetur ne impellatur ultro agnoscent quicumque adverterint quid sit differentiae inter Deum et Dei opera: videbunque Deum et principium et finem esse operibus suis; at non sibi. Neque enim vel consultat, vel quasi consultat, quibus mediis ad finem perveniat; necque finem ullum intendit sibi, seu ad quem ipse se referat, et ad cujus assecutionem mediis quibusdam opus habeat; nec tali vel intentioni vel deliberationi acceptum referre debemus mundum hunc adspectabilem, aut etiam invisibilem et Angelicum, quasi ipse inde auctior cumultatiorve ad seipsum rediturus esset, aut aliquid emolumenti et splendoris reportaturus." In the summary that precedes this chapter, Gibieuf himself sums up his thought on this point as follows, *De Libertate*, summary IV: "Deus non movetur ad agendum a Fine; etiam Seipso. Deus non processit ad creandum mundum ex consultatione et electione."

59 See the analysis of the doctrine of both *Summas* in chapter II above.

60 Gibieuf, *De Libertate*, II, 8, title: "Haec Dei libertas in processionibus temporalibus, ultimo confirmatur, insignioribus quibusdam testimoniis scripturae, Divi Dionysii et Platonicorum." It is not necessary to consider testimony taken from Holy Scripture. There is no doctrine during this period that is not amply provided with it. As for the texts of Proclus and Iamblicus cited by Gibieuf, they are quite far from holding the doctrine that they are supposed to validate. Gibieuf leads them to it by dialectical artifice. The same must be said for the passages from pseudo-Dionysius, as the reader will realize by the one that we will quote below.

been his preferred authority, and Gibieuf devotes himself to demonstrating that the ancient theologian, who had been an authority for St. Thomas, held the same doctrine as Gibieuf's teacher. The accounts that pseudo-Dionysius gives of the Platonic comparison between the Good and the sun seem to have especially seduced Gibieuf, and he insists on it several times. Just as the sun that illuminates us does not send us its light in consequence of reasoning and choice, and since, by the mere fact that the sun is, it illuminates everyone who can perceive its light, so the Good in itself, which is to the sun what a sublime archetype is to its obscure image, diffuses the rays of its universal goodness by the mere fact of its existence and makes them fall upon everything. That is not exactly what Gibieuf maintains, and there is some difference between saying that God diffuses his goodness without deliberation or choice and saying that he has created everything without deliberation and choice.[61] But Gibieuf does not look so closely, and since his hunger for authority is so great that he even shelters himself under St. Thomas's, it is understandable that he is comfortable with the neo-Platonists in whom he at least finds comparisons and expressions similar to his own. Moreover, by skillful appeals he often succeeds in making them produce the meaning he is trying to find. Gibieuf owes them above all his point of departure. The detail of the deduction by which he makes the rejection of final causes result from it, is certainly his.[62]

In this way, we are faced with a notion of the divine essence quite different from St. Thomas's, one from which certain metaphysical consequences begin to emerge and whose novelty we cannot help noticing. Despite Gibieuf's attempt to lessen the disagreement, it remains in its

61 Gibieuf, *De Libertate*, II, 4, 5, p. 317: "Declarat hanc veritatem [*scilicet*: Deum non moveri ad agendum a fine] Divus Dionysius allato Solis exemplo; ut sol noster inquit capitulo 4 *De Divinibus Nominibus* in principio, non ex ratiocinatione aut electione, sed eo ipso quod est, illuminat omnia quae lumen ejus percipere possunt, secundam propriam cujusque rationem: sic et Bonum ipsum, quod supra Solem est sicut supra obscurum imaginem excellens archetypum, ipsa sua existentia omnibus quae sunt, radios universae Bonitatis immittit." Cf. other reference to Dionysius in the same sense: II, 8, 8, pp, 338–339. Cf. Migne, *Patrologia Graeca*, vol. III, columns 693, 698–699, 822, and 823. [Translator: the columns correspond to *De Divinibus Nominibus*]. For the Scholastic interpretation of these texts, see St. Thomas, *De Veritate*, 23, 1, reply to objection 1.

62 Here is how Gibieuf extracts his own doctrine from pseudo-Dionysius's comparison: Gibieuf, *De Libertate*, II, 4, 5, p. 317: "Secundo simile est, quod sicut sol non deliberat nec eligit, sed ipsa sua bonitate et existentia, puta hoc ipso quod est, in id incumbit: ita Deus non consultat etiam secum, sed ni abundantia superinfinitae bonitatis, ad extra sese diffundit, nolens solus divitiarum suarum possessor esse."

entirety. Certainly, Gibieuf thoroughly proves that, for St. Thomas and for Gibieuf himself, God cannot set himself ends that are outside his essence and that, consequently God's will does not depend on an alien end that would come to limit it from the outside. That is the common ground, moreover, a purely negative one, on which Catholic theologians necessarily agree. But Gibieuf goes further. He suppresses any shadow of deliberation and choice in God. He denies that God pursues any kind of end, not even his own goodness. An irreducible opposition exists between the two doctrines. That is perceptible enough for Descartes to identify with Gibieuf, whereas he does not recognize himself in St. Thomas. The opposition is explained by a profound difference in the spirit that moves Cardinal de Bérulle's theology and the spirit that moves St. Thomas's.

The two theologians start from the fundamental unity of the divine nature but their approach differs perceptibly in treating this unity. We are already familiar with St. Thomas's attitude. He knows perfectly that the divine reality surpasses us infinitely and exceeds our finite understanding on every side. Consequently, he knows that all theological attempts to comprehend and explain it perfectly will result in failure. No name adequately signifies the divine nature, which comprises everything in its indivisibility, and yet St. Thomas does not hesitate to bring analysis to bear on this perfect unity of God. If God is infinitely above us, it is no less true that we have a divine character conserved in creation and a resemblance to the creator. Therefore, if it is not permissible to conclude from man to God, it is equally illicit to deny any analogy between man and God. What we say of the creator, the names we attribute to him *analogice dicuntur secundum analogiam creaturarum ad ipsum*.[63] If the terms we use are incapable of characterizing God in himself, they can still give us a certain knowledge with which we are to make do here on earth. If we know how to use our language and strip it of the meaning that is necessarily constricted by being proportioned to the creature, we can characterize God by certain words taken in their proper sense and not metaphorically.[64] Even when St. Thomas indicates the distance that separates humans from the creator, he still is concerned not to elevate God so much that he totally escapes our grasp.

63 St. Thomas, *Summa Theologiae*, part I, question 13, article 5. [Translator: These words seem to be a paraphrase; but see: "... ". . . huiusmodi nomina dicuntur de Deo et creaturis secundum analogiam... . . . Et sic, quidquid dicitur de Deo et creaturis, dicitur secundum quod est aliquis ordo creaturae ad Deum ..."]. . ."]

64 St. Thomas, *Summa, Theologiae*, part I, question 13, article 3. [Translator: see especially reply to objection 3.]

Gibieuf's attitude is totally different. In him, as in de Bérulle, we feel a constant concern to exalt God, to raise him higher, a kind of fervor to push him back as far as possible into the infinite. The calmness of Sscholastic exposition seems to leave Gibieuf completely cold. God must no longer be spoken of as an object of knowledge. In consequence, God is spoken of as being the fullness of all reality, and all that we can say is that he appears to us as the infinite source of being, truth, and goodness, in which our finite minds are blinded, lost, and destroyed. That is why Gibieuf raises his style to the heights of his enthusiasm. Superlatives and capital letters in Gibieuf's work have a real methodic value. Where St. Thomas calmly declares, *in Deo est liberum arbitrium,* or, *Deo liberum arbitrium habere competit,*[65] Gibieuf strikes up a hymn to divine freedom: *Liber est Deus, immo liberrimus, et si quid liberrimo liberius esse potest!*[66] Gibieuf has neither words enough, nor long enough, nor elevated enough to celebrate God's grandeur. Very far from thinking that certain names correspond properly to the creator, insofar as they signify a positive reality, Gibieuf judges that those who exalt him most are still very far from expressing his perfections. When you say that God is the One, the Universal, the All, you do not approach him; rather, such words leave you as far as possible from his true nature.[67]

Let us not think that we are dealing with a mere terminological question. Under the refusal to use the same expressions, we can easily perceive fundamentally different tendencies. What drives the new theology is the concern to make humans feel their complete dependence on God at the same time as the whole distance that separates them from him. The creature must be reminded that between the finite and infinite that is God, or as Gibieuf says superinfinite, there is an irreducible difference of nature, and that the difference must be kept present in the mind of the creature that wants to speak worthily of its creator. The constant danger, to which we are exposed when we apply the method of analogy to God, is to fall into anthropomorphism. It is extremely important for someone who wants to form an adequate idea of divine grace, to strip any anthropomorphism from the notion of the nature of God. Gibieuf devotes his best efforts to this, and it is also what separates Gibieuf irreducibly from St. Thomas, despite what he may

65 St. Thomas, *Suma contra Gentes*, book I, chapter 88, see title of article.

66 Gibieuf, *De Libertate*, II, 1, 1, p. 289.

67 Gibieuf, *De Libertate*, II, 1, 14, p. 298: "Nomina negativa supponunt positiva: cujusmodi sunt in Deo, Unum et Universale, sive Omne quamquam et illa quam longissime a Deo absint."

take from St. Thomas. St. Thomas starts from man, and by passing to the infinite, reaches God. Gibieuf starts from God and by limiting and breaking up the infinite, descends to man. From this difference of spirit and method stems the opposition of their conclusions. For Scholasticism, the understanding and will are human qualities and perfections. Humans are superior to other creatures by having an understanding that reaches the universal, a free will, and by proposing ends and gathering the appropriate means to accomplish them. Therefore, St. Thomas believes he honors God by attributing to him some perfections analogous to the understanding and the will, and by proposing God as the end of God's own activity. Since deliberation and choice are human qualities and perfections, we will attribute them to God, simply by taking them to the infinite. By contrast, for Gibieuf, since the understanding and will are distinct in humans and reciprocally limit each other, they cannot be attributed to God.[68] Since we act by deliberation and choice, nothing of the sort is found in our creator's infinite essence. All these perfections of the creature vanish upon entering into the immensity of the One.

The opposition between Gibieuf's doctrine and that of St. Thomas is, therefore, quite noticeable. Its similarity to Descartes' doctrine is no less conspicuous. There are still real differences between them. The first and most observable is that in Gibieuf we do not find the notion of God creator of eternal truths. Descartes' concern to escape from Scholastic discussions on the infinite is necessary for the doctrine of God creator of eternal truths to be deduced from the neo-Platonist conception of the One. Furthermore, it is undeniable that Descartes' deduction is presented with a balance and rigor that Gibieuf's deduction does not attain. In Descartes, the denial of distinction of the will and understanding follows from the affirmation of the One. From the denial of the distinction, ultimately follow, on the one hand, the creation of the eternal truths, and on the other hand, the rejection of teleology. The route taken by Gibieuf is less direct and less regular. It starts from the definition of freedom by amplitude and seeks the root of this amplitude in unity. Then it descends back to amplitude to conclude from amplitude to absolute independence and absence of any limit. From this absolute independence it follows that God has no beginning or end, and from the fact that God does not pursue ends, Gibieuf concludes that God does not proceed by deliberation or choice, that is to say, he does not proceed by understanding and will. Here Gibieuf indirectly connects God's absolute unity to the rejection of teleology and by way of amplitude. Accordingly,

68 On this point, see the last two pages of chapter 1, part II.

the differences are real, but the similarities are much more important. In Gibieuf as in Descartes, we will find the same care to separate clearly the realms of the infinite and the finite. In both we find the same refusal to start from humans to draw conclusions about God. Before all else, in Gibieuf's view, as in Descartes', God is an infinite power of production from which all good and all existence flow. Like Descartes, Gibieuf refuses to admit even a shadow of distinction in God, however light that shadow might be, or to fracture God's perfect unity by introducing inclinations, reasoning, deliberations, or choices. Lastly, like Descartes, Gibieuf situates a creative power at the origin of the world, whose activity is displayed in the order of efficient causality and not at all in the order of teleology. In the face of such similarities, it is very difficult to admit that the confluence is the work of chance, and it would be appropriate to compare the circumstances in which the two doctrines were established and perhaps discover some explanation of these unusual resemblances.

In the first place, it is appropriate to exclude any hypothesis about direct influence of Gibieuf's book on Descartes' thought involving the doctrine of divine freedom. Such a supposition is chronologically impossible. Only at the end of his controversy with Mersenne, does Descartes learn about the kinship of his ideas to those of Gibieuf. Through a reference provided by his correspondent, Descartes recognizes his own opinions "absolutely" in the summary report that Mersenne makes of those ideas. This is a most pleasant revelation for Descartes, but it is a surprise. He is even unaware that Gibieuf has published anything, and he resolves to read Gibieuf's book as soon as possible. On the other hand, Descartes is quite convinced that he has contributed an entirely new opinion on the nature of divine freedom, but from this time on, this conviction affords him worry rather than gratification.[69] We see him express his pleasure to Mersenne at no longer feeling isolated in a dangerous position. However, several months later, since Mersenne is no longer in Paris, Descartes has not yet been able to obtain *De Libertate*,[70] and it is in the course of the following year that, having finally received Gibieuf's book, he will read part of it quickly and declare

69 Letter to Mersenne of May 27, 1630; I, p. 153, lines 14–23: "Concerning God's freedom, I absolutely share the opinion that you tell me has been expounded by Fr. Gibieuf. I did not know that he had published anything, but I will try to get his treatise from Paris at the first opportunity in order to see it, and I am greatly reassured that my opinions follow his, because that assures me that they are not so extravagant that no capable men hold them."

70 Letter to Mersenne, November 4, 1630; I, p. 174, lines 20–29.

himself very satisfied.[71] By that point, it has been a long time since Descartes had set down his thoughts about this question in the letters to Mersenne that we have analyzed. Consequently. Gibieuf's book is not the source from which Descartes draws his notion of God's freedom.

The similarities we have reported between the doctrines of Descartes and Gibieuf are not, however, inexplicable. First of all, we can give a very general initial reason that has already been noted and that it is important to recall here. These two doctrines have a common source, which is de Bérulle's theology. Descartes and Gibieuf were both students of Scholastic philosophy and theology; both came to have the Cardinal as their confessor and teacher. We know the relations between Descartes and his spiritual director. We are sure that the bonds uniting Gibieuf to his superior were just as close. In regard to the doctrine of the founder of the Oratory, both are converts, and both take the point of departure for their metaphysical speculation from that doctrine. The two doctrines that we have compared resemble each other like two branches from a common trunk, whose species would be the neo-Platonic doctrine of the One.

We can go further. If Descartes does not get his notion of divine freedom from *De Libertate*, perhaps he gets it from Gibieuf himself. This hypothesis at least has the merit of being chronologically possible, and there are reasons that incline us to accept it. During his stay in Paris from 1626 to 1628, Descartes frequents not only de Bérulle, but also most of the priests whom the Cardinal had brought together at the Oratory of rue St. Honoré, and who lived under his direction. Baillet's testimony on the point is in perfect agreement with what Descartes' correspondence shows: during his stay in Paris our philosopher develops relationships with the principal priests of the Oratory. De Condren, de la Barde, de Sancy, were among them, but a special position must be kept for Fr. Gibieuf: "equally skilled in philosophy and theology," whose company by virtue of this skill must have been particularly agreeable to Descartes.[72]

71 Letter to Mersenne, October 1631: I, pp. 219–220.

72 Baillet, *Vie*, I, p. 139: "Fr. Guillaume Gibieuf, doctor by the Sorbonne, priest of the Congregation of the Oratory was also one of the principal friends Descartes made during his three year stay in Paris. This Father was equally skilled in Philosophy and Theology. But he was not the only one of this congregation with whom M. Descartes developed familiarity. There were also very special relations with Fr. de la Barde, Fr. de Sancy, and Fr. de Condren, who was the second general of the congregation afterwards; to say nothing of Cardinal de Bérulle, who acquired a very special affection and esteem for our philosopher."

We may suppose that Descartes more than once attended the very special kind of recreation that the regulations of the Oratory provided for the fathers after dinner, a walk in the courtyard and, during the walk, philosophical and theological conversations in which everyone took part. Under the constant direction of Cardinal de Bérulle, a spirit that animated all the members of the new congregation and constituted the Oratory's moral unity was formed.[73] In addition to Baillet's testimony, which encourages us to think that the relations between Descartes and Gibieuf were especially close, there is a tradition in the oOratory that Gibieuf played the role of adviser and moderator for Descartes. The historian Edme Cloyseault, who speaks based on his memories and his "conversations with the elders," echoes this tradition. "The famous Descartes greatly desired to make his acquaintance and to establish a friendship with him," Cloyseault tells us of Fr. Gibieuf, "He made several visits to him, and he often consulted with him about the new systems dealing with philosophical matters that the liveliness of his mind produced. And we are obliged to Fr. Gibieuf for the number of perceptions that he suppressed, which were not at all compatible with the principles of theology and which might appear opposed to the rules of faith."[74]

But on this point we have something more compelling. Descartes' correspondence proves not only that he was in contact with Gibieuf from 1626 to 1628 but even that these relations were rather close and, something of fundamental importance, that they were philosophical in nature. After 1629, we see Gibieuf recur to Descartes to request him to get his father's support for Fr. de Sancy, who had dealings with the parliament of Rennes. Therefore, although Fr. de Sancy was acquainted with Descartes, he judged it preferable to transmit his request through Gibieuf, who doubtless was a closer friend. Descartes' answer is particularly significant. After having thanked Gibieuf for remembering him, Descartes reminds him that he had promised to correct a little philosophical treatise and even, according to a mere polite formula of the time, to "give it the final polish." Therefore, it is certain that Gibieuf had been the confidant of Descartes' philosophical projects and that he was aware of Descartes' first *Meditations on First*

73 Michel Houssaye, *le P. de Bérulle et l'Oratoire de Jésus, 1611–1625*, Paris: Plon, 1874, pp. 154–156.

74 Cloyseault, *Recueil des vies*, p. 153.

75 By contrast, we have already seen that Gibieuf had not spoken to Descartes about the book he was preparing. This is astonishing, and, it surprised Descartes. We see only two hypotheses to explain it. One is that Gibieuf conceived the idea of his book and executed it out between the end of 1628 and the end of 1629, that is to

Philosophy.[75] How then can we think that before confiding his plan to construct a system to the Oratorian, Descartes had not conferred with him about what he proposed to introduce in it? It was an excellent moment for Descartes to put his mind at ease on one or another of his conceptions, and he gives us to believe that he had more than one conversation of this type with Gibieuf. The Oratorian finally agreed to review Descartes' treatise. All testimonies agree on the point that Descartes and Gibieuf were in continuous contact from 1626 to 1628 and that Descartes' future metaphysics was one of the chief subjects of their conversations. These good relations did not stop there, and we will have occasion to return to them. Let us simply note the most visible traces of this in their correspondence. Some months later, Descartes advises Ferrier to approach Gibieuf or de Sancy and "importune them" to be granted accommodations in the Louvre.[76] Before having read Gibieuf's book, he insists on informing him more especially than the others that he is studying "something other than the art of firing weapons."[77] Later we have proof that they are in agreement on the most important points of metaphysics,[78] and Descartes will get Gibieuf to actively support the *Meditations*.[79] Lastly, when Descartes is attacked on the question of divine freedom, he shields himself behind Gibieuf's authority, since he has written nothing "that fails to agree with what he [Gibieuf] put in his book *De Libertate*."[80] On Gibieuf's side, we find the same good will and the same signs of friendship. The Oratorian takes up Descartes" cause. He spreads the *Meditations*; he defends them, and he becomes involved in getting them approved by the body of doctors

say, after Descartes' departure, but this is \ implausible, because of the work's size and careful composition. The second is that he told no one about his projects in order not to alarm the Jesuits, who would not have failed to provoke difficulties and perhaps would have prevented the book's publication by invoking the Papal decrees that put a stop to the dispute. The Jesuits must have tried to do that to *Augustinus*, as we will see. The second supposition seems completely credible to us and will no doubt appear acceptable when we have examined the bitterness that the struggle on this point had taken on. (Cf. Part II.)

76 Letter to Ferrier, October 8, 1629; I, pp. 32–33.

77 Letter to Mersenne, November 4, 1630; I, p. 174.

78 Letter to Mersenne, March 31, 1638; II, p. 97. See also letter to Mersenne, May 27, 1638: II, p. 147.

79 Letter to Mersenne, September 30, 1640; III, p. 184. See also letter to Mersenne, November 11, 1646; III, pp. 239–240.

80 Letter to Mersenne, April 21, 1641; III, p. 360. See also letter to Mersenne, June 23, 1641; III, p. 385.

of theology of the Sorbonne.[81] But no testimony is more instructive or more interesting than that first short letter of 1629, where the possibility is established of Gibieuf's philosophical influence on Descartes in general and in particular on his notion of God's freedom.

This influence must be taken as confirmation and, in certain aspects, clarification of the influence de Bérulle had on Descartes. Doubtless it was mutual and deserves rather the label of cooperation. What can be supposed with great plausibility is that together they worked out the program of a new metaphysics and a theodicy differing from the Scholastic version. The method is less discursive than Scholasticism: it is more concerned with constantly rising to the intellectual intuition of principles; it is convinced that truth does not consist of a discursive chain, but is found in an intuitive vision; and that the only genuine demonstration is the one that makes the conclusion appear in the heart of the principles. The theodicy is completely founded on the consideration of the infinity and the unity of God, and concerned above all to make humans bow before the incomprehensibility of the infinite essence and to introduce no shadow of division into this essence. We do not know to what degree their conversations foment the development of these principles or what suggestions they make to each other regarding divine freedom. But one point remains perfectly certain. During the three years that immediately precede Descartes' elaboration of the notion of divine freedom, he was in contact with two men to whom he owes a general conception of the divine essence, very different in spirit from the one held by his teachers at La Flèche, and from which his doctrine of God's freedom was to emerge. Therefore, we can situate this doctrine's source within the Neo-Platonic theology restored by de Bérulle and Gibieuf.

Ultimately, it would seem that two different interpretations could be historically justified. In a first hypothesis, the Cartesian notion of divine freedom would be conditioned by what is most original and most personal in Descartes' thought: it would flow naturally from the system's inner logic, and without going beyond our philosopher's own works, we would discover its necessity. It would have to be admitted, then, that once sketched in Descartes' mind, at least in its general lines, the physics would have been the connecting thread in the construction of the metaphysics. In this hypothesis, the structure of Descartes' philosophy in what concern's God's freedom would be explained by the necessity of metaphysically justifying the physics

81 Letter to Mersenne, June 23, 1641; III, p. 388; Descartes, Letter to de Launay, July 22, 1641; III, p. 419. Descartes, Letter to Gibieuf, January 19, 1642; III, p. 472.

of efficient causes. By expressing ourselves in this way, we would say nothing contrary to the conception of science that Descartes fashions. We know how closely the truths of the sciences are intertwined according to him, and to what point they suppose and condition each other. Therefore, it is natural to think that, since he had achieved mathematical certainty and indisputable results in physics, Descartes wished to determine the metaphysical propositions presupposed as true by these physical truths. This interpenetration seems to agree with the secret ambitions that Descartes himself confessed, and it is evident that our philosopher was eager to connect the demonstrations in physics in the *Principles* to positions established by the *Meditations on First Philosophy*.

But if we assume a different viewpoint, we could attribute a totally different origin to the Cartesian notion of God's freedom. We would no longer consider the conception in its internal structure and dependence on the rest of the system, but in relation to a more general philosophical tendency encompassing and explaining it. At the moment when Descartes' ideas take shape and for some time previously, the neo-Platonic current that we can follow through all of medieval philosophy[82] seeps into many theological circles. We can pick up its traces and follow its progress a little bit everywhere around our philosopher. In the general philosophical situation, however, the Oratory is one of the particularly active and interesting centers of propagation. Its founder Cardinal de Bérulle was brought up on St. Augustine, a confessed admirer of the Platonists and permeated with their doctrine. Far from this being one individual's peculiar, accidental form of thought, it seems that it is identified with the spirit of the new order. In the Oratory, one breathes a Platonic atmosphere. Now, in this Oratory a doctrine about God's freedom appears, essentially agreeing with Descartes' own doctrine. This theory, which seems closely aligned with the new physics, arises at the same time in circles where the new physics is still unknown. Moreover, Descartes himself encounters the doctrine in those circles. Several times he pictures a period of his life in which he perceived the general plan of his philosophy, without having anything at hand to achieve it. Descartes

82 On this point see the works of François Picavet, who has devoted himself to showing this current's importance and continuity in opposition to historians who see only Aristotelianism in medieval philosophy. Cf. especially, *Esquisse d'une histoire générale et comparée des philosophes médiévales*, Paris: F. Alcan, second and revised edition, 1907, *passim*, and *Roscelin, philosophe et théologien, d'après la légende et d'après l'histoire, sa place dans l'histoire générale et comparée des philosophes médiévales*, Paris: F. Alcan, 1911, pp. 30 ff.

frequented the author of that system similar to his own, and we know that he underwent his influence. Finally, the Cardinal was his confessor, and during a three- year period Descartes was in a position to receive the neo-Platonic seeds with which his director was imbued and the notion of divine freedom that naturally flowed from them. From that point of view, this notion would be explained without difficulty, and it would be unnecessary to recur to the system's internal needs. Descartes simply would have been the Oratory's lay missionary.

If these two interpretations are equally supported by the texts and can equally be justified, it is because they are both true, and far from contradicting, complete each other. They constitute two different but equally legitimate viewpoints on Cartesianism. Seen from the inside, Descartes' thought appears to us in all its logic and its rigorous structure. But if we then understand the structure of this tree of science that Descartes describes for us and that he tries to cultivate, and if we can next perceive its general structure and the structure's relation with the slightest details, something still remains unknown and unexplained: the nature of the soil in which it takes root, the elements that the tree takes from its surroundings and that explain its growth. In the particular case that we are examining, it would be as mistaken to consider Descartes a thinker divorced from his environment as to drown him in it, to ground him so thoroughly in his environment that we can no longer distinguish his essential characteristics, the marks of his indisputable originality.

It is not true that Descartes' need to justify his physics give gave him the ability to create all the elements of a new metaphysics. His creative genius could not bring out of nowhere the elements of a notion of divine freedom that was so different from the one Scholasticism taught. Neo-Platonism, in the guise in which the Oratory had elaborated it, offered him these elements. It is equally false that Descartes was simply a neo-Platonist, more brilliant or more rigorous than the others. He occupies a very different place in the movement. De Bérulle is a theologian above all. Gibieuf is a theologian. Mersenne and de Silhon, who are both rather deeply impregnated by Platonism, are a theologian and a metaphysician who openly pursues apologetic goals. We find exclusively religious interests in all of them and the concern to defend or expound a disputed point of doctrine. Apologetic concern is hardly evident in Descartes, and, although it is very difficult to be precise about what place it holds in itshis mind, we can affirm without hesitation that it is relegated to the background. His metaphysics is still very theological, and it could hardly be otherwise in a person who wants to prove God's existence. But the apologetic itself is not the ultimate goal he pursues. From the Scholastic hodgepodge and multitude of disputed questions, he selects a very small number whose solutions he attempts to renew. The choice itself is not at all arbitrary or guided by the concern to come to the aid of a threatened Church. Descartes advances securely in the Scholastic labyrinth with its obscure controversies, holding the connecting thread that guides him: the authentic physics he intends to construct. That is what distinguishes Descartes from his contemporaries and his predecessors, and that is what constitutes the peculiar originality of his neo-Platonism. Therefore, it is impossible to separate the two viewpoints when we want to understand his metaphysics. By combining them, on the contrary, we can see the law that governs the establishment of the doctrine of divine freedom. It essentially consists of a justification of the new physics by metaphysical conceptions that Descartes finds in his environment. It is an adaptation of the Oratory's theology to the physics of efficient causes.

Part II

Human Freedom

Chapter One
Error

The problem of human freedom cannot be isolated from the rest of Cartesian philosophy. Descartes did not attack the problem for its own sake. It is only because he wanted to resolve the problem of error that he came to raise the question of human freedom and offer a solution. We must study the nature of the problem of error and situate it within the *Meditations on First Philosophy*. We will then more readily understand the terms in which Descartes posed the problem of freedom and under what influences he posed it.

The *Cogito* assures Descartes that he is a thinking thing and that the soul is only thought. Where does this certainty come from? From the fact, answers Descartes, that I clearly and distinctly conceive that nothing can belong to the soul except thought. I discover within myself the criterion of all certainty: what I clearly and distinctly conceive is true. Thereafter, nothing remains but to go on to the discovery of corporeal things, if some scruple does not make me hesitate on this point. What guarantees that my clear and distinct ideas are not mistaken? When I consider them in themselves, an invincible habit leads me to consider them true, but this habit is not a demonstration. In short, it remains possible that these clear and distinct ideas are illusions and errors. Until the contrary is proven, I must suspend my judgment on this point. Still, how am I to prove by an irrefutable demonstration that my clear and distinct ideas are true? I must return within myself and search again in my thinking soul. I already confusedly suspect that I do not exist by myself. I see that I am finite and limited. My thought, my soul, is not explained by itself. It requires the existence of a necessary and perfect being who created me and who is the total efficient cause of everything I am. Therefore, it is no longer I who am the guarantee of what is positive and real in me; it is God. My clear and distinct ideas are something; they are realities created by God and created with the striking characteristic of necessarily bringing about my assent. But a dilemma arises. Either my clear and distinct ideas are true, as I believe, or else they are false. If they are false, God deceives me. But he cannot deceive me, since his essential perfection implies his perfect veracity. Therefore, my clear and distinct ideas are true. The truth of clear and distinct ideas does not simply rest upon an inner feeling, an irresistible one, but which in a finite, imperfect being could ultimately be no more than a tendency to error. It rests upon an inner feeling that cannot deceive us, because it comes from God and participates in divine veracity.

However, we must be assured of this divine guarantee of our knowledge. That is the price of true science. Passing through God is not to follow a detour; it is to move onto the straight path, the only one that leads to true physics. By entering more deeply into the *Cogito* and my own nature, the Third Meditation already leads me to certainty about the existence of God. No difficulty would remain, if I did not find a great number of errors within me. I am sure God exists. I am also sure that in his supreme perfection he cannot want me to be deceived. But if so, how will I explain the existence of error? As long as I fail to demonstrate that God is in no way involved in my errors, a suspicion will remain, however slight, that God deceives me, and I will not be able to affirm that my clear and distinct ideas are true. The Fourth Meditation is dedicated precisely to establish this thesis.

Let us contemplate this true God in whom all the treasures of science and wisdom repose. We cannot fail to discover some path that takes its point of departure in him and will lead us surely to knowledge of those corporeal things whose nature we do not know.[1] We know that God is good and that he cannot have condemned us to error. But, how does he let us be deceived, even if only rarely?[2] Descartes' answer may give the impression of a slightly uneasy theological experiment,[3] when considered in itself, independently of the environment that explains it; yet, each line of it presents a familiar, clearly defined meaning for contemporary readers.

To relieve God of any responsibility in regard to our errors, Descartes denies that these errors possess positive reality, however minimal. If error is a mere nothing, God cannot be accused of having created it, and nothing allows its presence in the work of creation to be attributed to any imperfection of the divine power or divine veracity.

As long as I consider God alone, says Descartes, I find nothing that condemns me to error. The real source of my error is not in God, it is in me, in the very imperfection that makes me not be God. Alongside the idea I have of a supremely perfect being, a real and positive idea, I discover another in

1 *Meditations* (Fourth Meditation); VII, p. 53.
2 *Meditations* (First Meditation); VII, p. 21, lines 11-–16.
3 Hamelin, *Le système de Descartes*, p. 163.

me that is negative: the idea of nothing, or if we prefer, the idea of what is absolutely destitute of the least shadow of any perfection. If I seek to situate myself between these two extremes, I appear to myself to occupy a kind of mid point.[4] I am not nothing, because I am a reality created by the Supreme Being and, as such, I do not find any defect in myself, anything that could be the cause of error. But, if the Supreme Being creates me, I am not this Supreme Being. I lack much to equal it, since I am a finite being. Therefore, I can say that I participate in nothingness through all that I lack in order to be equal to God's supreme reality. The origin of my errors is found precisely in this non-being in which I participate. It is chimerical to imagine error as a kind of positive reality that God has deposited in me, which would be his work. Error does not imply a special capacity to be deceived that would be conferred on me by God. On the contrary, error comes from the fact that certain positive qualities are not in me and that I am a finite, limited being. I am deceived by reason of what I am not, not by reason of what I am, and my having the capacity for error measures the gap that separates me, an incomplete, deficient being, from God, the perfect and absolute reality.[5]

This way, Descartes vindicates God from the accusation that he created error by denying any reality to error. The mere observation of the limits necessarily imposed on the creature suffices to explain all its imperfection in general[6] and error in particular. Descartes has no need to dream up the solution to the problem he has posed. He has found it ready- made in theology. After having received it from his teachers at La Flèche in St. Thomas's form, he had recently met it again under the more Augustinian and Neo-Platonic guise Gibieuf gave it. This doctrine is the source of the whole beginning of the Fourth Meditation.

4 *Meditations* (Fourth Meditation); VII, p. 54, lines 13—24 [Heffernan, p. 152]: ". . . animadverto . . . nihili, sive ejus quod ab omni perfectione summe abest, negativam quamdam ideam mihi observari et me tanquam medium quid inter Deum et nihil, sive inter summum ens et non ens ita esse constitutum ut, quatenus a summo ente sum creatus, nihil quidem in me sit, per quod fallar aut in errorem inducar, sed quatenus etiam quodammodo de nihilo sive de non ente participo, hoc est quatenus non sum ipse summum ens, desuntque mihi quam plurima, non adeo mirum est quod fallar."

5 *Meditations* (Fourth Meditation); VII, p. 54, lines 24—30 [Heffernan, p. 152]: "Atque ita certe intelligo errorem, quatenus error est, non esse quid reale quod a Deo dependeat, sed tantummodo, esse defectum; nec proinde ad errandum mihi opus esse aliqua facultate in hanc finem a Deo tributa, sed contingere ut errem, ex eo quod facultas verum judicandi, quam ab illo habeo non sit in me infinita."

6 *Quintae Responsiones*; VII, p. 374.

Let us note first the exact problem that Descartes wants to resolve at this moment. It is easy to see that our philosopher is far less worried about explaining error than explaining evil. What Descartes wants to explain is not the possibility of error as such, but the possibility of error insofar as it is an evil. How can rational human creatures formed by a perfect God be subject to error and afflicted by such imperfection? Above all, how will we not trace this imperfection of the creature back to its creator?

Gibieuf provides a solution taken from St. Augustine to the problem posed in these terms, which Descartes in his turn will take from him. In fact, Descartes read *De Libertate* before the final version of the *Meditations*. On May 27, 1630, he learned from Mersenne that Gibieuf had written a book in which the problem of divine freedom was treated and resolved in a spirit very close to that of Descartes. At this moment, there was no question about the problem of evil or the problem of human freedom.[7] Descartes had no other reason to see Gibieuf's book than the desire to confirm his own agreement with the Oratorian on one of the most sublime points of metaphysics, where he most feared not being followed. But his pleasure was so great that he resolved to obtain a copy of *De Libertate* and let Gibieuf know how much he approved his opinions.[8] Moreover, it seems that Gibieuf too was eager to get his book to Descartes the following year. Descartes was busy with other issues when he received it, and only read a small part, but with great delight, completely subscribing to Gibieuf's view.[9]

At that moment surely Descartes read the section that dealt with divine freedom, since he had conceived the desire to read the book on the occasion of a controversy about that problem. Nothing permits us to claim that he immediately read something dealing with the problems of evil and human freedom, but everything leads us to believe that he did so subsequently, and ended

7 Letter to Mersenne, May 27, 1630; I, p. 153.

8 Letter to Mersenne, November 4, 1630; I, p. 174.

9 Letter to Mersenne, October 1631; I, pp. 219–220: "I finally received the book you did me the favor of sending and very humbly thank you. I have read only a very little of this book of Fr. Gibieuf, but I greatly value what I have seen and completely subscribe to his view. M. Rivet has asked me to lend it, which is why I have not read it all; also that now having my mind completely occupied with other thoughts, I believed I would not be capable of understanding this subject well, which, in my opinion, is one of the most sublime and difficult of all metaphysics. If you see Fr. Gibieuf, I beg you not to inform him that I have received his book: because my duty would be to write him already to thank him; but I would be very agreeable to waiting two or three months yet, in order to send him news about what I am doing in the same letter."

by becoming acquainted with all parts of the book that could interest him. We have just seen that Descartes owned his personal copy of *De Libertate*; we further know how much he wanted to win Gibieuf's approval and that he would later take cover behind the Oratorian's authority to defend the doctrine of human freedom contained in the Fourth Meditation. Before running risks in a strictly theological area, Descartes believed he needed to take precautions and not put anything forward that he could not support with the authority of a theologian, if the need arose. To know that his notion of human freedom was in complete agreement with what Gibieuf had written, Descartes necessarily had to read other parts of *De Libertate* than what dealt particularly with God's freedom. We are certain that he knew Gibieuf's conception of human freedom. The comparison of texts that follows permits little doubt that he was familiar with the chapters dealing with the problem of evil.

If we further ask what could have led Descartes to incorporate the Oratorian's doctrine into his metaphysics, we cannot answer without entering the realm of hypotheses unaccompanied by proof. We do not think this was a calculated move on Descartes' part. As relates to human freedom, the calculation would have been defective, because by winning over Gibieuf, Descartes alienated many other theologians and not the least influential ones. As relates to the doctrine on evil, the calculation had no basis, because at bottom this was everyone's doctrine and was no more peculiar to Gibieuf than to St. Thomas. The truth is surely simpler. During the final revision of the *Meditations*, Descartes came up against the problem of error considered as evil. He then remembered reading *De Libertate* in 1631. The book was at hand, and he turned to it. In the course of this second, more careful reading, Descartes perceived that the book contained ready-made solutions, acceptable for problems that only had indirect interest and on which he did not want to delay. Descartes had long known these solutions that Gibieuf brought to mind. His teachers at La Flèche had taught them, supported by the authority of St. Thomas. He now encountered them again supported by the authority of St. Augustine. This, therefore, was a completely uncontroversial doctrine, and Descartes ran no risk by adopting it. Surely, this is why Descartes gave it preferential treatment. It only remained to change some terms to adapt this whole theology to the problem of error that Descartes was posing, and he had time for that. In 1629 he had sketched out his "little treatise on metaphysics." In 1630 he had *De Libertate* in his possession. He was to do the definitive revision of the *Meditations* only in 1639.[10] Thus

10 See Adam, *Vie et oeuvres*; XII, pp. 289 ff.

Gibieuf's solution to the problem of evil and the problem of human freedom came to furnish Descartes with the framework of the Fourth Meditation.

Concerning the problem of evil more particularly, Gibieuf's doctrine was what St. Thomas took from St. Augustine, who himself received it from Plotinus.[11] In St. Augustine's teaching, the creature can only achieve the good because it participates in God, who created it. When, by contrast, it has fallen into evil, it is not that it participates in a certain positive nature of evil; it is simply that it is deprived of some good.[12] There exists no real nature of evil in which the creature could participate, but since the creature has been drawn from nothing and created from nothing, it can only adhere imperfectly to the supreme good. If God had drawn us from the divine nature, we would remain immutably attached to it, and we would never will evil. Therefore, we must say that God is the author of all goods and of no evil. God is the author of all goods, because he is the author of the natures capable of achieving them. By contrast, in the measure in which these natures commit evil, when they spontaneously separate themselves from good, they bear the stamp of their origin, not that of their creator; not of the supreme good that created them, but of the nothing from which they have emerged. Therefore, in us, evil is the stamp of the nothing from which we come. *Nothing* is not a reality, but the complete absence of reality, and since what is nothing can have no author, evil has no author.[13]

If evil is nothing in respect to God, it is an absurd question to ask what is the efficient cause of evil. Since evil is a mere defect, it could only have a deficient cause. God is the cause of our will insofar as it adheres to the supreme good, but not insofar as it turns away from it. No one seeks to see shadows or hear silence. Similarly, there is no reason to look for the cause of what is nothing.

11 For the dependence of St. Augustine on Plotinus see Grandgeorge, *Saint Augustin et le néo-platonisme*, p. 116.

12 On this point see Joseph Mausbach, *Die Ethik des heiligen Augustinus*, Freiburg im Breisgau: Herder, 1909 and 1929, vol. I, pp 105 ff.

13 St. Augustine, *Contra Julianum*, book I, chapter 3, Quoted by Gibieuf, *De Libertate*, II, 19, 13, p. 416: "Creatura bonitatis capax est, participatione boni a quo facta est. Malitiam vero capit, non participatione mali, sed privatione boni, id est non commiscetur naturae quae aliquid malum est, sed quia deficit a natura quae summum et incommutabile bonum est, propterea quod non de illa, sed de nihilo facta est. Alioquin nec malam voluntatem habere posset nisi mutabilis esset; mutabilis porro natura non esset, si de Deo esset, non ab illo de nihilo facta esset. Quapropter bonorum author est Deus, dum author est naturarum, quarum spontaenus defectus a bono non indicat a quo factae sunt sed unde factae sunt; et hoc non est aliquid, quoniam penitus nihil est, et non potest authorem habere quod nihil est."

Evil is something that we never know by reason of its own natures, but only as privations of this or that nature.[14] All that can be said about the origin of evil is that, ultimately, the divine nature can never fail anywhere or in any point whatever, while finite natures like ours, drawn from nothing, can fail.

Descartes must have first encountered this constant doctrine of St. Augustine at La Flèche, but integrated into St. Thomas's general philosophy. For both theologians, evil is not a reality produced by God's creation in any degree. It is a simple absence of good. Is not everything that has any reality in things a particular good? Consequently, it is evident that being as such cannot be the opposite of good, or, what amounts to the same thing, that evil as evil cannot be taken as a being in any degree.[15] Therefore, it is enough to contrast evil to good, which is its contrary, to discover its nature, just as we define shadows by opposition to light. The doctrine acknowledges that everything desirable is a good and that perfection and being are goods, since everything tends toward its being and toward its own perfection. It follows that evil is neither a being nor a nature nor a form, since it is the contrary of perfection. Evil can only consist of the absence of a good, and it is one and the same thing as to say that evil is not good and to say that it is not a reality. To suppress one term entails suppressing the other: where there is not good, there is not reality.[16]

Of what order is this absence of good that defines evil? If it is true to say that all evil is an absence of good, it is not true to say the reverse, that

14 St. Augustine, *De Civitate Dei*, book XII, chapter 7; quoted by Gibieuf, *De Libertate*, II, 19, 13, pp. 416–417: "Nemo ergo quaerat efficientem causam malae voluntatis; non enim est efficiens sed deficiens, quia nec illa effectio est sed defectio; deficere namque ab eo quod summe est ad id quod minus est, hoc est incipere habere voluntatem malam. Causas porro defectionum istarum, cum efficientes non sint sed deficientes, velle invenire, tale est ac si quisquam velit videre tenebras vel audire silentium, quod tamen utrumque nobis notum est: neque illud nisi per oculos, neque hoc nisi per aures, non sane in specie sed in speciei privatione. Nemo ergo ex me scire quaerat quod me nescire scio, nisi forte ut nescire discat quod sciri non posse sciendum est. Ea quippe quae non in specie sed in speciei privatione sciuntur, si sic dici potest, quodammodo nesciendo sciuntur, ut sciendo nesciantur."

15 St. Thomas Aquinas, *Quaestiones Disputatae de Malo*, question 1, article 1, body of article.

16 Thomas Aquinas, *Summa Theologiae*, part I, question 48, article 1, end of body of article: "Unde non potest esse quod malum significet quoddam esse aut quamdam formam seu naturam. Relinquitur ergo quod nomine *mali* significetur quaedam absentia boni. Et pro tanto dicitur quod *malum neque est existens, nec bonum*; quia cum ens, in quantum hujusmodi, sit bonum, eadem est remotio utrorumque."

all absence of good is an evil. It is appropriate to distinguish between absences of a negative and of a privative kind. When a nature is presented to us as lacking some good, we must ask ourselves whether this good is this nature's proper good, or if it is the proper good of another nature. In the second hypothesis, this absence certainly ought to be considered purely negative. For example, it is in this sense that the goat's swiftness or the lion's strength is absent from human nature. The purely negative absence of a good that a nature need not possess cannot be taken as an evil.[17] Evil appears only when the absence of a good constitutes a privation, understanding privation as the absence of a quality in a determined subject that the subject ought to possess.[18] The absence of sight in a blind person constitutes genuine privation, and thereby it is demonstrated to be an evil. The same holds in all possible cases: evil is never a simple negation, the absence of any good whatsoever, but a privation, the absence of a good that is the proper good of a certain being and the lack of a quality that it ought to possess.[19]

Accordingly, when Descartes considers evil as mere nothing and pure privation of a good, he can take his doctrine either from St. Thomas through his teachers at La Flèche or from St. Augustine through Gibieuf. However, it is fair to affirm that the opening of the Fourth Meditation is certainly directly tied to Gibieuf's Augustinianism. In Descartes' text, we can pick out a comparison that belongs to St. Augustine in particular and figures visibly and prominently in *De Libertate*. Descartes certainly does not take it from St. Thomas, who, to our knowledge, never used it. By contrast, Descartes could not have read the chapters Gibieuf dedicates to the problem of evil without encountering it.

Let us refer to paragraph three of chapter one to hear Gibieuf on evil. Here we discover the source of Descartes' well-known comparison in which

17 St. Thomas, *Summa Theologiae*, part I, question 48, article 3, near beginning of body of article: "Non autem quaelibet remotio boni malum dicitur. Potest enim accipi remotio boni et privative et negative. Remotio igitur boni negative accepta mali rationem non habet, alioquin sequeretur . . . quod quaelibet res esset mala ex hoc quod . . . non habet velocitatem caprae, vel fortitudinem leonis."

18 Eustachius a Sancto Paulo, *Summa Philosophiae*, I, part 2, pp. 153 and 177: "Est autem privatio non quaelibet formae carentia, sed ea quae reperitur in subjecto apto ad talem formam."

19 St. Thomas, *Summa Theologiae*, part I, question 48, article 5 reply to objection 1: "Dicendum quod quia malum privatio est boni, et non negatio pura . . . non omnis defectus boni est malum sed defectus boni quod natum est et debet haberi." Cf. similarly, *Summa Theologiae*, part Iª-IIªᵉ, question 25, article 2, body of article, and *Summa Theologiae*, part Iª-IIªᵉ, question 36, article 1, body of article.

humans are represented as a kind of middle between God and nothing, that is to say, between the Supreme Being and non-being. For example, in order to understand what the nature of an evil like corruption might be, let us imagine two extreme terms, being and non-being, and let us suppose something, for instance, a living being, in the middle. Next let us ask this: as long as this living being is formed, when it is born, when it grows, gets nourishment, grows stronger, improves in appearance, becomes adult, in the measure in which it subsists and maintains itself, toward which of these two terms does it tend, being or non-being? No one doubts that this body, even at its very beginning, is already something, but it will also be granted that the more it acquires its form, beauty, vigor, the more it also *is* and the more it tends toward being. Let us suppose that this living body comes to be corrupted and to decline from this flourishing state. It languishes; its strength wanes; it grows ugly; the bond that unites its members and all its organs in a harmonious whole is loosened. To the question to what extreme does it tend at this moment, being or non-being, no one will hesitate to answer that this body goes to its destruction in the measure in which it is corrupted and that all that goes to destruction, goes to non-being. On the other hand, let us consider that God is immutably and incorruptibly being, and that what we call *not being anything*, is absolute non-being.

So, if being and non-being are posited thus, and if we agree that all growth is movement toward being, while all corruption is movement toward non-being, it becomes easy to know what every corruptible nature takes from God and what it takes from nothingness. Growth comes to it from God, since all growth makes it be, and God is the pre-eminent being. Corruption, on the contrary, which draws it toward non-being, toward what is nothing, evidently comes to it from nothingness. With that, we see clearly that evil is nothing real in creatures and participates in the nature of nothingness. As it is only nothing, it has no origin but nothingness, that is to say, its origin is the creature insofar as it participates in nothingness.[20] Therefore, the

20 Gibieuf, *De Libertate*, II, 16, 3, p. 384: "Sic etiam Divus Augustinus liber contra epistolam fundamenti capitulis 39 et 40 sumens pro exemplo corruptionem rerum caducarum quam ad malum pertinere fatentur omnes, pertinere etiam ad non ens, sic manifestissime ostendit. Si quis nondum credit ex nihilo esse corruptionem, proponat sibi haec duo, *esse* et *non esse*; deinde velut in medio constituat aliquid, puta corpus animalis et hoc secum quaerat: dum formatur illud corpus, dum nascitur, dum augetur ejus species, nutritur, convalescit, roburatur, decoratur, firmatur, in quantum manet et stabilitur, in quam partem tendat, utrum ad *esse*, an ad *non esse*? Non dubitabit quidem esse aliquid in ipsis etiam primordiis; sed quanto magis

Cartesian notion of evil considered as mere nothing, and what we could call Cartesian optimism, goes back to Gibieuf and through him to St. Augustine. But we still only know its essential grounds, and this extraordinarily likeness that we have observed between our philosopher's doctrine and that of the theologian will only accentuate it more in the measure that we see the consequence emerge that each of them deduces from their common principle.

The very simple solution to which they have arrived does not remove all difficulties. To say that error in us comes from nothingness rather than the faculties God gave us, but from the absence of ones we do not possess, is certainly to attribute a purely negative nature to error in regard to God. This deficiency that belongs to the creature as such is merely pure nothing in regard to God. But in regard to humans, this absence of a good that is the origin of error in us seems to be the absence of a good that we ought to possess, *carentia perfectionis debitae*, not a simple negation but a privation.[21] If the errors we commit come from limits imposed on our reason, then we lack knowledge that we should have.[22] Moreover, if we are created by God, and if it is true that the more skillful the worker is, the more perfect his works are, we can only think that God gave us some faculty that is not

forma, et specie et valentia constabilitur atque formatur, tanto magis fieri ut sit, et in eam partem tendit, qua positum est esse. Nunc ergo incipiat corrumpi debilitetur omnis ille status, langescant illae vires, marescat robur, forma faedetur, dissiliat compago membrorum, contabescat et defluat concordia partium; quaerat etiam nunc, quo tendat per istam corruptionem, utrum ad *esse* an ad *non esse*? Non puto usque adeo caecum et tardum, ut dubitet quid ipse respondeat, et non sentiat quanto magis quisque corrumpitur, tanto magis ad interitum tendere, omne autem quod ad interitum tendit ad *non esse* tendit. Cum ergo Deum incommutabiliter et incorruptibiliter *esse* credendum sit; et cum ista proposueris *esse* et *non esse*, atque cognoveris quanto augetur species, tanto quidque tendere ut *sit*, quanto autem magis augetur corruptio, tanto magis tendere ut *non sit*; quid dubites dicere in unaquaque natura corruptibili quid in ea sit ex nihilo, cum species secundum naturam sit, corruptio contra naturam, quia species aucta cogit *esse*, et Deum fatemur *summe esse*; corruptio vero aucta cogit *non esse*, et constat quod *non est*, nihil esse. Quibis verbis clarissime ostendit malum creaturae ad non esse sive ad Nihil pertinere et sicut ad nihilum pertinet, ita a nihilo esse: sive a creatura prout ex nihilo facta est, quod inferius declarabitur."

21 *Principia*, I, 31: "Nec esse res [*scilicet*, errores] ad quam productionem realis Dei concursus requiratur; sed cum ad ipsum referuntur esse tantum negationes, et cum ad nos privationes."

22 *Meditations* (Fourth Meditation); VII, pp. 54-–55 [Heffernan, p. 154]: "Non enim error est pura negatio, sed privatio, sive carentia cujusdam cognitionis quae in me quodammodo esse deberet."

perfect in its kind. God could have created us infallible: he did not do so. We know that what God wants is always best. Does that force us to believe that it is better for humans to be fallible than infallible?

Descartes could find a two-pronged answer in St. Thomas, and his philosophical training should have given him the way to justify and confirm his optimism. If God, who is all-powerful and who is sovereign providence, allowed evil and imperfection to subsist in his work, that is because divine providence does not extend just to this or that particular individual, but to the whole universe. Evidently it would not be good for God, the providence of the universe, to prevent a particular evil at the risk of endangering the good of the whole. Therefore, it must be recognized that evil can be a serious defect in a particular individual and at the same time good for the totality of things.[23] We ought not to situate ourselves in the perspective of the individual to appreciate the reason that there is this or that evil, but in the perspective of the other individuals that the absence of this or that evil would rob of this or that good, and above all in the perspective of the whole, which would lose something of its beauty and its harmony. The imperfection of a creature could be necessary for the perfection of another. If God were to suppress an evil, some goods might become impossible, and ultimately every evil is the other side of a good. Fire is not produced without air being corrupted. Lions will not live without devouring donkeys. The justice that the defenders of right so admirably demonstrate and the admirable patience of so many victims would have not place in the world, if injustice and iniquity could not occur.[24]

A second reason comes to complete this first one. It was necessary that God not create all things alike and that he should introduce some

23 St. Thomas, *Summa Theologiae*, part I, question 22, article 2 reply to objection 2: "Ad secundum dicendum quod aliter de eo est qui habet cura alicujus particularis, et de provisore universale; quia provisor particularis excludit defectum ab eo quod ejus curae subditur quantum potest, sed provisor universalis permittit aliquem defectum in aliquo particulari accidere, ne impediatur bonum totius. Unde corruptiones et defectus in rebus naturalibus dicuntur esse contra naturam particularem; sed tamen sunt de intentione naturae universalis, in quantum defectus unius cedit in bonum alterius vel etiam totius universi . . ."

24 St. Thomas, *Summa Theologiae*, part I, question 42, article 2, toward the end. "Unde multa bona tollerentur, si Deus nullum malum permitteret esse . . . Neque etiam laudaretur justitia vindicantis, et patientia sufferentis, si non esset iniquitas persequentis." [Translator: This reference seems incorrect, because I, 42, 2 deals with the relation of the Son to the Father in the Trinity. The same point in is made in I, 22, 2 reply to objection 2: "Si enim omnia mala impedirentur, multa bona deesent universo . . . nec esset patientia martyrum, si non esset persecutio tyrannorum."]

inequality into the universe. This inequality allows different species of things to be arranged according to a hierarchical order of increasing perfection. For example, mixed bodies will be seen as more perfect than simple bodies, animals as more perfect than plants, and humans as more perfect than other animals. In addition, in each of these different orders we discover some species more perfect than others, and divine wisdom introduces inequality at the same time as distinction among things, and that happens for the greater perfection of the universe.[25] Let us apply this principle to the particular problem of moral evil, and its consequences will be easily deduced. Being good to the point of never committing evil is a certain degree of perfection in a thing. Being subject to evil and to sin is a different degree of perfection. For the universe to be perfect and all possible degrees of perfection to be represented, it will be appropriate that certain beings cannot commit evil, but that, alongside them, there exist others that can commit it. With that, the presence of evil in the world is fully justified.[26]

No doubt, Descartes had just re-encountered these two arguments of St. Thomas in Gibieuf, but this time supported by the authority of St. Augustine, from whom St. Thomas had only taken them, clarifying them. For Gibieuf, evil abounds in the world, if we consider it in relation to creatures and to their natures. However, if we consider evil in relation to divine providence, everything is good. All the things that appear bad to us from this first viewpoint, appear good from the second, that is to say, if they are considered as means, since they all serve to make some good possible.[27] This doctrine is the very same as St. Augustine's, who declares that the all-powerful and supremely good God would not allow anything bad to be in his work, if his power and his goodness were not such that he was able to make

25 St. Thomas, *Summa Theologiae*, part I, question 47, article 2, end of body of article: "Sicut ergo divina sapientia est causa distinctionis rerum ita et inaequalitatis. Non enim esset perfectum universum, si tantum unus gradus bonitatis inveniretur in rebus."

26 St. Thomas, *Summa Theologiae*, part I, question 48, article 2, end of body of article: "Ita perfectio universi requirit ut sint quaedam quae a bonitate deficere possint, ad quod sequitur ea interdum deficere. In hoc autem consistit ratio mali, ut scilicet aliquid deficiat a bono. Unde manifestum est quod in rebus malum invenitur sicut et corruptio, nam et ipsa corruptio malum quoddam est." Cf. *Summa Theologiae*, part I, question 49, article 2, body of article.

27 Gibieuf, *De Libertate*, II, 22, 10, p. 441: "Videlicet, etsi multa mala sint, relata ad creaturas et naturas earum, ad providentiam tamen comparata, omnia bona sunt, saltem per modum medii, quia omnia ad bonum aliquod conferunt."

good come out of this evil itself.[28] The divine Trinity, which is supremely, equally, and immutably good, created everything; and yet creatures are neither supremely nor equally, nor immutably good. However, creatures individually considered are good and collectively considered are excellent, because their harmonious diversity constitutes the wonderful beauty of the universe. The beauty and harmony are such that what we call *bad* enters into the order and naturally assumes its place, so that it makes the good that the world possesses dearer and more lovable when we compare it to what is bad and defective in it.[29]

Necessity of particular evils as the condition of general good, usefulness of certain differences and even inequalities among the different component parts of the world with a view to achieving superior harmony — we meet these two arguments again in the Fourth Meditation. Their extraneousness within Descartes' system is all the more apparent because, at the point in Descartes' deduction where these arguments are found, they can only be inserted by means of a dialectical trick, an expedient. Both arguments in fact involve the consideration of the totality of creatures, and even if we do not go so far as to consider the universe taken collectively and as a whole, in order to apply them, we cannot keep from at least considering another creature than the one whose imperfection is at issue. In the Fourth Meditation, Descartes still does not know whether a universe and creatures other than him exist. In delving into the *Cogito*, he discovers himself to be limited, imperfect, and subject to error. Therefore, he poses the question of evil very legitimately and correctly. But, if he does not need to go out of himself to pose the question, he needs to do so in order to solve it. He needs to do so

28 Gibieuf, *De Libertate*, II, 22, 9, p. 439: "Altera autem pars, quod Deus permittit mala ut inde eliciat bona, constat ex Divi Augustini *Enchiridii*, capitulis 11, 95, 96, 99 et 100. *Neque enim Deus omnipotens cum summe bonus sit, ullo modo sineret mali esse aliquid in operibus suis, nisi usque adeo esset omnipotens et bonus, ut bene faceret etiam de malo.*"

29 Gibieuf, *De Libertate*, II, 22, 6, pp. 437–438: "At enim Deus is est qui lucem et tenebras ordinavit, jussitque mane et vesperam diem unum esse, ita ut tenebrae ipsae, Deo ordinante, conferant ad pulchritudinem splendoremque dici, ut notavit Divus Augustinus *De Genesi ad Litteram Imperfectus*, capitulo 5 citato, et *Enchiridii ad Laurentium* capitulo 10. *Ab hac summe et aequaliter et immutabiliter bona Trinitate, creata sunt omnia; et nec summe, nec aequaliter, nec immutabiliter bona; sed tamen bona etiam singula; simul vero universa, valde bona; quia ex omnibus consistit universitatis admirabilis pulchritudo. In qua etiam illud quod malum dicitur, bene ordinatum et loco suo positum, eminentius commendat bona, ut magis placeant et laudabiliora sint, dum comparantur malis.*"

at least if he wants to resolve it with St. Augustine and St. Thomas's arguments, since these arguments consist of compensating for the evil that each of us discovers within himself by means of the good or the felicitous diversity that it introduces into things. At the cost of this irregularity, of which he is aware and does his best to dissemble, Descartes still prefers to utilize these two arguments that theology offers him, and he inserts them into his deductive chain.

According to Descartes, therefore, in order to appreciate the perfection of God's works, we ought to consider the whole universe in its entirety and not simply one of its parts. It may happen that we may see a thing taken in itself to be very imperfect, whereas we see it in all its perfection when set in the whole of which it is just a part. Although at the point to which we have come we have not yet affirmed the existence of anything outside of ourselves and God, the mere consideration of divine power makes us understand that God must have or could have created other realities than ourselves. That is enough for us to have to consider ourselves, not as isolated creatures, but as only being each one a mere part in the totality of things. By taking this perspective, we will know that it is impossible for us to gauge whether in relation to the totality of the universe, the error to which we are subject increases or diminishes our perfection. Despite the imperfections of its parts, the world is *collectively* perfect,[30] and we do not know whether our errors may contribute to making the world more perfect in totality.[31] Moreover, the shock we feel when we find we are imperfect is caused by our custom of considering humans to be the center of the universe and monarchs of creation. When we come to know that the world, as genuine physics demonstrates, transcends humans on every side, and that the earth is only a point by comparison to the universe, we will no longer be surprised at not playing the leading role in creation and of not being looked upon as perfect characters. In reality, we are only parts in the totality of things. It is true that, when we are considered in isolation, being subject to error makes us seem less perfect than if God had created us infallible. On the other hand, it may be that the perfection of the universe is augmented by that weakness. Perhaps the world is better if some of its parts are fallible, while others are

30 Letter to Mersenne, May 6, 1630; I, 150.

31 *Meditations* (Fourth Meditation); VII, pp. 55--56 [Heffernan, p. 154]: "Occurit etiam non unam aliquam creaturaram separatim, sed omnem rerum universitatem esse spectandam, quoties an opera Dei perfecta sint inquirimus; quod enim forte non immerito, si solum esset, valde imperfectum videretur, ut habens in mundo rationem partis est perfectissimum."

infallible, and perhaps that is better than all things being absolutely similar among themselves.[32] Here, in a more dubitative guise, we meet the same argument as in St. Thomas.

But Descartes adds another argument to these considerations, the paradigmatic Cartesian argument, which rests upon the systematic refusal to try to discover final causes. When we reflect upon the nature of the question we have posed, we easily discover the reason on account of which, properly speaking, it is ultimately unanswerable. To ask why God has created humans subject to error, to pose the question, "Why evil?" is to try to peer into those ends of God that a finite being cannot discover. This sort of question is unanswerable for us and surpasses us. It would not be at all surprising that the reason for error and evil should remain always hidden from us.

Again Descartes gets this quintessentially Cartesian argument from Gibieuf; more exactly, reading Gibieuf, it must have occurred to Descartes to use it at this point. Like Descartes, Gibieuf gets to the point of determining a certain number of reasons why God permitted evil, and these causes are the goods to which the evils permitted by God can lead. But, if pushing further, we ask why God permits that such and such goods were the consequences of evil, we are no longer asking about the end of the evil that God permitted, but the end of the divine will itself that permitted it. We are forbidden to seek God's ends, and besides, the search has no object. Let us hear St. Augustine against the Manichaeans: "They want to know the causes of God's will, while God's will is the cause itself of all that exists. If God's will has a cause, something exists that preceded God's will, which cannot be admitted. To one who says: 'Why did God want to create heaven and earth?' we must answer, 'Because he wanted to.' If he asks why God willed that, he is asking us to indicate something that is greater than God's will. There is nothing that surpasses it. Let human temerity keep within its just limits and give up looking for what is not, because it would no longer find what is." To this passage Gibieuf adds the comment that not only did God's will not have a cause considered in itself and insofar as God's will is absolute, as God, but also it does not even have a cause insofar as it leads to producing

32 *Meditations* (Fourth Meditation); VII, 61 [Heffernan, 164]: "Et facile intelligo me, quatenus rationem habeo totius cujusdam, perfectiorem futurum fuisse quam nunc sum, si talis a Deo factus essem. Sed non ideo possum negare quin major quodammodo perfectio sit in tota rerum universitate, quod quaedam ejus partes ab erroribus immunes non sint, aliae vero sint, quam si omnes plane similes essent. Et nullum habeo jus conquerendi quod eam me Deus in mundo personam sustinere voluerit, quae non est omnium praecipua et maxime perfecta."

this or that object outside of itself. If it were otherwise, there would be something prior and superior to the divine will that would push it and draw it to a determined object rather than to another. This is what St Augustine observes in the passage above and what he rejects. Therefore, let us renounce all questions of the type, "Why did God want this or that?" These are questions that can be raised about humans, whose will is moved and directed by a higher end. But to raise them about God is to offend his divine majesty.

Perhaps it will be objected that God does nothing and wants nothing in an irrational manner. Therefore, there is a reason that accounts for why he wanted and did all he did and wanted. The answer is that in the practical order, the reason flows from the end, as in the speculative order, discourse flows from principles. Therefore, a thing that has no higher end to which it is submitted and which, to the contrary, is the end of all things, could not by nature act in a rational manner, but only in a supra-rational manner. It does act in an irrational manner, if by that we understand that reason is not involved in any way in divine action, but not, if we understand it in the ordinary way, as meaning an irregularity or inferiority in this activity. God's activity is not rational, not that it is inferior to rational activity but, on the contrary, because it is infinitely higher than the rules of reason. Let us regard this point as unshakably true: it is useless to want to account for the divine will and to search either for why God does good or why God permits evil. Whether the divine will permits or acts, it is the grounds of reason and not reason that is the grounds of the divine will.[33]

33 Gibieuf, *De Libertate*, II, 22, 14, pp. 442–443: "Quod si interroges curiosus, quae causa sit propter quam Deus permiserit mala hos omnes exitus habitura? Jam non mali permissi finem scire optas, sed ipsius divinae voluntatis permittentis, quod et nefas est quaerere, et impossibile esse. Audi enim Divum Augustinum (Libro I *De Genesi contra Manichaeos*, capitulo 2). *Causas voluntatis Dei scire quaerunt, cum voluntas Dei omnium quae sunt, ipsa sit causa. Si enim habet causam voluntas Dei, est aliquid quod antecedat voluntatem Dei, quod nefas est credere. Qui ergo dicit: quare Deus fecit coelum et terram? Respondendum est ei, quia voluit. Voluntas autem Dei causa est coeli et terrae, et ideo major est voluntas Dei quam coelum et terra. Quis autem dicit: quare voluit facere coelum et terram? Magis aliquid quaerit quam est voluntas Dei: nihil autem majus inveniri potest. Compescat ergo se humana temeritas, et id non est non quaerat, ne id quod est non inveniat.* Non modo non datur causa voluntatis Dei secundum se et prout est tam absoluta quam Deus, sed nec prout terminatur extra se ad hoc aut ad illud objectum secundarium: alias esset aliquid prius et superius divina voluntate, quod illam impelleret, ut in hoc potius objectum ferretur quam in aliud: ut loco proxime citato refert et rejicit Divus Augustinus. Apage ergo hujuscemodi quaestiones: quare Deus hoc aut illud voluit?

The problem of the presence of evil in the world is resolved through all these arguments, and Descartes, who faithfully follows St. Augustine, St. Thomas, and Gibieuf on this point, does not lack authorities to protect him. But this very general solution does not suffice for him. The special problem that concerns him is still posed even after the previous explanations. Among all the guises that evil can take, there is one, error, which particularly interests Descartes. To establish absolutely that error is not imputable to God, the preceding arguments are not enough. Despite the summons that has been issued to us to refrain from vainly trying to discover God's ends, despite the assurances that we are given that our imperfection harmoniously contributes to the perfection of the universe, an inner feeling remains, stronger than all the arguments: the feeling that error comes from the privation of a perfection that we ought to possess: *carentia perfectionis debitae*. To remove this last scruple, it is necessary to discover how errors are produced. The analysis of the act by which we commit them, will make us see that God has not denied us anything he owed us, and that, on the contrary, he has taken care to place the remedy alongside the malady.

De homine ista quaeri possunt, cujus voluntas finem habet supra se a quo movetur ac dirigitur: de Deo autem non nisi cum injuria divinae ejus majestatis. At enim, inquies, Deus nihil facit aut vult irrationabiliter: quare oportet dari rationem propter quam Deus facit et vult omnia quaecumque vult et facit. Respondeo rationem in practicis esse derivationem quamdam finis, sicut discursus in speculativis est deductio principiorum. Quapropter ei qui nullum supra se finem habet, sed ipse est omnium finis, non convenit agere juxta rationem, sed supra rationem. Agitne ergo irrationabiliter? Ita dici posset, si irrationabiliter diceret quacumque rationis exclusionem. Sed si in communi sensu sumatur, ut significet statum ratione inferiorem, clarum est non posse Deo attribui, cujus nimirum operandi modus rationem et illius regulas infinite supereminet. Maneat ergo hoc firmum et inconcussum, divinae voluntatis frustra rationem quaeri, et quamobrem Deus vel operatur bona, vel permittit mala. Divina voluntas sive operans sive permittens, fundamentum est rationis, non ratio fundamentum divinae voluntatis."

Chapter Two
The Relations of Understanding and Will Judgment

Thus it is that Descartes comes to examine himself more closely and no longer seek *why* but *how* errors are committed.[1]

Our soul is something that thinks, but not all the thoughts that we discover in it are of the same nature. Basically, we can distribute or, more precisely, arrange our different modes of thinking into two general groups that include all those modes. One way of thinking consists in knowing by the understanding, the other in making up our minds voluntarily. Under perception or operation of the intellect, we are going to include sensing, imagining, and finally pure intellection. By contrast, desiring, hating, denying, doubting, must be considered as so many different manifestations of wanting. Once this general distinction is admitted, which furthermore agrees with Scholastic doctrine,[2] it remains to be decided whether error originates in the understanding or in the will. We perceive, firstly, that error does not reside in the understanding. By the understanding we only perceive the ideas upon which we can bring judgments, and, properly speaking, no error is found in it, if we consider it precisely and separately from the will. No doubt, we find understandingtunderstanding limited and lacking the ideas of an innumerable host of things, which, however, exist. But the absence of ideas constitutes a simple negation, not a privation. It is impossible to offer any reason proving that God ought to give me a greater faculty of knowledge than the one with which I am endowed, and although I know God is as skilled an artisan as there could be, I do not think he is bound to confer on each of his works the perfections that he can give to certain of them.[3]

1 *Meditations* (Fourth Meditation); VII, p. 56 [Heffernan, p. 156]: "Deinde ad me proprius accedens, et qualesnam sint errores mei (qui soli imperfectionem aliquam in me arguunt) investigans. . ."

2 *Principia*, I, 32, and also *Meditations* (Third Meditation); VII, pp. 36–37.

3 *Meditations*, (Fourth Meditation); VII, p. 56 [Heffernan, p. 156]: "Atque quantumvis peritum artificem esse intelligam, non tamen ideo puto illum in singulis ex

Error comes neither from my understanding, nor does it depend on my will. No error can slip into my will considered in itself or into my desires. Even if the object of my desires is bad or my desires have no object, it is no less true that I desire,[4] and consequently, I find no privation in my will of the perfection I ought to possess. Quite the opposite, my will is by far the most perfect of my faculties because it is free with an unlimited freedom. When I consider my restricted and limited understanding, I can immediately conceive another, which would be far superior to it. Better yet, I conceive a supremely perfect and infinite intellect, which is none other than God's intellect. Whichever of my faculties I may examine — understanding, imagination, or memory — I find it infinitely far from God's. All the faculties that are immense and infinite in him are restricted and limited in me. My will alone is not bound in this way. Its freedom is so broad that I can conceive none superior to it. God's freedom is superior to mine in that it is more efficacious and more enlightened, but disregarding understanding and power, which are joined in God, the divine will is not superior to mine. I am as free as can be to affirm, to deny, to pursue a goal, or to turn away. Indeed, once God wanted to give me a will, he could not give me less than what I discover in him, because it seems that, since the will only consists of a single thing and its subject is indivisible, its nature is such that nothing can be taken from it without destroying it. Considered formally and precisely in itself, my will is therefore infinite like God's and it is the will primarily that makes me know that I bear his image and likeness. It would be completely unreasonable to claim to discover some privation in it.[5]

suis operibus omnes perfectiones ponere debuisse, quas in aliquibus ponere potest." Also see V, Index, article 8. [Translator: It is not clear what this refers to. There is an Index of Doubts in the *Quintae Responsiones*, but it is not divided into articles. Nor is Gilson's *Index Scolastico-Cartésien* divided into numbered sections and numbered articles.]

4 *Meditations* (Third Meditation); VII, p. 37.

5 *Meditations* (Fourth Meditation): VII, p. 57 [Heffernan, p. 158]: "Sola est voluntas sive arbitrii libertas, quam tantam in me experior, ut nullius majoris ideam apprehendam; adeo ut illa praecipue sit, ratione cujus imaginem quamdam et similtudinem Dei me referrre intelligo. Nam quamvis major absque comparatione in Deo quam in me sit, tum ratione cognitionis et potentiae quae illi adjunctae sunt, redduntque ipsam magis firmam et efficacem, tum ratione objecti, quoniam ad plura se extendit, non tamen, in se formaliter et praecise spectata, major videtur . . ."

Meditations (Fourth Meditation); VII, p. 60 [Heffernan, pp. 162,164]: "Non habeo etiam causam conquerendi, quod voluntatem dederit [*scilicet*: Deus] latius patentem quam intellectum; cum enim voluntas in una tantum re, et tanquam in indivisibili consistat, non videtur ferre ejus natura ut quicquam ab illa demi possit . . ."

In proposing this doctrine, Descartes only advances after taking precautions. When he considers that free choice is the most evident stamp left by God on his work, he is not affiliating himself with St. Thomas or the theologians of the Thomistic school. The tendency of his teachers at La Flèche was not to emphasize the excellence of the will. In their eyes, that was just one perfection among many others, all of which testified equally that we have been made in the image of God.[6] But Descartes was not without precursors. One might think that the excellence of the gift bestowed upon humans by the creator when he conferred free will upon them had been pointed out by some priest, and perhaps Descartes received this doctrine in the course of some sermon.[7] But it is customary to attribute this sort of claim mainly to St. Bernard who, like Descartes, linked it to the thesis of free will's quasi infinity. For Bernard the theologian, as for our philosopher, free will is protected from any reduction and any defect in its own essence, and we bear the image and likeness of our creator through this free will, similar to God's in its perfection. The only difference is that St. Bernard seems to start from our resemblance to God to conclude the infinity of our free choice, whereas Descartes, on the contrary, seems to deduce the completely special likeness we have to God on this point from the excellence of free choice.[8] But the two theses are certainly the same, and in both cases the tie that binds them is equally tight.

6 Conimbricenses, *De Anima Separata*, I, 5: "Quapropter, tum Plato in *Alcibiade*, tum Porphyrius apud Boetium, referente Eusebio libro 11 *Praeparationis Evangelicae* capite 14, non de Adamo aut alio singulari homine, sed de omnibus celebrarunt esse illos inter caetera animantia ad Dei imaginem conformatos. Cum ergo secundum naturam suam homo sit Dei imago (enitet autem illa potissimum in cognoscendi et appetendi capacitate illimitata, in dominio indifferentiaque actuum suorum, in cupiditate ingenita aeternitatis . . ."

7 Théophile Raynaud, *Calvinismus Bestiarum Religio*, Preface. [Translator: Raynaud's book initially appears under the name of Antoine Rivière, O.S.A., *Calvinismus Bestiarum Religio*, apud S. L. Lefebvre, 1630.] "Nec profiteri dubitavit Gregorius Nyssae, Pontifex, vir plane magnus et doctrinae cum eloquentia certantis laude notissimus: *liberum voluntatis arbitrium honorem esse divino aequalem*, et ornamentorum quae maxima in nobis ac plurima enitent, facile princeps."

8 St. Bernard, *De Gratia et Libero Arbitrio*, chapter 9, article 28, col. 1016 in *Patrologia Latina*, vol. CLXXXII, cols. 999–1030: "Puto autem in his tribus libertatibus [what we have by nature, what grace confers upon us, and what we will have in glory] ipsam ad quam conditi sumus conditoris imaginem atque similitudinem contineri . . . Hinc est fortassis quod solum liberum arbitrium sui omnino defectum seu diminutionem non patitur, quod in ipso potissimum aeternae et incommutabilis divinitatis substantiae quaedam imago impressa videatur."

The main point is the assimilation of human freedom to divine freedom, or more exactly, of the human will to the divine will. Descartes could rightly invoke St. Bernard and shield itself himself behind his authority. In St. Bernard's treatise on grace and free choice, he attributes freedom from necessity equally to all rational creatures, good and bad, and to God. This freedom, our will itself insofar as it is incoercible, is equal in God and creature. The only difference separating them is the divine power, infinitely superior to human power, which consequently makes God's freedom infinitely more efficacious than that of humans. But, considered in itself independently of the power added to it, freedom is no greater in angels than in humans, nor less in humans than in God.[9] Purer in angels than in devils, better ordered in one who is good than on in one who is wicked, more powerful in God than in humans, freedom always and everywhere remains the same, full and entire. The reason is easy to grasp. Considered in itself, free choice does not consist either in science or in power. When God creates us free, he does not want to make us all-knowing, or all-powerful, but only to give us the will. Therefore, the differences that can be manifested in knowledge or power among different beings entail no inequality in their freedom. If we are sinners, while God is not, it in no way follows that we are less free than he. If, by ourselves, we are impotent to deliver ourselves from weakness and sin, it is not because our freedom in itself is inferior to God's but simply because we possess neither the infinite knowledge nor the infinite power that accompany freedom in God.[10]

9 St. Bernard, *De Gratia et Libero Arbitrio*, chapter 4, article 9, cols. 1006–1007: "Verum libertas a necessitate aeque et indifferenter Deo universaeque tam malae quam bonae rationali convenit creaturae. Nec peccato nec miseria amittitur vel minuitur; nec major in justo est quam in peccatore, nec plenior in angelo quam in homine. Quo modo namque ad bonum per gratiam conversus humanae voluntatis consensus, eo libere bonum, et in bono liberum hominem facit, quo voluntarius efficitur, non invitus pertrahitur; sic sponte devolutus in malum, in malo nihilominus tam liberum quam spontaeum constituit, sua utique voluntate ductum, non aliunde coactum ut malus sit. Et sicut coelestis angelus aut etiam Deus ipse permanet libere bonus, propria videlicit voluntate, non aliquae extrinseca necessitate, sic profecto diabolus aeque libere in malum et corruit et persistit, suo utique volutario nutu, non alieno impulsu. Manet ergo libertas voluntatis, ubi etiam fit captivitas mentis, tam plena quidem in malis quam in bonis, sed in bonis ordinatior; tam integra quoque pro suo modo in creatura quam in creatore, sed in illo potentior."

10 St. Bernard, *De Gratia et Libero Arbitrio*, chapter 8, article 24, col. 1014: "Manet ergo etiam post peccatum liberum arbitrium, etsi miserum, tamen integrum. Et quod si per se homo non sufficit excutere a peccato sive miseria, non libri arbitrii

It is hardly likely that Descartes knew these passages directly from St. Bernard. We see no time of his life at which the reading of the *Treatise on Grace and Free Choice* might be situated. But the great similarity of the two doctrines makes the hypothesis of indirect dependence highly probable. We do not hope to determine with certainty the intermediary through whom this dependence might have been established, but, in the absence of a sure intermediary, we can indicate a possible and even rather likely one, Mersenne. From Mersenne, whether during metaphysical and theological conversation or by reading one of his friend's works, Descartes might have known the doctrine of St. Bernard that we just recalled. Commenting on the phrase from Genesis, "Let us make man in our image and likeness," Mersenne, as usual, assembles signs of the likenesses that humans can have to God. The ninth likeness described is precisely the one St. Bernard had indicated; humans are like God by their free will, and in our freedom we perceive a kind of omnipotence by which we can want all that God himself wants.[11] Evidently, St. Bernard's doctrine is very attenuated and reduced here, but ultimately it is still quite recognizable and, in particular, it has kept two essential traits that Descartes in turn is going to introduce in the *Meditations*: the affirmation of equality between divine and human freedom that exists from a certain point of view and the affirmation that this equality constitutes an eminent sign of our likeness to God.[12]

signat destructionem, sed duarum reliquarum libertatum [*scilicet*, Gratiae et Gloriae] privationem. Neque enim ad liberum arbitrium, quantum in se est, pertinet aut aliquando pertinuit posse vel sapere, sed tantum velle, nec potentem facit creaturam nec sapientem, sed tantum volentem."

11 Mersenne, *Quaestiones Celeberrimae in Genesim*, Paris: Cramoisy, 1623, in folio, chapter 1, verse 26, question 15, column 1052. "Nona sententia constituit imaginem Dei in libero arbitrio, de quo Divus Bernardus, sermone 80 *In Cantica*, et capitulo 1 *De Meditatione Conditionis Humanae*. Quicquid enim volumus per arbitrium volumus, adeo ut nescio quam omnipotentiam in libertate agnoscere possimus . . ." Mersenne accompanies these lines with a rather fanciful commentary of his own concoction. Plausibly, he summed up St. Bernard by memory and unsuccessfully sought the passages we have quoted above, because his references are no more felicitous than his commentary. Sermon 80 of the *Sermones in Cantica* propounds this kind of doctrine only rather vaguely. Sermon 81, which Mersenne does not quote, would almost be more instructive. As for the treatise to which Mersenne remits us, Migne considers it apocryphal. It is found in vol. CLXXXIV of *Patrologia Latina* under the title *Meditationes Piissimae de Cognitione Humanae Conditionis*. Moreover, it contains nothing really interesting.

12 We must note that this doctrine is very clearly stated in St. Bonaventure, *In Sententias II*, distinction 16, article 2, question 3: "Qualitas in qua principaliter assimilatur

But there remains a point indicated by Descartes but not mentioned by St. Bernard. Freedom is one and, as it were, indivisible. One cannot diminish it without destroying it, so that, considered in itself, it could not be less in humans than in God. To whom does Descartes owe this conception of our freedom's invisibility? — To his teachers at La Flèche and beyond his philosophical instruction, to St. Thomas. It is true that St. Thomas does not consider free choice the most evident way humans resemble God because, in his eyes, the understanding is always more noble than the will. Still, St. Thomas at least recognizes explicitly that, if we consider our freedom in itself, it is not less in us than in God. The affirmation that freedom is equal in all rational creatures and in God is based on argument in St. Thomas's doctrine identical, at bottom, to what Descartes was pleased to take from him.

According to St. Thomas, what differentiates human, angelic, and divine freedom is not the difference of wills. That difference stems from the antecedents that determine the conditions in which the will acts. They are two: the nature of the being that wants and its mode of knowledge. The freedom of the being under consideration varies along with its antecedents. God's nature is different from the nature of the angel or human. God is uncreated; he is his own being and his own good. From that it follows that his nature can have no deficiency either in regard to its being or to its goodness. By contrast, the angelic or human nature is created, drawn from nothingness and thereby subject to committing evil. From that comes the first difference between the free choice of God, who is infallible and impeccable, and the free choice of humans, who are subject to sin. Since the mode of knowledge is different in God, the angel, and humans., Hhumans have confused and obscure knowledge incapable of reaching the truth without passing through the intermediary of discourse, and uncertainties and difficulties in discernment and judgment arise from there. But in God and in angels, the knowledge of truth is simple, independent of any discourse and of any searching, free of any doubt and any difficulty in discernment and judgment. That is the source of the promptness and ease with which divine free choice, for example, proceeds to its election

anima Deo, est in voluntate sive in affectione," We will point out other similarities involving the notion of judgment. But did Descartes know St. Bonaventure? Nothing permits us to affirm that. De Bérulle and Gibieuf knew him well, but in their writings we find no trace of Bonaventure's influence on these two points. There remains only the very risky hypothetical suggestion of verbal transmission of the doctrine through them. We do not dare to do more than suggest it.

and its decision.[13] But the difference cannot reside in the essence of free choice considered in itself. Freedom is not a quality extrinsic to the will that comes to be added from outside; it is the will itself considered as unaffected by any constraint. Therefore, if for the will being free is simply not being constrained, freedom is only simple negation in this regard. Negations and privations cannot be increased or diminished by themselves but only by their causes or according to some condition that is added to them.[14] Therefore, if divine freedom is superior to human freedom by reason of the essence of the mode of knowledge, or ultimately by the power that is connected to it, nevertheless, when considered it in itself, it does not appear to be less in humans than in God.

Therefore, by using theological conceptions from different sources, Descartes establishes this first conclusion: error is not found either in our understanding or in our will considered in isolation. It remains to find out whether error comes from the cooperation of understanding and will in one and the same activity, namely, judgment. To situate completely Cartesian thinking on this point, we must first sort out certain elements of theological provenance, which Descartes unknowingly retains and which have determined his general notion of the relations of understanding and will.

According to the doctrine of St. Thomas that Descartes had been taught, the will by its own nature always acts with an end in view. The end is what the agent's movement tends toward. If the agent attains the goal he proposed, we say that he has attained his end. In the opposite case, we say that the end

13 St. Thomas, *De Veritate*, question 24, article 3, second half of body of article: "Aliter tamen invenitur librum arbitrium in nobis et in Angelis et in Deo: variatis enim prioribus necesse est posteriora variari. Facultas autem liberi arbitrii duo praesupponit, scilicet naturam et vim cognitivam. Natura quidem altruism mode est in Doe quam in omnibus et in Angelis. Natura enim divina increata est, et est suum esse et sua bonitas; unde in eo non potest esse defectus aliquis nec quantum ad esse nec quantum ad bonitatem . . . Cognitio etiam alterius modi invenitur in homine quam in Deo et in angelis. Homo enim habet cognitionem obumbratam, et cum discursu notitiam veritatis sumentem; unde accidit ei dubitatio et difficultas in discernendo et judicando . . . et ideo Deus et Angeli habent promptam electionem liberi arbitrii; homo vero in eligendo difficultatem patitur propter incertitudinem et dubitationem."

14 St. Thomas, *Summa Theologiae*, part I, question 59, article 3, reply to objection 3 end: "Tamen verum est quod ipsa libertas, secundum quod in eo consideratur quaedam remotio coactionis, non suscipit magis et minus, quia privationes et negationes non remittuntur nec intenduntur per se, sed solum per suum causam, vel aliquam affirmationem adjunctam."

has been missed.[15] It is easy to establish in consequence that every agent that acts, acts in view of good. If an agent does not tend to produce a determined effect, every effect would be indifferent to it. What is indifferent to producing several effects does not tend to produce one rather than the other; therefore it does not act. This is to say that every being that acts tends to produce a determined effect,[16] and this effect is what we call its end. For a being to tend toward a determined end, this end must be suitable, since it would tend not to an end if this suitability did not exist. What suits a being constitutes a good for it. Therefore, it is the same to say that every being acts in view of a determined effect that is its end, and to say that it acts in view of something good.[17] Consequently, it must be admitted that the good is the will's proper object. This is a point all the more firmly established since to want consists of nothing but a certain inclination of the being that wants toward the object of its will. Everything constitutes a certain good, insofar as it is a being and a substance, and therefore only the good can be wanted.[18] In the eyes of St. Thomas, such is the primary and also the essential characteristic of the will; by its very nature, it is to be an inclination toward the good.[19]

But how does the good that the will desires appear to it? The understanding presents that good to the will, and in this sense the will is subordinated to the understanding. A human will is a rational will since humans are endowed with reason. The appetite by which things lacking reason tend towards their good is called "natural," like the appetite by which the stone

15 St. Thomas, *Summa contra Gentes*, book III, chapter 2 beginning.

16 St. Thomas, *Summa contra Gentes*, book III, chapter 2 second paragraph beginning *Item*: "Si agens non tenderet ad aliquem effectum determinatum omnes effectus essent ei indifferentes . . . impossibile igitur esset quod ageret. Omni igitur agens tendit ad aliquem determinatum effectum, quod dicitur finis ejus."

17 St. Thomas Aquinas, *Summa contra Gentes*, book III, chapter 3, second paragraph: "Id autem ad quod agens determinate tendit oportet esse conveniens ei; non enim tenderet in ipsum nisi propter aliquam convenientiam ad ipsum. Quod autem conveniens est alicui est illi bonum. Ergo omne agens agit propter bonum."

18 St, Thomas, *Summa Theologiae*, part I^a II^{ae}, question 8, article 1 near beginning of body of article. ". . . appetitus nihil aliud est quam quaedam inclinatio appetentis in aliquid . . . Cum igitur omnis res, in quantum est ens et substantia, sit aliquod bonum, necesse est ut omnis inclinatio sit in bonum."

19 Cf. St. Thomas, *Summa Theologiae*, part I, question 48, article 5 body of article second paragraph; also, I, 19, 2, beginning body of article; likewise, I^a II^{ae}, 1, 6, body of article; again, I^a II^{ae}, 9. 2 beginning body of article; and lastly, I^a II^{ae}, 20, 1, end of body of article.

tends down. In beings endowed with sensible knowledge, we find the animal appetite itself subdivided into concupiscible and irascible appetites. Finally, in beings that know by the understanding, we find the intellectual or rational appetite, which is the will.[20] That is to say that the human will is an inclination toward the good that the understanding grasps.[21] Incapable of wanting in a vacuum the will requires a good, an end that is represented to it and toward which it directs its desires. Nothing is wanted without being known.[22]

Consequently, our understanding exerts a very real and very effective influence upon the will. We say that the object acts in a certain manner upon the act that tends toward it in the measure in which the object fulfills the role of formal principle in relation to this act. The very first formal principle is being and truth in general, which is the object of the understanding. The understanding thus acts on the will by determining its act according to the highest formal principle, which is truth. We shall say that the understanding moves the will insofar as it presents its object to it if, by *moving*, we understand the determination of the potency to act.[23] Therefore, in election or voluntary choice, the understanding plays the role of motor, while the will is the thing moved. In the measure in which the good apprehended by the understanding determines the will, the understanding plays an active role, and the will plays a passive role."[24] Moreover, this same action of the understanding upon the will is what makes the human will a free will, a free choice. Certain things lack judgment, like falling stones and in general all beings lacking knowledge. Other beings act after a judgment, but a judgment that is not free, which is the case of the brute animals. A lamb that sees a wolf certainly judges that it has to seek safety, but this is by a natural judgment, not by a free judgment. It acts following pure instinct. By

20 St. Thomas, *Summa contra Gentes*, book II, chapter 47.

21 "Voluntas cum sit inclinatio consequens intellectus apprehensionem . . ." St. Thomas, *Summa Theologiae*, part I^a^ II^ae^, question 8, article 1, body of article. [Translator: This is certainly the sense of the article, but I have not found this phrase.]

22 Conimbricenses, *De Anima*, III, 13, 2, 2: "Nihil volitum quin cognitum." See also Eustachius a Sancto Paulo, *Summa Philosophiae*, I, 2, p. 38.

23 St. Thomas, *Summa Theologiae*, part I^a^ IIae, question 9, article 1, last paragraph of body of article: "Sed objectum movet determinando actum ad modum principii formalis... . . . Primum autem principium formale est ens, et verum universale, quod est objectum intellectus; et ideo isto modo motionis intellectus movet voluntatem, sicut praesentens ei objectum suum."

24 St. Thomas, *Summa Theologiae*, part I, question 82, article 3, response to objection 2, last sentence: "Hoc modo intellectus prior est voluntate, sicut motivum mobili, et activum passivo; bonum enim intellectum movet voluntatem."

contrast, humans act after having determined by a judgment what they ought to seek or avoid, and this judgment is free because it does not stem from a natural instinct leading in a certain particular case to a certain determined action. It follows from an examination by reason. Indeed, in all contingent matters, reason can equally push its way toward opposite conclusions. Argumentation and syllogistic dialectic sufficiently prove this. Particular human actions must be placed among contingent matters. So, the judgment delivered by reason is not determined, and as different actions correspond to different judgments, it follows that humans are free by the mere fact that they are endowed with reason.[25]

If the action of understanding on will is very certain in St. Thomas's view, we can say that it is no less so in Descartes. Descartes never questions the Scholastic proposition, "The will tends toward the good." Whether he supposes it implicitly or he enunciates it explicitly, he frequently appeals to this fundamental proposition.[26] It would be pointless to quote passages from Descartes in which this Scholastic notion is implied. It constitutes the very basis of the critique of freedom of indifference. We shall see it always present and always active in the Cartesian doctrine of freedom. If the will naturally tends toward the good, it necessarily follows that by its very nature it is closely tied to the understanding. The understanding must present its object without which the judgment would become impossible. As Descartes says, there is no sign that our will is determined to what our understanding does not notice in some manner.[27] Therefore, will is necessarily subordinate to understanding. However obscure, however confused our knowledge of things may be, it is still necessary in order that our will be determined to bring judgment. The will tends by itself toward one object that is its proper object, namely, the good. But the understanding must first apprehend this good. It must be recognized that we want nothing that we do not first conceive in some manner, and our natural light teaches us that the understanding's

25 St. Thomas, *Summa Theologiae*, part I, question 83, article 1, body of article.

26 Moreover, the translator of the *Meditations* enunciated it in a passage where it is supposed, *Sextae Responsiones*, VII, p. 432: "Evidens est ipsum [*scilicet*: hominem] eo libentius ac proinde etiam liberius, bonum et verum amplecti, quo illud clarius videt." The translation comments on the passage as follows: "and since the will is such that it can only naturally turn him toward what is good, it is manifest . . ." etc., *Méditations Métaphysiques*; IX, p. 233.

27 *Principia*, I, 34: "Atque ad judicandum requiritur quidem intellectus, quia de re quam nullo modo percipimus, nihil possumus judicare."

knowledge must always precede the will's determination.[28] But does it suffice to speak of mere priority of the understanding in relation to the voluntary decision? For that it would be necessary to admit that the understanding's knowledge only presents its object to the will without exercising a true action upon it. In reality, things happen quite differently. If it is true that we cannot want anything about which we do not know something in some manner, it is no less true that the understanding not only reveals the good to the will, but also that it acts on the will and pushes it toward the good. Therefore, it would be mistaken to represent the will as indifferent in the face of the good that the understanding reveals to it. At the same time that the understanding is enlightened, and in the measure in which it is enlightened, the will feels that a strong inclination toward the good arises within itself.[29] Like St. Thomas, Descartes acknowledges an action of the understanding upon the will, since for both thinkers the understanding contains the formal reason that can entail the will's assent.[30] This notion, which we encounter frequently in the Fourth Meditation, although implicitly, is however revealed by the different terms that Descartes employs to express the understanding's action on the will. Sometimes the will is presented as receiving an impulse from the understanding toward the good that is its object;[31] sometimes the will is presented as stirring the understanding and giving it movement.[32] Always, the real efficient action of the understanding upon the will is affirmed, and we shall see how far Descartes dares to advance on this path, once he

28 *Quintae Responsiones*; VII, 377: "Atque sic fateor quidem nihil nos velle de quo non aliquid aliquo modo intelligamus." *Meditations* (Fourth Meditation); VII, p. 60 [Heffernan, p. 162]: ". . . lumine naturali manifestum est perceptionem intellectus praecedere semper debere voluntatis determinationem."

29 Letter to Mesland, May 2, 1644; IV, p. 115: "It seems certain to me that *ex magna luce in intellectu sequitur magna propensio in voluntate*."

30 *Secundae Responsiones*; VII, p. 147: "Quippe distinguendum est inter materiam sive rem ipsam cui assentimur, et rationem formalem quae movet voluntatem at assentiendum."

31 *Meditations* (Fourth Meditation); VII, p. 59 Heffernan, pp. 160, 162]: "... ". . . cognitio... . . . sufficit ad assensionem meam in contrarium impellendam." Also *Meditations* (Fourth Meditation); VII, p. 58 [Heffernan, p. 158]: "... ". . . nulla me ratio in unam partem magis quam in alteram impellit . . ." Also Letter to Mesland, May 2, 1644; IV, p. 155: ". . . it knows fewer reasons that push it to choose one part rather than the other." Lastly, Letter to Mesland, February 9, 1645; IV, p. 173, lines 14–17.

32 *Secundae Responsiones*; VII, p. 147.

starts. However, holding to this point of view alone would condemn us to imperfect knowledge of the relations of understanding and will. If the understanding really acts effectively on the will, the reverse is no less true: the will in turn acts on the understanding.

It might seem, St. Thomas says, that the will is incapable of acting on the understanding, since what is moved can only move its mover by accident. But the term "mover" can be taken in two different senses. In the first sense it relates to ends, and this is what we use when we say that the end moves one who seeks it. In this sense, it is the understanding that moves the will, because the good grasped by the understanding is the will's proper object and determines the will as its end. In the second sense, we say of something that it moves another in the measure in which it acts on it to communicate movement to it effectively. Accordingly, what produces a change moves what undergoes it; what impresses an impulse moves what receives it; and the will moves the understanding just as it always moves all the faculties of the soul. If we compare all our active faculties to each other, the one that tends to the universal end will necessarily be seen as acting upon those that tend to particular ends. The will's object is precisely the good, that is to say, the end in general. Therefore, since every power of the soul tends toward a particular good that is its own good, like sight toward the perception of colors and understanding toward the knowledge of the true, the will, whose object is the good in general, must act on all the faculties of the soul and on the understanding in particular.[33]

From that, it is easy to perceive how important is the role played by the will. The will is what makes each human faculty pass into act. We have said that its action upon the entire soul, except the vegetative functions, which are not subject to it, comes from the fact that its object, the good, is the highest end. It is consequently necessary to admit that we comprehend because we want to; that we imagine because we want to, and so on. Our understanding's movement comes to it from the will, and

33 St. Thomas, *Summa Theologiae*, part I, question 82, article 6: "Alio modo dicitur aliquid movere per modum agentis . . . et hoc modo voluntas movet intellectum . . . Cujus ratio est quia in omnibus potentiis activis ordinatis illa potentia quae respicit finem universalem movit potentias quae respiciunt fines particulares . . . Objectum autem voluntatis est bonum et finis in communi. Quaelibet autem potentia comparatur ad aliquod bonum proprium sibi conveniens sicut visus ad perceptionem coloris et intellectus ad cognitionem veri. Et ideo voluntas per modum agentis movet omnes animae potentias ad suos actus."

it is by reason of our voluntary determinations that our intellectual, imaginative, and other faculties can pass into act.[34] Accordingly, a series of actions and reactions is produced between the understanding and the will, which, furthermore, are not at all incompatible or contradictory. To harmonize them, it suffices to show that the understanding and will really act on one another, but in different relations. If we consider the objects of the will and of the understanding, we see that the object of the understanding is the first principle in the genus of the formal cause, since it is being and truth. Furthermore, the will's object is the first principle in the genus of the final cause, since the will's object is the good, and all ends are included under the good, as all forms that the understanding grasps are included under the true. It follows that insofar as the good itself is a form graspable by the understanding, it is included under the true *qua* particular truth and that reciprocally, insofar as the true is the end of the understanding's operations, it is included under the good *qua* particular good.[35] The origin of movements of the faculties of the soul can be referred to the understanding or to the will according to the point of view we adopt. If we take the perspective of the specification of acts by reason of their object, we \ locate the first principle of the soul's movement in the understanding. But if we situate ourselves in the perspective of the fulfillment of acts, then the origin of movements is not located in the understanding but in the will.[36] Therefore, it is evident that the understanding and the will are not moved reciprocally in the same relationship. That is, we can maintain that, while the understanding moves the will *qua* formal cause and also *qua* final cause (since the understanding represents its object, the good, to the will), by contrast, the will moves the understanding *qua* efficient cause and also *qua* final

34 St. Thomas, *Summa contra Gentes*, book I, chapter 72, in the second paragraph, beginning *Item*: "In virtutibus motivis et habentibus intellectum, primo invenitur voluntas; nam voluntas omnem potentiam applicat ad suum actum. Intelligimus enim, quia volumus; imaginamur quia volumus, et sic de aliis."

35 St. Thomas, *De Malo*, VI, 1, paragraph begins *Ad evidentiam*: "Unde et ipsum bonum, in quantum est quaedam forma apprehensibilis, continetur sub vero quasi quoddam verum; et ipsum verum, in quantum est finis intellectualis operationis continetur sub bono ut quoddam particulare bonum."

36 St. Thomas, *De Malo*, VI, 1, continuation of note 35: "Si ergo consideremus motum potentiarum animae ex parte objecti specificantis actum, primum principium motionis est ex intellectu . . . si autem consideremus motus potentiarum animae ex parte exercitii actus, sic principium motionis est ex voluntate." Cf. *Summa Theologiae*, part I^{a} II^{ae}, question 9, article 1, reply to objection 3.

cause, since the end is both what the agent achieves and what determines it to act.[37]

Descartes does not depart from St. Thomas on this centrally important point for what concerns the explanation of freedom. Just as we have seen him admit an action of understanding on will, we also see him acknowledge with St. Thomas the will's action on the understanding. *Intelligimus quia volumus*, we read in the *Summa Theologiae*, *imaginamur quia volumus et sic de aliis*.[38] In the treatise on *The Passions of the Soul*, Descartes expresses himself identically. It is the will that applies our soul to the imagination of unreal beings. We imagine monsters and chimeras because we want to imagine them. The same holds for the understanding. We examine and understand what is intelligible, because we want to. All of our soul's operations are submitted to determinations of our will. "When our soul applies itself to imagining something non-existent, like representing an enchanted palace or a chimera, and also when it applies itself to considering what is solely intelligible and not imaginable at all, for example considering its own nature, the perceptions it has of these things depend primarily on the will that makes it perceive them."[39]

Therefore, the will is the active principle of the soul. The understanding has a passive role in regard to the will. Clearly, it is not difficult to show that Descartes attributed an active role to the soul and real influence upon the understanding. The real difficulties arise rather from his sometimes making this role so great and the influence so preponderant that no room remains for the understanding's reciprocal action upon the will. We know that Descartes spoke readily of an impulse impressed by the understanding on the will, a kind of movement that the understanding communicates to the will by revealing the good to it. However, other apparently contradictory passages seem to reduce the understanding to the most absolute passivity, and only acknowledge authentic activity in the will's determination. Just as

37 St. Thomas, *Summa contra Gentes*, book I, chapter 72 at "*Item. in virtutibus*" Cf. *Summa Theologiae*, part I, question 82, article 6, body of article. Also: Eustachius a Sancto Paulo, *Summa Philosophiae*, I, 2, p. 40: "Respondeo primo non esse absurdum idem respectu ejusdem esse movens et motum in diverso genere causae. Finis enim est id quod ab agente fit, et tamen idem movet agens ad operandum. Atqui in re proposita intellectus movet voluntatem in genere causa formalis externae, voluntas vero intellectum in genere causae efficientis et finalis."

38 St. Thomas, *Summa contra Gentes*, book I, chapter 72, about halfway through the chapter.

39 Descartes, *Passions of the Soul*; I, 20.

the different kinds of thoughts that we perceive in the soul can be grouped under two main types and are related either to the understanding or to the will, they can also be considered either as active or passive. All the soul's thoughts are either actions or passions. Descartes' classification seems very simple: only the soul's wishes are actions; all the other kinds of thoughts are passions.[40] How can such claims be reconciled? If it is true that only the will is active in the soul, how can we admit that the understanding exerts any action upon the will?

Descartes nowhere manifests a concern to achieve this harmonization. While Scholastic philosophers took care to demonstrate that in this reciprocal action of understanding and will *non est idem movens et motum secundum idem*, Descartes seems not to have perceived the difficulty. In the absence of an explicit solution offered by our philosopher, we will examine the texts to find the elements of a solution and an explanation for such a contradiction.

First of all, we could allege that the texts, in which the term *action* is not found, seem to suppose an influence of the understanding on the will. Understanding pushes the will, Descartes says. The understanding stirs it up, communicates impulses to us, but nowhere do we find the theses set out about the understanding's activity and the will's passivity. Therefore, we might admit that in Descartes' own thought this supposed activity does not exist. The understanding perceives the good. The will then really determines itself to accept it, but the origin of this voluntary determination would be rather in the will's freedom than in the object the understanding presents to it. Some texts seem to justify this interpretation. It is evident, says Descartes, that a great propensity in the will follows upon a great light in the intellect.[41] But everything depends on the meaning assigned to the term *sequitur*. Nothing demonstrates that, by the term, Descartes wants to signify a real, effective action of the intellect. Let us simply translate: "Following a great light in the understanding, a great propensity arises in the will." Still, there are reasons that might turn us away from this option, and it seems difficult to reconcile the hypothesis of the understanding's absolute passivity in Cartesian philosophy with the texts. Moreover, the mere definitions of action and

40 Letter to Mesland, May 2, 1644; IV, p. 113 "I make no more difference between the soul and its ideas than between a bit of wax and the different shapes it may receive. As receiving different shapes is not properly an action, but a passion in the wax, it seems to me that receiving this or that ideas is also a passion in the soul, and that only its wishes are actions."

41 Letter to Mesland, May 2, 1644; IV, p. 116.

passion, as Descartes understands them, will be enough to convince us that the intellect is not absolutely passive.

"I am obliged to write here as if I were treating a matter thant no one before me had treated."[42] With these words Descartes resolutely abandons all the teachings of his predecessors at the start of the treatise on the *Passions*, teachings so meager and, moreover, so hard to believe that we can only hope to discover the truth in these matters on the condition of abandoning the beaten paths. Descartes immediately adopts the Scholastic definition of action and passion in its general sense. All that is produced, every fact, every event can be considered from two standpoints. In regard to the subject that makes the event happen, it will be an action. In regard to the subject to which the event happens, it will be a passion. Therefore, action and passion are not two events, two different facts, but one and the same event considered sometimes in the one that produces it, and sometimes in the one that undergoes it.[43] Descartes knows and says that his definition does not essentially depart from that of the "philosophers." In passing from Scholasticism to Cartesianism, that concept of passion had to shed all of the theories about the relations of matter and form with which it was burdened. According to Scholasticism, to act is to impose a form, to undergo is to receive a form.[44] Descartes distrusts these notions of form and matter, potency and act. They badly disguise ideas that are neither clear nor distinct. They often obscure primary concepts, known by themselves, that can only lose when cloaked in so many explanations. So, as we see, Descartes substitutes the simpler concept of *fact* (or event) for the concepts of form and of matter. But if we consider this notion of *what happens* more closely, we see it come near to Scholastic doctrine on many points concerning the relations of action and passion.

For both philosophers the essential thing is to establish the fundamental identity of action and passion, to make very evident that the same fact always and necessarily implies the activity of what produces it and the passivity of what undergoes it. More than once, Scholastic philosophers seem to devote themselves to distinguishing the two terms, action and passion, and to make an effort to forestall any confusion. Yet, at the very instant when they distinguish them, they seem forced to bring them closer. Although

42 Descartes, *Passions of the Soul*, I, 1.

43 Descartes, *Passions of the Soul*, I, 1.

44 Suárez, *Disputationes Metaphysicae*, disputation 48, section 1, number 1: "Est passio receptio alicujus formae."

movement is the common act of what moves and what is moved, one thing is to receive a movement and another one to produce it. These two categories, action and passion, must be distinguished.[45] To produce a movement is to act, to receive it is to undergo, but action and passion are not only different in that. They are one, single act considered now in its origin, now in its term. They are the modes of one same reality, and it is impossible to introduce a real distinction between action and passion.[46] No essential disagreement can arise between Descartes and Scholasticism on this point, since Descartes refuses to separate action from passion. Every fact is an action in regard to what happens, a passion in regard to the subject to which it happens. It is no less impossible to separate action from passion than to separate cause from effect. Just as we can affirm that there is no effect without a cause, we can affirm that there is no passion without action and reciprocally. For example, how can we say that a shoe that keeps on moving moves after a tool has struck is passive in regard to the tool, although the tool has ceased to strike it? Therefore, it must be admitted that action and passion can reside in absolutely separate subjects and even that the passion can last in a subject when the active subject no longer exists. If the instrument not only stops striking the shoe but even existing, will the shoe therefore be passive in regard to what does not exist? On this account, it might be denied that any action is produced in the world. All events could be considered as passions resulting from primitive actions produced at the origin of the world in the instant of creation. This connection falls, however, when we deny that action and passion are really distinguished. They are only one, same thing that is called action when it is related to the *terminus a quo*, passion when it is related to the *terminus ad quem* or i*n quo* and there is not an instant of passion, however brief, without corresponding action, and the reverse.[47]

45 St. Thomas *Summa contra Gentes*, book II, chapter 57, paragraph begins *Praeterea*: "Licet motus sit communis actus moventis et moti, tamen alia operatio est facere motum et recipere motum. Unde et duo praedicamenta ponuntur, *facere* et *pati*."

46 Suárez, *Disputationes Metaphysicae*, disputation 48, section 1, number 3: "Est communis et vera sententia, actionem et passionem non distingui realiter proprie et rigorose. Haec est sententia Aristotelis, III, *Physicae*, capitulo 3, ubi ait actionem et passionem in re esse eumdem actum seu motum, differreque penes diversos respectus... Actio et passio sunt modi ejusdem rei; ergo non possunt inter se habere realem distinctionem."

47 Letter to Hypersaspistes, August, 1641; III, p. 428: "Cum vero dicitur turbinem in seipsum non agerem, dum se circumvolvit, sed tantum pati a verbere, licet absente, vellem scire quo pacto unum corpus ab alio absente, pati possit, et quomodo actio

Unquestionably, the adversary Descartes wants to silence here is Scholastic philosophy, but it must be observed that he fights it with its own arguments. When Descartes denies that we cannot really distinguish between movement impressed by the agent of movement and movement received by the patient, he is applying the doctrine of identity of action and passion.[48] According to Scholasticism, action and passion are united in a single movement or, if we prefer, in a single change that is common to them. It is contradictory for a subject to undergo a passion without it being imposed by the action of another subject, because there is no effect without a cause. This event, this fact, or this change, in the very measure in which it refers to what produces it, is an action in the proper sense of the term. Reciprocally, by the very fact that the change produced depends on the action of a certain subject, another subject must necessarily undergo it, and it must necessarily be a passion in its regard, with the result that the action and the passion can never be separated.[49] This is Scholastic doctrine, and it is also, one must recall, the conclusion of the first article in the treatise on *Passions*. Therefore, it is difficult to claim that Descartes does not acknowledge an active role for the understanding in regard to the will. Judgment, as Descartes conceives it, supposes the cooperation of understanding and will, and in the judgment, the apprehension of the good by the understanding in some measure and some fashion entails that there should be consent of the will. Given that, how could we maintain that the understanding is not active in regard to the will and the will passive in regard to the understanding for Descartes? When action is defined as a fact considered in regard to what produces it, can an active role be denied to the understanding, which is always the

et passio ab invicem distinguantur... Semper autem existimavi unam et eamdem rem esse, quae cum refertur ad terminum *a quo* vocatur *actio*, cum vero ad terminum *ad quem* sive *in quo* recipitur vocatur *passio*: adeo ut plane repugnet, vel per minimum temporis momentum, passionem esse sine actione."

48 Conimbricenses, *De Generatione et Corruptione*, I, 3, 6: "Omnes actio est idem re, cum termino, et passio non distinguitur realiter ab actione cum simul ambae concurrunt."

49 Suárez, *Disputationes Metaphysicae*, disputation 48, section 1, number 9: "Actio et passio ita conjunguntur realiter in uno motu seu mutatione, ut nec actio a passione, nec passio ab actione separabilis sit... . . . quia repugnat pasionem fieri in aliquo subjecto quin ab aliquo agente procedat, quia non potest esse effectus sine causa; hoc autem ipso quod ab agente procedit invenitur in illa mutatione vera ratione actionis . . . E converso etiam non potest esse actio ex subjecto . . . quin hoc ipso inferat passionem, nam si ex subjecto fit, in subjecto recipitur terminus ejus et in eodem fit: ergo est passio et receptio ex parte talis subjecti: sunt ergo omnino inseparabilis passio et talis actio."

reason of the will's determinations? Reciprocally, if the passion is only the same fact considered, no longer in relation to what produces it but to that in which it is produced, we cannot say that the will is always active. On the contrary, its determinations always depend on the impulse that it receives from the understanding, when the understanding reveals its object, the good, to it.

The terms *impulse* and *movement* themselves are no longer employed by Descartes to eliminate the hypothesis of a real action properly so-called, of the understanding upon the will. The terms *impellens et impulsum* or *movens et motum* do not exclude the meaning of the terms *action* and *passion*. To the contrary, these different manners of expression are synonyms in Descartes' view. Descartes thinks that the model of action and passion is found in local movement. Each movement must be considered as an action in regard to that one of two bodies that moves the other and as a passion in regard to that one of the two bodies that is moved. When we extend the meaning of these two terms to immaterial things, we simply mean that something analogous to movement is produced in them, which is called action in regard to what moves and passion in regard to what is moved. This is how volition is an action of the soul, and intellection or vision is a passion.[50] When Descartes says that the will is active and the understanding passive, he means to indicate that the will produces something analogous to movement in the understanding. We have the right to conclude the reciprocal. That is, when Descartes says that the understanding pursues or moves the will, by these metaphors taken from movement, he indicates that understanding is active there, in contrast to the will's passivity. Perhaps it will be granted to him all the more readily, as Scholastic philosophers already employ metaphors of this kind with the very explicit intention of designating the relation of action to passion.[51] Accordingly, everything invites us to take

50 Letter to Regius, December 1641; III, pp. 454–455: "In rebus corporeis omnis actio et passio in solu motu locali consistunt, et quidem actio vocatur, cum motus ille consideratur in movente, passio vero cum consideratur in moto. Unde sequitur etiam, cum illa nomina ad res immateriales extenduntur, aliquid etiam motui analogum in illis esse considerandum; et actionem dicendam esse, quae se habet ex parte moti, ut intellectio et visio in eadem mente."

51 Eustachius a Sancto Paulo, *Summa Philosophiae*, I, 2, p. 38 "Hoc igitur loco asserimus voluntatem ab intellectu moveri quoad speciem actus quia intellectus proponit voluntati objectum a quo tanquam a principio formali externo actus voluntatis speciem sumunt. Ubi adverte bonum cognitum non solum sese habere ad actus voluntatis ut causam formalem externam, prout illis tan quam terminus ad quem referuntur, speciem tribuit, sed etiam ut finem quatenus motu metaphorico allicit voluntatem."

the terms used by Descartes in a strict sense and to think that he has retained the Scholastic notion of the understanding's activity in regard to the will. We need to reconcile the contradictory affirmations and explain that, having inherited the Scholastic doctrine of the reciprocal action of understanding and will, Descartes only recognizes movement of the will as an action of the soul.

The only possible explanation of this contradiction seems to be bound up with the particular goal that Descartes pursues in the treatise on the *Passions*. In the Fourth Meditation, our philosopher does not have to employ the terms *action* and *passion*. In that place, this completely Scholastic language would risk misleading the reader, who would not have failed to interpret the terms in the same sense as that in which the Scholastics usually took them. St. Thomas recognizes a dual kind of activity of the intellect in regard to the object it apprehends and in regard to the object it clarifies. Descartes certainly admits that the understanding is active in regard to the will, at least in a certain sense, but he maintains by contrast that this same intellect is passive in relation to the object. In the treatise on *Passions*, the essential issue is to explain in what the soul's activity and passivity consists in regard to exterior objects, in particular to explain from what bodily actions come these movements of the soul that are called the *passions*. At this stage, what interests Descartes is no longer the reciprocal action of understanding and will, but the question of activity or passivity of the whole soul in regard to the body. It is understood that the terms *action* and *passion* take on a very peculiar sense in his thought. Descartes finds himself led to restrict the sense of these terms in order to adapt them to the problem that concerns him. What he will understand by *action* is a certain kind of thought that is immediately in the power of the soul and upon which the body can only act indirectly. By *passion*, he will no longer simply understand a fact considered in regard to the subject that undergoes it, but all sorts of perceptions: thoughts different from the first ones, absolutely dependent on the body's action, and which can only be moved directly by the body except in those cases where the soul itself is the cause of these perceptions. In the first kind of thoughts, the soul's volitions have been recognized. In the second, the perception of the object by the senses, imagination, and the perception of the movements of our will are grouped.[52]

52 Descartes, *Passions*, I, 41: "And in these two kinds of thoughts that I have distinguished in the soul, some of which are its actions, namely its wishes, the others its passions, taking this word in its most general meaning that comprises all sorts of

Moreover, each time that Descartes affirms our understanding's absolute passivity and acknowledges an active role for the will alone, he defines the understanding's passivity not by relation to the will but by relation to its object. A body can never directly modify our wills. First, there must be some perception or imagination subsequent to which the will determines itself, and this is why we can say that the will is active. By contrast, the soul cannot act directly on perceptions or imaginations: here the body is necessary as an intermediary and this is why we can say that perceptions are passive in a general way. Therefore, our perceptions' passivity must be understood on the one hand from their passivity in regard to the things they represent and on the other hand in regard to the body, where the traces of our previous perceptions are conserved. Lastly, that passivity is understood in regard to the innate disposition of the soul and the movements of the will. In all these cases, the soul is passive exactly as a bit of wax that receives different figures that other bodies imprint on it, and also those that result from its own qualities or from the movement the wax conserves after it has been imprinted on it.[53] By defining the understanding's passivity in perception, Descartes opposes the Scholastic notion that sees an act in every apprehension of the true by the soul.[54] But to affirm passivity, even absolute passivity, of the intellect in relation to its object does not make every claim about the intellect's activity, at least relative activity, impossible in relation to the will. These two theses of Descartes do not exclude each other, since they are posed on different levels and, despite apparently contradictory passages, it remains true to say that the Cartesian notion of the relations of understanding and will are the same as those of St. Thomas himself. Descartes retains the doctrine of reciprocal activity and passivity of understanding and will imparted by his teachers at La Flèche. This same doctrine constitutes the basis of the conception of judgment developed in the Fourth Meditation. At first sight, it might seem that Cartesian thought sets itself up in flagrant contradiction to St. Thomas's thought. Descartes is generally considered to have been the first to highlight the will's role in judgment. St. Thomas, on the contrary, is regarded as having held a purely intellectualist notion of

perceptions, the first are absolutely in its power and can only be indirectly changed by the body, whereas, by contrast, the latter depend absolutely on the actions that guide them, and they can only indirectly be changed by the soul, except when the soul itself is there their cause."

53 Descartes, *Passions*, I, 17. See also Letter to Mesland, May 2, 1644; IV, pp. 113–114.

54 Letter to Regius, December 1641; III, p. 455.

judgment, and there is no lack of texts to support it. Some historians congratulate Descartes for this innovation;[55] others blame him for it.[56] We are inclined to think that at least two considerations wrest something of its novelty from the Cartesian doctrine.

In the first place, it ought to be noted that Descartes' principal modification of St. Thomas's doctrine consists of a change or rather displacement of name. Descartes extends to error what St. Thomas's doctrine said about sin. And if, instead of reserving the term *judgment* to what St. Thomas called *judicium*, we agree that what Thomas called *electio* is to be included and described under *judgment*, we get all of judgment as Descartes conceived it. This extension to error of what St. Thomas taught about sin is explicable, because error and sin are two different aspects of one and the same problem. The problem of sin is the theological version of the problem of error, as the problem of error is the philosophical version of the problem of sin. We should, therefore, not be surprised to see a theologian like St. Thomas bring the whole weight of his analysis to bear on the question of sin, while a philosopher like Descartes insists on the question of error. That does not mean that both of them are unaware that at bottom the two problems are combined.

St. Thomas explicitly notes that ignorance and error are found at the origin of many of our faults. Deceived by a false judgment we take evil for good, and it is then that we sin.[57] Not only is moral evil an error committed in seeking good, but also error in itself and in its essence has the same nature as sin. Ignorance is not a sin, but the same does not go for error. Ignorance is only the absence of knowledge. Error is more than that: it consists of an approbation given to what is false instead of what is true. Therefore, error adds an act to simple ignorance. The ignorant are not deceived when they form a judgment on what they do not know. Moreover, as sin essentially consists of an act, we must recognize that error has the same nature as sin.[58]

55 Fouillée, *Descartes*, p. 149.

56 Maumus, *Saint Thomas d'Aquin et la philosophie cartésienne*, I, p. 361.

57 *Summa Theologiae*, part I, question 63, article 1, reply to objection 4, beginning: ". . . sicut homo peccat eligendo adulterium quod secundum se est malum. Et tale peccatum semper procedit ex aliqua ignorantia vel errore; alioquin id quod est malum non eligeretur ut bonum."

58 St. Thomas, *De Malo*, III, 7, a few lines from the beginning: "Error autem est approbare falsa pro veris; unde addit actum quemdam super ignoratiam. Potest enim esse ignorantia sine hoc quod aliquis de ignotis sententiam ferat, et tunc ignorans est et non errans; sed quando jam falsam sententiam fert de his quae nescit, tunc

If we find a tendency to approximate error to moral evil, it is no less certain that in Descartes the inverse tendency is clearly felt, and that he tries to assimilate moral evil to error. If we believe the synoptic summary of the *Meditations*, nothing would be further from Descartes' mind than to identify these two problems. When Descartes speaks in the Fourth Meditation of the errors that are committed in distinguishing true and false, he never thinks of sin. He is a philosopher simply using the lights of his reason to discover the truth and not a theologian concerned with what involves faith and morals.[59] But Descartes does not articulate his authentic thought in this place, he simply takes a precaution. Descartes adds a prudent restriction to the *Meditations* following advice from Arnaud, a hypersensitive theologian on the subject of grace. Why would Descartes confuse intellectual error and moral error? — objects Arnauld. Much can be lost this way, and there is nothing to gain. Descartes' real teaching concerning the error that is committed in pursuit of the true and the false is not the same when the issue is the error that is committed in pursuit of the good and the evil.[60] This would be a useless confusion, given the goal Descartes sets himself, and what is worse, dangerous because it gives a handle for disputes.[61]

Arnauld prevails. The appeal to Descartes' prudence was not made in vain, and through the intermediary of Mersenne, he grants Arnauld the required satisfaction.[62] In reality, Descartes' authentic thought was completely different, and he never dreamt of giving two different solutions to the problem of error and sin, but he wanted to remain within the limits of philosophy as much as possible, and the fear of engaging in thorny theological questions was the only cause of his reserve.[63] Again, he had done only what he could in the summary, but in the text of the *Meditations*, certain expressions

proprie dicitur errare. Et quia peccatum in actu consistit, error manifeste habet rationem peccati." Cf. *Summa Theologiae*, part I, question 17, article 1.

59 *Meditations*, Synopsis; VII, p. 15, lines 6–12.

60 It will be clearer below what might be troubling Arnauld on this point. Descartes ends the Fourth Meditation by concluding that not being deceived does not depend on us. That is strictly defensible for a Jansenist, but it would be completely indefensible to maintain that we still have the power to abstain from sin. Grace still is necessary and from the start.

61 *Meditations*, Fourth Set of Objections; VII, p. 215, p. 15, lines 6–12.

62 Letter to Mersenne, March 18, 1641; *Meditations*, Fifth Set of Objections; VII, p. 334, lines 10 ff.

63 Nothing kept me from speaking of the freedom that we possess to follow good or evil, except that, as much as possible, I wanted to avoid theological controversies and stay within the limits of natural philosophy.

escape the author belying the summary's restrictions. Sometimes Descartes speaks of grace at the same time as of the natural light, sometimes he speaks of the search "veri et boni," thus openly combining the two problems of evil and of error.[64] All these expressions prove the degree to which the two questions continue to be inseparably linked and combined in his mind. Ultimately, like St. Thomas, Descartes deems not only that the same explanation is valid for error and for evil, but also that error is an evil. On this point he is appropriately sure of being in agreement with the theologians: those who without knowledge of the situation, pass some judgment, sin.[65]

It is important to note acknowledge this agreement but also to immediately immediately the note its impact. The passages where St. Thomas considers error to be a kind of sin are infrequent and too inconspicuous to be considered the origin of the amplification of the Scholastic doctrine of sin carried out by Descartes. However, they have real importance to Descartes as a shield. St. Thomas teaches that error participates in the nature of sin, and Descartes can present himself as following St. Thomas and teach that the act by which we commit error is the same act by which we commit sin. This is the argument that we see him employ in his responses to objections.

This is not to say that Descartes only had to harvest the assimilation of error to sin from Scholasticism, and consequently the assimilation of judgment to election. We detect passages in St. Thomas where the will's role in judgment is indicated and that perhaps encouraged Descartes along the path he had taken. But this is only a hypothesis. It is not likely that Descartes studied the text of the *Summa* closely enough to pick up such brief and fleeting indications. What he knew well was not St. Thomas's authentic doctrine with all the nuances that he introduced into it as a theologian, but the simplified outline that Scholastic teaching had retained from it. According to this outline, whose general tendencies do correspond to the thought of St. Thomas, we find before judgment a deliberation that is the work of the understanding. The opinion or judgment would come after deliberation, both produced by the understanding. Lastly would come the election or acceptance by the will

64 *Meditations*, Fourth Meditation; VII, p. 58, lines 1–5 and 10. See also VII, p. 60, lines 28–31.

65 *Secundae Responsiones*; VII, p. 147: "Et quis unquam vel Philosophus vel Theologus, vel tantum homo ratione utens, non confessus est, eo minori in errando periculo nos versari, quo clarius aliquid intelligimus, antequam ipsi assentiamur, atque illos peccare qui causa ignota judicium ferunt." For what concerns St. Thomas, cf. *Summa Theologiae*, part I, question 17, article 1, and also *Summa Theologiae*, I[a] II[ae], 75, 5 at *Responeo.*

of the judgment produced by the understanding. With the judgment, the possibility of error is introduced, the responsibility for which falls back upon the understanding. With election, the possibility of sin is introduced, whose responsibility belongs to the will. In the eyes of Descartes' contemporaries and surely for a long time in Descartes' own eyes, this was the true doctrine and also St. Thomas's doctrine.

If Descartes extended to the problem of error Scholasticism's solution to the problem of sin, it was surely for internal reasons stemming from the requirements of his own system. We know the particular perspective in which Descartes places himself. The problem that concerns him is that of error, but error considered as an evil. He wants to prove that God did not inescapably condemn us to error and that, when creating us capable of being deceived, God also conferred on us the power of not being deceived if we are firmly resolved to avoid error.

St. Thomas had not posed this precise problem. He most certainly thought error is an evil but did not opine that the presence of this evil in the world required a particular explanation. The general arguments that we have recorded and that Descartes was to take up for his own use suffice to exonerate God of any responsibility in this connection. Inequality among creatures is necessary, and consideration the universe taken *collectively* rather than of the individual or even the species sufficiently legitimates the presence of evil in general in the world and the presence of error in particular. Error is explained above all by the fact that humans are creatures, that is to say, finite and limited beings, deficient because drawn out of nothingness, and consequently incapable of attaining perfection in the order of knowledge or any other. To say that humans are subject to error and to say that they are humans is exactly the same. Therefore, St. Thomas is not especially scandalized by the presence of error in human nature, which, furthermore, is compatible with his conception of knowledge. For him, as for Scholastic philosophies in general, the proper domain of human thought is not the certain but the probable. Apart from mathematical knowledge and revealed truths, we only attain probabilities, although the different orders of human knowledge can be graded according to their increasing or decreasing probability.[66] Between absolute truth and absolute error, there is room for a number of degrees in which truth and error are mixed in varying proportions, and in the majority of cases this is the only kind of knowledge available to humans.

66 Conimbricenses, *Commentary on the Physics, Proemium*, 5, 4; and Suárez, *Disputationes Metaphysicae*, disputation I, section 5, numbers 22–26.

For Descartes things are completely different. The probable is not enough for him, and in his eyes the probable and the false blend together. Mathematics provided Descartes with his model of knowledge, and he wants to reconstruct the whole edifice of science on its model. Consequently, he suppresses the different degrees of probability that Scholasticism recognizes and that form the scale over which different sciences are distributed. Truth and error come face to face. The presence of error becomes a scandal, and if error were to be found invincible, there would be reason to make a just reproach against the creator's impotence or against his malice. Then God would be the great deceiver, since, having given us the desire of always reaching truth, he would not have bestowed the power on us to do so. So the difference that separates the doctrine of error in St. Thomas and in Descartes measures the difference of their requirements in the matter of certainty. St. Thomas never had the idea of a human knowledge whose parts would all be absolutely and definitively certain. Knowledge like that would be more than human, and God does not need to be justified for not having created us so that we could arrive at such knowledge. Descartes, on the contrary, thinks that such a science is possible or, properly speaking, that there is no other science possible, and that, ultimately, if God granted him life enough, he would construct it himself. He quite sincerely believed he was not mistaken and that he had never written anything that not waswas not as certain or even more certain than mathematical truths.

For this kind of science to be possible, not only was it necessary that error not be the natural human condition, but furthermore it was necessary that humans be infallible *de jure*. And according to Descartes, they are. If a simple error that is inevitable remains within the confines of human knowledge, God forces us to be deceived, and he is nether neither all-powerful nor all good. Such a consequence is evidently absurd, but it still is important to completely demonstrate its absurdity. Its demonstration is the analysis of the conditions in which the error that gives the absurdity is produced. For error to be always avoidable, it must always be within our power to not commit it. For that, in the last analysis, our will must be master of the conclusion from our judgment. This is what Descartes has to demonstrate if he wants to establish the possibility not only of a complete science, but an entirely and rigorously certain one.

Descartes can take the demonstration of this possibility from Scholastic philosophy. St. Thomas had to resolve a problem similar in all its aspects, that of sin. According to Catholic theology, humans are exactly in the situation in relation to sin that Descartes wants them to be in relation to error.

Humans are fallible in the sense that they can sin, but they are not obliged by nature to commit a single fault. Just as according to Descartes humans can think all their lives without error, according to Catholic theology they can act all their lives without committing a single sin. A life like that supposes a series of extraordinary assists from God, but it is ultimately possible. It certainly must be so because, if there is a single truly inevitable fault for a human, whatever his efforts of will may be, God himself would be responsible for the sins committed by that human. In reality, matters do not occur this way, as St. Thomas establishes with his doctrine of *electio*. Between the false judgments of an understanding ruled by concupiscence and passion and the acts that we carry out, free will is interposed. Accepting or rejecting the propositions of our understanding is always within our power, and humans become the only ones responsible for their failures through the free acceptance of their acts. This is precisely what resolves the problem Descartes posed. It is enough for him to push the judgment back to the instant where it is accepted by the will, that is to say to call *judgment* what St. Thomas called *election*. We can observe simultaneously the difference of terminology that separates the theologian from the philosopher and the extraordinary parallelism between their doctrines' content.[67]

We know what the nature of our judgments is, according to Descartes, and consequently the nature of our errors. Two causes converge for their production, our faculty of knowing and our faculty of choosing or free choice; in other words, our understanding and our will. Judgment is a complex act, and the error that comes from it cannot be attributed either to the understanding considered in itself or to the will taken in isolation. For there to be error or sin, understanding and will must concur in a single act: the understanding deliberating and presenting to the will the ideas upon which its election will bear.[68] As long as I cannot conceive the ideas of things, it

67 Moreover, St. Bonaventure clearly introduces the will into judgment, *In Sententias*, II, distinction 5, part 1, dubium 1: "Judicium importat actum rationis regulatum secundum imperium voluntatis." Also: *In Sententias* II, distinction 25, part 1, article 1, question 6: "Quantumcumque enim ratio deliberet in eam partem terminatur definitivum judicium quam praeoptat voluntas." We have already said why we do not insist on the possible influence of St. Bonaventure. But, we see that here that the difference is only in terminology. The core of St. Thomas and St. Bonaventure's doctrine is identical.

68 *Meditations*, Fourth Meditation; VII, p. 56 [Heffernan, p. 156]: ". . . adverto illos [*scilicet*: errores] a duabus causis simul concurrentibus dependere; nempe a facultate cognoscendi quae in me est, et a facultate eligendi, sive ab arbitrii libertate, hoc est ab intellectu, et simul a voluntate."

is impossible for me to be deceived. But error appears when judgment appears, that is to say, as soon as the decisions of our will come to be added to the simple knowledge of things we get through our understanding. Still, was it not to be feared that confusion would be introduced between two powers of the soul that have very different natures? How do we attribute a role in judgment to the will, by itself blind? Would it perhaps be better to attribute all that is knowledge and judgment to the understanding and reserve to the will the election following upon the judgment? That is an objection in one of Pierre Gassendi's queries,[69] and it is what Henricus Regius in turn objected in the 1647 *Program*, when he specified that the faculty of judgment ought to be attributed to the understanding alone.[70] Descartes knew the doctrine. It was what he had been taught at La Flèche as belonging to St. Thomas. But he had weighty reasons to modify it as he did. According to him, beyond the perception that is necessary for there to be judgment, an affirmation or negation is still needed to give the matter furnished by the understanding. We know by experience that this affirmation or this negation is always in our power. We are free to withhold our assent and to deny it to what our understanding perceives. Therefore, the assent, that is to say, the act that constitutes judgment, ought to be referred not to the understanding's perception, but to the will's determination.[71]

With this stroke, Descartes gets the solution to the problem he has laid out. Error is only found in judgment. Judgment depends on our will, and our will is free. We are always free to not commit errors, if we use our will well. For that, it is enough to never grant our assent to false or even simply doubtful propositions of our understanding. It will suffice that we never make any judgment on what we do not perceive clearly and distinctly. That is always in our power. It depends on us alone to avoid haste and bias, and consequently, we cannot make God responsible for our errors under any

69 *Quintae Responsiones* In Meditationem IV, Dubitatio III, Instantia 1; VII, p. 404: "Vitandae confusionis gratia debere intellectum et voluntatem ita distingui, ut quidquid cognitionis et judicii est ad intellectum pertineat; quidquid appetitionis electionisque ad voluntatem."

70 "XVI. Cogitatio mentis est duplex: intellectus et voluntas. XVII. Intellectus est perceptio et judicium." VII, p. 345.

71 *Notae in Programma Quoddam*; VIII, p. 363: "Ergo enim cum viderim, praeter perceptionem, quae praerequiritur ut judicemus opus esse affirmatione vel negatione ad formam judicii constituendam, nobisque saepe esse liberum ut cohibeamus assentionem, etiamsi rem percipiamus: ipsum actum judicandi, qui non nisi in assensu, hoc est, in affirmatione vel negatione consistit, non retuli ad perceptionem intellectus, sed ad determinationem voluntatis."

pretext. The act that constitutes the form of error comes from bad use of our free choice. That is where we really find the privation from which this evil comes, and again this privation is only found in the act by which we commit error in the measure in which it proceeds from us, but not in the faculties God gave us nor in our operation itself, insofar as it depends on God's concurrence.[72]

We have resolved the problem in what concerns our faculties in themselves. They are what they must and can be. Our understanding is finite as befits a creature. Our will is infinite as befits an indivisible faculty that cannot be diminished without being destroyed. As the only possible origin of error, there remains bad use of faculties that are good considered in themselves. We are deceived when we affirm or deny what we do not conceive distinctly, whether we are entirely deceived by affirming a false proposition or whether falling into the truth by choice we commit the fault of deciding despite our understanding's ignorance. Whatever the kind of error we commit, no privation is found in it that is imputable to the cooperation God provides. Even if the acts we carry out are bad, they are entirely good and true in the measure in which they depend on God. The privation that constitutes the formal reason of error and sin is only privation in relation to us, who use our free choice badly; in relation to God it is simply negation. The evil in our acts comes from us but they contain nothing but good insofar as they depend on God's cooperation.[73]

Let us compare what St. Thomas teaches about sin with this doctrine of error that Descartes presents. The human will leads naturally toward good. On this point, there is no difficulty. There is never reason to deliberate in order to know what the end of our will is going to be. By the very fact that an end is imposed as the good to achieve, it is exempt from any deliberation. Insofar as it is discussed in the opposite direction and remains doubtful, it does not yet authentically play the role of end. Therefore, every end as such, presents itself as already determined,[74] and consequently the

72 *Meditations*, Fourth Meditation; VII, p. 60 [Heffernan, p. 162]: "Atque in hoc liberi arbitrii non recto usu privatio illa inest quae formam erroris constituit: privatio, inquam, inest in ipsa operatione, quatenus a me procedit, sed non in facultate quam a Deo accepi, nec etiam in operatione quatenus ab illo dependet."

73 *Meditations*, Fourth Meditation; VII, p. 60 [Heffernan, p. 164]: "Nec denique etiam queri debeo quod Deus mecum concurrat ad eliciendos illos actus voluntatis, sive illa judicia in quibus fallor: illi enim actus sunt omnino veri et boni quatenus a Deo dependent . . ."

74 St. Thomas, *Summa Theologiae*, part I[a] II[ae], question 14, article 2, reply to objection 1.

deliberation that preceded the choice can bear on the end itself, but only on the means to arrive at that end.[75] On the other hand, such deliberation is absolutely inevitable. Every time we are dealing with doubtful, uncertain matters, reason avoids making its judgment without prior examination. Our acts are particular, contingent, and, because of their very variability, uncertain in nature. An investigation by reason is necessary before every decision, and the name *consilium* or deliberation is given to its investigation.[76] This deliberation falls under the domain of reason. It belongs to reason to discuss by what means we can arrive at a certain end and to present the matter to the will upon which to exercise its choice. Nevertheless, the deliberation itself depends on the will in some measure. To deny that dependence, we would have to misunderstand the close relations that unite the will to the understanding. Let us consider these two powers, whose respective acts are ordered at the same time in relation to one another among themselves. The act of each of these powers could receive its denomination from one or the other indifferently. Deliberation is surely the work of reason, but it also bears the stamp of the will, which has a certain role in it. Will always furnishes the matter for deliberation, since humans deliberate on what they do or not dodo not want to do. Furthermore, the will provides the initial motive of deliberation. Someone deliberates on means, because he wills the end. Therefore, it is right to define deliberation as *a will that seeks to be enlightened*,[77] although from the first moment of our analysis, the will appears to us to be the determining element of the election.

Nevertheless, in its very essence, deliberation remains the paradigmatic work of the reason. The same must be said about judgment. Judgment, *judicium rationis* as St. Thomas often calls it, is the conclusion, or one of the conclusions,

75 St. Thomas, *Summa Theologiae*, part Iª II, question 14, article 2, body of article: "Unde cum consilium sit quaestio, de fine non sit consilium, sed solum de his quae sunt ad finem."

76 St. Thomas, *Summa Theologiae*, part Iª IIªᵉ, question 14, article 1, body of article: "In rebus autem dubiis et incertis ratio non profert judicum absque inquisitione praecedente, et ideo necessaria est inquisitio rationis ante judicium de eligendis. Et haec inquisitio consilium vocatur."

77 St. Thomas, *Summa Theologiae*, part Iª IIªᵉ, question 14, article 1, reply to objection 1 end: ". . . in consilio, quod est actus rationis, apparet aliquid voluntatis, sicut materia quia consilium est de his quae homo vult facere, et etiam sicut motivum: quia ex hoc quod homo vult finem movetur ad consilium de his quae sunt ad finem . . . Ita Damascenus dicit . . . quod *consilium est appetitus inquisitivus*, ut consilium aliquo modo pertinere ostendat et ad voluntatem, circa quam et ex qua fit inquisitio, et ad rationem inquirentem."

that closes deliberation. Therefore, it essentially falls within the realm of reason and precedes the will's election. In this way the conclusion of the syllogism that establishes what we ought to do (and that constitutes judgment) has a relationship of antecedent to consequent with the election by the will.[78]

But the conclusion of the deliberation is not yet complete with the judgment alone. The will's acceptance must be added to the judgment performed by reason.[79] This acceptance constitutes the consent or the election, and it is here that the will intervenes in the guise of free choice. The expression *free choice* designates nothing but a power of election that is based on the reason's deliberations, and this is why the election can be called a sort of judgment. Let us see what its nature is exactly. When the reason makes its judgment, the will can accept it by consent or by election. By consent (*consensus*),[80] the will adheres to one of the objects that are offered to it and consequently to one of the deliberation's possible conclusions. In truth this conclusion was present in the understanding, but a special act that fixes the will's choice is added to the simple knowledge that the understanding grasped of it.[81] It may happen that the deliberation leads us to observe that several means can lead us to our end. If the different means at hand all satisfy us equally, we give our consent to each of them, and in that case it is necessary that election come to be added to consent in order to finish the deliberation.

Given several means that suit us, election consists of choosing one of them rather than the others. In the case where a single means seems satisfactory to us, that is to say, where our understanding proposes a single

78 St. Thomas, *Summa Theologiae*, part I^{a} II^{ae}, question 13, article 1 reply to objection 2: ". . . conclusio etiam syllogismi qui fit in operabilibus, ad rationem pertinet; et dicitur *sententia* vel *judicium*; et ob hoc ipsa conclusio pertinere videtur ad electionem tanquam ad consequens."

79 St. Thomas, *Summa Theologiae*, part I, question 83, article 3, objection 2 and reply to objection 2 "Praeterea, liberum arbitrium dicitur quasi liberum judicium. Sed judicare est actus cognitivae virtutis. Ergo liberum arbitrium est potentia cognitiva. . . Ad secundum dicendum quod judicium est quasi conclusio et determinatio consilii. Determinatur autem consilium primo quidem per sententiam rationis et secundo per acceptationem appetitus . . . Et hoc modo ipsa electio dicitur quoddam judicium, a quo nominatur *liberum arbitrium*."

80 St. Thomas, who situates himself in the perspective of sin, more readily employs the expression *consent*. Descartes, who situates himself in the perspective of error, more readily employs that of *assent*, but he does not exclude *consent*, and St. Thomas considers the two terms synonyms. Cf. *Index Scolastico-Cartésien*, article "Assentment," pp. 28–31.

81 St. Thomas, *Summa Theologiae*, part I^{a} II^{ae}, question 15, article 1, body of article.

judgment to us, there is no real difference between consent and election. The only difference that can be introduced between them is a difference of reason. By consent, our choice is brought to bear on an action that suits us. By election, we prefer this action to others that do not suit us.[82] But the most frequent case is when several possible acts are offered to us, and then we must add (to the consent that we give to each of them) the election by which we chose one in preference to the others. Even in such a case, consent and election do not really differ by nature. Both consist of an act of the will, and election is ultimately only consent in the second degree. In certain of St. Thomas's disciples, this shadow of a distinction between consent and election, which the *Summa* retains, vanishes, and we find the two terms employed indifferently. In fact, they end by being considered synonyms.[83]

However, let us consider the act that brings its definitive conclusion to the deliberation, namely election, and let us seek to specify its nature. Every election involves a part that goes back to reason or understanding and a part that goes back to will. Election obviously depends on the cooperation of these two faculties.[84] Election is nothing but the complete act by which the will is determined, and that includes at the same time the reason's deliberations and the will's decision. Reason and understanding are required in order for there to be deliberation in the way we have set out, with judgment on what seems preferable to us. The will is required for there to be acceptance of the judgment rendered by the understanding. From this cooperation of understanding and will comes a single act that is called *election*.[85]

82 St. Thomas, *Summa Theologiae*, part I^{a} II^{ae}, question 15, article 3, response to third objection: ". . . electio addit supra consensum quamdam relationem respectu ejus cui aliquid praeelegitur; et ideo post consensum adhuc remanet electio. Potest enim contingere quod per consilium inveniantur plura ducentia ad finem . . . sed ex multis quae placent praeaccipimus unum eligendo. Sed si inveniatur unum solum quod placeat, non differunt re consensus et electio, sed ratione tantum."

83 Toletus, *Commentarium in tres libros De Anima*, Lyon: Veyrat, 1602, p. 636: "Praeterea in voluntate est actus quod dicitur consensus seu electio. Propositum enim bonum ab intellectu, ut diximus, potest voluntas velle et non velle: cum autem vult, illa acceptatio dicitur consensus et electio."

84 St. Thomas, *Summa Theologiae*, I^{a} II^{ae}, 13, 1, beginning body of article: ". . . in nomine electionis importatur aliquid pertinens ad rationem, sive ad intellectum, et aliquid pertinens ad voluntatem."

85 St. Thomas, *Summa Theologiae*, I, 83, 3, near beginning body of article: "Ad electionem autem concurrit aliquid ex parte cognitivae virtutis, et aliquid ex parte appetitivae . . . Ex parte quidem cognitiva requiritur consilium, per quod dijudicatur quid sit alteri praeferendum. Ex parte autem appetitivae requiritur quod appetendo acceptetur quod per consilium dijudicatur."

It remains to be determined whether the substance itself of the act that concludes the deliberation goes back to the understanding or to the will. To decide, it must be noted that the substance of an act depends simultaneously on its matter and its form. Among the acts of the soul, an act that goes back to a certain power in its matter still can get its form and receive its specification from a higher order power, because the lower is ordered always in relation to the higher. If, for example, someone carries out an act of strength for the love of God, this act is truly an act of strength in its matter, but it is an act of love in its form and, consequently, it is substantially an act of love. Let us apply this reasoning to the election, and we may observe that in its substance, it is an act of will. Evidently, in some manner, the understanding furnishes the matter of the act by proposing the judgments for acceptance by the will. But to give the form of election to this act, a movement of the soul toward the good it chooses is necessary. This movement belongs to the will. The election, therefore, must be referred ultimately to the will, not to the understanding.[86]

It is always in our power to carry out an act or not carry it out. Allowing for grace, to which we have to return, we are always the sole authors of our good actions as well as of our bad ones, and in no case can responsibility for sin go back to God. It could be objected that God gives his cooperation to each of our actions and that, consequently, he contributes to the act by which we commit sin. But the effect of every deficient second cause only depends on the first cause for the being and perfection that it contains, not for the imperfection and defect. For example, in someone who limps, his motor faculty causes whatever movement there is, but the lack of straightness observable is caused not be by the motor faculty, but by the leg's deformation. The same goes for evil and sin. God is the cause of every action insofar as it is an action. Sin is assuredly an action, but an action that involves a certain defect by its very nature. This defect is caused by the created second cause, free choice, insofar as it departs from the order of the first agent, that is to say from God. Therefore, God is the cause of the act of the sin, but he is not the cause of the sin, because he is not the cause of what is defective in the act.[87]

86 St. Thomas, *Summa Theologiae*, I^{a} II^{ae}, 13, 1, end of body of article: ". . . substantia actus materialiter se habet ad ordinem qui imponitur a superiori potentia; et ideo electio substantialiter non est actus rationis sed voluntatis; perficitur enim electio in motu quodam animae ad bonum quod eligitur. Unde manifestus actus est appetitivae potentiae."

87 St. Thomas, *Summa Theologiae*, I, 49, 2 reply to objection 2: "Dicendum quod effectus causae secundae deficientis reducitur in causam primam non deficientem

This whole line of argument, in Descartes and in St. Thomas, supposes that the fact of our freedom is admitted. It is important to establish that for the proof to be complete. This same freedom required for humans alone to be responsible for error and sin must present the occasion for a new reproach to be addressed to the Creator. Why has he created us free, since our freedom is a means for us to be deceived and to do evil? Why not have compelled our understanding to only consent to clear and distinct ideas, and, on the other hand, to consent to these ideas each time they present themselves? Descartes is ready to pose this objection and has the way to resolve it. At the very moment in which he composes the Fourth Meditation, a great furor breaks out around him about a doctrine according to which the power to sin is neither freedom nor even an element of freedom. According to the theologians who teach it and who appeal to both St. Thomas and St. Augustine, being free consists precisely in not sinning. If this doctrine is true, Descartes gets the solution to his problem. The reproach brought against God for having made us subject to error by giving us freedom falls by its own weight, when freedom resides in our not being deceived. It is to establish this thesis that Descartes introduces the critique of the freedom of indifference in the Fourth Meditation.

quantum ad id quod habet entitatis et perfectionis, non autem quantum ad id quod habet de defectu. Sicut quidquid est motus in claudicatione causatur a virtute motiva; sed quod est obliquitatis in ea non est ex virtute motiva sed ex curvitate cruris. Et similiter quidquid est entitatis et actionis in actione malo reducitur in Deum sicut in causam; sed quod est ibi defectus non causatur a Deo, sed ex causa secunda deficiente."

Chapter Three

Critique of the Freedom of Indifference

Its Sources

If there is a question about freedom in Scholasticism, it is posed less about the fact of freedom than about its nature. Are we free? This is a point of dogma that nobody dares to dispute. To deny freedom is to overturn all morality and all religion, to make useless all deliberations, commandments, prohibitions, and rewards as well as punishments.[1] Theologians sometimes add another argument to the traditional ones. It bases our freedom on the experience humans can have of it. Beyond any reasons, we experience a certain power to act or not act at our pleasure.[2] As it pleases us, we can remain standing or sit, go in one direction or another, consent or not to sin when the occasion presents itself, turn our mind toward the consideration of our faults to deplore them or to be distracted about them. Therefore, it would be pure nonsense to deny free choice. It would be as senseless to believe someone who denied free choice against their own experience as to believe one denying that a white paper placed in front of him is white. The two facts are equally evident.[3] Our natural lights furnish decisive reasons in favor of our will's free choice.

To say that we grasp our freedom in the experience of our will is to say that will and freedom are identical. Voluntary and free are just one and the same thing. There is a proportion between voluntary and intellectual faculties:[4] Understanding and will are to one another what will and free choice

1 St. Thomas, *Summa Theologiae*, part I, question 83, article 1, beginning of body of article. Also, St. Thomas, *De Malo*, 6, near beginning of body of article.

2 Eustachius a Sancto Paulo, *Summa Philosophiae*, I, part 2, p. 49.

3 Luis de Molina, S.J., *Corcordia Liberi Arbitrii cum Gratiae Donis: Divina Praescientia, Providentia, Praedestinatione*, Lisbon, Apud Antonium Riberium, 1588 (Antwerp: 1595; electronic resource, Alexandria, VA: Alexandria Street Press, 2007), 14, 13, 23, 1.

4 St. Thomas, *Summa Theologiae*, part I, question 64, article 2, especially paragraph beginning *Ad inquirendum*, and I, 80, 2.

are to each other. To understand consists in the simple perception of a thing. It is right, therefore, to say that principles are understood, since they are understood in themselves without any discussion. By contrast, reasoning properly consists in passing from the knowledge of one thing to the knowledge of another. So, we truly reason about conclusions, because we know them starting from principles. The same goes for what involves the will. The will in itself only includes the simple appetite for some object. Therefore, in this sense, we want an end, because an end is always desired for itself. By contrast, to choose freely is to desire a thing with a view to getting another. Properly speaking, we only choose means. There is a parallelism between understanding and reason, on the one hand, and will and the faculty of choosing freely, on the other. But to understand and to reason are only one single power of the soul. Reason is to intelligence what acquisition is to possession, and movement is to rest. Between those terms there is only a difference in perfection.[5] That amounts to saying that to will and to choose freely belong to the same faculty of the soul, and we must conclude that will and free choice are just one faculty.[6] Therefore, to declare an action human, voluntary, or free is to say the same thing: these three terms imply one another.[7] Of all the Scholastic arguments put forth in favor of free choice, Descartes only retains the appeal to our personal experience. To base himself on the consideration of moral laws and the legitimacy of sanctions would be an error in method, since none of these questions has yet been posed at the beginning of the Fourth Meditation. At that point we possess the knowledge of our soul and of God, but this knowledge suffices for us to be able to affirm our free choice because, if we examine our soul, we discover within it the freedom of our will as an authentic first notion, known of itself.[8] Even more, the other arguments that can be alleged become

5 St,. Thomas, *Summa Theologiae*, part I, question 79, article 8, middle of first paragraph, body of article: "Patet ergo quod ratiocinari comparatur ad intelligere sicut moveri ad quiescere, vel acquirere ad habere: quorum unum est perfecti, aliud autem imperfecti."

6 St. Thomas, *Summa Theologiae*, part I, question 83, article 4, near end of body of article: "Ejusdem potentiae est velle et eligere. Et propter hoc voluntas et liberum arbitrium non sunt duae potentiae, sed una."

7 Eustachius a Sancto Paulo, *Summa Philosophiae*, vol. I, part II, p. 37: "Intellectus dicitur principium humanarum actionum, non tantum qua est facultas, cujus actiones elicitae possunt esse humanae, hoc est voluntariae seu liberae . . ."

8 Letter to Mersenne, December 1640; III, p. 259: "You are right to say that we are as sure of our free choice as of any other first notion, because it is genuinely one of them."

useless by the sole fact of this one: freedom is one of those things that everyone must experience in himself and that are hardly demonstrated by reasoning. If someone should deny it, he must be left to himself until in his turn he has had the experience.[9] Since the freedom of our will appears to us every time we descend into ourselves to consider it, it follows that it is impossible to establish any difference between will and freedom. Voluntary and free are just one and the same thing,[10] and that is why Descartes constantly uses one term for the other in the course of the Fourth Meditation.[11] There is no difficulty about the fact of freedom, and, since Descartes finds the theologians in agreement, he has no perilous options to make. But his position is completely different concerning the nature of freedom. In what does free will consist? The theologians and the Scholastic philosophers had not been able to establish that definitively. The problem's whole difficulty came from its close connection to the controversies that had arisen on the question of grace and had become acrimonious even before the Jansenist polemic. What interested the theologians was not the psychological problem of the relations of understanding and will in the free act. If the solution to this problem had not entailed, or seemed to entail, serious consequences in relation to the dogma of grace, the controversy would have ended, perhaps not even arisen. But events transpired quite differently. What did the nature of grace have to be for our freedom to receive it without, thereby, being destroyed, and how must we understand the nature of our freedom, for it to be able to be submitted to grace without being annihilated? This was the thorny question that reignited St. Augustine's controversy against Pelagius and became a battlefield for theologians from different schools. Is the solution of the problem of human freedom that Descartes offers in the Fourth Meditation exempt from the intellectual currents that divided the theologians of his time? Or, on the contrary, was not that solution historically dependent on the notorious controversy *de auxiliis gratiae*?

9 *Quintae Responsiones*, VII, p. 377: "Talia enim sunt ut ipsa quilibet apud se debeat experiri potius quam rationibus persuaderi . . . Ne sis igitur libera, si non lubet [*scilicet*: o caro] ergo certe mea libertate gaudebo, cum et illam apud me experiar . . . Majoremque forte apud alios merebor fidem, quia id affirmo quod expertus sum, et quilibet apud se poterit experiri, quam tu, quae idem negas ob id tantum, quod forte non experta sis."

10 Third Set of Objections, Reply 12; VII, p. 191: ". . . nemo tamen, cum seipsum tantum respicit, non experitur unum et idem esse voluntarium et liberum."

11 *Meditations* (Meditation Four); VII, p. 57, lines 11–12 [Heffernan, p. 158]: "Sola est voluntas, sive arbitrii libertas . . ."

It is impossible to pick out a fact or a book in the history of the sixteenth century that, strictly speaking, constitutes the point of departure for this controversy. After St. Augustine's struggle with Pelagius, the question never fell into oblivion, and we can record its traces through the whole history of medieval philosophies. But the Protestant heresy unquestionably gives it new currency. It pointedly raises the question of the relationship between divine grace and human free will. By denying everything to free will in order to concede everything to the grace that predestines, this heresy pushed the Catholic doctors who fought it to exaggerate the part that corresponds to human freedom in the work of our salvation. The members of the Society of Jesus felt particularly compelled to defend free will. They constituted a company of soldiers who could be sent at a moment's notice to all the points where the faith was threatened. In Germany, the Jesuits fought the Protestants; in Belgium, they fought the followers of Baius, who also misinterpreted free choice and seemed to exaggerate its dependence on God's grace. One can understand that apologetic necessity called forth a certain number of doctors from the Jesuit ranks, concerned with establishing harmony between freedom and divine grace by particularly insisting on the role that corresponds to freedom in the work of salvation. In order to resolve this difficulty, the Jesuit theologians chose from among different possible solutions the one usually designated by the name of *Middle Science* (*Scientia Media*) that allots the greatest possible role to our freedom. It seems that a clear form of this doctrine is found for the first time in the Portuguese Jesuit Pedro Fonseca, though without the name that would make it famous. From his teaching it passes into Bellarmine and Lessius, who taught at Louvain; into Gregory de Valencia, who taught at Ingolstadt; into Prudencio de Montemayor, who taught at Salamanca, where the Dominican Bañez's violent opposition was to arise; and lastly, into Molina, who taught at Coimbra, and was to give the doctrine its finished version along with the name under which it would be attacked and defended. What made Molina's doctrine particularly interesting is that its author had become clearly aware of the consequences that his theology of grace entailed in relation to human freedom. Simultaneous to the spread of Middle Science through the active propaganda of the Jesuits, the conception that the very essence of our freedom resides in indifference to opposite acts filtered into the same minds. Theological teaching served as the vehicle for more properly philosophical speculation from which it found its rational basis and support. At the core of the controversies conducted on apparently religious grounds, it is easy to perceive the underlying philosophies, certain theses independent of any revelation, to which the opposing sides constantly appeal. From a metaphysical point of view, this whole theological war is reduced to the conflict of two incompatible notions of freedom. For some, who take the name of Thomists, freedom is defined by the absence of con straint. For others, who invoke Molina, besides the absence of constraint, freedom requires the absence of determination. This is why the controversy continues and has no internal reason to end. Descartes knew the second of these doctrines first. Therefore, let us see what notion of freedom was implied by Molina's theory.[12]

According to this theologian, freedom is defined by its relation to necessary determination. A free agent is one who, when all conditions required for his action are given, can act or not, or carry out one of two contrary actions, with the reservation the he could carry out the other.[13] The wills of the blessed who see God in heaven and cannot break away from him, are not free wills. Likewise, in this life, acts that spring up suddenly without our will having the time to stop them are not free. Therefore, the will is only free in the case where it would be possible for it not to carry out the act that it carries out. From that stems a two-sided character of freedom. The possibility in which the will is situated to act or not to act is called freedom with regard to the exercise of the act (*libertas quoad exercitium actus*). If the will can, in addition, make its choice bear indifferently upon a certain act or the contrary one, freedom with regard to the specification of the act then makes its appearance,[14] and it is full and perfect freedom.

On account of this notion of freedom, Molina combats with all his might against the doctrine that grace is efficacious in itself. To be free, we might say, is to have the possibility of an indifferent will.[15] If the will cannot resolve itself for a good act without the help of efficacious grace, and if with this help it cannot fail to decide, our free will is destroyed. When God's decrees are given, our will no longer possesses the indifference to determine itself or not, and to determine itself for this act rather than for that other one, without which it cannot

12 Molina, *Concordia*.

13 Molina, *Concordia*, 14, 13, 2: "Illud agens *liberum* dicitur, quod positis omnibus requisitis ad agendum, potest agere et non agere, aut ita agere unum ut contrarium etiam agere possit."

14 Molina, *Concordia*, 14, 13, 2: "Quod si simul possit elicere indifferentur vel contrarium actum, cernitur etiam libertas quoad speciem actus, ut vocant, quae plenae et perfectae libertatis rationem habet."

15 Molina, *Concordia*, 23, 4–5, 1, 7: "Potentiam quippe liberam esse non esse aliud quam posse indifferentur elicere hic et nunc, et non elicere actum . . ."

have genuine freedom.[16] Therefore, we must give up this doctrine that makes do with a will unable to choose its own decisions. Every time that the will can choose and does not, we affirm that it is free in its refusal to choose. This not willing is a very real act that can cause sins of omission. Likewise, we consider that the act of volition is free each time the will chooses when it could refrain from doing so, not by reason of an inadmissible intrinsic quality of the will itself, but because it could have refrained from determining itself to the act it has chosen. This indifference is the necessary condition for the will to be capable of virtue and vice, of merit and demerit, of praise or blame, of reward or punishment. From this standpoint, we can easily differentiate what corresponds to grace in the supernatural act and what corresponds to our will. Considered in itself, grace acts necessarily by its nature and not freely. Therefore, all our acts are supernatural insofar as they are produced by grace, but they cannot get their character of being free from it. Inversely, these same acts are free insofar as they are produced by a will that could have refused to produce them, but they do not get their supernatural character from the will. Therefore, in the free act, what is supernatural comes from God, and what is free comes from us. To say that our freedom depends on the gift of grace is to destroy it.[17]

If the very essence of freedom consists in the act's indifference, it follows that freedom is only found in the will prior to our determination and in the precise moment in which it is determined. Then it is indifferent to every determination and could naturally determine itself otherwise than it does. But as soon as we consider it at any instant already determined to one of two opposites, it implies a contradiction that it should not be at the same instant determined, and consequently it is no longer free in regard to this same determination. It must be said with Aristotle and Boethius: "That which is, while it is, cannot not be."[18] So we cease to be free at the same time as to be indifferent.

16 Molina, *Concordia*, 14, 13, 53, 4: "Quibus datis nunquam in voluntate ipsa relinquitur facultas ad se indifferenter determinandum aut non determinandum, vel ad se determinandum in unam aut alteram partem, quod tamen ad veram libertatis rationem omnino est necessarium."

17 Molina, *Concordia*, 23, 4–5, 1, 7.

18 Molina, *Concordia*, 14, 13, 53, 4: "Quia potius, idcirco libere operatur [*scilicet*: voluntas] libereve se determinat ad operandum, quia prius natura est indifferens, ut ita se determinet aut non determinet; atque adeo quando se determinat, potest non se determinare; postquam vero in aliquo instanti intelligitur jam ad unum determinata, implicat contradictionem e non determinasse in eodem instanti, ac proinde jam non est libera ad non ita se determinandum."

There is no doubt that Descartes knew this doctrine of freedom in his youth and that even he accepted it for some time. Educated in a Jesuit school at the very moment when the controversy was at its most acrimonious, he was a student of philosophy just after the victory achieved by his teachers.[19] At La Flèche, Descartes certainly learned the doctrine of Middle Science and the conception of human freedom it implies. The question was too dear to the members of the Society of Jesus for its philosophy teachers not to have tried to transmit some Molinism in their teaching. The *Conimbricenses* authors did not hesitate in this matter. Molinism had its place, and a prominent place, in the course in Natural Philosophy in the context of the relation that humans, considered as second causes, maintain with God, considered as first cause. St. Thomas's well known opinion on physical premotion was presented for review and found support from some authorities; it was explained by the Thomist comparison between God, who applies our will to its act, and the logger, who applies his ax to the tree. The *Conimbricenses* authors condemn this doctrine, as was to be expected, and reject it for the same reasons advanced by Molina, to whom the commentators ultimately remit for more extensive explanations.[20] Moreover, even if Descartes did not learn this doctrine in the philosophy program, he did so beyond question from the religious instruction and rudiments of theology that he received. The topic was a classic and inevitable, particularly in a period when the struggle against the Protestant heresy was heated and harsh. Descartes had certainly witnessed this question resolved, and resolved in a Molinist sense: How are divine foreknowledge and human freedom harmonized, and what is predestination for the just? The influence this teaching had on Descartes' thought does not seem to have been deep, since he was to abandon the doctrine in the Fourth Meditation. Furthermore, another influence was going to weigh on him that would quickly erase the earlier one: that of the Oratory,

19 In August 1607, Pope Paul V declared the Molinist doctrine to be free of suspicion. The Jesuits received the decree with rejoicing, and it was a motive for celebration, principally in Spain. Jesuit schools had three days of vacation. Festivities were held in which fireworks alternated with plays and masses of thanksgiving. They went so far as to erect triumphal arches that bore the legend *Molina victor* in gold letters. Cf. Théodore de Règnon, S. J., *Banes et Molina, histoire, doctrines, critique métaphysique*, Paris: H. Oudin, 1883 chapter 1.

20 Conimbricenses, *Physica*, 2, 13, 1 and 2: ". . . Quia si res creatae nihil omnino absque praevia illa excitatione moliri queunt, sequitur excitari invitarique a Deo voluntatem, etiam ad actus vitiosos, quod nemo dicat. Plura ad hanc opinionem refelledam habes apud Ludovicum Molinam, in sua *Concordia* questione 14, articulo 13, disputatione 26."

through the involvement of Cardinal de Bérulle and the first priests of his new order.

In 1630, the Oratory entered the conflict. Gibieuf's *De Libertate* appeared, and at that moment the new congregation openly placed itself among the adversaries of Molinism. In this work Gibieuf intended to provide the thought of Cardinal de Bérulle, the spiritual director Descartes had chosen. The Cardinal especially blamed the defenders of Middle Science for having invented this doctrine to flatter human reason, to exalt nature and make concessions to it.[21] Since de Bérulle could approve neither the mentality nor the doctrine that flowed from it, he had charged Gibieuf with speaking in his name[22] and giving systematic form to the numerous indications scattered throughout his works.[23]

"Jesus Christ," said de Bérulle, "gave everything for grace. St. Augustine gave everything to grace."[24] With their example, de Bérulle wanted to grant only minimal concessions to human nature. He went back to Plotinus's theory of the double movement to make us understand in what the movement of grace attracting us to God consists. At the moment of creation, the hand of God forms us as to our body, but he brings us forth from his innermost spirit as to our soul. At the same time that God makes us come forth from himself, "he impresses upon us an instrument of returning toward him." Thereby, he creates us daily, in nature and grace, since the movement

21 Gibieuf, *De Libertate*, dedication.

22 In his dedication, Gibieuf affirms: "Primum enim id jussit non semel Parens optimus Cardinalis Berullius." Furthermore, de Bérulle died October 2, 1629, and Gibieuf sent his manuscript to Rome before November 9 that same year." Cf. Louis Batterel, *Mémoires domestiques pour servir à l'histoire de l'Oratoire: les pères de l'Oratoire recomendables par la piété ou par les lettres*, I, p. 242. Consequently, the book was written while de Bérulle was alive and, without any doubt, with his assent. [Translator: Batterel, 1680–1752, secretary of the Congregation of the Oratory, seems not to have actually published this six- volume work, which was apparently edited and published for the first time by Augustin Marie Pierre Ingold, starting in 1902.]

23 Principally de Bérulle, *Discours de l'état et des grandeurs de Jésus*, which, among many others, bears the approval of Jansen, doctor and ordinary professor of the University of Louvain. [Translator: There are actually two Cornelius Jansen or Jansenius, both professors of theology at Louvain and both ended their lives as bishops. The first 1510–1576, an exegete, was bishop of Ghent; the second, 1585 (or 1586)–1638 was bishop of Ypres, and more importantly the founder of Jansenism. Gilson obviously refers to the latter of the two.]

24 Guillaume Gibieuf, *Mémoire pour servir à une nouvelle édition des ouevres de notre B. Père*, Archives Nationales, manuscript 223.

of return that God impresses on us is nothing other than grace in itself. To abandon oneself to grace, therefore, is not a violent movement for the creature; it is to follow a natural moment and "consent to its origin."[25]

By following the movement that puts us back into God's hands we become free. It is by servitude to God that we reach true freedom. The creature is subject to threefold servitude. Derived from and dependent on God, it must perpetually look upon him as its sovereign. Corrupted by original sin and made the child of Adam, it becomes the slave of sin and the devil. It can only escape this second servitude by the third, that of grace. It corresponds to us to submit ourselves to it by the free choice of our will. According to how we will, we make ourselves slaves either of the devil or of Jesus Christ, "and our duty is to use all the power we have to bind ourselves to him, since the best and holiest use of our freedom is to put it into his hands, taking account that the more we become his the more we become free."[26]

At the same time that this state of servitude in relation to grace makes us free, in some manner it makes us share in God's own nature, he who tends to draw everything to himself and to his unity.[27] By grace, we rise above human nature up to divine nature.[28] We must recognize two emanations in Jesus, one of which derives from the other. By the first, Jesus emanates from his Father. By the second, grace emanates from Jesus, and the nature of the first emanation can make us know what the second is. Just as the Son and the Spirit live in the bosom of the Father, and they only subsist in their relationship with him who is their principle and their origin, so all "created sanctity," that is to say all humans insofar as they receive grace, have life and subsistence in Jesus Christ as their principle. Grace is "a perfect imitation, a living portrait, and a formal participation in Divinity."[29] That is why we ought to place ourselves in this happy state of servitude in regard to God, which alone will assure our salvation. De Bérulle, moreover, is quite ready to use himself as an example for us, and frequently he places himself in the hands of God through pious gestures.[30] The exaltation he brings to this giving and abandonment of self does not know Molinism's prudent restrictions. There is no concern to retain some independence for human freedom. On

25 de Bérulle, *Discours*, column 1135.
26 de Bérulle, *Discours*, column 1148.
27 de Bérulle, *Discours*, column 156.
28 de Bérulle, *Discours*, columns 165, 166. Cf. columns 172, 173, 1136.
29 de Bérulle, *Discours*, column 166.
30 Cf. de Bérulle, *Discours*, columns 168, 169.

the contrary, it is essential no longer to live and act, except in God, to be directed and possessed by him entirely.

Still, de Bérulle did not directly take a position against Molina. He preferred the less brilliant but more efficacious endeavor of spiritual direction to public controversies. Gibieuf had to try to gain victory for the position after a hard fight. De Bérulle busied himself primarily with making St. Augustine's doctrine penetrate into the hearts of his disciples. He found the opportunity for it in the community meetings, where he gave the Oratory the general directives that were supposed to guide its spirit according to his desires. He then followed more private paths and, in individual conversation or direction, he fought against Molina's doctrine with all his strength.[31] Gibieuf was better situated than anyone else to talk about it. He had begun by admitting Middle Science himself, and if we believe one of his biographers, he had fallen "into exaggerated Molinism."[32] De Bérulle contented himself with praying for him and gently joking: "You seem to me to be a poor Christian. "You are not grateful enough to Jesus Christ. You surely have a greater obligation to him than you believe." One day Gibieuf suddenly felt "as if the scales fell from his eyes" and since then no longer understood how he could have held his former opinions.[33]

This new convert did not hide his zeal in spreading his new convictions. Moreover, Gibieuf was not a man of half-convictions or half-measures. He wanted to publish *De Libertate* so that all would share in his superior's insights on the question of grace, deeming it preferable to expound the thought of such a great man as best he could rather than to keep impotent silence.[34] After vain efforts to obtain approval from Rome, which would have been considered almost an official condemnation of Molinism,[35]

31 Gibieuf, *De Libertate*, dedication.

32 Gibieuf, *De Libertate*, I, 36, 4. Cf. *Biographies de différents pères de la Congregation*, Archives nationales, manuscript 220.

33 Cloyseault, *Vie de plusiers pères*, I, pp. 141–143.

34 Perhaps he also felt some pleasure in taking a stand against the Jesuits, who had previously treated him harshly. Cf. de Bérulle, *Lettre à Richelieu contre les Jésuites*, Migne, column 1596.

35 In October 1629 Gibieuf sent his book to his friend Fr. Bertin to obtain the approval of the Master of the Sacred Household. Paul V's decree confirmed by Urban VIII declaring the controversy closed was cited against the request. The Pope's nephew Cardinal Barberini made the same objection, and although Gibieuf claimed that the issue in his book was primarily about freedom, the approval was denied. See Batterol, *Mémoires domestiques*, I, p. 242. The book was merely presented to the Pope on July 21, 1630.

the book appeared, offering a doctrine on the burning issues of freedom, grace, and predestination that could hardly fail to appear bold and odd.

From the outset, the new conception of freedom was put under the patronage of St. Augustine. The whole book was intended to be just a commentary on this fundamental proposition of the revered Doctor: the more we are enslaved to grace, the freer we are, and if not sinning is a great freedom, not being able to sin constitutes the highest freedom.[36] To establish this theme Gibieuf wanted to get to the very heart of the question and refute the false notion Molina had formed about freedom.

Gibieuf's two supporters, whose names significantly appeared at the beginning of such a work, interpreted the Oratorian's thought in this way. The book appeared to them, first of all, to be a radical condemnation of freedom of indifference. One of the two, Cornelius Jansen, congratulated Gibieuf for having gone back to the authentic notion of free choice that the ancient Fathers had held and for having soundly refuted the defenders of indifferentism.[37] The other, Jean du Verger de Hauranne, abbot of Cyran, expanded upon Gibieuf's Platonic vein, praising him for having eliminated

36 Gibieuf, *De Libertate*, dedication. We are eager to point out the very great interest of Gibieuf's book from the point of view of the origins of Jansenism. We will indicate an approach by giving the information we have been able to gather regarding the relations of de Bérulle and Gibieuf with Jansen and Saint-Cyran. The Cardinal's Oratorian historians, both ancient and modern, speak very cautiously about this. The Oratory is not proud of these memories.

See however, Houssaye, *Le cardinal de Bérulle et le cardinal de Richelieu*, conclusion, which is interesting but partial. Cf. on this point some indications in René Rapin, S.J., *Mémoires du P. René Rapin de la Compagnie de Jésus sur l'église, la societé et la cour*, edited from the autograph manuscript by Léon Aubineau, Paris: Gaume Frères et J Dupey, 1865 (reprinted Farnborough: Gregg, 1972), I, pp. 102–103 and note 1, pp. 156–157. See also Charles-Augustin Sainte-Beuve, *Port-Royal*, Paris: Rendeuel, 1840–1859, vol. I, book I, chapter 11, pp. 299, 318–319.

Except for the contemporary polemicists nobody seems to have suspected Gibieuf's role. We have to concentrate especially on the problem of freedom, but chapter 22 of book I offers several more interesting points of approximation to those who would like to establish a doctrinal comparison with *Augustinus* on predestination. Wilhelm Kahl, *Die Lehre*, perceived *De Libertate*'s importance in relation to Descartes, but knew only its title.

37 Approbatio Cornelii Janssenii . . . professoris Lovaniensis, in Gibieuf, *De Libertate*: "Veram arbitrii Libertatem antiquis Scriptoribus notam, non esse sitam in illa Philosophica indifferentia agendi, quae vulgo praedicatur, multis praeclaris et solidis rationibus hic liber astruit et adversae opinionis defensores confutat."

the notion of freedom of indifference, a purely Scholastic notion rather than a Platonic and therefore divine one. [38]

In these approbations, we recognize the influence of Michael Baius and of his condemned doctrine, in which the criticism of indifferentism was a necessary part. The future founders of Jansenism already sought to shield their cause with the name of the ancient Fathers and of St. Augustine.[39]

An oddity that lets us anticipate what the whole doctrine of the Oratorian will be is that Gibieuf defines freedom as de Bérulle had defined grace.[40] We already know how Gibieuf conceives divine freedom. God's freedom is only the superabundance of his essence, the greatness of his being; in a word, it is his infinity. To be supremely free is to be supremely infinite. There is no freedom without infinity, and someone is truly free who not only possesses all things but even *is* all things.[41] At the same time, we see that what is perfectly free is supremely indifferent,. Infinite freedom necessarily entails absolute indifference, and this is the case of God. Since things are not in the relation of principles, ends, or means to God but of mere effects that he produces by completely gratuitous love, it follows that God is indifferent to all things. Humans, on the contrary, come out of a principle, since God created them. They tend to an end, since God is the end of all nature. Therefore, they are under the jurisdiction of a master to whose direction they must bend entirely and in all their acts. From there it follows that humans are bound to act in conformity to the rule that is imposed on them and to always submit their will to an end. Therefore, it is the very essence of divine freedom to be indifferent and the very essence of human freedom that each act be subordinate to an end.[42] Let us go more deeply into the reason for this distinction.

38 "Indifferentiam quam non Platonica, id est divina, sed Peripatetica disceptatio in puram Libertatem jam pridem induxerat, hic auctor ita eliminat, ut mirum sit eam aliquot retro saeculis, adolescentiori Scholae usque adeo placuisse." Signed: Johannes Vergerius Auranus, abbas Sancti Cigirani, in Gibieuf, *De Libertate*. [Translator: Hauranne was an abbot in the sense that he held the Abby of St. Cyran in *commendatio*.]

39 Gibieuf had met Saint-Cyran and Jansen in Paris, where they studied together at the Sorbonne in 1605. Cf. Sainte-Beuve, *Port-Royal*, I, p. 293.

40 According to Gibieuf, *De Libertate*, I, 1, 1, freedom is an innate idea.

41 Gibieuf, *De Libertate*, I, 34, 2.

42 Gibieuf, *De Libertate*, I, 12, 3: "Quia enim Deus nec finem habet nec principium ac nullum proinde superiorem, cujus directioni subdatur, ideo cum agit, ut a principio nullo dependet, ita nec ad finem tendit, unde oritur ut ejus indifferentia ad agendum et non agendum, creandum, etc., sit indifferentia absoluta . . . At contra

If we ask the philosophers what human freedom consists in, they will all answer with one voice that it consists in the power to choose between two contradictory opposites or to carry out either of two actions.[43] If, on the other hand, we question the doctors of the Church, we will observe that they express themselves quite differently. Philosophers can only talk about the freedom they know, and that is why they speak of freedom of indifference. The early Fathers and the Doctors, by contrast, speak to us of a freedom that Christ has brought us and that the apostle Paul, as faithful interpreter of Christ's doctrine, preaches to us. Freedom, they tell us, consists in our state when we submit ourselves to the power of God and we are enslaved neither to sin nor to creatures; when we do not belong to the devil or the world or to ourselves, but to God alone. Hearing these two very different explanations, we might initially believe that there are two freedoms. However, that is not at all the case, because they are only two parts of one and the same freedom. The error committed about this issue comes from the essence of human freedom being denatured by attributing an absolute indifference to it that only belongs to God. It is not that there is no indifference in human freedom. There is, and the pagan philosophers are right to find it there, but the gospel comes precisely to teach us that this indifference is evil, since it is the sign of a will that does not fix itself definitively and totally to the law of its creator. In other words, indifference of the will is a supreme perfection in God, but in humans, indifference of the will that refuses to submit to the divine rule, far from constituting authentic freedom, is the sure sign of its depravity. If indifference is found in the will, it is only because we are creatures and imperfect beings. It only constitutes a deficiency in it and measures the distance that separates us from God to whose rule we must adhere steadfastly.[44] Indifference is found in our freedom, but it does not constitute it.[45]

quia homo principium et finem habet ac superiorem cujus regimini universaliter et in omnibus suis actibus subditur, ideo cum agit dependenter a regula agere tenetur, et ad finem tendere." Cf. *De Libertate*, I, 6, 11.

43 Gibieuf, *De Libertate*, I, 35, 1.

44 Gibieuf, *De Libertate*, I, 1, 1: "Adeo ut indifferenter se habere ad agendum et non agendum posthabito ordine finis, qui regula est appetitionum nostrarum, non sit vera libertas sed spuria et verus libertatis defectus."

45 Gibieuf, *De Libertate*, I, 30, 10: "Et quamquam indifferentia ad varios actus in causa secunda libera reperiatur, non tamen tanquam quid quod ad ejus libertatem pertineat, sed tanquam conditio creaturae. Indifferentia illa si proprie loquimur in libertate nostra reperitur, non ad eam pertinet."

To make the essence of our freedom consist in absolute indifference, God would have to be included among the things towards which the human will is indifferent in its natural state. Being separated and independent from God is not the rational creature's natural state. It is the state in which we are maintained by this unfortunate indifference that confers on us the power of sinning and abandoning God. The movement of our real freedom is totally different. It leads us directly to God and, instead of being the indifference about which we have been told, it is the sure movement of a soul that submits itself to God and gives itself to him. It becomes God, and in some way shares in his infinity.[46]

When we are thus transformed in God, we become free like him. Nothing dominates us. We raise rise above all the weaknesses of creatures. We live submitted to our creator alone. To be submitted to him who is our supreme and only genuine Good is to be submitted to the domination of none other than ourselves. It is to be great; it is to be invincible. It is to rise above everything.[47] If we wanted to define human freedom by its essence, we would say: to be free is to participate in the infinite. If we wanted to define human freedom in its cause, we would say: to be free is to serve God.[48]

It is easy to understand now why indifference cannot be considered the very essence of freedom. If our unfortunate power of sinning could be extirpated, nothing that constitutes freedom would be taken from us. To the contrary, freedom would be purified of its defect and blemish.[49] This is what divine grace works in us, at least in a certain degree. In the very measure in which God irrevocably determines us toward the good by his grace, he increases and confirms our freedom rather than diminishing it.[50] We should not pay attention here to the objections of those who believe freedom consists in indifference. They say that if our ultimate goal prescribed and defined all acts to the least circumstances, so that no room was left to indifference, no room would be left to freedom either. But this is contradictory reasoning. To imagine that the suppression of our indifference necessarily entails the suppression of our freedom is to misunderstand the nature of the choice by which the exercise of free will is manifested. If it is true that the determination of the will by its end is equivalent to the suppression of freedom, it immediately follows that voluntary choice, the election that

46 Gibieuf, *De Libertate*, I, 34, 2.
47 Gibieuf, *De Libertate*, I, 34, 7.
48 Gibieuf, *De Libertate*, I, 34, 1.
49 Gibieuf, *De Libertate*, I, 31, 10.
50 Gibieuf, *De Libertate*, I, 28, 5.

is the proper act of free choice, is not a free act. The consequence is rigorous because every election is determined by an end. Therefore, if the will's determination by its end, that is to say the suppression of our indifference, entails the suppression of our freedom, it must be acknowledged that the will's choice itself is not free and that our freedom itself is not free. That is an astonishing consequence from a principle that leads to consider as unfree the natural act of our freedom, unless we regard the consequence as laughable.[51]

This is not the only difficulty that the defenders of freedom of indifference come up against. If, as they claim, freedom consists in the indifference in which we can be in regard to our actions, how do they explain that we are still free at the moment itself when we act? No doubt they take reference in subtle distinctions. Before we are determined, say these theologians, we are indifferent and consequently free. Immediately upon being determined, we are freer because we are no longer indifferent. But this is a sophism. A choice must be made to get out of the dilemma: at the moment when I act, am I free or have I been free? If I *have* been free, then there is only freedom in regards to acts that have not yet occurred. If I am free, then freedom consists in something other than absolute indifference in regard to actions.[52]

So, Gibieuf and Molina give profoundly different solutions to the same problem. For both theologians the whole issue is to establish harmony between human freedom, on the one hand, and divine foreknowledge and cooperation, on the other. But while Molina shows himself primarily concerned with making the case for humans, Gibieuf is primarily concerned with making the case for God. Molina starts from a notion that situates human freedom in indifference to the acts and to the choice of acts. That is what *Concordia* is intended to maintain, even under the impact of grace and of God's predestination. The problem is to satisfy the demands of theology while safeguarding the will's indifference. Regarding grace, the solution

51 Gibieuf, *De Libertate*, I, 1, 3: "Neque hic audiendi qui causantur libertatem hujusmodi esse ut indifferentia exposcat; et si omnia a fine ultimo praescribantur ac definiantur usque ad minimas circumstantias, ut nihil indifferentiae superit, sic neque libertatis. Si enim res ita habeant ut determinatio quae est a fine libertatem perimat, in primis electio quae est immediatum ac proprium exercitium liberi arbitrii, electio inquam qua electio, libertatis expers erit; quia ut superius ostendimus, nulla electio nisi prout a fine determinatur. Quis autem non aut obstupescat aut rideat, ipsum proprium libertatis exercitium, libertate privatum esse."

52 Gibieuf, *De Libertate*, I, 1, 6: "Confirmatur iterum hoc dilemmate: dum enim ago, vel liber sum, vel fui ante; si hoc ergo libertas est respectu actuum futurorum tantummodo; si illud quaerenda igitur alia libertas quam quae in indifferentia absoluta ad agendum." Cf. Gibieuf, *De Libertate*, I, 24, 3.

forces itself on Molina. For grace to leave us free, it must leave us indifferent. Therefore, its efficacy depends not on a divine decree, but on the free consent of our will. Is this consent itself foreseeable, and can God know it from all eternity? — Without doubt. — But the consent only depends on me, and I am free. — God can infallibly foresee a free act. God possesses certain knowledge of an uncertain event. — That is incomprehensible; but then the infinite penetration of divine knowledge is incomprehensible.

In Gibieuf's view, the mystery subsists, but it is displaced. God gives us grace, Gibieuf thinks, and God foresees our acts. How can he? If God gives us grace, the reason is simple: without it we can do nothing. — But are we free? — Yes. Therefore this grace itself is what constitutes our freedom. Likewise, if God foresees our acts, then God, without whom we can do nothing, has decreed that we will accomplish them. — But don't these acts have to be free? — They are free. — But that is incomprehensible. — Indeed, divine omnipotence cannot be understood.

Molina and Gibieuf put us in the position of having to choose between two mysteries. The first asks that we admit that God foresees the undetermined. The other asks that we admit that the being infallibly determined by God remains free. On the one hand, mystery of power; on the other hand, mystery of knowledge; mystery for mystery, it seems that the choice would have no consequences. That is not the case, however. The first of these mysteries concedes a great deal to humans. The second gives everything to God. If God foresees our free acts, divine foreknowledge is subordinated to the different decisions of our will. God observes our actions. He does not determine them. If, by contrast, God foresees our acts, because he has decreed them, our acts do not depend on us, either in the choice we make about them or in carrying them out. The freedom that they still very much want to grant us is no longer that indifference that the divine power respected. It is only the acknowledgement of the absolute domination of God over the creature. We go where it pleases God to lead us. We freely follow him where his irresistible will has decreed we should be drawn, and we can only tell him:

> Ipse quidem studui bene de pietate mereri,
> Sed quidquid potui, gratia, Christe, tua est.
> Quid sum? Nil. Quis sum? Nullus. Sed gratia Christi
> Quod sum, quod vivo, quodque laboro facit.[53]

53 "Returning to St. Augustine," one of his biographers says, "Gibieuf composed these verses that were a kind of motto." *Biographies de différents pères de la Congrégation.*

Which position was Descartes going to take in this conflict of greatly divergent and even radically opposing theological opinions? By the time that he was composing the *Meditations*, he had read *De Libertate* in 1631, and we know he was thoroughly persuaded,[54] to the point that it won him to the Thomist doctrine of freedom. Baillet adverts to this in terms that initially seem obscure, but about whose meaning no theologian could be misled: "It will suffice," Baillet says, "to observe that as regards indifference and freedom, he professes to be in perfect agreement with St. Thomas, whose explanation resembles his not a little."[55] Let us translate that sentence into modern language. In that period, agreeing on freedom with St. Thomas was to be a Thomist. To be a Thomist was to reject Molina. If Baillet's testimony is correct, Descartes must have opposed Molinist indifferentism and joined the Thomist camp with Bañez, de Lemos, Álvarez, and the first priests of the Oratory. Moreover, we find an energetic critique of indifference in the Fourth Meditation.

Still, the first definition of freedom seems to favor Molinist indifference. According to Descartes, it merges freedom of contradiction (*quoad exercitium actus*) and of contrariety (*quoad speciem actus*). It is power *ad utrumlibet.* Being free is to do something or not do it according to one's pleasure, that is to say, affirm or deny, pursue or flee from the same object.[56] But Descartes immediately completes his definition, and going beyond the mere standpoint of indifference, he situates our freedom in the fact that we come to affirm or deny, pursue or flee what our understanding proposes to us, without our feeling determined by any external constraint to do it.[57] Therefore, he abandons the requirement of the absence of determination for our freedom and is satisfied by the simple absence of constraint. With this feature, we can already affirm that he abandons Molina's doctrine, and the texts that follow leave no room for doubt. For us to be free, it is not necessary for our will to be able to turn indifferently to either one of the two parts. To the contrary, the more we feel drawn toward one of them, whether by the evident knowledge that we have of the true or good that is found there, or because God has disposed our inner thought to will it, the more we choose

54 See the discussion above in Part II, chapter 1.

55 Baillet, *Vie*, II, p. 516.

56 *Meditations* (Meditation Four); VII, p. 57 lines, 21–23.

57 *Meditations* (Meditation Four); VII, p. 57, lines 23–27 [Heffernan, p. 158]: ". . . vel potius in eo tantum quod ad id quod nobis ab intellectu proponitur affirmandum vel negandum, sive prosequendum vel fugiendum, ita feramur, ut a nulla vi externa nos ad id determinari sentiamus."

it freely. Neither divine grace nor natural knowledge ever diminishes our freedom; rather, they very much increase and strengthen it, precisely by the fact that our indifference is diminished.[58]

We recognize the doctrine Descartes upholds here. Freedom does not reside in the power of choosing between two acts or in the power of acting or not acting indifferently, but in the natural or supernatural movement by which freedom chooses one of the acts and carries it out in preference to the other. Therefore, there are degrees in our freedom, and freedom grows in the measure that the action of the understanding upon the will becomes more intense, since this action can emerge either from the natural light that reveals the good and the truth to us, or from divine grace that sweeps us along. Nothing is lacking in Descartes' Thomism. By saying that we choose an act all the more freely when divine grace more powerfully sweeps us along to carry it out, one opposes Molina's doctrine with absolute clarity. By extending to the understanding's natural action what Thomist theologians said about the supernatural action of grace, Descartes simply gives the right of citizenship in philosophy to this doctrine, which previously had been essentially theological: everything that diminishes our indifference increases our freedom.

This is not to deny that the indifference of the will plays a role and has a place in freedom. In Descartes' view, the will certainly manifests a kind of freedom when it is indifferent to several acts, but it is a very imperfect freedom, the lowest grade, in a sense. This indifference that we feel when we are not pulled to one side rather than to another by the weight of some reason, is proof of lack of knowledge rather than a perfection of the will. Here we find the faithful transcription of Gibieuf's fundamental thesis: *Indifferenter se habere ad agendum et non agendum posthabito ordine finis, qui regula est appetitionum nostrarum, non est vera libertas.*[59] Descartes does not hesitate to admit a hypothesis very similar to what Gibieuf had already proposed, which pushes the doctrine to its ultimate consequences to make it better understood. A familiar Thomist argument consists of invoking the case of the blessed in heaven, who adhere to divine truth and goodness

58 *Meditations* (Meditation Four); VII, pp. 57–58 [Heffernan, p. 158]: "Neque enim opus est me in utramque partem ferri posse, ut sim liber, sed contra, quo magis in unam propendeo, sive quia rationem veri et boni in ea evidenter intelligo, sive quia Deus intima cogitationis meae ita disponit, tanto liberius illam eligo; nec sane divina gratia, nec naturalis cognitio unquam imminuunt libertatem, sed potius augent et corroborant."

59 See above in this chapter.

immutably in such a way that they are perfectly free without experiencing the least indifference in their will. Descartes transforms what for Gibieuf is a reality in heaven into a hypothesis that he supposes is achieved on earth, when he says: "If I always knew clearly what is true and what is good, I would never have trouble deliberating about what judgment and what choice I ought to make, and thus I would be entirely free without ever being indifferent.[60] This is Gibieuf's doctrine secularized. Descartes does not take very strict care to eliminate theology from his exposition. What he says about the indifference in regard to truth, which is the source of error, he extends to the indifference in regard to good, which is the source of sin. He explicitly declares that the action of the natural light of the understanding parallels the action that grace exerts upon the movements of our will.

To explain his notion of free choice, Descartes takes an example, and he finds it without needing to go outside the *Meditations*. I can consider the *Cogito*, says Descartes, as the very prototype itself of free judgment. I was trying to find out whether it was possible for me to affirm the existence of anything in the world with certainty. Now, it appeared to me that I could not pose such a question without existing myself, and my will was immediately determined to affirm my own existence. It is not that some external constraint came to impose the affirmation on me, but the judgment "I think therefore I am" was imposed with such force on my understanding that I could not refrain from affirming it. There is no indifference in this and yet perfect freedom. The movement that drew me toward the judgment, and in which I feel no indifference, comes from the fact that the great light that dominated my understanding made a great inclination be born in my will. I believed with all the more ease and freedom as I found myself less indifferent.[61] Leading the reader's thought back to the fundamental problem whose solution he is preparing at this point, Descartes adds:

60 *Meditations* (Meditation Four); VII, pp. 58 [Heffernan, p. 158]: "Indifferentia autem illa, quam experior, cum nulla me ratio in unam partem magis quam in alteram impellit, est infimus gradus libertatis, et nullam in ea perfectionem, sed tantummodo in cognitione defectum, sive negationem quamdam, testatur; nam si semper quid verum et bonum sit clare viderem, nunquam de eo quod esset judicandum vel eligendum deliberarem; atque ita quamvis plane liber, nunquam indifferens esse possem."

61 *Meditations* (Meditation Four); VII, pp. 58–59 [Heffernan, p. 160]: ". . . non potui quidem non judicare illud quod tam clare intelligebam verum esse, non quod ab aliqua vi externa fuerim ad id coactus, sed quia ex magna luce in intellectu magna consecuta est propensio in voluntate, atque ita tanto magis sponte et libere illud credidi, quanto minus fui ad istum ispsum indifferens."

> On the contrary, at present I do not know merely that I exist insofar as I am something that thinks, but a certain idea about corporeal nature is also present to my mind: this makes me doubt whether this nature that I think about, which is in me or rather is that by which I am what I am, is different from this corporeal nature, or else whether both are just the same thing. Here I suppose that I still do not have any reason that persuades me of one rather than the other: whence it follows that I am entirely indifferent to denying or affirming or even abstaining from rendering any judgment about it.[62]

It is evident in this case that indifference is nothing but our ignorance about the side that it is appropriate to choose and that it cannot constitute authentic freedom.

Moreover, in order to specify the nature of this indifference, let us say that if it always consists of a certain ignorance, it does not necessarily consist of absolute ignorance. Our will can be indifferent without its object being totally unknown to us. For there to be indifference in the will, it is enough that there is not perfect clarity in the understanding. Each time that we deliberate about an object that is not perfectly known to us, our will is in a state of indifference, and in more or less great indifference as we more or less clearly know the object that is proposed to us. If the reasons that incline us to bring judgment are only simple conjectures, however plausible they may be, the mere thought that they are only conjectures, and not certain and indubitable reasons, immediately inclines us to make the opposite judgment. Moreover, this is what Descartes already experienced in his early meditations. As soon he discerned that all the prior knowledge that until then seemed very certain to him, was doubtful in some aspect, he immediately considered it false.[63] If simply probable knowledge sufficed to eliminate the will's indifference, the prior judgments would have no reason to vary. If, however, Descartes felt impelled to deny judgments that are not entirely certain, then the indifference of the will would immediately appear with the uncertainty of reason. Certainty alone can eliminate it.

This nature of human freedom is closely linked to our condition of finite, created beings. Our freedom cannot consist in indifference for the simple reason that we are humans and consequently creatures naturally

62 *Méditationes Métaphysiques*; IX, p. 47.

63 Letter to Mersenne, December 11, 1643; IV, p. 59.

subordinated to God. To hold that our will's perfection consists in indifference is to confuse the condition of creature with that of creator, and any objection that is based on a possible or necessary analogy between divine freedom and human freedom is vitiated at its root. It is contradictory to suppose that the divine will was not indifferent from all eternity to all that is, has been, or could be. Nothing is prior to God or to his will. The true and the good are equally subject to him, and it is he who created them. The unity of his will, his power, and his understanding brings all things into being, essences just like existences, and consequently nothing can limit or restrict his will's supreme indifference. But in what concerns humans, the issue is posed in totally different terms. Humans find the nature of the good and the true already determined by God. Besides, his will could have no other proper objects than this good and this truth. Human freedom, therefore, consists in the movement by which we are led to embrace them. The indifference that is introduced into our will only signals our ignorance about the good and the true established by God. In the measure in which we make clear and distinct knowledge replace the uncertainty, in that same measure we make better use of our authentic freedom.[64] In this way, Descartes establishes the harmony between his notion of divine freedom and his notion of human freedom. This is still pure doctrine of Gibieuf. In *De Libertate* Descartes finds a doctrine of divine freedom closely related to his own. He takes his own doctrine of human freedom from it, along with the transition from divine to human freedom that lets them be harmonized.

Descartes followed the process of indifference with a detailed critique. He considered difference to be an uncertainty of the will subordinated to a deficit of the understanding. The more irresistible the movement that pushes our will toward a certain act, the more our will must be considered free. Would it not be a strange notion of freedom to confuse it with our ignorance, in such a way that to be free we would have to act at random without knowing what we ought to do? If, as is certain, indifference is the sign of a certain

64 *La Géometrie*, book II; VI, pp. 431–433: "Quantum ad arbitrii libertatem, longe alia ejus ratio est in Deo quam in nobis. Repugnat enim Dei voluntatem non fuisse ab aeterno indifferentem ad omnia quae facta sunt aut unquam fient . . . Sed quantum ad hominem, cum naturam omnis boni et veri jam a Deo determinatam inveniat, nec in aliud ejus voluntas ferri possit, evidens est ipsum eo libentius, ac proinde etiam liberius, bonum et verum amplecti, quo illud clarius videt, nunquamque esse indifferentem, nisi quando quidnam sit melius aut verius ignorat, vel certe quando tam perspicue non videt, quin de eo possit dubitare." For Gibieuf's text see, note 42 above in this chapter.

freedom, it can only be the least perfect and lowest kind. Freedom consists not in this indifference considered in itself, but of the adherence of our will to the good and the true that the understanding presents to it or that divine grace makes it embrace. For all those who read the critique of freedom of indifference at the moment in which the *Meditations on First Philosophy* appeared, it was doubtless evident that the philosopher who had written those pages was an adversary of Molina in the controversies about grace.

Chapter Four

Human Freedom in the *Principia Philosophiae*

When we search the *Principles* for clarification of Descartes' criticism of freedom of indifference, we may initially experience some surprise at not finding it. This criticism, one of the fundamental components of the Fourth Meditation, seems to have vanished in the *Principles*. Yet, the same problem is posed in both works and receives the same solution. As in the *Meditations*, in the *Principles* Descartes devotes himself to demonstrating that God is not responsible for our errors and that these errors, which come from bad use of our free choice, do not keep our clear and distinct ideas from being true. But while in the *Meditations* the critique of freedom of indifference seems to ground the whole demonstration of this thesis, in the *Principles* it is carried out without the term *indifference* being used more than once. A very simple explanation of this change comes to mind. Descartes adverts that, in a general way, the order and relative importance of subjects treated will not be the same in the *Meditations* and the *Principles*. Consequently, there is nothing surprising in our not finding a certain number of arguments in the first book of the *Principles* that were found in the *Meditations*. Still, let us observe that the difference in the order of subjects treated is unimportant.[1] As to the development allotted by Descartes to various questions that are discussed in both treatises, in general, the discussions carried out in the *Meditations* are not greatly reduced in the *Principles*. The problem of free choice constitutes a particular case. We are no longer dealing with a change of order or of proportion, but a change of content. In what concerns the question of freedom of indifference more particularly, we do not find a reduction but suppression. In the period when the *Principles* appeared, a suppression of this type might already be deemed significant. Moreover. Descartes does not limit himself to suppressing his criticism of freedom of indifference. He disavows it. The term *indifference* appears just once and it is employed as a synonym of freedom. Far from contrasting the terms as in the *Meditations*, Descartes deliberately merges

1 See Adam, *Vie et oeuvres*; XII, pp. 370–71 on this point.

them.[2] For his readers, an indication like that would be sufficient. It must not be forgotten that the term *indifference* was a rallying cry during this period. In the *Meditations*, Descartes battles against freedom of indifference, and therefore opposes Molina. In the *Principles*, on the contrary, he says: "We are sure of the freedom and of the indifference that is within us." Therefore, in his view, indifference either constitutes freedom or is an indispensable element of freedom. Descartes is now a follower of Molina. He makes such a declaration in connection with the problem of harmonizing free choice and divine preordination. This time, no one can be misled. Descartes is not a Thomist and has nothing in common with that school. On the one hand, we are sure that God has preordained everything, and on the other, we are sure that this preordination leaves our freedom and our indifference intact. Father Gibieuf witnesses his old disciple denying that divine preordination suppresses our indifference, as if he feared to see our freedom vanish at the same time. To explain this silence and this discrete but perfectly clear repudiation to which Descartes certainly thought his readers would pay attention, we must consider the particular goal that Descartes pursued in the *Principles*, and the direction that the controversy on grace had taken at the time.

One of the most constant preoccupations that tormented Descartes was to assure the success of his philosophy. Whatever scorn for Scholasticism he displayed, perhaps quite sincerely, he did not cease to envy its marvelous destiny, and sometimes he seemed to express himself as if Aristotle's prestige kept him awake at night, an astonishing plight for a man, all of whose writings are taken for oracles today.[3] Sometimes Descartes' biting irony may even reveal certain spite.

Whatever Descartes' feelings about Aristotle were, it is an established fact that his ambition was to dethrone Aristotle and reign in his place as the undisputed master. According to the custom of the time, to replace Aristotle it was necessary to redo his work and build a *Philosophia Universalis* or *Summa Totius Philosophiae Complectens Quatuor Partes: Logica, Metaphysica, Physica et Moralis*. Descartes visualizes his system on this plan. If he wants to demolish Aristotle's edifice and construct another, unshakable one on the ruins, he does not put the legitimacy of this approach in doubt for an instant. An unyielding adversary of Scholasticism on each particular

2 *Principia*, I, 41. ". . . libertatis autem et indifferentiae quae in nobis est, nos ita conscios esse, ut nihil sit quod evidentius et perfectius comprehendamus."

3 Letter to Plempius, February 15, 1638; I, 522.

point, Descartes does not imagine that philosophy could be conceived other than as Scholasticism itself conceived it. The great tree of science that Descartes wants to make spring forth from previously leveled ground, will include as many branches as necessary to replace the philosophy courses in schools and universities. Metaphysics will follow genuine logic, then physics, and from this branch medicine, mechanics (which constitutes the only new offering), and lastly "the final degree of wisdom," ethics.[4] Let us add that Descartes does not doubt for an instant that on all these points he can furnish demonstrations as certain as in mathematics, definitive and unshakable, and that it will be understood that once this "body of philosophy" is established, nothing will remain but to teach it indefinitely and to develop its beautiful arrangement in all schools and universities. Descartes not only embraces this dream of "true philosophy," triumphant in a far-off future and ruling in the schools where Aristotle triumphed previously, but he hopes that even during his lifetime he will see its fulfillment.

There was a hard battle to be waged. Aristotle reigned over education, and within education the Jesuits ruled. For Descartes' philosophy to be disseminated and replace Scholastic philosophy, he absolutely needed to get the Society of Jesus on his side. With their powerful schools and their many connections in the university, only the Jesuits could accomplish the rapid and sure triumph of the new philosophy. Descartes knew that, and the most important effort that he made to conciliate the Jesuits was the composition *ad usum scholarum* of *Principia Philosophiae*.[5] Still, he had not begun by trying to woo them. For a time, vexed when his *Meteors* did not receive sufficient deference and were not introduced into the curriculum,[6] and irritated by Bourdin's attacks, Descartes thought of exploiting the rivalry that existed between the Sorbonne and the Jesuits. At that juncture, his plan consisted of obtaining official approval for his metaphysics from the Doctors and, armed with that support, hurling a formidable weapon against Jesuit philosophy, with the objective of making his philosophy's superiority burst forth and immediately open the doors of schools to him. For the stroke to be decisive he had to bring it to bear on the very heart of the evil. Without revealing his whole project to Mersenne, Descartes pretended to be preparing himself for the objections that the Jesuits were to make against the *Meditations*. Under the pretense of "keeping himself

4 *Principes de la philosophie*; IX, p. 14. Also, *Principia, preface*.

5 Letter to Schooten, September 1639?; II, p 577.

6 Letter to Huygens, March 1638; II, p. 50; also letter to Mersenne, July 27, 1638; II, p. 267–268; also letter to Mersenne, July 30, 1640; III, p. 126–27; also letter to Mersenne, September 15, 1640; III, p. 178.

in readiness," he requested that Mersenne indicate the philosophy courses "most followed" in the Order's schools. Unfortunately, the Conimbricenses, Toletus, and Rubius were very long. By contrast, Eustachius a Sancto Paulo had written a relatively short compendium, which was the best work of this kind.[7] Descartes must have decided to reveal his real plan to Mersenne, who immediately objected that it would be difficult for Descartes to refute a philosophy whose adherents had professed such different opinions. That was no longer Descartes' intention. He simply wanted to destroy the foundations of the edifice and he responded to Mersenne: "All the foundations about which they are in agreement among themselves can easily be overthrown. With that done, all of their particular disputes will seem fatuous."[8] To carry out this plan, Descartes wanted to draw up all the principles of his philosophy in the form of theses. The elaboration with his conclusions and reasons that demonstrated them would form an authentic "Course of Philosophy." In the same volume, after the first course, an "Ordinary Philosophy Course" would be printed, for example, that of the Feuillant Eustachius a Sancto Paulo. Notes composed by Descartes would follow each section. In these notes, the different Scholastic opinions on this same question would be assembled and criticized, and perhaps at the end there would be a "comparison of these two philosophies." This project had to be thought out and executed in silence. If alerted, the Regents of the schools would do everything to intercept it. The Sorbonne also might be roused and refuse the approval that Descartes desired and would "help his plan extraordinarily." Once the *Meditations* were approved, the physics could not fail to be accepted, because "this little bit of metaphysics" contained "all the principles of my physics."[9]

7 Letter to Mersenne, September 30, 1640; III, p. 185.

8 Letter to Mersenne, November 11, 1640; III, p. 232.

9 Letter to Mersenne, November 11, 1640; III, p. 233. The Adam-Tannery edition publishes a long letter, number 222; III, p. 253, which was not dated by Clerselier. Adam-Tannery dates it December 1640, but we believe it ought to be dated considerably earlier. In this letter, Descartes appears to open up to Mersenne about his project for the first time. "But I cannot explain free will, except by giving my whole philosophy, and, between the two of us, I will tell you that I am beginning to make a summary of it in which I will put the whole Course in order, so as to have it printed along with a summary of Scholastic philosophy like that of Fray Eustachius" (Letter to Mersenne, December 1640; III, p. 259). This letter is certainly earlier than letter 220, where Descartes speaks to Mersenne about his plan and of the campaign he wants to mount against the Jesuits, as if Mersenne were informed about the matter. More importantly, Mersenne had already indicated Raconis' textbook as usable for Descartes' plans (Letter to Mersenne, September 15, 1640; III, p. 251).

The difficulty was above all to find a Scholastic philosophy course that could serve for the project. The two characteristics that Descartes required were that it be brief and generally accepted.[10] Fr. Raconis' course, which Mersenne had proposed to Descartes, was less suited to his project than that of Eustachius a Sancto Paulo. The length of the Conimbricenses excluded their utilization. The Feuillant Eustachius remained, but he had the serious handicap of not being a Jesuit, and given Descartes' general objective, he would have liked "much better to deal with the great Society than with an individual," since he did not doubt that he could demonstrate that his reasons "could withstand their arguments as well as those of others."[11] While waiting for his choice to be finally settled, Descartes began to compose his course. There was no hurry, since he needed to give the Sorbonne time to examine the *Meditations* and formulate approval. Descartes' work was presented to the Doctors only after March 4, 1641.[12] Several months slipped by while Descartes' friends mounted a campaign to obtain the Doctors' approval. Gibieuf particularly seems to have been actively involved in it, and our philosopher even had hopes of the favor of receiving this approval by the intermediary of the Duchess of Aiguillon, Richelieu's niece.[13] However, the negotiations were laborious, and at the end of July 1641, Descartes, whom Mersenne no doubt led to foresee failure, began to assume the detached air of a man who had never taken this business to heart.[14] The dangerous

Nothing in the remainder of the letter, and notably in the reference to the trouble des Argues [Desargues] is taking to catechize Bourdin, conflicts with our chronology. Furthermore, in letter 220, Descartes has seen Raconis' textbook. In letter 214 of November 11, 1640, Descartes, to whom Mersenne has already suggested it, had not yet seen it. Lastly, in the passage analyzed above (Letter to Mersenne, November 11, 1640; III, p. 233), Descartes only clarifies a project. The proof of this is that Mersenne has already raised the objection about the difficulty that the diversity of Scholastic doctrines would make for Descartes. Therefore, letter 222, where Descartes secretively confides his new project to Mersenne, is prior to letter 214 (III, p. 230), and consequently ought to be pushed back before November 11, 1640.

Let us add that from October 28, 1640 (date of a lost letter written to his father), Descartes had conceived the desire to refute Jesuit philosophy. Baillet *La vie de M. Descartes*, I, p. 512. Cf. Adam-Tannery, III, p. 329. Around this time, Descartes also must have confided his project to Mersenne.

10 Letter to Mersenne, November 11, 1640; III, p. 234.

11 Letter to Mersenne, December 3, 1640; III, p. 251.

12 Letter to Mersenne, March 4, 1641; III, pp. 328–29.

13 Letter to Mersenne, June 23, 1641; III, p. 388.

14 Letter to Mersenne, July 22, 1641; III, p.416,

passages were revised. The answer to Arnauld was trimmed. Nothing happened, and the Body of the Sorbonne finally refused to give its approval. This was a great disappointment for all of Descartes' supporters. All of them counted upon the support of the Sorbonne, so much so that the first edition of the *Meditations*, completely ready at the moment, appeared with the notice: *Cum Privilegio et Approbatione Doctorum*. Since only the approval was missing, Mersenne announced the bad news to Descartes by expressing his indignation against those whose maneuvers and misinformation had brought the refusal. Descartes remained above everything like someone whom such events did not affect. But under this apparent detachment from his work about which he had "entirely ceased to think" for a long time, under the haughty scorn he professed toward those who showed themselves incapable of understanding his reasons, deep disappointment and silent rage can be perceived seeping through.[15]

This development spoiled all Descartes' plans. Without official approval from the Doctors of the Sorbonne, it became imprudent to embark on open warfare against the Society of Jesus. His position in the battle would have been completely different, had he been able to demonstrate to his adversaries that the physics they rejected necessarily flowed from metaphysical principles that the Sorbonne had approved. Since Descartes lacked this support, it only remained for him to undertake a suitable retreat.

From the moment when he was denied approval by the Doctors, Descartes gave up his plan to refute a course of philosophy accepted in Jesuit Schools and no longer considered this project except as a threat that it was useful to leave standing in order to check the boldness of the members of the Order. Rumor of the project had already spread and the Jesuits had some knowledge of it. Bourdin, who according to Descartes must have been given the assignment by his superior, had come to talk to Mersenne about Descartes' plan to attack the philosophy that the Jesuit schools taught. In the course of this conversation, the Jesuit had exchanged threat for threat, and he offered Descartes a kind of compromise. If the philosopher agreed not to write against the Society of Jesus, Bourdin would not publish his pamphlet, which was to constitute the *Objectiones Septimae*.[16] In his own interest, Descartes should not forget that it was easy for the Jesuits to destroy

15 Letter to Mersenne, September 1641; III, pp. 436–37. Cf. also p. 437, note b. The bad humor that Descartes' editors notice, is easy to explain at this point. Letter to Pollot, October 6, 1642; III, p. 577, lines 1–17.

16 Letter to Mersenne, December 22, 1641; III, p. 465, lines 13–19.

his reputation completely and that the combat would not be between equals.[17] In transmitting these propositions, Mersenne expressed his fear of seeing Descartes involved in dangerous business, but our philosopher reassured him and declared that he was not frightened. Except that, as if by chance and after a long time, Descartes "entirely dropped the plan of refuting" a philosophy "so absolutely and so clearly destroyed by the mere establishment of his own."[18] He only wanted to reserve for the future the right to follow up on a threat whose efficacy he observed with satisfaction.[19] For the rest, in a letter that Descartes emphatically desired should be made known not only to Bourdin but also to the Father Provincial,[20] he disavowed the project attributed to him of writing against the priests of the Society of Jesus. This announced the abandonment of his original project from which he only retained the publication of a *Course*, or better *Summa*, of philosophy. Again he specified that this *Summa*, although very different from the ones the Jesuits used, would not be published in a spirit of contradiction but exclusively out of love of truth.[21] In reality, Descartes continued to pursue the same goal; only his tactic had changed. Since he could not introduce his philosophy into the schools by an armed takeover, he was going to try to open doors by means of guile.

Descartes neglected no way to reach his goal. First, since the threat of writing against the Jesuits seemed to have frightened them so much, despite Descartes' official disavowal, Mersenne was to keep that salutary fear alive among them. Although Descartes did not then intend to do so, if the Fathers employed "abuse and calumny" toward him, he could very well pick "one of their *Courses of Philosophy* to show its errors."[22] As for the pamphlet

17 Letter to Mersenne, December 22, 1641; III, p. 467: "Denique mirror quam maxime Reverendum Patrem Bourdin Reverentiae Vostrae significasse suos perfacile posse famam omnem meam delere, sive me infamem redderem tum Romae tum aliis omnibus in locis. (Non melius haec verba latine possum reddere: Reverend Father Bourdin certainly made me see how they could easily make you lose his reputation at Rome and everywhere.)"

18 Letter to Mersenne, December 22, 1641; III, p 470.

19 Letter to Mersenne, December 22, 1641; III, p. 470, lines 2–7. See also, p. 466, lines 10–12 in the same letter.

20 Letter to Mersenne, December 22, 1641; III, p. 470, lines 24–26.

21 Letter to Mersenne, December 22, 1641; III, p. 465: "Miror Reverendos Patres Societatis sibi potutisse persuadere mihi contra ipsos scribendi animum esse: hoc enim a moribus meis vitaeque instituto, et a perpetua mea in ipsos observantia, quam maxime est alienum."

22 Letter to Mersenne, January 19, 1642; III, p. 481.

with which Bourdin threatened him, Descartes showed he was not afraid by publishing it himself under the name *Seventh Objections*, accompanied by his own *Responses*.[23] At the same time, he began a labor of peaceful introduction and of cutting the bridges between Bourdin and the rest of the Order. It was impossible to obtain official Jesuit approval at once, but at least it was necessary that Bourdin's attacks should not be considered an expression of the Society of Jesus' disapproval. So, in a letter of fundamental importance on this point, Descartes tells Fr. Dinet that he had never considered that Bourdin's unfair attacks and calumnies expressed the feelings of such a prudent and pious Society.[24] Furthermore, Descartes did not hide how attacks by Bourdin, mathematics teacher at the best school in the world, could harm the propagation of his philosophy in schools. Would it not be believed that Bourdin had been assigned by the Jesuits to judge Descartes' philosophy?[25] From that, were not all the Jesuit priests throughout the world going to accept Bourdin's opinions and calumnies without having read Descartes? Even more, almost everyone would have given credence to these false opinions on the credit they give the Society of Jesus. This had already happened in the case of the *Discourse* and of the *Treatise on Meteors*. Since the Jesuits, always occupied in their teaching, could not read every new book; they accepted the opinion of the first member of the Society who became acquainted with a new publication and made his judgment known. Bourdin, who violently attacked the *Meteors*, was the cause that none of the priests, who taught that part of physics every year in the schools, had taken the trouble of reading the first part of Descartes' book. This way, through the ill will of a single member of the Society, the success of the true philosophy had been delayed.[26]

At the same time, Descartes laid down paths for his new treatise of philosophy and sought to open schools to it. He announced his intention to change style. He recalled how, at the end of the Fourth Responses, his

23 Letter to Mersenne, December 22, 1641; III, p. 466, line 17 to p. 467, line 3. Cf. Letter to Huygens, January 31, 1641; III, p. 523, lines 6–12. Also, Letter to Mersenne, March 1642, III, p. 543; and letter to Bourdin, September 7, 1642; III, p. 575.

24 Letter to Dinet, VII, p. 564, line 10 to p. 566 line 11. See *Objectiones Septimae*, note; VII, p. 453, lines 8–18.

25 "Multi enim sibi persuaderent illam unum ex universo vestro corpore fuisse delectum ad judicem de meis [*sicilicet*: opinionibus] ferendum . . ." Letter to Dinet, VII, p. 571.

26 Letter to Fr. Dinet; VII, pp. 573–74.

philosophy had shown itself capable of explaining the mystery of transubstantiation, insofar as is possible, and he made bold to resolve as reliably all the difficulties of this kind.[27] Finally, he emphasized the peace and calm that his true philosophy's adoption would introduce in the schools, since the clear vision of truth would leave no place for doubt or dispute. Everything made the acceptance of the true philosophy and its propagation in education desirable.[28] After this manifesto, Descartes set about accomplishing his plans.

His first concern was "to make [his physics] learn to speak Latin." To better signal his intention and introduce his philosophy into Scholastic conversations more easily, Descartes initially wanted to call it *Summa Philosophiae*. It would get the attention of his persecutors, both ministers and Jesuits.[29] At the same time, he made an effort to establish and maintain relations with some influential priests in the Society of Jesus. Vatier sent him the assurance that he disagreed in voice and heart what had been done against him. He openly supported Descartes' explanation of transubstantiation, and contrary to rumor, he denied that he had even contemplated writing against Descartes.[30] Three or four months previously, our philosopher had tried to interest Fr. Charlet in his situation,[31] and in fact Fr. Dinet, who had recently arrived from Rome, sent word to Descartes that Fr. Charlet cherished and esteemed him, that his letter *Admodum Reverendo Patri Dinet* was worthy of him and of his generosity, and lastly that Fr. Charlet would write Descartes regarding his studies and the affection he demonstrated for the Society of Jesus.[32] Accordingly, a perceptible truce was noticeable in Descartes' relations with the Jesuits, and while praising them, he thought that they were waiting for the publication of his philosophy to take a stand.[33] Moreover, around this same time, he discovered a relative by marriage who was a Jesuit and who seems to have taught mathematics in Paris. It was a good opportunity to attempt reconciliation with Bourdin. Descartes took

27 Letter to Fr. Dinet; VII, p. 581, lines 3–18.
28 Letter to Fr. Dinet; VII, pp. 581–82.
29 Letter to Huygens, January 31, 1642; III, p. 523.
30 Letter to Mersenne, November 17, 1642; III, p. 591. See Letter to Vatier, also of November 17, 1641; III, pp. 594–97.
31 Letter to Vatier, November 17, 1642; III, p. 595, lines 11–16.
32 Letter to Mersenne, January 4, 1643; III, p. 609.
33 Letter to Mersenne, January 4, 1643; III, p. 609, lines 10–14. Cf. also Letter to Mersenne, March 23, 1643; III, p. 639: "I certainly think that Fr. Bourdin has been silenced in order to await my Philosophy."

advantage of it and expressed his desire to see himself "in his good graces" if that were possible.[34] Just after the *Principles* had been printed, Descartes answered Mesland's objections about freedom and transubstantiation to the best of his ability and in the most conciliatory spirit. Any Jesuit won over was a great advantage for Descartes.[35] Finally, the *Principles* appeared. Descartes distributed as many copies as he could among members of the Society of Jesus and devoted himself actively to promoting the *Principles*. As he dreaded the jealousy of the school directors toward a philosophy other than the one they taught, Descartes tried to tie the Order's prestige to teaching his philosophy. His *Principles* were based on reason in such a way that "the most prudent person" ought to "glory in being the first to bring favorable judgment upon them."[36] He sent a copy to Fr. Dinet "of this unfortunate philosophy that some have tried to smother before its birth."[37] In a radical change, Descartes had great satisfaction in having the honor to be received by Bourdin, all the more since the latter had "made him hope for the favor of his good graces."[38] Following his visit to Bourdin during his trip to Paris, Descartes pursued the overtures he was making to Bourdin to the point of constituting him the dispenser of Descartes' philosophy among the members of the Order. Vatier, Fournier, Mesland, Grandamy, and up to a dozen Jesuits received copies of the *Principles* from the hands of Bourdin.[39] Charlet, Dinet, and Bourdin replied,[40] and in the thanks Descartes directs to Charlet, he finally puts his cards on the table. The special confidence he had in this priest's benevolence and authority encouraged him to do so. He naively gave all the reasons why he would be "extremely distressed to be at odds with any of the members" of the Order: first, his own inclination and the consideration of his duty. Beyond that, the path he had taken "by publishing a new philosophy" meant that he could "benefit so greatly by their benevolence and, by contrast, be at such a disadvantage through their coldness" that he would have to be deemed out of his mind for it not to be believed that he

34 Letter to P. . ., 1643; IV, p. 66.

35 Letter to Mesland, May 2, 1644, IV; pp. 111–20. See also letter to Grandamy of the same date, May 2, 1644; IV, pp. 121–22.

36 Letter to Charlet, October 1644; IV, p. 140–41.

37 Letter to Dinet, October 1644; IV, p. 142.

38 Letter to Dinet, October 1644; IV, p. 142, line 17 to p. 143, line 5.

39 Letter to Fr. Bourdin, October 1644; IV, pp. 143–44.

40 Letter to Charlet, February 9, 1645; IV pp. 156–58. Letter to Dinet of the same date, February 9, 1645; IV, pp. 158–60. Letter to Bourdin also of the same date, February 9, 1645; IV, pp. 160–61.

desired their friendship.[41] Without question, his philosophy was "so grounded in demonstrations" that it could not be doubted that in time it would be received and approved by everyone, but Descartes would very much like to "live long enough to see that time" and the Jesuits could help him. If their benevolence invited them to examine the Principles, Descartes noted:

> I dare to anticipate that they will find some things that seem true to them and that can easily be substituted for some common opinions and serve advantageously to explain the truths of Faith, even without contradicting the text of Aristotle, that they will not fail to accept them, so that in a few years, the philosophy will acquire all the reputation that without that happening it would take a hundred years to acquire. I confess having some interest in this. For, since I am human like other people, I am not of those indifferent individuals who do not let themselves be affected by success. And this is also something in which you can greatly oblige me.[42]

The history of *Principia Philosophiae* is completely dominated by preoccupation with the Jesuits. The *Principles* was a book intended to be taught, which would assure the rapid dissemination and success of the true philosophy in the near future. It is for this purpose that our philosopher conceived and carried out the problem of organizing a *Course* or *Summa* that "the lowliest master can teach."[43]

Therefore, it becomes easy to explain Descartes' attitude toward the question of freedom in the *Principia*. In composing his *Philosophy Course*, he must devote himself to increasing his chances of success in every way possible. One of the first conditions for his physics to be accepted in Jesuit schools was that its metaphysical foundations be acceptable to members of the Order. With much greater reason, Descartes had avoided introducing anything into his course that might be regarded as criticism of theological doctrines in favor within the Society of Jesus. Criticism of freedom of

41 On this point, cf. also letter to Dinet, February 9, 1645; IV p. 159: "Because, since I became involved up in writing a Philosophy, I know that your society can do more than the whole rest of the world to make it valued or scorned."

42 Letter to Charlet, February 9, 1645; IV, pp. 157–58.

43 Letter to Mersenne, December 1640; III, p. 260. lines 4–5.

indifference would be precisely that sort of thing. Freedom of indifference is Molina. If there is a case in which one could observe the union of the Jesuits that Descartes liked to recall, it was certainly that of the controversies about grace. By attacking the freedom of indifference, and consequently Molina, Descartes attacked the whole Society of Jesus, whose self-respect was very much at stake in the quarrel and was very sensitive on the point. Therefore, it was necessary to choose. The *Principles*, like the *Meditations*, could present a developed explanation of the nature of freedom and a criticism of freedom of indifference. In that case resistance on the part of the Jesuits was anticipated. Or, the point would be glossed over, indifference would even be reintroduced stealthily, and thereby the reception of true philosophy in Jesuit schools would be facilitated and its dissemination in education would be assured. As we have seen, Descartes was very greatly concerned about his philosophy's immediate success and fastened onto the second option. To be more confident of opening the doors of Jesuit schools to his physics, he reinserted indifference into authentic freedom.

Moreover, he could do so without modifying the essential lines of his metaphysics, and even without disowning what he had written about the nature of freedom. It sufficed to pass over the point in silence and to throw responsibility for error back onto the bad use of our freedom. This is why the general thrust of the demonstration stays the same in the *Principles* and in the *Meditations*, despite the total omission of any criticism of freedom of indifference. The issue raised is evidently the same: proving that our clear and distinct ideas are true. To demonstrate that, it is enough to consider that God, who is perfect, could not deceive us. If we were deceived in what we see clearly and distinctly to be true, then God himself would deceive us. But he is not a deceiver. Therefore, our clear and distinct ideas are true.[44] But the difficulty remains of how it come to pass that we are deceived? Is it sure that God is not a deceiver and that he is not the cause of our errors to any degree? In order to resolve the difficulty, it will be immediately demonstrated that our errors are nothing from God's point of view and that they are real defects, privations, only from our own point of view.[45] From there, Descartes simply picks up the argument of the *Meditations*, and the only differences that can be seen are in matters of detail and expression. Error does not come from our understanding. Its limitation, something natural in a created understanding, only condemns it to ignorance of certain things,

44 *Principia*, I, 29–30.
45 *Principia*, I, 31.

not at all to error. Error comes from the dominance of our will over our understanding. But this dominance depends on the nature of our will, and it even constitutes the main human perfection, which is the power of acting freely. Therefore, our understanding is limited and finite. In some manner, our will is infinite and, since it easily extends its judgments beyond what we perceive clearly and distinctly, we are deceived. The defect, from which error comes, resides in our actions and not in our nature. This nature is such that it pleased God to give it to us and, such as we received it, it does not condemn us to error. Error comes from the bad use that we make of it.[46] Consequently it is not legitimate to affirm that God has condemned us to error, since not being deceived depends only on us. If God is not a deceiver, we can affirm that everything that we know clearly and distinctly is true. Descartes has changed nothing in the Fourth Meditation as a whole, but through opportunism, he has abandoned the notion he had previously held about the nature of our freedom.

Perhaps some distaste will be felt at admitting that Descartes modifies his doctrine in this way for quite evidently self-seeking reasons. Surely, the explanation of the change of attitude that we just presented hardly enhances our philosopher's honor. Let us say that an element of opportunism cannot be discounted in the reasons that explain Descartes' abandonment of the position he adopted in the Fourth Meditation. Descartes wanted his doctrine to be taught, and for that he consented to make certain seemingly necessary sacrifices. The composition of the *Principles* bears obvious traces of some of them. The earth's movement is explained there with an abundance of precautions and expedients that give the exposition an indisputable self-seeking slant. It has been demonstrated that Descartes' caution on this point was excessive and out of proportion to the danger he ran.[47] But there are more precise signs of his particular desire to obtain the good will of the Jesuits. It is well known that Descartes is not lavish in his references and that proper names are infrequent in his writings. This is true in general and can be verified as regards the *Principles of Philosophy*. In more than 300 pages Descartes cites ten proper names. Not counting Aristotle, Democritus, Ptolemy, Tycho Brahe, and Copernicus, who were unavoidable, we are left with the names of five scientists: Gilbert, Grassius, Pontanus, Regiomontanus, and Scheiner. Gilbert and Regiomontanus are not relevant, but we

46 *Principia*, I, 33–38.

47 On this point see the solid and perfectly conclusive chapter of Adam, *Vie et oeuvres*; XII, pp. 165–79.

know that Grassius or Grassi,[48] and Pontanus[49] were Jesuits. Scheiner was a Jesuit, and Descartes takes care to mention that fact as well as the excellence of Scheiner's observations on sunspots, whose exactness leaves nothing to be desired.[50] Three Jesuits out of five scientists cited in 300 pages is truly a high proportion, and it is hardly permissible to think that it was by chance. Let there be no doubt: in omitting his criticism of freedom of indifference and in disowning what he wrote in the *Meditations*, Descartes acted on self-seeking motives.

These motives were real, but it must be added that they were not the only ones. If we situate Descartes in the circumstances in which he found himself when he composed the *Principles*, the stance he takes there is hugely clarified and takes on a fairly different appearance. To understand it, we ought to consider what criticism of freedom of indifference had become after the appearance of *De Libertate*. This story will take us away from Descartes only in appearance, because it will carry us beyond the problem posed by *Principia Philosophiae* toward a solution of the difficulties that Mesland's letters raise on the nature of freedom.

48 *Principia*, III, 128 note. On Grassi, see Letter to Du Puy, January 5, 1645; IV, p. 151 a.

49 On Pontanus see *Principia*, III, 128 note and IV, p. 151 a.

50 *Principia*, III, 35.

Chapter Five
Freedom of Indifference from *De Libertate* to *Augustinus*

By embarking his philosophy on the so-called Thomistic path that de Bérulle and Gibieuf had just opened up to him, Descartes involved himself in something risky. It would get progressively worse to the point where on occasion even Gibieuf lamented having committed himself to it. Descartes could not help being affected by the turn events had taken. At stake here was not simply an author's self-regard and personal sensitivity, but his entire human and Christian conscience. Between 1641 and 1644, that is, in the interval that separates the *Meditations* from the *Principles*, something new had occurred, whose importance was beginning to be understood. In its evolution, Thomism was turning into Jansenism, and Descartes was not the only Thomist to be frightened by that.

To understand the mentality of the period, we must take up the history of the controversy on grace at the point where we left it, that is to say, at the appearance of *De Libertate*. Gibieuf's book was not designed to ease the quarrel. Independently of the work's actual content, it often presented ideas in aggressive language, making long personnel personal attacks that could not help but irritate the Society of Jesus. Evidently, Gibieuf considered that Paul V's decree, renewed by Urban VIII, which forbade any harsh language and any accusation of heresy, was inoperative. Not only did Gibieuf openly and nominally attack theological glories of the Society, like Lessius, Molina, Vázquez, and others, but he even offered reasons that, according to him, explained the success of Molinism with an unflattering summation that deeply offended the Jesuits. Furthermore, Gibieuf employed an argument of which Jansen was to make notorious use. He rejected Molinism as the old, condemned Pelagian doctrine, and this accusation of heresy greatly irritated his adversaries. The Society of Jesus did not accept being attacked with impunity and would defend itself soon.

If we believe some histories, the Jesuits immediately did everything to get Rome to condemn Gibieuf's book.[1] The testimony of these histories is too partial for us to be able to trust them absolutely, but it is highly plausible that things proceeded in this fashion. It was an ordinary tactic during the period and the habitual weapon of theologians. Still, the tactic failed, and the blow was not delivered. Gibieuf would never be condemned. But while the Jesuits lobbied at Rome they worked to defend themselves, the opportunity to respond was too good to pass up. The same year *De Libertate* was published, another Oratorian priest, William Chalmers, published a book that vigorously attacked middle science.[2] The Jesuits would take advantage of the fact that Gibieuf's sometimes clumsy attacks were exposed to challenge as violating the Papal decrees, and at the same time settle another problem.

In 1630, Théophile Raynaud, a theologian whom the Society of Jesus sometimes found embarrassing, published a short, very crude work under the name of one of his students against the adherents of Thomism in general and Domingo Bañez in particular.[3] Both the thesis and the reasoning intended to establish it are simple. All Thomists were Calvinists and brute animals. Reynaud even tried to force his adversaries to acknowledge this: Humans are distinguished from beasts by free choice above all. Therefore, he who denies free choice considers himself to be a beast.[4] That was the book's core. The rest was a fabric of more or less well-organized quotations with which Raynaud intended to prove that all theologians of Bañez's school

1 These histories are suspect of partisanship and of being unfavorable to the Jesuits. See Batterel, *Mémoires domestiques,* I. p. 245. See also M. Géry, *Apologie historique des deux censures de Louvain et de Douay, Cologne,* Nicholas Schouten, 1678, p. 143. [Translator: *Géry* is believed to be a pseudonym of Pasquier Quesnel.]

2 Fr. William Chalmers, born in Aberdeen, Scotland, entered the Oratory in 1627. He published *Gulielmi Camerarii Scoti Congregationis Oratorii Domini Jesus Presbyteri, Selectae Disputationes Philosophicae, in Tres Partes Distributatae. Pars Prima, Praecipuas Disputationes Logicae et Moralis Philosophiae Complectens*, Paris: Charles Chapelain, 1630. Chalmers treats freedom in Ethics, question 4, and discusses middle science in question 9 of the second part.

3 *Calvinismus Bestiarum Religio, et Appelatio pro Dominico Banne Calvinismo Damnato, per Reverendum Patrem A. Rivière, Doctorem Parisensem. Ordinis Sancti Augustini*, Paris: 1630. *Editio Altera Parisiensi Nitidior: Benedicite Omnes Bestiae et Pecora Domino (Daniel 3),* Lyon: Claude Landry, 1630. Reprinted in Théophile Raynaud, *Opera*, vol. XV (Lyon: Horatius Boissat et Georgius Remeus, 1665–1669. [Translator: A reproduction is also available as Antoine Rivière, *Calvinismus Bestiarum Religio*, Kessinger, 2009, 194 pp.]

4 Raynaud, *Calvinismus*, p. 2.

were only disciples of Calvin at bottom. Gibieuf and Chalmers were then swept up in the general reprobation, but without being named. The skirmish was not very dangerous, but it gave time for more series serious attacks to be prepared.[5]

The first proper refutation of *De Libertate* appeared in 1632 in the form of an anonymous book, serious and pondered in tone, whose doctrine was closely argued and solid. The anonymity hid Fr. Annat, one of the most formidable Jesuit polemicists.[6] Except for an appendix devoted to refuting Chalmers, the whole body of the work was explicitly directed against the doctrine of *De Libertate*.[7] As his title (*Exercitatio Scholastica Tripartita*) announced, Fr. Annat's refutation was divided into three parts: suspect propositions, contradictory propositions, and fabrications, above all in what concerns the authorities with whom Gibieuf tried to protect himself. The attack was serious. This was not a hastily composed pamphlet out of ordinary material, but instead a very precise refutation, especially geared to Gibieuf's books and intended to shed light on the novel and very special character that assured the Oratory's theologian a particular place among the defenders of Thomist doctrine. Fr. Annat's great merit in the affair was to understand that *De Libertate* marked a novel development of Thomist doctrine, that Gibieuf's book had put forth something different.

Today, no doubt, the discovery may seem easy. By calling his book *De Libertate*, Gibieuf announced clearly that he was going to shift the ordinary focus of the discussion. Many saw the choice of title only as a device to divert Rome's attention and avoid censure. However, there was something else. Gibieuf offered a new doctrine of freedom along with a more or less overt criticism of middle science. This new doctrine constitutes the basis and the foundation of this analysis. Annat saw that, and he already showed

5 Furthermore, the little book by Raynaud, who all too evidently took no notice of the Papal decrees, was put on the *Index of Forbidden Books* in 1633.

6 François Annat was born February 5, 1590. He entered the novitiate February 16, 1607. He taught philosophy and theology at Toulouse for 13 years. He was Rector of the schools at Montpellier and Toulouse and Assistant for France to the Superior General of the Jesuits. In 1654 he was Jesuit Provincial and Confessor to Louis XIV. He became famous for his struggle against Jansenism. He died at Paris on June 14, 1670.

7 *Eugenii Philadelphi Romani, Exercitatio Scholastica Tripartita, contra Novam Rationem Tuendi Physicas Praemotiones Liberorum Agentium, Eorumque Libertatem Exponendi Quam Auctor Operis De Libertate Dei et Creaturae Nuper Invexit.* Cum appendice ad Guillelmum Carmerarium Scotum, Cadurci: Jean d'Alvy, 1632 in octavo.

it emphatically in his full title: *Exercitatio Scholastica Tripartita contra Novam Rationem Tuendi Physicam Praemotionem Liberorum Agentium, Eorumque Libertatem Exponendi.* What the Jesuit primarily saw in Gibieuf's book is certainly what constituted its originality and novelty: an unusual notion of human freedom.[8]

The position Annat took was excellent, and his criticism must have had an impact. In *De Libertate* Gibieuf offered a defense of physical premotion before which more than one Thomist surely shrank back. To begin with, the book's general tone was stamped with a mysticism[9] that could not please everyone, even among the most ardent adversaries of Molina. De Lemos, Álvarez, and many other Thomists were subtle, vigorous dialecticians, but calm, with very balanced temperaments, without the effusive passages and high-mindedness in de Bérulle's style, which Gibieuf felt he had to interject constantly into his exposition. This was the Oratory's trademark, and it was not obvious that it was going to win the trust of the Dominicans. In the second place, the book's content itself was such as to trouble some defenders of St. Thomas. That definition of freedom as "amplitude," "the infinite," "not so much possessing everything as being everything," sounded like a novelty never heard before. As theologians who called themselves Thomists, they deemed themselves pulled a bit too far away from St. Thomas, After all, the matter was not very clear. The freedom Gibieuf talked about and attributed to humans, in certain cases became so tenuous and so hard to grasp that the Thomists might be troubled by it.

Until Gibieuf, Molina's adversaries agreed on the appropriate answer to give when Thomism was accused of ending up in Calvinism and suppressing freedom: to take refuge in the distinction between composed sense and divided sense. How could a predestined person be free, if he could carry out no action contradicting his predestination? The person predestined by God remains free *in sensu diviso*, although he is not free *in sensu composito*. In human freedom, act and faculty can be distinguished. To consider act and faculty in freedom at the same time is to consider freedom in *sensu composito*. To consider the act and the faculty separately is to consider freedom *in sensu diviso*. It is now very easy to answer the accusation of Calvinism: someone predestined remains free *in sensu diviso*, because his faculty of acting remains free; it retains the power to sin and to persevere in the sin, if

8 Annat, *Exercitatio*, preface: ". . . novas etiam et insolitas cogitationes in expondenda libertatis natura . . ."

9 Annat, *Exercitatio*, p. 146.

it wills. But this person is no longer free *in sensu composito*, because his voluntary power cannot decide itself for any act contrary to his predestination. Therefore, predestination only determines the nature of the acts and leaves the faculty entirely free.[10] If someone asks that this marvel be explained, it is absolutely necessary to recur to God's omnipotence. The foreknowledge by which God knows, for example, that Peter will consent to grace does not take the power away from Peter to refuse it if he wills, but only the act by which he would refuse it and, consequently, leaves his freedom intact too. Likewise the eternal absolute, efficacious decree by which God decides that the assistance of his operative grace will determine Peter's consent, does not suppress Peter's power to refuse it if he wills. God only acts by his grace in such a way that although humans could freely refuse grace, still, in fact they do not refuse it.[11]

Perhaps the solution is only verbal, but whatever the explanation is worth, for Catholic theologians it had at least the merit of retaining the name of freedom. Above all, it maintained something of freedom of indifference. Not that Thomists confused indifference and freedom in the slightest. They severely criticized freedom of indifference,[12] but they admitted that a minimum of indifference was necessary to be able to speak of freedom. Even the will of someone predestined by God is still a power *ad utrumlibet*, in the sense that the efficaciousness of the grace that determines the choice of this or that act does not prevent human freedom considered in itself from being able to make another choice. Let us understand this essential contradiction well, because it is key to the Thomist position. God determines the act, although the faculty is still a power of choice. Certain indifference cannot be eliminated from freedom, and it is an integral part of the essence of freedom. It is the influence that is the opposite of the *necessary* determination of a free act or a free power to one of two opposing terms.[13] Gibieuf assumes the obligation of eliminating even this Thomistic remnant of indifference and of extirpating it from our freedom. In his view, the Thomists' distinction is superfluous and it is only true to a certain degree.

10 On the point, see Diego Álvarez, de *Auxiliis Divinae Gratiae et Humani Arbitriis Viribus, et Libertate, ac Legitima Eius cum Efficatia Eorumdem Concordia, libri duodecim*, Lyon: Horatius Cardon, 1611, book IX, disputation 94, article 3.

11 Álvarez, *De Auxiliis*, book IX, disputation 94, article 3. Cf. also book II, disputation 5, articles 4–5.

12 Álvarez, *De Auxiliis*, book XII, disputation 116 at *Confirmetur* et article 3.

13 Álvarez, *De Auxiliis*, book III, disputation 22, article 36.

Let us recall Gibieuf's general thesis: to be free is to be unable to sin. Those who are in the state of complete indifference are at the lowest level. They choose everything they want, and since nature is corrupt, they spontaneously choose evil. Above this first group come those whose faculties God leaves indifferent, while he determines certain acts. They are freer than the previous group, and they are free precisely *in sensu diviso*, as the Thomists say. But above them come those whom God has really filled with his gifts. They are no longer indifferent about this or that act, or in what concerns their faculty of acting. They are predetermined *in sensu composito*, and in removing all indifference from them, God has given them the most perfect and supreme freedom. From that, according to Gibieuf, comes the necessity of a new definition that acknowledges no room for indifference in authentic freedom. We see can what position Gibieuf is taking in regard to his predecessors. Molina's freedom is the freedom of pagans, indifference to good and evil. The Thomists' freedom is semi-freedom, because it is partial liberation in regard to sin. Freedom, as Gibieuf conceives it, is absolute liberation, immovable and definitive adhesion to God, formal participation in supreme perfection. By presenting such a doctrine, Gibieuf felt that he was continuing in one Thomist sense, but also that he was departing from the Thomist tradition. To use his own expression, he brought the content of certain previously admitted principles into the light.[14] Some Thomists must have been frightened by the consequences they quite suddenly saw emerging from their principles. It had to be admitted that one could be free, although neither the execution nor the choice of actions was in our power *in sensu composito*. Already confronted with the *sensus divisus*, Molina's followers cried Calvinism. What would they say against a claim to reconcile necessary and efficacious predetermination of our faculties and our acts with freedom? Several drew back, as Annat indicates.[15] There are good reasons to believe he spoke the truth on this point. Many must have refused to cross the road that separated Thomism from Jansenism. Some refused to follow a theologian who had already half traversed it.

To this novel and false doctrine Annat wants to oppose quite simply Molina's conception of human freedom that had become that of his whole order: freedom of indifference. Against Gibieuf and with all Molinists, Annat protests that outside freedom of indifference there is no salvation, against Gibieuf, who combats the conception. Otherwise, we inevitably

14 Gibieuf, *De Libertate*, I, at the end of last chapter.

15 Annat, *Exercitatio*, p. 262.

fall into barely disguised Calvinism. On this point Annat's indictment is precise and terrible. He constantly offers passages from Calvin chosen with a discernment that few Molinists demonstrate in the controversy. As for Gibieuf's texts, when they seem to lack clarity, Annat has no trouble deducing propositions out of Gibieuf's system to be condemned.[16] That is the ordinary method in such cases, and by this procedure, Annat establishes that Gibieuf goes further than Calvin in the negation of freedom. The only remedy is simply to return to freedom of indifference.[17] The attack on *De Libertate* was insistent, and its author was in a dangerous position.

Some weeks after the appearance of Fr. Annat's book, [18] Fr. Théophile Raynaud returned to the fray, but this time he signaled his attack and in particular concentrated only on the book that Gibieuf had just published.[19] Evidently, Raynaud did everything in his power to adopt a grave demeanor and write a serious work, and he partially succeeded. It must be recognized that his argumentation evinces a certain subtlety that is useful in these matters, and that his criticism is sometimes rather penetrating. But his weakness for theatrics takes over from time to time, and then Fr. Annat's haughty reproaches yield to astonishingly truculent rhetorical devices.

The work opens with an epistolary dedication, in which our Jesuit reveals his enemy and sets out his project. Those he attacks are not heretics properly speaking, but imprudent and short-sighted people, who for the last two years have fallen into the excesses of a novel opinion, whose consequences lead to the destruction of that without which we not only would we not be Christians and Catholics, but even humans. With that Raynaud links his new book to *Calvinismus Bestiarum Religio*, and he immediately begins

16 Annat, *Exercitatio*, pp. 17–18.

17 The following are the principal passages in which Annat defends the freedom of indifference against Gibieuf's attacks: pp. 17–18, 33, 72–73. He contrasts Gibieuf with St. Augustine, p. 34. He answers Gibieuf's claims regarding the causes that favored the success of Molinism, pp. 151 ff. Lastly, in a skillful maneuver, he implicates Gibieuf and de Bérulle, whose beatification would hardly be possible if he professed the doctrine of *De Libertate*, p. 145.

18 Annat's publication "privilege" is dated Saint-Germain-en-Laye, August 3, 1632. Fr. Raynaud's is dated Paris, November 5, 1632.

19 Théophile Raynaud, *Nova Libertatis Explicatio ad Lucem Obscurissimis Quibusque Theologicis Difficultatibus affundendam Nuper Adinventa et Duobis Liris proposita, Hac Antistropha Tratactione Discussa* a Theophilo Raynaud, Societis Jesus Theologo. Accessit examen novae theologiae, negantis concursum Dei nobiscum ad actos liberos. Paris: Sebastien Chappelet, 1632 (one quarto volume, 579 pp.).

his exposition.[20] Several of his arguments are identical to Annat's, since in this period many arguments belong less to the theologians than to their party. However, Raynaud's refutation is not completely lacking in originality, and its particular merit is shedding light on the internal connection between the two parts of Gibieuf's book, the close relation that unites his notions of human freedom and God's freedom. That brings Raynaud to a specific condemnation of Gibieuf ' 's conception of freedom. If Annat had the merit of indicating that the most important point of the new doctrine was there, Raynaud adds the value of pushing its analysis and discussion much further.

According to Raynaud, true freedom is neither eminence, nor amplitude, nor infinity. Firstly, the term *eminence* is of no use here. But Raynaud is aware that Gibieuf intends to introduce the new doctrine under the patronage of a Cardinal, so it is understandable that he constantly uses it.[21] As for amplitude or infinity, it is not clear what relation they might have with freedom. What could this infinity of the will be? If we admit that a faculty is so much the more noble as its object is more extended, we will be led to think that the understanding is nobler than the will. We will even say that it is more extended, and consequently more free, according to Gibieuf's own principles.[22]

Let us concede that freedom consists of amplitude and infinity. From Gibieuf's own point of view, his position is still untenable. In what does this amplitude of our free faculty consist, if not in the power of acting or not acting, or choosing this act in preference to that other one? This amplitude is precisely ordinary indifference, which Gibieuf would like to excise from freedom. Freedom must not be defined simply by amplitude, but by what is most ample in freedom, that is to say by active indifference, which alone serves to establish it.

It is customary to raise a seemingly irrefutable objection against this freedom of indifference: if freedom consists of indifference, how can we describe the freedom of the blessed in Heaven, who in a single, eternal, immutable, and not at all indifferent act, adhere to the divine essence in the perpetuity of their love? The solution to the problem is very simple, and the Doctors have adopted it as their common opinion long ago. The blessed in Heaven are not free to love or not love God, which explains that they are

20 A kind of mock prologue precedes the discussion properly speaking of the doctrine set forth by Gibieuf. In the prologue Raynaud's imagination is given free rein.

21 Raynaud, *Nova Libertatis Explicatio*, p. 40.

22 Raynaud, *Nova Libertatis Explicatio*, pp. 43–44.

not indifferent.[23] Therefore, on this point, we have no reason to abandon the common conception, which makes freedom consist in the power to shift the decision indifferently toward either one of two terms.[24]

By contrast, let us consider this new kind of freedom that is proposed. It is difficult to accept it as more than merely verbal. According to Gibieuf, the more God determines us, the freer we are. To be determined by God, we are told, is to be determined from the outside. Freedom consists of the human will's formal participation in the essence of divinity. Therefore, to be free would be to emerge from one's own essence and pass into the essence of God, who then is no longer a stranger to humans nor a being external to them, but their own being and the heart of their hearts. We can participate in divinity and lose ourselves in it without going out of ourselves. Therefore, the infinity that the human will acquires by raising itself to God would be a shared divinity and, yet, would constitute the very soul of our freedom.[25] But here Reynaud reluctantly stops, in spite of himself, because it is impossible to criticize Gibieuf's way of philosophizing enough. For Gibieuf's answer to the objection, "If God determines us, we are not free," to be satisfactory, God and humans must be admitted to come to constitute together only one single essence, which is heretical.[26] If, on the contrary, this transposition of humans into God is presented as metaphorical and partial, not real and total, Gibieuf's answer loses all value.[27]

In reality [continues Raynaud], these pretended definitions by amplitude, infinity, and participations of humans in God are simply mystical jargon, snares for the naive, excellent for stupefying feeble minds or shaking up the conscience of weaklings. But men whose heart and doctrine are solid hardly value this nebulous language, bad seed from which weeds spring, fertile kernels that often engender errors in abundance.[28] No doubt this kind of language flatters the one who employs it. It presumes a higher personality, who has gazed into the heart of things and who possesses lights that not everyone has. This flaunting affectation of extraordinary mystical phrases tends toward that presumption.[29] But for a healthy stomach, all this is weak

23 Raynaud, *Nova Libertatis Explicatio*, pp. 54–55.
24 Raynaud, *Nova Libertatis Explicatio*, p. 62.
25 Gibieuf, *De Libertate*, I, 17, 9 and 10. Raynaud, *Nova Libertatis Explicatio*, p. 81.
26 Raynaud, *Nova Libertatis Explicatio*, pp. 82–83.
27 Raynaud, *Nova Libertatis Explicatio*, p. 308.
28 Raynaud, *Nova Libertatis Explicatio*, p. 140.
29 Raynaud, *Nova Libertatis Explicatio*, pp. 217–218.

gruel. Upright minds see only mysticism and Platonism there,[30] deceitful alchemy, a false glitter destined especially to dazzle simple souls, which certain Catholic doctors use only too much when they treat the mysteries of religion.[31]

To crown this whole critique, we re-encounter the classic objection, the favorite argument of Molinists: *Substantia novae sententiae foetus Calvini.*[32] Raynaud first establishes this claim by a dialectical discussion,[33] and also by authorities, some of whom are rather vague and others rather unexpected. He mentions in a general way great men who have viewed physical premotion as being close to Calvin's doctrine.[34] As an argument *a contrario*, he mentions Martin Kemnitz, one of Luther's most intrepid drinking companions, who reproached Jesuit fathers at Cologne with falling into Pelagianism by granting the powers to humans of turning down God's call and the summons of his grace.[35] That lets us judge how true it is that those who make the same objection against the Molinists concur with Calvinists and Lutherans.

Such are the main complaints leveled by Raynaud against *De Libertate.* He seems rather satisfied with his work. Gibieuf's amplitude and infinity seem to him to have received blows from which they will not rise again. Gibieuf's freedom has been pulled down. Raynaud has shattered Gibieuf's shield, made him drop his arms, and has even de-clawed him.[36] It was a job well done.

Gibieuf, however, did not consider himself completely disarmed and immediately thought about publishing a reply. The "privilege" obtained in 1633 for *Libertas Vindicata* has been found among Gibieuf's papers. It is not clear whether this book was ever written or if it was written and destroyed by Gibieuf himself.[37] The fact remains that except for the privilege and two approvals, no trace of this work has been located. The most

30 Raynaud, *Nova Libertatis Explicatio*, pp. 292–300 are obviously directed against de Bérulle.

31 Raynaud, *Nova Libertatis Explicatio*, p. 305.

32 Raynaud, *Nova Libertatis Explicatio*, p. 114.

33 Raynaud, *Nova Libertatis Explicatio*, pp. 116–117.

34 Raynaud, *Nova Libertatis Explicatio*, pp. 272–273.

35 Raynaud, *Nova Libertatis Explicatio*, p. 273.

36 Raynaud, *Nova Libertatis Exercitatio*, p. 254.

37 The second hypothesis would seem easier to reconcile with Batterel's affirmation that the originals of the approbations by two doctors of the Sorbonne were attached to the privilege. He does not give their names. Batterel, *Mémoires domestiques*, I, p. 250.

plausible hypothesis is that, whatever happened, William Chalmers informed Gibieuf that he had a completed reply that he was going to publish. Gibieuf avoided a useless dispute and suppressed his book or desisted from writing it.

Raynaud had not confronted Chalmers, but Annat had vigorously attacked him in an appendix to *Exercitatio*. He reproached not only Chalmer's doctrine, but also his attitude toward the Society in whose care he had been brought up.[38] Chalmers was goaded into the contest, and in the year 1634 he answered for Gibieuf and for himself in a new treatise especially devoted to the defense of physical premotion against Fr. Annat's book.[39] From that moment the discussion dragged on to its end. Just as Chalmers answered for Gibieuf, Raynaud would answer for Annat.[40] Then silence fell upon this affair, and the battle continued in another venue.

After the publication of *De Libertate*, Gibieuf must have been intrigued by the strange personality of one of his book's approvers, Jean du Verger de Hauranne, the Abbot of Saint-Cyran. Gibieuf had known him for a long time.[41] In 1621, Fr. de Condren, whom de Bérulle had sent to Poitiers to lay

38 Annat, *Exercitatio*, pp. 326–327.

39 *Antiquitatis de Novitate Victoria, sive Justa Defensio Praemotionis Physicae contra Impetitiones Pseudo Eugenii Philadelphi Romani*, per Reverendum Patrem Guillelmum Camerarii Scoti. Fastemburg: Petrus Baretius et Joannes Altemius, 1634 in quarto.

40 *Non Causa ut Causa, Subjuncta Vera Causa. Elenchus Sophismatis* Guillelmi Camerarii Scoti, Fastemburg: Petrus Baretius et Joannes Altemius, 1635. Published under the name of Fr. du Pasquier, doctor in theology, former student of Raynaud. Reprinted with Raynaud's name, *Opera*, vol. XVII, pp. 135–152.

41 We have a very interesting firsthand document about Gibieuf's relations with Saint-Cyran, which has not yet been utilized, at least to our knowledge. It is a manuscript, in the Arsenal Library *Recueil sur le jansénisme*, containing "Sentiment du Père Gibieuf de l'Oratoire touchant le jansénisme," manuscript 2009 (55 T. F.). Gibieuf's memoir against Jansenism, or rather against Saint-Cyran, since Jansen was not at issue at this time, occupies folios 21–45. The margin of folio 21 of the memoir relates the manuscript's history. "The Bishops of Ipre [Ypres] and the Abbot of Saint-Cyran approved Fr. Gibieuf's books on freedom in the year 16 . . . [sic], but since, in his dealings with them, Fr. Gibieuf recognized their pernicious sentiments, he formed the plan to make a history of this naissant heresy. He drew up this memoir on the subject, but because his many occupations prevented him from dedicating himself to it, he looked to Fr. Amelotte. To this end, he put his memoir written in his own hand into the hands of Monsieur de Reuty on order to hold it for Fr. Amelotte, who made a copy of it and sent the manuscript back to Monsieur de Reuty. The latter having died without returning the manuscript that Fr. Gibieuf had

the foundations for a house of the Oratory, made the acquaintance of Saint-Cyran, who was attached to the Bishop of Poitiers, de la Rocheposai.[42] No doubt de Condren was struck by Saint-Cyran's good qualities and introduced him to his superior, de Bérulle. The two theologians were able to meet again in 1621 between March and November during a trip Saint-Cyran took to Louvain to see Jansen. De Bérulle was greatly impressed by the enigmatic Saint-Cyran. He observed his "unusual scholarship, much more than ordinary knowledge of Scholastic philosophy and theology, extensive reading in the Fathers, his lively, penetrating, and hard-working mind," and was captivated by so many good qualities: "By his exceptional charity, he also has an ardent desire to become a useful laborer for the Church."[43] So de Bérulle immediately proposed to use Saint-Cyran for the greatest good of the Church, and, who knows, for the greatest good of the Oratory. Unfortunately, by this period, Saint-Cyran greatly cherished the project of utilizing de Bérulle himself and the Oratory for a general renewal of the Church that he planned.[44] Neither side would succeed. Both sides were confronted with

confided to him, Fr. Gibieuf took care to have it sought in the papers of the deceased, but it was not found. Only Fr. Amelotte's copy remains, which he sent to me this year of 1675 in the month of August." The manuscript, moreover, bears the date of 1638, which seems to be that of the memoir's composition.

42 Gibieuf, "Sentiment," p. 21: "The Reverend Father de Condren, who had known him at Poitiers introduced him to the reverend Father de Bérulle . . ." Gibieuf does not indicate a date, but Saint-Cyran seems to have come to Poitiers in 1618. In 1620 he received the Abby of Saint-Cyran-en-Brenne whose bishop resigned it in his favor. As for Condren, he was sent to Poitiers in 1621, where he spent a year and a half preaching and confessing. The bishop must have introduced them to each other as two priests that he esteemed. Therefore date of their encounter could only be 1621 or at the very latest, 1622. On Condren's mission at Poitiers, see Cloyseault, *Recueil des vies*, I, pp. 209–212.

43 Gibieuf, "Sentiment," p. 21.

44 On this point see le Sieur de Préville, *La Naissance du jansénisme découverte*, 1654. We find this collection extremely interesting in what concerns Jansen and Saint-Cyran's attitude toward the Oratory. We believe that the texts contained in the collection establish that Saint-Cyran tried to trick the Oratory and win it over to his plan. Cf. pp. 18–19 on the matter of vows; pp. 44–45, 49, 64, 67, 78, 82 on the assistance given by Jansen to the establishment of an Oratory in Flanders; pp. 31, 35, 64, for his expectations based upon the Oratory; pp. 35 and 38 for Jansen's approval of de Bérulle's *Discours*. It is also clear that even before Jansen's death, he and Saint-Cyran lost all hope in this area. The Oratorians did not have "hierarchical" spirit, pp. 86, 143; and they distrusted Jansen, pp. 120 and 123. We set aside the question of the authenticity of Jansen's letters and of the introduction that accompanies them. It would take us too far off course to work out a direct proof of that.

personalities too powerful to let themselves be absorbed. De Bérulle did not keep Saint-Cyran from the path on which he had set out. Saint-Cyran did not succeed in pulling the Oratory into the Jansenist movement. Still, at the beginning he had the impression that everything was going perfectly well. De Bérulle and the priests of the Oratory appeared to be so close to the plan Saint-Cyran had laid out, that their cooperation seemed assured. On both sides there was the same fervor in spiritual life, the same desire for the renovation of the clergy, the same veneration for the Fathers of the Church, especially St. Augustine, the same estrangement from Molinism and the same antipathy toward the Jesuits. The two sides coincided on so many points, and yet they were not to reach an understanding. As long as the issue was only St. Augustine, grace, or the Jesuits, everything was fine, but when the question was resistance to the Holy See and a possible struggle against the Pope, the difficulty began. What always separated the priests of the Oratory from Jansenism was their unshakable desire to follow the directives of Rome and submit to all the decisions of the Papacy.[45]

As to *De Libertate* in particular, Jansen and Saint-Cyran had been quite concerned about the appearance of the book, whose publication they awaited with curiosity. Jansen especially had already been working on *Augustinus* for a long time and seemed quite uneasy about this unexpected competitor.[46] However, he was reassured upon reading it, and the work gave him the impression of an improved Thomism, a new kind of "Thomistry" committed to the good path, but stalled halfway to the truth. At that moment, just one part of the book satisfied him, the critique of freedom of indifference.[47] Apart from that, *De Libertate* could not replace *Augustinus*. It did not push the doctrine of predetermination far enough, and even from the philosophical point of view, which seemed to be Jansen's own, the book had not "gone at the business adequately." Still, Jansen approved of many things and judged that

With this reservation, we can observe that in the passage where Saint-Beuve mentions it he expresses no doubt, Saint-Beuve, *Port-Royal*, 3rd edition, I, pp. 287 ff. Saint-Beuve admits their authenticity on the testimony of Rapin, who gives the history of the publication, and whose explanations on this point Saint-Beuve reproduces. Moreover, the Jansenists tried to interpret the letters in their own sense but not, to our knowledge, to deny their authenticity. Cf. *Lettres de M. Cornelius Jansénius à M. Jean du Verger de Hauranne*, with comments by François du Vizier (Gerberon), 1702.

45 Gibieuf, "Sentiments," pp. 22 ff.

46 Préville, *La Naissance*, p. 82.

47 Préville, *La Naissance*, pp. 85–86.

the book made "great openings."[48] He sent his approbation. But Saint-Cyran could obtain nothing more from him. Despite very pressing entreaties, Saint-Cyran never convinced Jansen to intervene in order to defend Gibieuf against Annat's and Raynaud's attacks.[49] Jansen was afraid of scandal and saw more to lose than to gain in the controversy. He found it difficult to excuse Gibieuf for having jeopardized the cause with his ineptitude and by proposing certain theses that would appear in *Augustinus*, without demonstrating them sufficiently. Jansen dreaded the thought that, as Saint-Cyran wrote him Gibieuf might speak out again.[50] Ultimately Jansen kept silent.

Jansen died in 1638, leaving the task of publishing his manuscript to Fromond. *Augustinus* appeared in 1640. The Oratory, which had distanced itself from Saint-Cyran in the interval, was going to be forced to involve itself in a new struggle so that its fate would not seem tied to that of Jansen, who had publicly approved Cardinal de Bérulle and Gibieuf. Furthermore, at the same time, all Thomists were going to be implicated, particularly Gibieuf, who had distinguished himself by his harsh criticism of freedom of indifference. Such a critique was an essential element of *Augustinus*; inevitably, it was going to bear the weight of the general disapproval that fell upon the whole book. Let us recall the third of the five propositions that would be condemned a few years later: "That in order to merit and to incur guilt in the state of fallen nature, it is not necessary for man to possess freedom that is opposed to necessity, but only the freedom that it opposed to constraint." To affirm that Gibieuf held this might provoke many theological arguments. There has been a four- decades- long discussion to find out whether Jansen taught this proposition. Therefore we will only try to establish whether it is found in Gibieuf. But it is at least legitimate to say that, like all Thomists and even a little more than they, he had taught something of the sort. God can necessitate the human will while leaving it free, and he determines it without constraining it. If this proposition is heretical, that mere fact may not necessarily make criticism of freedom of indifference heretical. Possible explanations remain, but the criticism is at least compromising and compromised.

Upon reading *Augustinus*, Gibieuf and the Thomism theologians must have felt this very clearly.[51] We might be tempted to dismiss Jansen's reproach

48 Préville, *La Naissance*, p. 88.

49 Préville, *La Naissance*, pp. 97, 117, 119.

50 Préville, *La Naissance*, p. 120,122.

51 Cornelius Jansenius, Episcopi Iprensis, *Augustinus*, Louvain: 1640, three books in one volume, in folio.

of Gibieuf for not having gotten to the heart of the matter. As we become familiar the doctrine of *Augustinus*, we are forced to admit that Jansen spoke the truth. Whatever the merits of Gibieuf's book, it must be agreed that even from the philosophical standpoint, *Augustinus* surpasses it everywhere, with its clarifications, additions, and greater depth. Let us set aside its innovations about grace and predetermination to consider solely its notion of freedom.

To eradicate Molinism and the Jesuits' relaxed doctrine, Jansen attacks the roots of the evil: the Pelagian heresy of which middle science is a kind of reincarnation. If we seek the origin of the Pelagian error, we find it in the fact that Pelagius and his disciples wanted to grant too much to free choice and overvalued it.[52] For them, free choice consists essentially of a kind of possibility or power of carrying out several actions indifferently. In Pelagian writings,[53] we constantly find that a misleading consideration of certain actions that are indifferent in themselves. Frequently, humans find themselves facing actions about whose commission or omission they are indifferent. When the Pelagians came to examine what our liberty is, no longer in relation to indifferent actions, but to virtue or vice, they want to maintain the possibility of our will's indifferently doing good or evil. This indifference seems so essential to freedom that they cannot understand that there can be a place for good and evil in our habits or actions without it.[54]

Therefore, for Pelagius and his disciples, our actions can only be moral if they are free, and if they are free, they are indifferent. In their view, being free is to be devoid of any necessity of the kind they call necessity of constraint. It must not be thought that by *constraint* they mean constraint properly speaking that breaks the will's resistance by violence. Rather, the constraint about which they speak is simply the subjection and submission of a free choice that can no longer want anything but good or evil, even if the will does not reject it. In that way, confusing everything, nature and violence, subjection, necessity, and immutable perseverance in good, they show clearly that constraint, as they conceive it, is simply the absence of indifference, the impossibility in which the will finds itself of breaking away at its pleasure either from evil or from good.[55] This is authentic freedom in their eyes, full and absolute indifference in regard to good and evil, to the degree that in the moment at which our soul is inclined to conserve what it

52 Jansen, *Augustinus*, I, column 91.
53 Jansen, *Augustinus*, I, column 93.
54 Jansen, *Augustinus*, I, columns 93–94.
55 Jansen, *Augustinus*, I, column 97.

possesses, or to acquire what it does not possess, it must be free, that is, indifferent to inclining or stopping itself. Otherwise, there will be no sin, nor evil will, and consequently, no possible acts of willing.[56]

Here the inconsistency of Pelagius and his disciples bursts forth. Provided that we grant them the indifference of the will, they ask nothing further to save free choice. Grant that the will is not compelled to a certain act, and they deem it free. This indifferent and dominating power of free choice, master of determining itself at its pleasure, has always been key for them. With it, no possible impediment for our freedom exists. If our will's indifference is safe — or given that this indifference always remains safe according to them — there is nothing to fear except that the vertigo of the passions or their alluring promises, by provoking us to this or that act, might attempt against our free choice. In their view, such movements are not causes that make actions necessary, but simply occasions of our consent or our rejection.[57] St. Augustine severely criticized the Pelagians for having attributed to our will essential indifference that cannot be lost, by which, whatever its state of grace or sin, of fallen or redeemed nature, the will can choose good or evil at pleasure, without being forced to want one or the other. Freedom of indifference constitutes something like the foundation of Pelagian doctrine upon which the whole edifice rests.[58]

Let us return to the Fathers" wholesome doctrine and to the sound notion of freedom. For the human will to be free, there is no need to attribute indifference to it, nor to exempt it from all necessity, but only to remove it from all constraint. It can be objected that this is a contradiction. Even free from all constraint, an act does not seem genuinely free if some necessity determines it, because the act is not in our power; we are not masters of carrying it out or not at our pleasure. Yet, it seems that this is an indispensable condition for there to be freedom authentically. How are we going to admit that an act is in our power and depends on us, if it is imposed on our will in such a way that we cannot abstain from it?

Let us be careful here. If we are unable to admit this point, that inability must be attributed not to the strength of the arguments put forward but to

56 Jansen, *Augustinus*, I, columns 184–185.

57 Jansen, *Augustinus*, I, column 322.

58 Jansen, *Augustinus*, III, column 367: "Gravissime fuisse reprehensos ab Augustino Pelagianos propter illam inamissibilem et quasi essentialem in omni statu liberi arbitrii indifferentiam ad bonum et malum exclusamque alterius partis necessitatem, ex iis quae libro 2 diximus intelligi potest. Haec est enim totius Pelagianae structurae basis pene praecipua."

the weakness of the human imagination that does not succeed in getting at the heart of the freedom of our voluntary acts. Considering all our voluntary actions, the philosophers have seen that they only appear free in the measure in which we can carry them out or not, according to our will. When the completion or cessation of an action does not follow the decision of our will, we declare that action to be outside our power, and consequently outside our freedom. We all have the innate, natural idea of freedom that an act is free if we can carry it out when we want and not carry it out when we do not want, so that the rule by which we measure our freedom is the will itself. Every faculty is called free in the measure that its acts depend on the will in their cessation or in their completion, and this is the proof: many movements are produced in us that are not voluntary, for example the obscene imaginations and movements of concupiscence and evil desires. By the very fact that they are not produced in us when we want them and that they are produced when we do not want them, they are out of our grasp and therefore outside our will.

This power of acting or not acting that is ordinarily called freedom, or indifference of contradiction, appears as something evident in all the acts that depend on our will and our freedom. This evidence is such that when we leave behind the consideration of actions to penetrate into the very seat of our freedom, namely the will or volition, we judge it absolutely necessary to encounter this same indifference in regard to every free movement always and everywhere. Since the definition of the free act involves the freedom of contradiction and supposes that we can act or not act, as we will,[59] we judge it impossible that the indifference that is essential to freedom should be lacking in any free act in particular. So far, this is perfect. But, observe the impotence of this imagination and the error that it entails. Just as we appraise the indifference of acts according to their dependence on the will that suppresses them at its pleasure or gives them free rein, we also gauge the freedom of this will according to another will different from it. When we want to evaluate a volition"s freedom, we do not confine ourselves to this volition itself, but, going further back, we indefinitely seek a prior volition upon which this volition depends and by reason of which it is free.[60]

59 Jansen, *Augustinus*, III, column 718: In his argumentation, Jansen rejects freedom of indifference of contrariety, because it is secondary and subordinated to indifference and freedom of contradiction. If we can carry out or not carry out the acts presented to us, *a fortiori* we can carry out this act in preference to that other one.

60 Jansen, *Augustinus*, III, column 718: "Sed in eo imaginandi imbecillitas et imbecillitatis error est quod quemadmodum illam contradictionis indifferentiam quae

From St. Augustine's viewpoint, which is ours, this interpretation of human freedom is certainly false. If by *will* is understood deliberate volition, the will is free by itself; that it not be free by itself, but only by another volition, implies contradiction. That is the sense of Augustine's words: the act is produced when we will it; it is not produced when we do not will it. Free will is justified by nothing other than itself. This manner of balancing our freedom should not be seen as a vicious circle or vacuous answer. An explanation like this is inevitable when we try to account for essences: there is no accounting for an essence; the will is free by essence. Therefore, we cannot claim to assign another reason to it than this one: the will is free by the very fact that it is the will.[61]

Besides, consider the contradiction into which the adversaries of this doctrine fall. They necessarily admit that the will can have reasons to determine itself without its freedom being thereby endangered, but do not admit that the will can have reasons to want an act immutably and definitively without there being a danger for its freedom. If freedom is fixed, it is destroyed. What will they say of God's freedom, whose full, immutable, and very wise will never changes because it never perceives any reason in the divine intellect to change? Continuing to will and to persevere in his resolution is no less a proof of freedom than choosing an act and deciding. The reverse is true: whatever inconstancy and mobility can be introduced into our freedom is proof of its insufficiency and weakness. Far from signaling our freedom's excellence, the capricious inconstancy of the will that we experience is a very sure sign of our soul's corruption. One cause of that is that sometimes inconstancy stems from ignorance of reasons for which it might be prudent to embrace a certain option; sometimes it comes from our inconstancy in persevering with the option we have wisely embraced. Our indifference is due either to our ignorance or to our inconstancy; the first makes us change by reason of the uncertain resolution we have just taken; the other makes us mistakenly change the wise resolution we had taken. If any hidden light shows itself in our mind, it is necessary for us to change or suspend our imprudent decision. If no new light is revealed, it corresponds

in omnibus actibus imperatis lucet, voluntatis jussu metiuntur cui ad nutum eos laxando vel cohibendo subsint; ita motuum volendi libertatem alia voluntate quam seipsa metiri volunt, ut sic videlicet in metienda libertate volitionis, nunquam in ipsa illa volitione maneamus, sed sine fine sursum semper ad alteram priorem ascendamus; ratione cujus haec postrema sit libera, dum priorem sequitur aut non sequitur, prout jusserit aut vetuerit."

61 Jansen, *Augustinus*, III, cols. 718–719.

to a prudent will to persevere in the same decision. The absence of these two vices, and consequently of any indigence, is what makes for the excellence of the divine will and of the wills of the blessed.[62]

Let us suppose that after ignorance and inconstancy have been uprooted from a creature's will, the will is immutably and perpetually good, that is to say, it is free with an immutable and perpetual freedom. That is the state of the blessed souls. Constantly attached to supreme justice, which is God, and invariably opposed to injustice, they persevere for eternity in the act of love that they have carried out once. Free of all feebleness, all uncertainty, and all ignorance, they love that justice above all, in all and always, in the midst of that full light, without perceiving the shadow of a reason that could turn them away from their final resolution. They love immutably because they will it; they are freed.

It is not surprising that we cannot picture such a state, because we experience nothing of the sort in our lives. That is why we retain some kind of scruple, as if the will of the blessed were drawn toward God by an irresistible impulse that would destroy all freedom in the will. Nevertheless, even considering the will as it is in human life on earth, it is easy to find in it some traces of such a state. Let us take a person of such perfect sanctity that nothing higher has ever been seen, or that someone more perfect could not exist outside of the direct vision of God. Let us suppose he has a complete horror of drunkenness, not only because of an irresistible physical and moral repugnance that would be purely natural but also by reason of his great virtues, and that he detests this vice like death. Let us ask him if he could get drunk. No doubt he will answer, "I could, if I wanted to." Let us insist, and ask him to want to and do so. There will be no promises, temptations, reasons, or threats that are capable of deciding him to it, not that he feels his will determined by a brutal tug that constrains him, but because he finds such absurdity and impurity in this vice that without a passion so violent that it takes away his use of reason, he will never make up his mind to change his

62 Jansen, *Augustinus*, III, column 720: "Quasi vero desultoria ista volendi inconstantia quam in nobis experiumur, perfectioni liberae voluntatis quicquam conferat, cum sit non libertatis, sed aegritudinis animi certissimum agumentum. Oritur quippe partim ex imperitia rationum et circumstantiarum omnium, propter quas aliquid prudenter amplectendum est, partim ex inconstantia non perseverandi in eo quod prudenter amplexi sumus, quarum altera facit ut priorem voluntatem juxta ratione, altera ut sine justa ratione, mutemus. Si enim nova lux oritur quae ante latuit, voluntas imprudens vel mutari vel cessare debet; si non oritur, voluntas prudens nec mutari nec cessare debet." Cf. Jansen, *Augustinus*, III, column 793.

decision. Still, it always seems to him, and rightly, that he could decide to, if he wills it. But he will never find any motive to do it, and he will never will it.[63] He is free, although he is not at all indifferent.

Moreover, the same proposition can be established by showing to what absurdities we arrive when we consider indifference to be necessary for authentic freedom. First, it would follow that the activity of grace in our souls would be absolutely contradictory to our freedom. Perfect grace perfectly suppresses our will's indifference, and grace is so much the less perfect as it suppresses this indifference less perfectly.[64] Therefore, if freedom consists in indifference, the grace that determines us to this or that act can only suppress our freedom. Perfect indifference is like a balance scale that a very slight jolt suffices to tilt toward one side or the other. This ease at being inclined indifferently to either side diminishes by the very fact of being inclined ever so lightly toward one of them. The more one weights down one of the two sides of the balance scale, the more difficult it will be to elevate the other side to such a degree that ultimately all of the forces of body and will together will not be enough. It is the same for the indifference of the will. The least movement of grace destroys perfect equilibrium. If grace is greater, this indifference diminishes. If grace is perfect, the indifference has completely disappeared.

There are other absurdities that flow from the same opinion. For example, it would be necessary to say that every movement of concupiscence diminishes freedom and that, consequently, we are not responsible for faults committed under the impulse of an overly strong temptation. Then, it will be said that habits, by suppressing our indifference, suppress our freedom, and that the faults will be so much less serious as they become habitual.

63 Jansen, *Augustinus*, III, 721: "Et tamen ei semper videtur, et sic revera est, quod hoc posset perpetrare si vellet. Sed nunquam rationes volendi invenit et ideo prudentem istam voluntatem mutare non potest."

64 "Nam, si perfecta gratia perfecte indifferentiam libertatis tollit, imperfectior imperfecte tollet . . . Gratia igitur quae facit facere, direct repugnant libertati, si libertas in indifferentia agendi et non agendi sita est. Nam illa indifferentia perfecta instar bilancis est quae facillimo nutu in alterutram partem impelli potest. Haec autem illo ipso diminuitur quo vel tantillum alterutri parti additur. Nam quo magis addideris, eo difficilius in alteram partem erigetur . . . Eadem prorsus est indifferentis voluntatis ratio. Minimus motus gratiae tollit perfectum aequilbrium, major minuit maximus penitus adimit" [Translator: Presumably Jansen, *Augustinus*, III, circa column 721]. On this point and all the other contradictions that freedom of indifference brings with it, see Jansen, *Augustinus*, III, book VII, chapter XIV in its entirety.

Finally, it will be affirmed that God and the blessed, who are confirmed in grace, are not free. Too many contradictions flow from the doctrine for it to be true, and we are necessarily led to reject it. Freedom is nothing of the kind, and if we want to delve into the inner sanctum where it dwells, we will find it where the will resides. Will and freedom are just one thing. No doubt many causes exist that determine our volitions. Besides the will considered in itself and in isolation, there must be something that makes it will and exercise its free choice.[65] That is the role of delectation. The will wants what delights it, and there is no will or volition that is not provoked by some delectation.[66] But whether this delectation is determined by the tendency of our fallen nature toward sin or by the light of grace that God sends us,[67] it has no other role than to make us will and consequently will freely, since will and freedom are just one thing.[68] The root of all this freedom that appears in exterior acts as well as in our interior activity resides in the will, by which alone all those acts are in our power. The will is free not by reason of some other will or volition, but by reason of its own essence in which freedom is necessarily included. Therefore, the will is free by essence and to say," The will is not free," is as contradictory as to say, "We can will without willing," or again, "We cannot do what we want in the acts submitted to our will." It is as contradictory as to say, "The will is not the will."[69]

Jansen's theology rests upon a philosophical infrastructure, all of whose elements are carefully arranged.[70] The principal element is a rigorous critique of Molinist indifferentism. It is hardly necessary to call attention to how obvious this infrastructure was and to the fact that Jansen did not try to conceal it in the least. On the contrary, in his view, the subject was

65 Jansen, *Augustinus*, III, column 734.

66 Jansen, *Augustinus*, III, column 721: ". . . nulla voluntas seu volitio exseri potest nisi delectatione aliqua suscitetur . . ."

67 See Jansen, *Augustinus*, III, book VII, chapters II and III on the role of delectation.

68 Jansen, *Augustinus*, III, column 736: "Delectatio efficit voluntatem et libertatem, hoc est facit velle et libere velle."

69 Jansen, *Augustinus*, III, column 622: "Est enim ipsa [*scilicet*, voluntas] radix totius libertatis, quae in omnibus actionibus sive externis sive internis apparet, propter quam solam illae in nostra potestate sunt. Itaque libera est voluntas, hoc est volitio, ratione sui, quia est essentialiter libera. Implicat enim contradictionem, ut voluntas non sit libera, sicut implicat ut volendo non velimus, aut non faciamus quod volimus; hoc est, ut voluntas non sit voluntas."

70 On the eminently philosophical character of *Augustinus*, cf. Fortunat Strowski, *Pascal et son temps*. 3 vols., Paris: Plon-Nourrit, 1907–1908 (re-edited 1921–1922), vol. I, p. 274.

fundamentally important. At bottom, the Pelagian heresy is a philosophical error about the true nature of our freedom, and in some manner, indifferentism is its main foundation, *basis poene precipua*. Therefore, the critique of freedom of indifference is also the main foundation of Jansenism, and *Augustinus* combats this false doctrine *mordicus* [with his teeth], since Pelagius sustained it *mordicus*.[71]

71 Jansen, *Augustinus*, II, column 458.

Chapter Six

Descartes and Nascent Jansenism

The singular fortune of *Augustinus* is well known. The Louvain Jesuits always had problems with Jansen, and they kept him under surveillance even after death. Anticipating difficulty, the executors of his will, who were his chaplain and two friends, Libert Fromond and Henricus Galenus, decided to infringe the papal decrees and print *Augustinus* without previously submitting it to Rome. However, the Jesuits managed to obtain the sheets as they were printed and tried to get a decree that would forbid the book's apparition as contrary to Paul V's brief renewed by Urban VIII. Despite the Jesuits' diligence, the book appeared before the decree condemning it. The 1640 edition published at Louvain was rapidly exhausted. At the same time, a second one was being printed, which appeared at Paris in 1641, and a third would follow shortly, in 1643 at Rouen. Having failed in their first attempt, the Jesuits tried to attack *Augustinus* on a different flank.

What had particularly troubled them in Jansen's book was the parallel he drew, and upon which he insisted, between their doctrine and that of the semi-Pelagians. They undertook to return the accusation. On March 22, 1641, the Jesuit Johannes Groll defended a thesis at Louvain with Fr. Joannes De Jonghe presiding, in which he exonerated the Society of Jesus from the accusation of Pelagianism and semi-Pelagianism brought by Jansen and tried to demonstrate that the doctrine of *Augustinus* was contrary to the definitions of the Council of Trent. The thesis with notes was immediately printed at Louvain and the same year re-printed at Paris by Chatelain.[1] These

1 We owe the notice of these theses to the kindness of the Conservator of the Catholic University of Louvain Library. We want to express our appreciation for access to this volume *in quarto* with the title: *Theses Theologicae de Gratia, Libero Arbitrio, Praedestinatione, etc.*, in quibus doctrina theologorum Societatis Jesu contra Cornelii Jansenii *Augustinum* defenditur; in VI capita divisae: Praeside Reverendo Patre Joanne de Jonghe, S.J. Sacrae Theologiae Professore. Defendet Joannes Groll ejusdem Societatis. Louvanii in Collegio Societatis Jesu, 22 [The date is handwritten.] Martii 1641, ante meridiem [These two words are handwritten.] apud Joannem Mersum, anno M.DC.XLI, cum superiorum permissione. The theses occupy pp. 1–124.

theses were a direct reply to the attack against Jesuit theologians. Through Groll, the whole Society of Jesus responded. The work, whose size was notably greater than that of ordinary dissertations, presented side by side in two columns Jansen's doctrine and the doctrine held by the *Theologi Societatis*. As one would very much expect, the full-fledged refutation did not spare the Jansenist notion of freedom.[2] Freedom of indifference was confirmed by weighty reasons, and an avalanche of quotations and references of all kinds overwhelmed Jansen's criticism of it.[3] We meet again the usual arsenal of arguments opposed to Thomism including its assimilation to Calvinism, and we also find the positions generally adopted by the Jesuits. We also find some newer arguments especially tailored to the theses that Jansen's doctrine has advanced. Among the indefensible errors of *Augustinus*, the Louvain *Theses* rise up against one in particular. It constitutes the radical denial of all Molinism: *Quod voluntarie fit, etiam si in necesssitate fiat, libere tamen fit.*[4]

This is the situation toward mid-1641. At this very moment the printing of the *Meditations on First Philosophy* is completed, and Descartes does not yet seem to feel himself in jeopardy. Let us specify certain dates. In 1630 after sharing his reflections on divine freedom with Mersenne, Descartes learns about the appearance of the book Gibieuf has just published. Toward October 1631, Descartes reads this book, which is still a complete novelty. We know what pleasure Descartes seems to have found in the reading. Gibieuf's ideas satisfy him, and Descartes "absolutely subscribes to his opinion." In 1631 the controversy that Gibieuf's book is going to generate has not yet erupted. At this moment, the Jesuits are plotting at Rome to get Gibieuf's book condemned, but there is no rumor of anything in the general public. Thereupon, Descartes stops corresponding with Mersenne on the question of freedom and generally seems to space out his correspondence to the point that during the period that goes from the end of 1631 to January 1637 only fourteen letters to Mersenne are recorded, all

Then, without transition other alleged theses begin, which are really a parody of Jansen (pp. 1–40). Two letters in Spanish that are petitions for judgment against Jansen follow (without page numbers). Lastly, a whole collection of items and parodies relative to the controversy these theses had provoked, notably Urban VIII's bull prohibiting both *Augustinus* and Joannes Groll's *Theses*.

2 Groll, *Theses Theologicae*, chapter 12, article 11, "De Libertate," pp. 52–64.

3 Groll, *Theses Theologicae*, p. 53: "Augustinus ejusque discipuli indifferentiam voluntatis ad utrumlibet, expeditam vinculo necessitatis antecedentis . . . agnovere."

4 Groll, *Theses Theologicae*, p. 101.

devoted to scientific discussions or to the condemnation of Galileo, about which Descartes was greatly concerned in 1634.[5]

1637 sees a very active resumption of his correspondence, but we get to 1640, date of the final version of the *Meditations*, without there having been any question of freedom. Nothing lets us think that Descartes is concerned with the problem. After 1630, when he spoke to Mersenne about divine freedom, the question was no longer discussed, and, moreover, Descartes never confided to his correspondent what he thought about human freedom. Notably, the *Discourse on Method* only brings in the problem superficially without Descartes pausing to take sides. He spoke to no one about the problem of human freedom, and we do not see that anyone spoke to him about it.

In 1640, when Descartes composes the *Meditations*, he is still occupied with Gibieuf's book, for which he professes great esteem and about whose fate he seems to be unaware. That is the disadvantage of the relative isolation in which he lives. Residing in France, Descartes would have known all about the history of *De Libertate* and the subsequent controversies it stirred up. He would have been familiar with Annat and Raynaud's books and the accusations of heresy brought against the new adversary of freedom of indifference. Finally, he would have known that since 1631 *De Libertate*'s doctrine, of which he had proclaimed himself a staunch advocate, had become more compromising and compromised day by day. But Descartes voluntarily isolates himself. He completes the final version of *Meditations on First Philosophy*, attacks and resolves the problem of human freedom without communicating any details to anyone. Still under the impression of a book he possesses and which, quite unusually, he likes, he utilizes those aspects of Gibieuf's work that seem most worthwhile to him, without suspecting any problem. Unfortunately, 1640 is also the year when *Augustinus* appears.

Descartes worked on the correction of the *Meditations* from November 1639 to March 1640.[6] Immediately after receiving the Objections of Caterus, he sent his manuscript to Mersenne with the Objections and the Responses. The letter accompanying the parcel is dated November 11, 1640.

5 A total of 29 letters have been conserved for the period that goes from January 1632 to January 1637, whereas for the year 1637 alone the number is 28, seven of which are addressed to Mersenne. This is evidently only indicative, because many letters could be lost, but it may be useful to keep it in mind.

6 On this point see Adam, *Vie et oeuvres*; XII, pp. 287–289, where all necessary references are found.

Augustinus had already appeared in September of the same year, and, if Mersenne was not already informed about it, he soon would be. Like all theologians of the period, Mersenne was interested in the controversies about grace and, without publicly taking sides, he did not pass up the opportunity to discuss it in private. The end of 1640 found Mersenne involved precisely in a discussion of this kind with his correspondent André Rivet.

Mersenne was a Molinist. Rivet was a Thomist and Augustinian and seemed completely ready to become a Jansenist.[7] Mersenne maintained that God does not want the damnation of anyone, but "that everyone is saved if he wills to cooperate with his salvation."[8] This thesis greatly scandalized Rivet, who wanted to force Mersenne to admit an Origen's paradise and "to place all the devils in it" or to acknowledge that, though God wanted to save everyone, he had not succeeded. As to the restriction, "if they cooperate in their salvation," it hardly seemed felicitous to Rivet: "Where does this operation and cooperation come from?" Why does not God operate and cooperate in everyone? Is he unable? If he so wished, could he not bend the will of all those who are being lost and withdraw them from their evil lifestyle? Why does he not do so? This is where his providence must be adored, and still we must heed what he commands without rising to heaven to enter his abode.[9] Rivet tried to convert Mersenne. Fortunately, assistance from heaven had just arrived and divine providence sent Mersenne an ally at that very moment. This ally was none other than *Augustinus*, Jansen's "great book," whose appearance had been communicated to his friend on November 10 of that same year, that is, the day before Descartes was to send the manuscript of the *Meditations* to Mersenne.[10]

7 Letter to Mersenne, October 1631; I, p. 220. Descartes knew Rivet and must have spoken with him more than once about these questions, because in October 1631 Rivet borrowed Gibieuf's book from Descartes, which Descartes was unable to read to the end for this reason.

8 On this point, see in the Bibliothèque Nationale Manuscript section, the Collection formed by Brother Hilarion de Coste of the original letters sent to Fr. Marin Mersenne (Fonds français, nouvelles acquisitions, 3 vols. numbers 6204–6206). Rivet's letter dated The Hague, November 25, 1640, is found in vol. III, folios 108 and 109. The phrase we cite in quotation marks here is underlined in the text. Therefore, it reproduces a fragment of Mersenne's letter. Rivet writes, folio 108, p. 204: "Consider, I beg you, where you are going in saying *that God* . . ."

9 de Coste, *Recueil*, vol. III, folio 108, p. 205.

10 de Coste, *Recueil*, vol. III, folio 108, p. 204: "I can only attribute to a special providence of God that, at the same time as you write your letter to me on the tenth of this month, which I have just received, I was answering your previous letters and

Mersenne must have read the two books within a short time of each other, and he did not fail to notice to what point, in certain regards, the critique of freedom of indifference contained in the Fourth Meditation was close to that in *Augustinus*. Descartes had obviously put himself in jeopardy, and Mersenne was troubled about it from the first attacks against *Augustinus*. Moreover, an opportunity presented itself to speak to Descartes about this. One of the theologians to whom Descartes had submitted the *Meditations* in order to obtain objections raised some difficulties against the notion of freedom Descartes proposed. Mersenne warned about the opposition Descartes would find in this quarter, but Descartes answered with some naiveté, that Gibieuf would certainly defend his cause on this point, because Descartes had written nothing that did not agree with *De Libertate*'s doctrine.[11] It seemed obvious that Descartes did not realize the changes that had occurred in the respective situations of the two parties. Mersenne insisted and strove to make Descartes understand that he was running the risk of being exposed to fierce attacks, perhaps even bringing difficulties on himself for getting involved in a dispute whose outcome could not be foreseen. To this good advice, Mersenne added a valuable memo. If Descartes absolutely held to his critique of freedom of indifference, let him at least be informed about the current state of the controversy. He asked whether Descartes had read the recently appeared *Augustinus*, and the Louvain Jesuit theses, which, by contrast, upheld freedom of indifference against Jansen. Descartes answered that he had seen neither of the two books and did not believe he needed to see them, but that it would be easy to find out where *Augustinus* had been printed in order to be able to obtain it in case of need. For the rest, Descartes persevered in his great confidence in *De Libertate's* doctrine and took shelter behind that book as behind an impregnable rampart.[12] Descartes would have been amazed if he had known that at that very moment, Gibieuf himself no longer felt secure.

Did Descartes read the Louvain theses and even Jansen's book? Nothing

mentioned the great book of Jansen, Bishop of Ypres, entitled *Augustinus*, where he deals at length with the doctrines of the human fall and reparation, with free will, grace and its efficacy, and with predestination and reprobation."

11 de Coste, *Recueil*, III, p. 360.

12 de Coste, *Recueil*, III, pp. 385–386 and 386–387: "As to what I have written about freedom, it agrees with what Reverend Father Gibieuf also wrote before me, and I am not afraid of any objection. I have not seen ... the Louvain theses or Jansen's book. But I would have no difficulty finding where it was printed in order to be able to find it, if I need to."

authorizes to affirm that absolutely, but at least we can say that there are strong probabilities that he did. The indecision apparent in his answer to Mersenne, the care he takes to find out the publisher"s name, although he often simply and flatly refused to read books that were recommended to him, the concern he always demonstrates in maintaining good relations with the Church and assuring himself of the approval of his doctrine by theologians — all this inclines us to think that Descartes must have become acquainted, not with the whole *Augustinus*, but at least the part of the book that dealt with freedom. At any rate, if he never read *Augustinus*, Descartes was warned. He knew that Jansen's work continued a doctrine of freedom similar to that in the Fourth Meditation. This was enough to put him on guard, because the great Jansenist polemics began in 1642, and no longer could one be unaware of the events unfolding in contemporary philosophy and theology.

Let us imagine what Descartes' state of mind might be after Mersenne warned him. Events accelerate. In Paris, by the end of 1642 Isaac Habert, who had been one of the warmest supporters of Gibieuf's book, changes sides, something the Jansenists greatly reproach, and violently attacks Jansen's book in resounding sermons.[13]

Saint-Cyran received the news of the sermons in prison at Vincennes. He wrote from prison to Arnauld in a prophetic mode to summon him to answer the sermons: "*Tempus tacendi et tempus loquendi*. The time to speak has arrived. It would be a crime to be silent, and I do not doubt that God would wreak some very visible and perceptible suffering upon your person as punishment for that."[14] All that was unnecessary to spur Arnauld to attack, and during 1643 the book *La Fréquente Communion* appeared, followed in 1644 by *l'Apologie de M. Jansenius d'Yprès, et de la doctrine de saint Augustin, expliquée dans son livre intitulé* Augustinus, *contra trois sermons de M. Habert théologal de Paris*. Simultaneously, the Jesuits responded at each step and even made the first move if necessary. The ardor with which they lashed out at *La Fréquente Communion* is well known, and the years 1643–1644 were completely employed in pursuing the polemic. Fr. Nouet's sermons, the *Lettres d'Eusèbe à Polémarque*, Fr. Pétau's book *la Penitence*

13 For the reproaches against Habert for having attacked Jansen after approving Gibieuf, see Géry, *Apologie historique de censures de Louvain*, second part, and Hermant, *Mémoires*, I, pp. 173 ff.

14 Letter of February 1, 1643; Hermant, *Mémoires*, I, pp. 183–185. (Hermant has 1642 erroneously.)

purlieu, a host of other treatises, parodies, or pamphlets, to which responses immediately followed, testify to the acrimony the controversy assumed. But the Society of Jesus mainly tried to obtain a condemnation that would fall upon the new sect from above. On August 1, 1641 the Jesuits obtained a decree of the Inquisition in Rome that forbade the printing and reading of Jansen's book, and despite the respectful protests of John Jansen, the author's nephew, the decree stood. From that moment, the defenders of *Augustinus*, especially at Louvain, did not cease to work to get the bull revoked. Cardinal Barberin would reiterate frequently to the Archbishop of Malines that the bull of interdiction had not been revoked and remained in full vigor.[15] This was not yet a condemnation of the doctrine, but it was an evident demonstration of suspicion that greatly perturbed the Jansenists.

Between 1641 and 1644, the general trend of the controversy was more and more unfavorable to Jansenism. It is also the time when all those who in one way or another felt implicated in the matter worked to demonstrate their orthodoxy and to distance themselves from Jansenism. Without mentioning Habert's attitude that constituted a complete reversal, the Thomists, and particularly the Oratory, showed some unease. They feared, what indeed occurred, that the Jesuits, seeing the occasion to implicate all their old adversaries, would proceed as if they identified Jansenists, Thomists, and Oratorians. On this point and at this moment, the Jesuits were triumphant. Molina"s doctrine, which for a long time some had attempted to render suspect, was now the only one evidently not Jansenist. As for Thomism, if it was not Jansenist, it might, strictly speaking, seem to favor Jansenism. The Jesuits presented themselves as the Society chosen by God to defend wholesome doctrine against the heresies that assailed the Church. Struggling on one flank against Calvinism and the Calvinist infiltrations that had given birth to Thomism, they confronted Jansenism on the other. The moment had come to compromise with the Jesuits, and that is what everyone did. Thomism no longer would have to defend itself against Molina, but (something much more delicate and difficult) against Jansen with whom the attempt had been made to confuse it. Thomism's vigor had been exhausted in the struggle, and we can say that as a living, active doctrine in the Church, Thomism at this moment was dead.

Gibieuf was one of the persons most seriously compromised in the affair. *De Libertate*, which, according to the supporters of *Augustinus*, agreed

15 This interdiction was renewed August 5 and 25, 1641, April 5, 1642, and July 8 1643. See Hermant, *Mémoires*, I, pp. 399–400.

in spirit with the doctrine they taught, was not forgotten. A certain chapter that Jansen had devoted to the appreciation of Gibieuf's book did not lend Gibieuf a very orthodox appearance.[16] Certainly, Jansen directed criticisms toward Gibieuf. Jansen refused to call Augustinian the doctrine of amplitude, which cannot be found in any of the six hundred passages of St. Augustine related to freedom. After eighteen years of assiduous and meticulous reading of Augustine, Jansen was incapable of attributing a doctrine to him that he had never seen. But, at the same time, he granted four essential points to Gibieuf on which *De Libertate* spoke the whole truth, and the first of these truths was Gibieuf's categorical denial that indifference constitutes an essential perfection of genuine freedom. Consequently, Jansen publicly stated that he and Gibieuf were in perfect agreement on the critique of freedom of indifference.[17] That was an approbation with which Gibieuf would have gladly dispensed. The first approbation that Jansen had directed to him at Saint-Cyran's request was already embarrassing enough.

This was beginning to be discussed in Gibieuf's circle, where some nervousness became apparent. Habert, the aggressive preacher who had issued the clarion call against *Augustinus*, caused a new scandal, at least in regard to the Oratory, by retracting the approbation he had earlier given to *De Libertate*. Denial of freedom of indifference was Gibieuf's peculiar heresy, to put the matter like a Jesuit of the period.[18] It constituted the core

16 This chapter, in which Gibieuf is not named but undoubtedly envisaged, is Jansen, *Augustinus*, chapter 16 of book VII, entitled, "Quomodo se habeat libertas arbitrii ad amplitudinem, eminentiam, independentiam, immensitatem, et similes voluntatis proprietates."

17 Jansen, *Augustinus*, book VII, chapter 16: "In primo quatenus auctor illius doctrinae, in hac amplitudinis assertione, satagit necessitatem illam indifferentiae ad bonum et malum, quam libertatem contrarietatis vocitant, a libertate secludere: sententia, juxta mentem Augustini est verissima. Hoc enim non solum illa loca quae ipse tangit, sed aliis plurimis quae produximus probari potest. Secundo, quod libertatem seu indifferentiam illam philosophicam contradictionis ad agendum et non agendum, non aliter putat esse necessariam, nisi prout ordo finis postulaverit, non minus Augustino consonat, qui sumum humanae libertatis in eo ponit ut peccare, hoc est a fine deviare non possit. Utrumque supra juxta doctrinam Augustini fusius asseruimus."

18 Batterel, *Mémoires domestiques*, I, p. 143, note "The Jesuit author of the *Bibliothèque Janseniste* says, p. 138, that in his *Théologie grecque*, p. 148, Habert retracted this approbation because of the Sorbonne decree that finds guilty of error those who deny human indifference to do good with freedom; this constitutes the core of Fr. Gibieuf's system and *his peculiar heresy* (underlined in the text). These are the words of Fr. de Colonna."

of his system, and Habert now saw the consequences to which this denial led. We must do justice to Gibieuf, who seems in this perilous situation not to have thought only of himself. His first thought seems to have been for the memory of Cardinal de Bérulle, somewhat touched by the Jansenist scandal. In the memoir that Gibieuf composed for a second edition of the Cardinal's works,[19] he devoted himself primarily to pointing out how far his superior always kept from the excesses of those doctors who imagined that all solutions to all problems raised by grace are found in St. Augustine's writings. But at the same time, Gibieuf worked to cover himself by expurgating passages from *De Libertate* that might seem dangerous. He prepared a revised and corrected second edition of his book. This edition met the fate of *Libertas Vindicata* and was never published. Perhaps Gibieuf was surprised by death. Perhaps he was brought to understand that since he enjoyed relative tranquility, it would be better to let silence pacify everything rather than re-awaken attention with a less than opportune publication. The fact remains that the project was not continued but ultimately abandoned.[20]

Did Descartes know the details of the polemics that surrounded *Augustinus* and the uneasiness that dominated the Thomist faction? His correspondence is silent on this point, and nothing permits us to affirm absolutely that he knew about the existence of any of the books directed by the Jesuits against Jansenist doctrine, beyond the Louvain theses. But that was enough to make up his mind. Since the opposite is implausible, we can admit that echoes of the quarrel reached him. Descartes knew two of the most important episodes of the controversy, if not in time to emend the text of the *Principles*, whose printing was complete by July 10, 1644, at least soon enough for him to be able to congratulate himself on the day of their appearance for having adopted a prudent, reserved attitude on the problem of freedom. By the beginning of April 1644, Descartes knew the difficulties within the environment where Arnauld was doing battle. During his trip to Paris he witnessed it, and, while the *Principles* were being printed, Fr. Mesland informed him about the appearance of Pétau's *De Libero Arbitrio* and about the doctrines it contained.

Through Fr. Picot, Descartes was aware of Arnauld's clashes with the Jesuits and the kind of defeat he had ultimately suffered. Descartes considered

19 The first edition of de Bérulle's works is dated 1644.

20 Batterel, *Mémoires domestiques*, I, p. 247 note: "Fr. Gibieuf had corrected and emended his book on freedom in order to publish a second edition" (Letter from Fr. Serry to Fr. Daniel in 1705, p. 66, where he quotes a curious addendum to his copy, *Mémoire de Bonardy*).

Arnauld one of the theologians most favorable to him, completely disposed to embark on the paths of Descartes' new philosophy. Descartes felt he could expect nothing good from those who persecuted Arnauld. His community of ideas and spirit with Arnauld on questions of theology, and the good disposition to follow him that Arnauld had demonstrated, encouraged Descartes to judge that they had the same enemies. Furthermore, he knew who these enemies were by having already experienced their unwillingness to accept true philosophy in their schools. Arnauld's travails seem to have affected him. One consolation was left: the thought that his writings did not touch upon theology proximately or remotely and that there could be no pretext on that score for finding fault with him.[21] That was Descartes' state of mind in 1644, and his stay in Paris that same year could only confirm it. There he certainly learned the details and the state of the controversy. Arnauld was forced into hiding for having refused to go to Rome to justify himself and, unable to see Descartes himself during July 1644, sent him a young clerical friend, Monsieur Wallon de Beaupuis "to offer him his services." Arnauld even made Beaupuis propose some new difficulty about Descartes" manner of explaining transubstantiation according to his principles, but rather to give the young cleric a subject for conversation with this great man than to obtain a response that Arnauld needed on the difficulty proposed."[22] Descartes could see the persecution of Port Royal with his own eyes, and that must have singularly confirmed his prudence.

Furthermore, Descartes was aware that the Jesuits were not satisfied with the Louvain theses and continued to mount a campaign against the opponents of freedom of indifference. In May 1644, Fr. Mesland wrote Descartes about *De Libero Arbitrio*, which Fr. Pétau had just published against Jansen and which would reappear incorporated into that renowned scholar's *Dogmata Theologica*. Mesland's opposition must have made Descartes pause to think. If a Jesuit who had shown such sympathy toward the new philosophy still could not help feeling some misgivings on this point where the honor of the Society of Jesus was involved, how much difficulty

21 Letter to Picot, April 1, 1644; IV, pp. 103–104: "Arnauld's trouble affects me more than my own [the affair of the Utrecht theologians]. For, I count him among those who wish me well; and I fear, on the contrary, that his enemies may be my own in large part. Still, I do not yet know the subject of the displeasure he could have caused them, and I console myself, because my writings do not touch upon theology proximately or remotely, and I do not believe that they could find any pretext in them for finding fault with me."

22 Baillet, *Vie*, II, pp. 129–130.

would others have raised against Descartes if he had persevered in his original attitude?[23]

Principia Philosophiae was worked out and published during this period. Descartes claimed to be sheltered from any attack from theological quarters, but he made the assertion without being absolutely certain of it, and perhaps partly to reassure himself. We know, moreover, that Descartes had implicated himself in some measure in the controversy, an imprudence that surely he regretted, he. The issue is to discover whether he would to persevere in his original attitude in this new work or, on the contrary, make an effort to attenuate the bad effect it might have produced.

There could be no doubt about Descartes' decision, since considerations other than those of mere prudence also must have pressed upon his mind. After the publication of *Meditations on First Philosophy*, the meaning and scope of certain doctrines had changed. In 1641 the criticism of freedom of indifference might simply have been disagreeable to the Jesuits. That was a blunder, but no more. In 1644, it became closely identifiable with a whole system on grace and predestination that appalled even many Thomists. Criticism of freedom of indifference was now the very foundation of *Augustinus*, a book prohibited by an often renewed interdiction, suspect, violently attacked on all sides, and under the shadow of a condemnation that was announced every day as to be effectuated on the morrow. In short, at this moment, criticism of freedom of indifference seemed to be an integral part of Jansenism. The question is whether Descartes was going to be implicated with this new party. Descartes would not be implicated, not just out of prudential motives, but also because he had nothing in common with Jansenism and had no settled conviction on the matter.

Let us consider the central point of the debate about grace: the problem of harmonizing divine preordination and our freedom. We can say that Descartes did not think seriously about this problem at all. When pressed during discussion, he would end by offering an *ad hoc* solution, but he did so unwillingly, careful to recall that there are questions beyond our grasp, and that we cannot claim to determine the nature of God by means of our reason alone.

On two occasions Descartes had an opportunity to explain himself, in circumstances such that, if he had any firm position on this point, he could not have refrained from expressing it. The first time occurred in a private

23 On Pétau's book and Descartes' attitude toward the doctrine of this Jesuit, see the next chapter.

conversation where Frans Burman, who was very concerned with theological problems, decidedly wanted to find out how Descartes reconciled divine immutability with the fact that God grants something or does not grant something according to our prayers. Descartes answered that God is perfectly immutable and has decreed from all eternity what he is going to grant or not grant, but with the restriction that he has decreed to give each thing in consequence of prayers of each person, in such a way that having decreed to only give us his graces in consideration of our good life and of our prayers, we must pray and live well if we want to obtain anything from God. The response did not commit Descartes to anything and could be accepted by any party. Burman was not satisfied by it and, wanting to obtain a more precise confession of faith, ended by making Descartes acknowledge that he was much more in agreement with the Gomarists, who attributed a great deal to God's power and little to freedom, than with the Arminians and the Jesuits among the Catholics, who conceded little to divine omnipotence and a great deal to freedom. Possibly Descartes was familiar with the controversies of Gomar and Arminius through conversations, but nothing lets us think that he had been influenced by them.[24] The very terms in which Burman expressed himself seem to indicate that the interlocutor imposed his conclusions on this subject on our philosopher rather than the latter being led by the natural bent of his own ideas.[25] Possibly also he had retained a slight inner preference for Thomism that became apparent when the question was pressed. Still, that is a hypothesis that the correspondence with Princess Elizabeth of Bohemia hardly seems to confirm.

By making our finite reason bow before the incomprehensible but very certain reconciliation of two contradictory truths in God, our freedom and divine preordination, Descartes thought he satisfied the requirements of theologians of all parties on this point. The objections came to him from an unexpected quarter. What might win over the allegiance of Catholic theologians stirred up serious difficulties in the mind of the Protestant Elizabeth. Nothing obliged her to accept these contradictory propositions. She would agree to that, only if Descartes (despite declaring himself incapable of so doing) harmonized them somewhat intelligibly. The question was raised in the context of clarifications about Ethics that Descartes sent Elizabeth.

24 Possibly Descartes had even been informed about them by Burman; IV, p. 316.

25 Conversation with Burman; V, p. 166: "Et ita quidem id ethice se habet, in quo author examinans rei veritatem vidit se convenire cum Gomaristis et non cum Arminianis, nec etiam cum Jesuitis inter suos."

Knowing that there is a God who is perfect and whose decrees are infallible, the philosopher concluded that we must "accept willingly everything that happens to us as being expressly sent to us by God."[26] Elizabeth had answered that this consideration could console us for misfortunes "that come to us in the ordinary cause of nature and the established order," such as losing one's goods by a storm or one's friends by death, but "not those imposed on us by humans, whose will seems entirely free to us, since faith alone could persuade us that God takes the care to direct wills and that he determined the fortune of each person before the world's creation."[27]

Descartes rejected the distinction. Faith alone teaches us about the grace by which God raises us to supernatural beatitude, but reason, and consequently philosophy, by itself suffices to demonstrate "that not the least thought can enter the human mind that God does not will and has willed from all eternity should enter." The certainty of divine preordination is based on the consideration of God's supreme perfection. Every effect that depends on human free choice depends on God as its first, immutable cause, because God "would not be supremely perfect if something could happen in the world that did not entirely come from him." It is not enough to say that God is the universal cause of all things in the sense in which that term is taken in Scholastic terminology. The sun is the universal cause of all flowers, but it is not the cause by which tulips differ from roses, since the production of these flowers does not depend totally on the sun's action, but also on that of some other particular causes. Therefore, a cause can be a universal cause without being a total cause. God, on the contrary, is the total cause of all the effects of the universe and consequently the total cause of those very things that depend on our free choice.[28]

In expressing himself so, Descartes merely takes the position he had adopted in the *Principles*: certainty about freedom, certainty about preordination, and reticence about their reconciliation. But this reticence no longer satisfied Elizabeth. Hardly interested about harmonizing freedom with the demands of a faith she did not share, she had strong curiosity about how Descartes would establish this harmony, if divine preordination were not a simple article of faith rather than a demonstrative certainty. That is why, when she saw herself obliged to acknowledge as a rational truth what she thought a truth of faith, despite the reticence that Descartes imposed

26 Letter to Elizabeth, September 15, 1645; IV, p. 291, lines 20–26.

27 Elizabeth to Descartes, September 30, 1645; IV, p. 302.

28 Letter to Elizabeth, October 6, 1645; IV, pp. 313–314.

on himself, she believed she could ask him for some explanation on this point.

Indeed, to Elizabeth, the reasons that proved God's existence did not seem sufficient to prove that God is the immutable cause, not only of all the effects that do not depend on human free will, but even of those that do. God's supreme perfection simply proves that, if God had wished, he could be the cause of all the effects that actually depend on us. For that, it would have sufficed for him not to give us free choice. But since God has endowed us with free choice, he did not want to be the immutable cause of all effects, and since he created us free, he wanted us to be independent at least in this sense.[29] Descartes could not accept a proposition like this for the simple reason that it was contradictory. It implies contradiction to say that God created humans independent. If humans are of such a nature that the actions of their will do not depend on the divine will, then God's power is finite. On the other hand, if God created humans with that kind of will, his power is infinite. Therefore, to say that God created humans independent is to say that he is finite and infinite at the same time, which implies contradiction. In reality, one must be satisfied to take as equally sure the certainty of our free choice, since we experience it in ourselves, and the certainty of the existence of an omnipotent God. It will suffice to know that "the independence we experience and feel in ourselves and that suffices to make our actions praiseworthy or blameworthy is not incompatible with a dependence of a different nature, according to which all things are subject to God.[30]

This compatibility is precisely what Elizabeth did not perceive. She certainly grasped the two terms, but it was "impossible to make them fit together." Contradiction for contradiction, it was difficult for her to understand that divine power was infinite and finite at once, and she could understand no better that our will could be free and tied to the decrees of Providence at the same time. Since Descartes seemed to perceive the possibility of a solution, she begged him to have the kindness of explaining it to her.[31] Descartes wanted to satisfy his distinguished correspondent and for the first and last time confronted this question, whose solution infinitely surpasses our limited human understanding, according to what he wrote in the *Principles*.

Let us first say that Descartes did not tax his imagination. He summons old memories from La Flèche and is content to adapt them to give the

29 Elizabeth to Descartes, October 28, 1645; V, pp. 322–323.

30 Letter to Elizabeth, November 3, 1645; IV, pp. 332–333.

31 Letter to Descartes, November 30, 1645; IV, p. 336.

appearance of a satisfactory solution. As is well known, to explain free will's "dependence and freedom," Descartes recurs to a comparison. Let us suppose that a king, who has forbidden duels and who knows with certainty that two gentlemen of his realm, dwelling in different cities, have quarreled and are so antagonistic that nothing will keep them from fighting if they meet. Suppose also that he gives each one a mission that brings them toward the town where the other is on a determined day. The king knows with certainty that the gentlemen will meet and will fight and will thus violate his prohibition. He even wills it in a certain sense. But can we say that he compels them? In no way, because the prior knowledge he has of their action does not determine that action at all, and his will to make them meet has not prevented them from fighting as freely as they would have done had they met by chance. What a king can do in this particular case, God can and does do in all cases in regard to all free human action, by reason of his infinite power. God, who can do everything and who knows everything "knew exactly what all the inclinations of our will would be; he himself put them in us; he also disposed all the other things that are outside us, to make these or those objects present themselves to our senses at these or those times, on which occasion he knew that our free choice would determine us to this or that thing; and he willed this, but he did not thereby will to compel it."[32]

Let us strip this explanation of the aristocratic allegory in which Descartes enveloped it.[33] We find Molina's middle science pure and simple. In this example, it is easy to recognize a particular application of the famous

32 Letter to Elizabeth, January 1646; IV, pp. 353–354.

33 It is possible that Descartes took the fable he used from a book of sermons, from a theologian, or even remembered it from the catechesis at La Flèche, but we have not found it in the works of any theologian that we have read. In any case, it is legitimate to see its origin in St. Thomas, in an image he frequently employs to explain the relation of chance to providence, *Summa Theologiae*, part I, question 116, article 1: "Respondeo dicendum quod in rebus inferioribus videntur quaedam a fortuna vel casu provinere. Continget autem quandoque quod aliquid ad inferiores causas relatum est fortuitum vel casuale, quod tamen relatum ad causam aliquam superiorem, invenitur esse per se intentum. Sicut si duo servi alicujus domini mittantur ab eo ad eumdem locum, uno de altero ignorante; concursos duorum servorum si ad ipsos servos referatur, casualis est quia accidit praeter utriusque intentionem; si autem referatur ad dominum, quo hoc praeordinavit, non est casuale sed per se intentum." — Cf. *Compendium Theologiae*, I, 137. By complicating the problem with the involvement of free choice and by resolving it through Molina's middle science, we get Descartes' development. Let us add that, in writing to a princess, it is fitting to employ a noble tone and replace slaves by gentlemen.

doctrine set out in *Corcordia Liberi Arbitrii cum Divina Praescientia*, which was certainly taught to Descartes when he received his religious instruction at La Flèche. Through his infinite knowledge, God foresees from all eternity what action we would freely carry out, according to whether we might be placed in these or those circumstances that God freely determines. The certainty of divine foresight and the choice made by God of the circumstances on the occasion of which we will take our determinations removes nothing from the absolute independence of our freedom.[34]

Surely desiring to settle this whole theological controversy once and for all, Descartes complicates his response by incorporating into the solution a completely different problem that had been discussed in his presence another time. To the question *Libertas arbitrii quo pacto cum divina praescientia cohaereat?* Descartes had added the question *Utram voluntas Dei semper impleatur?* The theologians see two very different problems there. Once admitted that God can foresee our acts without determining them, it still must be explained how God can manifest two apparently contradictory wills at once: one by which he ordains or forbids certain actions, the other by which he places us in circumstances such that we freely contravene his ordinances and prohibitions. To use Descartes' example, how can God forbid dueling and at the same time put men in circumstances where he knows with certainty that they will fight?

Descartes gets out of the difficulty by a distinction he borrows from theology: "As two different degrees of will can be distinguished in this king, one by which he willed that those gentlemen should fight, since he has made

34 On this point, cf. Molina, *Concordia*, question 23, articles 4 and 5, disputation 1, memb. 11: "Praeexistente in Deo ante omnem liberum actum suae voluntatis ratione ejus ordinis rerum, auxiliorum et circumstantiarum quem ex sua parte elegit, nec non finitorum aliorum, qui sua omnipotentia esse poterant, praevidente item quid in unoquoque eorum pro libertate arbitrii creaturarum esset futurum, ex hypothesi quod ipse eum ex sua parte vellet eligere; utique neque quod Deus hunc potius ordinem elegerit quam alium... in solam liberam ac misericordem voluntatem Dei est referendum, qui pro suo beneplacito id ita voluit." And also: "Cum ergo quod Deus eminentia, illimitataque sui intellectus perfectione, praesciat quid pro cujusque arbitrii libertate sit eventurum, nihil de libertate ejus adimat, sed perinde indifferentem illum relinquat ut in quam maluerit partem se flectat, ac si praescientia in ipso non praeextetisset; eo quod non, quia id praescivit, idcirco arbitrium se flectere debeat in eam partem, sed quia sua libertate se est inflexurum, Deus id praesciverit, praescivissetque contrarium, si pro eadem libertate esset futurum; profecto nihil hac praescientia impediente, eadem libertas ac facultas perveniendi in vitam aeternam, aut ab ea deflectendi, inconcussa perseverat."

them meet, the other, by which he did not will it, since he forbade duels; so theologians distinguish an absolute and independent will in God, by which he will that all things happen as they happen, and another that is relative and that relates to the merit or demerit of humans, by which he will that his laws be obeyed."[35] Considered in its core, this distinction does not belong specifically to any school. Plainly indicated by St Thomas,[36] it is found in different terms in all the theologians who take up this question. It is capable of a favorable interpretation in both theses, according to whether this absolute will is taken to be based upon simple prescience of free acts (Molinist interpretation), or upon the arbitrary decree made from all eternity by God that determines the nature of our actions in advance (Thomist thesis). By accepting this distinction, Descartes does not identify with any party, but, by the terms in which he frames it, it can be said that he seems to take it rather in the form Molina had given it.[37] However this may be, Descartes'

35 Letter to Elizabeth, January 1646; IV, pp. 353–354.

36 St. Thomas, *Summa Theologiae*, I, question 19, articles 10 and 11.

37 Here is how Diego Álvarez a theologian of the Thomist school, presents this distinction (*De Auxiliis*, book V, disputation 33, article 5): "Ad tertium respondetur, Deum voluntate antecedente, seu voluntate signi, quae est voluntas secundum quid, velle ut omnes universaliter observent ejus praecepta; non autem id vult voluntate consequente, alias omnes adimplerent Dei praecepta: nam voluntas Dei absoluta, seu consequens semper empletur." Here is the form Molina gives it (*Concordia*, question 19, article 6, disputation 2): "Sit prima conclusio: Quicquid Deus vult voluntate absoluta, semper impletur. Haec est de fide. Ut vero melius intelligatur, dilucidius probetur, sciendum est Deum duobus modis velle aliquid voluntate absoluta. Uno, sine ulla dependentia ab arbitrio creato, qua liberum arbitrium est. ejusmodi voluntas, absoluta Dei est quae propriisime appellatur voluntas Dei efficax, cui nulla creatura resistere valeat, idque sive Deus quod ita vult, exequatur per seipsum solum, ut fuit creatio orbis; sive interventu causae secundae, etiamsi voluntas humana aut angelica ea sit, cui necessitatem potest inferre. Comparatione tamen ejus, quod ita exequeretur voluntas creata non haberet rationem liberi arbitrii, eo quod in facultate ipsius non esset facere oppositum . . . Altero modo dicitur Deus velle aliquid dependenter quidem ab arbitrio creato, qua liberum est, atque adeo sub conditione, si creatum arbitrium id etiam velit . . . Hac ratione Deus optimus maximus vult omnia bona, quae per arbitrium nostrum sunt futura, non solum voluntate conditionali, si nos quoque ea velimus, sed etiam voluntate absoluta, quatenus ipsi praevidenti ea futura placent; eademque divina ejus ac singularis bonitas per arbitrium nostrum intendit ac vult. Quod autem haec etiam absoluta Dei voluntas semper impleatur, ex eo est manifestum, quia nititur certitudini praescientiae divinae, quod ita res futura sit per nostrum arbitrium, consequiturque in Deo eamdem praescientiam . . . Secunda conclusio: non semper impletur quod Deus voluntate conditionali vult. Conclusio haec ex dicta disputatione praecedente est manfesta. Vult

answer puts an end to the discussion Elizabeth had started. Was the princess satisfied by the solution proposed to her? Or, as is more probable, did she deem it useless to prolong a discussion that departed from the realm of philosophy to enter the inextricable difficulties of theological controversy? The fact is that she did not address any other request for clarification to Descartes. What particularly interests us in this controversy is the absence of commitment that Descartes demonstrates. A Thomist with Burman and a Molinist with Elizabeth, Descartes defends any solution according to the circumstances and he only resigns himself to defending one of them when he is compelled and forced by his interlocutors' insistence. After that, the attitude he adopts in the *Principia* is easily conceived. First of all, we comprehend his abandoning the criticism of freedom of indifference. By holding the doctrine he expounded in the Fourth Meditation too insistently, Descartes would risk being taken for a Jansenist. We have just seen that he is not at all Jansenist. No doubt, he goes a little far in this sense, since, not content with being silent, he retracts. An irreducible element of self-interest must be acknowledged in his attitude, and yet, on his behalf, it must be admitted that more than one theologian was beating a retreat at the same time and abandoning his earlier position.

Next, we understand the role played by the chapters Descartes devotes to harmonizing divine preordination with human freedom in the first book of *Principia*.[38] If we divorce this work from the conditions in which it was written, those chapters are difficult to explain. No one required Descartes to account for his opinions on this point, and nothing obliged him to explain them. It would have been very easy for him than to declare the human will free without undertaking to justify the harmony of divine preordination with our freedom. In this period it was very much understood that every Catholic — and we know that Descartes prided himself on being one — admitted as a truth of faith the harmony of these two truths, whatever the nature of that harmony might be. On the other hand, the two chapters play no role in his argumentation. They are previews, and we wonder what they are supposed to do in the discussion of the problem of error that Descartes is trying to clarify at this stage. The fact is that this passage is not addressed to the metaphysicians of today but to the theologians of his time. In chapters 40 and 41

enim ejusmodi volitione omnes homines salvos fieri, nec tamen omnes salutem assequuntur. Vult item sua praecepta et consilia observari, quae tamen passim contemnuntur."

38 *Principia*, I, 40–41.

of *Principia*, book I, we must see less the affirmation of personal doctrine than a profession of faith imposed by the circumstances. Nothing in Descartes' conscience was opposed to that. To the readers of the *Meditations*, who had ranged him among the Thomists and perhaps were going to range him among the Jansenists, Descartes simply sends the message that his declaration on the nature of error is not allied to any doctrine on predestination. He is neither Molinist nor Thomist on predestination, and if his words have led to misunderstanding on this point, he begs that it be rectified. As a philosopher he neither has nor can have any opinion on these questions. — No doubt, some political calculation enters into a declaration of this kind, However, it must be acknowledged that Descartes had the right to be unburdened of an unfair suspicion and to publicly abjure parties to which he was never genuinely committed.

Chapter Seven
Descartes and Father Pétau's *Dogmata Theologica*

This clear but discrete disavowal by Descartes did not liberate him from all difficulty. The text of the Fourth Meditation remained, and, before the appearance of the *Principles*, a Jesuit correspondent, Fr. Denis Mesland, thought to ask Descartes for an explanation. Like all the members of the Society, this Jesuit could not fail to share Molina's perspective. The quarrel on grace was a matter in which Dominicans and Jesuits considered their collective honor to be at stake. Mesland took the occasion of the recent publication of a treatise on grace by Fr. Denis Pétau to expound to Descartes at least the outline of his notion of indifference and freedom.[1] Although Mesland's letter is lost, with the help of Pétau's book, it is easy to reconstruct the objections it contained.

Fr. Pétau was known as a historian and scholar rather than a philosopher. He wanted to combat Jansen's book as a scholar. Pétau's *De Libero Arbitrio* is a fabric of texts aimed at making it evident that Jansen's doctrine is not

1 Dionyisii Petavii, S.J., *De Libero Arbitrio*, libri tres, in folio, Paris: Cramoisy, 1643. This reference provided by Descartes' editors, surely following Sommervogel, is completely correct. However, we have requested the book unsuccessfully at the Bibliothèque Nationale and the Mazarine Library, whose holdings of early editions in seventeenth- century theology are so extensive. Still more important, the Mazarine Library possesses the catalogue printed by Cramoisy, who published Pétau's book. This prospectus makes no mention of *De Libero Arbitrio* that Pétau supposedly published in 1643, nor, furthermore, of any work of the same type that he published at another time during his life. It must be sought in Fr. Pétau's *Dogmata Theologica*, whose first three volumes appeared in 1643 but were dated 1644. Three books from *Dogmata Theologica* dealing with free choice were printed separately and published with the date 1643 under the special title we have recalled. Doubtless under pressure to move quickly against *Augustinus*, Pétau accelerated the publication of this part of his work, which appears with the general privilege granted to *Dogmata Theologica*. The Municipal Library of Tours possesses a copy of this printing dated 1643, which, if we can generalize from our own experience, must be extremely rare.

St. Augustine's or the doctrine of the other Church Fathers, but actually Luther and Calvin's. Fr. Pétau knows just one kind of argument: the argument from authority, and his procedure consists of crushing each of Jansen's propositions under a mound of texts. But, upon reaching the end of book II, Pétau finally feels a philosophical scruple and seeks to define with some clarity the term *indifference* that he has constantly employed from the start of his work.[2] As Pétau acknowledges, this is a difficult task, because there are few ideas more confused than this one and few ideas more in need of analysis. What do we understand by this *indifference* that we introduce into the definition of freedom? What do we mean by affirming that a will is free when it is indifferent to acting or not acting, to choosing this or that side?[3]

Taken in this strict sense, the word *indifference* involves the notion of a certain situation and designates the condition of being placed between two terms without being necessarily determined to either one of them. For example, we call what is neither good nor bad *morally indifferent*. In this sense, the free will is called *indifferent* when it is placed between two things without being determined of itself to choose one and reject the other. That can come about in two ways, so that there are two kinds of indifference: one that is innate and essential, of which the very essence of freedom consists; the other is adventitious and only completes the first. This indifference is to freedom what accidents are to a nature that they complete and perfect by permitting and facilitating its deployment and exercise. Therefore, the term *rational* can have two senses. In one sense, to be rational is essential to humans and cannot

2 What turns out to be Descartes' source through Mesland's initiative is book III, chapter 11, to which chapter 12, which contains some interesting passages, can be added. In the notes that follow, we intend to give all the passages from these two chapters than can facilitate the comprehension of the famous letters of Descartes to Mesland.

3 Pétau, *De Libero Arbitrio*, III, 11, 1, p. 222: "Sed quoniam nuperi istius coryphaeus dogmatis [*Read*: Jansenius], post antiquorum allata pro eo testimonia, quaedam et sibi objecta dissolvit, et contra communem et catholicam objecit ipse sententiam; paullulum in ea conflictione operae ac studii ponere statui: ut ad ea, quae pro se illi firmissima putant; certe in omni, qui habetur hac de re, privato publicoque sermone prae se ferunt, parata sint quae ex adverso dicantur, ex omni superiore doctrina per partes articulatimque digesta. Ac primum illud, in quo jactare se potissimum et insistere solent, explicandum est, quid *indifferentia* sit illa, quam in libertatis definitionem ponimus; cum liberum dicimus arbitrium *indifferens* ad agendum esse, vel non agendum; ad hoc vel illud eligendum. Est enim anceps istius vocabuli significatio: et in hac ambiguitate latebra quaedam est insidiosae calumniae, quam in apertum proferri, ac notari interest Catholicae veritatis ac fidei."

be separated from human nature whose constituent difference it is. In another sense, this term designates an accident, a complementary characteristic of human nature: the power and the faculty of reasoning that children do not yet possess and that is degraded in the insane.

Let us apply this distinction to the problem of freedom. There is a natural indifference, essential to freedom, that consists of the power of choosing one of two opposite terms. In other words, when the adjudication of reason has proposed one of two terms as being preferable to the other, the will can still choose either without being drawn to it by any necessity that determines it. We understand the sense in which the Fathers of the Council of Trent understand it: human free choice gives its assent in such a way that it could refuse it, if it willed. That is said without prejudging the question of finding out which of two equally orthodox parties that conduct a subtle controversy on the text gives the best interpretation of it. There is a second kind of indifference in which the will is found when it can opt between two terms but is not especially drawn toward either one. The will then tends toward each of them with an equal propensity and is in the state that is called *state of equilibrium*. Such is the case when two equally convenient roads take us where we want to go. No reason inclines us to choose one rather than another, and our choice is subordinated to the absolute option of our will.[4]

4 Pétau, *De Libero Arbitrio*, III, 11, 2, p. 222: "Sic igitur habendum est, *indifferentiae* nomini proprie subjectum esse notionem hanc, uti medium quemdam statum, et interjectum inter duo significet: quorum ad neutrum necessario determinatur. Ita enim in iis que ad mores spectant, *indifferens* dicitur quod nec bonum nec malum . . . Hoc sensu indifferens voluntas *libera* dicitur, cum inter hanc rem et illam media est, ut ad neutram eligendam at rejiciendam sese ipsa determinat. Hoc autem duobus fit modus: et est *indifferentia* duplex. Una est a natura insita, οὐσιώδης, in qua libertatis essentia posita est. Altera est adventitia, et quaedam prioris abolutio. Sic enim accidentia complementa velut naturae perfectionesque dicuntur; quod illi proferendae et exercendae sui facultatem et facilitatem tribuunt. Quem admodum *rationale* duplicitur sonat; et alterum est οὐσιώδης homini nec ab eo separari potest est enim indifferentia naturam hominis constituens. Alterum est accidens, et quaedam naturae perfectio: ut est ratiocinandi vis et facultas quae nondum est in infantibus, in amentibus est laesa.

"Naturalis indifferentia libertatis in eo consistit, ut tam unum quam huic oppositum eligere possit. Sive, ut cum arbitrio rationis unum illi praeferendum alteri proponitur, ad utrumvis inclinare se possit; nec ad unum necessitate ulla determinante trahatur. Quod eo sensu intelligi volumus, quo Tridentini Patres decreverunt, *sic assentiri liberum hominis arbitrium, ut possit dissentire si velit.* Nec enim praejudicium de alterutra parte facimus illius controversiae, quae jamdudum magna et acuta ingenia, salva catholica veritate in scholis exercet.

Only the first of these two kinds of indifference is essential to freedom. As for the second, it can be more or less, or even completely, absent, without any prejudice to the first, which is the essence of freedom. The natural inclinations that we carry at birth, the habits that constant repetition of the same acts strengthen, and illnesses and troubles of all kinds often act upon our will and, like weights that burden it, make it veer in a certain direction. Therefore, it will be helpful to remember that there is a native or innate indifference that is called *indifference of election*. There is another accidental and adventitious one that could be called *indifference of propensity or inclination*.

A dual sort of determination corresponds to these two kinds of indifference, one absolute and the other relative. That which would suppress the natural and essential indifference in freedom will be called *necessity or absolute determination*. Let us note first that such necessity is purely hypothetical and corresponds to no reality. It would consist either of simple necessity, suppressing all power of choosing and of deliberating, or of violent necessity, forcing the choice of evil actions, which would suppress all freedom in the will if it were possible that freedom should be constrained and destroyed. That is contradictory and impossible, and therefore absolute determination is imaginary and fictitious. The other species of determination is purely relative, and it comprises every force and every necessity that produces external constraint and violent impulse on the will. Pain, physical suffering, imminent harm, and the appearance of danger will constitute relative determinations. Also included here are violent impulses of concupiscence, other impulses called *passions*, and in a general way everything that saps the soul's strength without thereby totally suppressing freedom of election or absolutely determining free choice. When the human will and soul are caught in the net of vice and reduced to slavery to sin and Satan, and undergo that interior struggle that the apostle Paul felt and lamented, they are in this state of slavery very much opposed to true freedom. Let us still observe that, however great may be the violence and impetuosity of the assault on freedom and however low it may fall, the impulse that these determinations communicate is never transformed into constraint and does not take away

"Altera est indifferentia, cum sic habet voluntas utriusvis optandi potestatem, ut neutram in partem sit affecta, sed paribus momentis in utrumque propendeat, quam Graeci ἰσορροπίαν, Latini *aequilibrium* nominant. Ut cum duplici via aeque commodo eo quo intendimus pervenire possumus, non magis in unam quam alteram tenendam propensi sumus; sed absoluta est ad eligendum voluntatis optio."

indifference, that is to say, the right and power of choosing any one of the terms proposed.[5]

This distinction, of which Pétau is rather proud, constitutes the clearest element in his personal contribution to the controversy on grace, and it also seems to have provided Mesland with the material for his remarks about the doctrine on human freedom taught by Descartes. In truth, this distinction is only a kind of compromise and it introduces less light than obscurity into the dispute. Pétau had rehearsed Jansen so much in order to refute him that he had become slightly Jansenist without knowing it. We cannot read this chapter of *De Libero Arbitrio* without being struck by the fact that Pétau accepts the results of Jansen's critique of freedom of indifference. Compelled, despite himself, by the close and vigorous criticism in *Augustinus*, Pétau is caught between his very fixed resolution to justify freedom of indifference and the dazzlingly evident fact that the portion of indifference that enters into our freedom marks its feebleness and uncertainty. Rather than frontally attack such an indisputable proposition, Pétau tries to integrate into Molinism Jansen's critique of freedom

5 Pétau, *De Libero Arbitrio*, III, 11, 3, pp. 222–223: "Haec autem indifferentia vel adimi ex toto potest, vel ab ea plus minusve recedi, integra manente priori, quae est libertatis essentia. Nam et naturalis affectus ab ortu ipso inditi, et habitus usu et actionum assiduitate roborati, et morbi ac perturbationes saepe voluntates impellunt, ac velut pondere quodam alteram in partem deprimunt. Meminerit itaque lector eruditus, indifferentiam aliam esse nativam et insitam, quae *electionis indifferentia* nominetur; aliam accidentem et adventitiam, quae *indifferentia propensionis vel affectus* dici poterit. Sic *determinatio* sive necessitas quae *indifferentiae* illi respondet, similiter duplex est: una est absoluta quae naturalem et οὐσιώδη tollit indifferentiam, cujusmodi est absoluta necessitas tam simplex quam violenta; tametsi haec intimam voluntatem nunquam afficit, ac proinde nunquam libertatem eripit, sed fictione sola et ὑποθετικῶς, si quidem esse posset in rerum natura, adversari et illam perimere dicitur. Altera est κατά τι et *quadamtenus*, vel, ut vulgo Scholae nuncupant, *secundum quid*; ad quam vis omnis et necessitas extrinsecus cogens, ac violenter impellens referri debet: ut sunt dolores, cruciatusque corporis, metus ingruentis mali ac proposita pericula, vehementes concupiscentiae motus et quae *passiones* vocantur; et innumera id genus alia, quae constantes animos saepe labefactant, nec tamen eligendi libertatem ex toto detrahunt, neque liberum arbitrium absolute determinant. Quo et servilis ille status animi ac voluntatis attinet, verae ac laudabili oppositus libertati, cum homo vitiis irretitus sub peccati ac Diaboli servitutem trahitur, et intestinum illud sentit ac domesticum praelium, quod in se magnus experiebatur ac lugebat Apostolus capitulo 7 ad Romanos. Haec enim omnia etsi magna vi et impetu libertatem quatiunt et in praeceps abripiunt, non tamen invitam dimovent, nec *indifferentiam*, hoc est utriuslibet amplectandi jus ac potestatem auferunt."

of indifference. The distinction we have just set out springs from this attempt.

This harmonization was not easy to accomplish. Given the respective positions of the two bands, Pétau could hardly avoid either seriously deforming Molina's doctrine by making important concessions to Thomism and even Jansenism, or falling into pure verbalism. We can ask what option the Jesuit definitively chose, but upon reflection, the answer is clear: he fastened upon the second solution. We underline the element of incoherence and uncertainty in Pétau's attitude, not with the purpose of reproaching him uselessly, but to show that Descartes seems to have been somewhat disoriented in the face of this incoherence. Part of the obscurity of his answer to Mesland comes from the effort he makes to give Pétau's doctrine a logical, precise meaning.

The Jesuit conceded that a kind of indifference, the same kind that Descartes and Jansen had criticized, is a defect and an authentic depravity in our freedom. Everything that human passions, concupiscence, and ignorance introduce into our judgments and our actions constitutes the indifference in question, an authentic slavery from which we cannot be delivered quickly enough. The equilibrium in which we may be between good and evil, without which we feel pulled toward one or the other, can be completely broken without any harm to our authentic freedom. In what does this authentic freedom consist? It is always indifference and power of choosing, but understood in a different sense that Pétau does not specify further. How, indeed, might he specify? After granting that equilibrium can be destroyed without the will thereby ceasing to be free, Pétau claims that the will, even completely pulled in a certain direction, remains indifferent in the exercise of its choice. From there, only the two following interpretations can be given of his thought. Either he simply calls *indifference* the movement by which the will is moved to embrace one side, in abstraction from any hesitation and any possible change in its decision; in this case it only retains the name of *indifference*, and Pétau's doctrine absorbs all of Thomism with something of Jansenism or alternatively, he retains an inalienable power that the will would have of changing side and decision in all cases, which makes us wonders what sense this distinction could have. If Pétau admits that the weight of reasons that pull our will toward a certain side leaves our freedom intact while suppressing our indifference, if he admits that this indifference *adimi ex toto potest* without any harm to or freedom, what does he understand by this power of changing sides that would remain to the will? When it is entirely pulled to one side, how could it decide for the other? It seems that we cannot avoid choosing here. The will can change sides and still remain a little bit indifferent, or else it is not at all indifferent, but then it could not change sides. To avoid contradiction, Pétau assigns two indifferences to humans, that both consist of choosing between two sides. Thereafter, his tactic against Jansen becomes simple. Every time Jansen has destroyed one freedom of indifference, Pétau exhibits the other in such a way that there always remains a freedom in Molina's favor.

Let us take an example. Jansen objects that if indifference is an integral part of our freedom, all movement of concupiscence and of the passions, all good or bad habits, by destroying indifference, will destroy freedom. Armed with Pétau's distinction here, even a child would be capable of reversing this objection. What is diminished or destroyed is not the indifference that is natural and essential for our freedom, but only the accidental indifference that in this case would be one more perfection added to freedom. The first indifference, that which is essential to freedom, remains intact; it undergoes no growth or diminution; but consisting of indivisible unity, it simply requires the power of consenting to one side, free from any necessity, in such a way that it can turn away from it if it wills; it is the power of choosing between two sides. By this very quick answer, with one stroke, we knock down the mass of arguments accumulated by our adversaries, and we impose silence on their loud talk.[6]

6 Pétau, *De Libero Arbitrio*, III, 11, 4, p. 223: "Haec quanto a nobis operae pretio animadversa notataque fuerint sciet, qui praecipua contrariae factionis argumenta in hoc uno verti cardine cognoverit, ut *indifferentiam* eximant e natura definitioneque libertatis. Ac sunt absurda quatuor quae adversus illam Dogmatistes novus [*scilicet* Jansenius] opponit tanquam consectaria communis opinionis: quae ex duplici constituta a nobis indifferentia facillime diluuntur. Nec est necesse dividi ac singillatim illa proponi. Est enim vis eadem omnium et una responsione solvuntur.

"Igitur si in indifferentia liberi arbitrii natura ponitur, sequi ex eo dicit, omnia illa quibus alterutram in partem voluntas trahitur, *repugnare arbitrii libertati, quoniam illam extrahunt ab indifferentia agendi, eamque determinate faciunt agere vel non agere, velle aut non velle. Tales sunt concupiscentiae motus: omnes iidem habitus et consuetudines animi sive bonae, sive malae, quae direct repugnant aequabilitati istius indifferentiae*. Vel puero facile etsi quam haec cassa sint et ludicra discere. Non enim quaecumque voluntatis indifferentia vel ad essentiam pertinet libertatis, vel istis rebus violatur ac minuitur. Sed sola illa, quae accidens est liberae voluntatis perfectio. Nam prior et naturalis nec ulla fit accessione major, nec decessione minor: sed in individuo posita, id unum postulat, nulla uti determinante necessitate *sic uni consentiat, ut dissentire possit si velit*: hoc est ut in utrumlibet ferri ac movere se possit. Quamobrem uno hoc ictu brevissiame responsionis totum illud genus labat argumenti, quod ex loco isto moliuntur, et magnis clamoribus intentant."

Such is the solution concocted by Pétau, upon which Mesland's letter invites Descartes to offer his reflections. Of the two possible interpretations of the Jesuit's peculiar doctrine, Descartes at once selects the pejorative one because, by elaborating Pétau's explanations in a Thomistic sense, it reduces the difference separating Pétau's doctrine from that of the Fourth Meditation to a question of words. Descartes' position at this moment is very clear. He refuses to see two indifferences, two powers of choosing, in human freedom. Our freedom only includes one power that sometimes is indifferent and imperfect by Pétau and Mesland's own admissions, sometimes perfect, which is to say, not indifferent. Thereafter, the question is only verbal. Pétau calls the indifferent will *free* and *imperfect*. Descartes prefers to call the perfect and non-indifferent will *free*. That is the difference that separates them. At bottom, they are entirely in agreement because both admit that indifference is an imperfection of the will.

Therefore, Descartes initially had the impression that Pétau's opinion, which Mesland seemed to support, was not far from his.[7] Moreover, at the same time as Descartes wanted to construe the opinion in his own sense, he simply sought to make a small effort at conciliation. Since Pétau wanted another kind of indifference to be acknowledged, one that comes from feebleness and ignorance of the understanding, Descartes indicated to Mesland that the text of the *Meditations* was not at all opposed. Descartes had not written that humans are indifferent when they lack knowledge, but only that the more we lack knowledge, the more indifferent we are. This last point is evident and acknowledged by all, even Pétau. Nothing prevents it being accepted, while also admitting that another kind of indifference remains possible, that indifference about which Pétau speaks that would be natural and essential to freedom.[8]

But, what constitutes this other species of indifference? It consists, they say, of the power the will has to always and in every case suspend our judgment. Descartes agrees but wants to know how judgment can be suspended. Does that occur while we clearly perceive the truth of a proposition or the

7 Letter to Mesland, May 2, 1644; IV, p. 115: "As for free choice, I have not yet seen what the Reverend Father Pétau has written; but, by the way you explain your opinion on the subject, it does not seem to me that my opinion is very far from yours."

8 Letter to Mesland, May 2, 1644; IV, p. 115: "Because, firstly, I beg you to observe that I did not deny that humans are indifferent when they lack knowledge, but exactly that they are that much more indifferent insofar as they know fewer reasons that might push them to choose one side rather than the other. No one, it seems to me, can deny this."

excellence of an action? It does not. It is certain that every great light of the intellect is followed by a great inclination of the will, in such a way that seeing very clearly that something is good, it is very difficult, even impossible for us to hold back the course of our desire, that is to say, our will's consent. Therefore, perfect light in the understanding suppresses any indifference in the will and any possibility of suspending judgment. But our attention is fluid. We do not think of the same thing for more than a moment, and when the issue is the reasons on account of which something seems good to us, we sometimes lose sight of them so that only the recollection of having desired the thing remains. If we add the fact that we can then represent contrary reasons that incline us to finding it bad, it will be understood that we can always suspend our judgment and even in certain cases we can replace it by the opposite judgment. Therefore, Descartes grants to Pétau the famous *ut possit dissentire si velit*, required by the Father of the Council of Trent for the integrity of our freedom.[9] At the same time, he concedes to Pétau that indifference can always be found in the choice of our judgments and our acts, but he grants it from a standpoint and in a sense that are his own, by subordinating the will's indifference to the understanding and imperfection of the intellect.

In any case, Descartes thinks he has established the agreement of his views and those of Pétau on the two points above. The essential point, the definition of indifference, remains. There, Descartes thinks that Pétau has conceded the match. Since, by Mesland's own admission, freedom does not consist of indifference understood in the Cartesian sense, and since, by contrast, it is agreed that this indifference is an imperfection and a defect in freedom, what remains is that freedom is the real positive power to determine oneself. Descartes admits that absolutely; he explicitly recognizes that this power is in our will. Therefore, at the heart of the matter, he agrees with

9 Letter to Mesland, May 2, 1644; IV, pp. 115–116: "And I agree with you when you say that someone can suspend his judgment; but I have tried to explain the means by which he can suspend it. For, it seems to me certain that, *ex magna luce in intellectu sequitur magna propensio in voluntate*, so that, seeing very clearly that something is appropriate for us, it is very difficult, and as I believe, even impossible, while we remain in that thought to stop the course of our desire. But, because the nature of the soul is almost to not be attentive to the same thing for a moment, as soon as our attention turns away from the reasons that make us aware that the thing is appropriate for us, and in our memory we only retain that it appeared desirable to us, we can represent some other reason to our mind that makes us doubt about it, and thus suspend our judgment and also perhaps even form an opposite judgment."

Mesland and Pétau. A simple question of words is involved here. The will contains a real, positive power of determining itself; that is the fact. It remains to find out in what case the will is to be called *free*. Is it when choice is accompanied by this indifference that is acknowledged to be an imperfection, or on the contrary when it is not accompanied by it? In both cases, it is the same power of the will's determining itself that is manifested. But in the first, it is imperfect, while in the second it is perfect, as we see by the blessed whose understanding only contains the light and whose will is contained in grace. Descartes prefers to call *free* all that is voluntary, even a voluntary determination that is completely perfect.[10] Pétau and Mesland restrict the term *free* to the indifferent will and deny freedom to the blessed. This is a mere question of words, and Descartes wants nothing more than to follow usage and precedent.[11]

After having cut through the fundamental difficulty, Descartes resolves some ancillary issues raised by Mesland. It had been objected that if, as the Fourth Meditation affirms, freedom consisted in the mere absence of constraint and not in a positive power of determining oneself, animals would be free since they act without being forced or constrained. Descartes concedes the argument in its entirety, since he has just explicitly acknowledged that the power of determining oneself is essential to freedom. Not having this power, animals are not free, and the absence of constraint in them is a pure negation that does not correspond to any positive power of self-determination. They do not have a will that could be

10 Note the perfect agreement on this point between Descartes and Jansen. See above, Part II, Chapter 5, note 61.

11 Letter to Mesland, May 2, 1644; IV, p. 116: "Since you do not situate freedom precisely in indifference, but in a real, positive power of determining oneself, the only difference between our opinions is verbal. I affirm that this power is in the will. But since I do not see that the power is different when it is accompanied by indifference, which you affirm is an imperfection, from when it is not so accompanied, and that in the intellect there is nothing but light, as occurs in the blessed who are confirmed in grace, I generally call *free* everything that is voluntary, and you want to restrict the term to the power of determining oneself that is accompanied by indifference. But, regarding names, I desire nothing so much as to follow usage and precedent."

It will be recalled that for Molinists, the blessed are not free, and it may be that Mesland recalled the affirmation explicitly repeated by Pétau, *De Libero Arbitrio*, III, 12, 22, p. 235: "Amor autem beatorum, cum in summum bonum ac finem ultimum feratur perfecte, et cujus modi in se est cognitum, non ex electione oritur: adeoque nec a libero arbitrio, cujus propria est electio."

constrained. Therefore, the absence of constraint in no way implies that they are free.[12]

Lastly, Mesland calls Descartes' attention to the theological consequences of his doctrine by asking if he would dare to explicitly extend the explanation he had given for error to the explanation of sin. Descartes accepts those consequences unhesitatingly. If he did not speak "of the freedom we have to follow good or evil" in the Fourth Meditation, it is because he wanted to avoid "the controversies of Theology"[13] as far as possible, but what he said about the role of indifference in error can be applied without difficulty to the role of indifference in sin. Just as we err in judgments when the obscurity of the understanding leaves our will indifferent, "there is indifference in everything in which there is the occasion of sinning."[14] Therefore, if it is impossible to sustain that indifference in the choice of judgments is a perfection, it is no less impossible to sustain that indifference is a perfection in the choice of actions. Indifference of the will, whether in regard to the true or in regard to the good, must always be considered the lowest degree of our freedom.

Will it be objected, as Mesland seems to have done, that indifference in Descartes' sense leaves no room for sin? Will it then become necessary to say that for an action to be truly bad, our understanding must necessarily have represented it to us as bad? Yet, we do not do evil only when our understanding is incapable of clearly deciding whether an act is good or bad and leaves our will in the state of indifference. If we saw, as is required, that a certain act is evil, and if our understanding discerned the place of this action with perfect clarity, our will would not be able to resolve to carry it out during this time. Just as it is impossible to see good without desiring it, it is impossible for us to see evil without hating it. But it can happen that we only perceive the evil confusedly, and we also know how fluid our attention is, which cannot be fixed upon the same object for a long time. It will loose lose sight of evil, as it lost sight of good. At that moment we will simply recall that a certain act seemed bad to us before; however, we will no longer perceive its malice at all nor the reasons that demonstrate that malice as evident. It is also at this moment that our will can resolve to carry out the

12 Letter to Mesland, May 2, 1644; IV, p. 117: "For animals without reason, it is evident that they are not free, because they do not have this positive power of determining themselves; but it is pure negation in them of not being forced or constrained."

13 Letter to Mesland, May 2, 1644; IV, p. 117, lines 6–10.

14 Letter to Mesland, May 2, 1644; IV, p. 117, line 11.

action. Therefore, the will's indifference is the condition of all sin, and as this indifference comes from the understanding's ignorance, every sinner is called ignorant.[15]

Lastly, it will be objected that if all indifference is excluded from our free actions, there will be no merit for us in acting well. It will be asked: if it is true that authentic freedom does not include indifference and that we infallibly do what we clearly see must be done, what merit remains in carrying out good actions? If I see the good and do it by the mere fact that I see it, I cannot fail to carry out this action, and consequently, I cannot be rewarded for it. No doubt, it must be agreed that when we see very clearly what must be done, we do it with no indifference, and yet, the objection is not compelling, since Jesus Christ acquired merits for his actions in this life, although he never was ignorant of what he ought to do.[16]

This argument invoked by Descartes is a direct appeal to Thomistic theology. It is the custom of Thomist theologians to contrast the freedom of Jesus Christ with freedom of indifference. If indifference is the very essence of freedom, the Thomists say, how do we explain that Christ was free, that by reason of divine knowledge and of his infallibility, he was never indifferent?[17]

15 Letter to Mesland, May 2, 1644; IV, p. 117, lines 10–21: "And I do not believe that to do evil, it is necessary to see clearly that what we are doing is bad. It is enough to see that confusedly or only to recall that we formerly judged that it was evil, without seeing it in any way, that is to say, without paying attention to the reason that proves it. Because, if we see it clearly, it would be impossible to sin during the time that we saw it in this way. This is why it is said that *omnis pecans est ignorans*."

16 Letter to Mesland, May 2, 1644; IV, p. 117, lines 21–24: "And we do not cease to merit, although seeing very clearly what must be done, we do it infallibly and without any indifference, as Jesus Christ did it in this life."

17 Perhaps at this juncture Descartes remembered a chapter of *De Libertate* by Gibieuf, the last theologian whom we are sure he read. Cf. *De Libertate*, I, 33, 1. Gibieuf posed the question thus: "Christus est impeccabilis; ergo non potest non observare omnia quae sibi a Patre mandantur; ergo non est liber, nam libertas importat indifferentiam ad agendum vel non agendum." He concluded by refusing to situate freedom in indifference, but instead, in conformity with the principles developed in the whole work, he situated Christ's freedom in the glorious impossibility of sinning. *De Libertate*, I, 33, 8: "Consistit etiam libertas in indifferentia ad multa, sed praecipue in adhaesione ad Deum; in respectu autem ad multa per adhesionem ad Deum et servato ordine ad illum, ita ut ordo ille sive adhaesio sit quasi forma et spiritus libertatis." Similarly, *De Libertate*, I, 33, 9: "Cum dicunt sequi Christum omnia fecere et velle necessario, intelligunt necessitatem quae ponatur libertati. Sequi autem

However convincing an appeal to this argument was, it still could not exempt Descartes from explaining more precisely what the merit is for infallibly carrying out what we see to be good. The instability of human attention is what furnishes the principle of his explanation. The will is determined to want the good while it perceives it, but it is only determined to will in the time in which it perceives it. In some measure, this time depends on our will. According to whether our effort to pay attention is more or less great, we can retrain this clear vision of good and of truth present to the understanding for a longer or shorter amount of time. Moreover, while it is very true that we cannot fail to do good while we perceive it, it is equally true that it does not depend only on our perceiving or not perceiving it. The reason for our actions' merit appears clearly from that. Since we can fix our attention on what our understanding represents to us as good or turn our attention away from it, it is a meritorious act to fix the understanding upon it and a bad act to turn it away. Therefore, merit consists for us of considering the good with such a sustained attention and to retain its clear and distinct idea so perfectly, that our will is infallibly determined to carry it out.[18]

On this point Descartes remains deeply imbued with the thought of St. Thomas, which he is content to utilize and adapt to his particular scheme. The fact is that Descartes takes from St. Thomas the notion of will that constitutes the basis for all the considerations above. The power the will possesses to pull the understanding away from the consideration of good, rests on the principle that the will cannot be constrained by any object to determine itself. Descartes explicitly acknowledges this principle of St. Thomas.[19] It is contradictory to

ex antecedenti, Christi actiones et voluntates necessario procedere illo genere necessitatis, hoc plane negamus, immutabiliter procedunt, et eo prorsus modo quo fines ordo et Patris aeterni consilium exigit: at non sine libertate. Necessitas enim quae ex subjectione ad inferior proficscitur servilitatem et privationem libertatis importat; at non ea quae ex subjectione at adhaesione ad Deum. Quinimo quanto creatura Deo subjectior est, tanto est liberior." Cf. likewise, Álvarez, *De Auxiliis*, book 12, disputation 116, ad Confirm. 3: "Christus Dominus libere obedivit usque ad mortem, et tamen, supposito praecepto ejus liberum arbitrium non habebat indifferentiam ad obediendum et non obediendum; alias potuisset peccare: ergo indifferentia ad utrumlibet non est de intrinseca ratione liberi arbitrii."

18 Letter to Mesland, May 2, 1644; IV, p. 117, lines 24–29.

19 St. Thomas, *Summa Theologiae*, part I, question 82, article 1, second paragraph body of article: "Haec igitur coactionis necessitas omnino repugnat voluntati." Also, St. Thomas, *Summa Theologiae*, I[a IIae] question 6, article 4, at *Sed contra* end: "Ergo voluntas non potest cogi ad agendum." Cf. Descartes, *Passions*, I, 41: "But the will is so free by its nature that it can never be constrained."

suppose that an act is at the same time constrained and voluntary, that is to say, free. By contrast, it is not contradictory for the will to be free although it is necessarily attached to its supreme end, which is beatitude. This natural necessity, very different from the necessity of constraint, is not at all incompatible with freedom. Completely to the contrary, in a certain sense it constitutes the basis of freedom. Therefore, the will wants the supreme good, which is beatitude, and it wants it necessarily. But here again, it is necessary to distinguish between the determination of the act as to its species and the determination of the act as to its exercise. The will cannot fail to want the supreme good, if it thinks about the supreme good. But it can still have recourse to not thinking about the supreme good.[20] At this same moment, the will is going to stop feeling the impulse that the understanding impressed on it and, if it pleases, will be able to turn away from the supreme good that it had clearly perceived for an instant at least. In his answer to Mesland, Descartes just applies to each particular good what St. Thomas says about the supreme good. The only personal consideration that Descartes adds is to remark that our merit would consist precisely of wanting to maintain the understanding's gaze upon the good in such a way that we are infallibly brought to carry it out.

But at the same time that Descartes appeals to the most authentic principles of St. Thomas, he manifestly moves away from Thomism and from the initial position that he had adopted under the influence of Gibieuf. Finding himself forced to give precise explanations about the problem that Mesland poses, Descartes offers a solution that meshes poorly with the doctrine in the Fourth Meditation. Descartes is not a theologian by profession, and he never delves into the problem of human freedom deeply enough to form very clear convictions on the problem, and especially not enough to reach a set of perfectly coherent answers. He resolves the difficulty from memory and only in the measure that it is posed to him, without ever going beyond the difficulties his own doctrine raises. All the misgivings arise his thought

20 St. Thomas, *De Malo*, question 6, article 1 about three quarters of the way through the body of the article: "Et propter hoc homo ex necessitate appetit beatitudinem, quae, secundum Boetium [libro III, *De Consolatione*, prosa 2] est status omnium bonorum congregatione perfectus. Dico autem ex necessitate quantum ad determinationem actus, quia non potest velle oppositum; non autem quantum ad exercitium actus, quia potest aliquis non velle tunc cogitare de beatitudine." St. Thomas, *De Malo*, question 6, article 1, reply to objection 7: "Et hoc solum est bonum perfectum, quod est beatitudo, quod voluntas non potest non velle, ita scilicet quod velit ejus oppositum; potest tamen non velle actu, quia potest avertere cogitationem beatitudinis, inquantum movet intellectum ad suum actum."

exhibits and all the restrictions that accompany his affirmations arise from that. From that also comes the obscurity that characterizes his letters to Mesland on the nature of freedom. His answers are more makeshift than a thoughtful expression of a mind sure of itself and master of the problem to which it is applied.

Mesland questions Descartes on a passage of the Fourth Meditation where he has adopted the Thomist position. Descartes can scarcely do anything but reaffirm himself, because he has no taste for spectacular retractions. That is why in his answer we find arguments that are characteristically Thomist from the philosophical and even theological standpoint. He interprets Pétau's thought in a Thomistic sense. From Thomism he takes the arguments drawn from the beatific vision and from the will of Jesus Christ. But in the course of his exposition Descartes introduces elements into his response, taken from St. Thomas, which were neither Molinist nor Thomist, and at the same time he perceives the difficulty he will have in harmonizing the whole. If our will cannot ever be constrained, and if it can always turn away from the supreme good, even when clearly perceived, what happens to the Thomist physical premotion and predetermination? What happens to the criticism of freedom of indifference? Is it necessary to grant to the Molinists that by fixing the choice of our intellect in a single act and by confirming it through grace in an immutable adhesion to the supreme good, God would withdraw its freedom at the same time as its indifference? That is in formal contradiction with the text of the Fourth Meditation. Descartes knows this, but pretends to forget. At the same moment in which he makes human merit consist in the voluntary consent that we give to the supreme good, he cannot help thinking of the fundamental Thomistic thesis that the reparative work of grace consists in preventing our will from turning away from it. Descartes also cannot fail to remember that he wrote something of the sort, although he immediately needs to imagine a harmony between these two statements that it is difficult to render compatible. He evades the issue by sacrificing the doctrine in *Principia*, whose printing is being completed at that time. "For the rest, I have not written at all that grace entirely excludes indifference, but only that it makes us incline more toward one side than the other, and thus it diminishes indifference, although it does not diminish freedom; from which it follows, it seems to me, that this freedom does not consist in indifference."[21]

The reconciliation is clever, but it costs Descartes a contradiction. In the Fourth Meditation he not only wrote that grace diminishes indifference

21 Letter to Mesland, May 2, 1644; IV, pp. 117–118.

without diminishing freedom, but that by diminishing indifference, grace confirms and strengthens freedom. While now he seems to admit that a minimum of indifference must be left to us by grace for us to remain free, in the *Meditations* he had written: "I could be entirely free without being indifferent in any way." At the beginning of his answer, Descartes opposes Pétau's doctrine but is now half converted to it. This uncertainty in his thought and this eagerness to embark upon the path of accommodation are only accentuated in the second response that Descartes directs to Mesland's objections dealing with the nature of our freedom.

Mesland, of course, was not satisfied with the answers of Descartes, who obviously had not grasped Pétau's thought.[22] By reducing the dual indifference proposed by the author of *De Libero Arbitrio* to a single power of determining oneself, we would be led, like Descartes himself at the start of his response, to make only purely verbal concessions to Molina's doctrine. Mesland set great store in Descartes' recognizing the reality of the two distinct indifferences that Pétau considered the specific remedy to all difficulties raised by Jansen. It even seems that Mesland wanted to obtain Descartes' official recognition of this distinction and professed adherence to Pétau's doctrine. A declaration of this kind could only advance Descartes' fortune and facilitate the spread of his doctrine within the Society of Jesus, something for which Mesland actively worked. We are very much inclined to believe that the second letter on freedom is nothing but this declaration. The impersonal, dogmatic tone Descartes adopts, the concessions made to Pétau's doctrine in particular and Molinism in general, invite us to see something other than a simple bit of correspondence. We are going to find the confirmation of the concessions that Descartes has already made and of such attenuations and explanations offered for doctrine in the *Meditations* that it becomes absolutely unrecognizable.

22 The response from Descartes that Mesland requested is printed in the complete works in three different forms: Letter to Mersenne, May 27, 1641 (III, p. 378); Notes on Letters 239 and 240 (III, p. 703); and Letter to Mesland, February 9, 1645 (IV, p. 173). We would add the following to the remarks with which the editors preface the last and most authentic version. It is extremely plausible, as Descartes' editors indicate, that this letter was written to Fr. Mesland to be shown to someone else, and this other person was surely a professional theologian. This is why Descartes uses Latin. We are inclined to think that this letter was destined to Fr. Pétau, whose doctrine Mesland seems to have been eager to reconcile with that of Descartes. So the Reverend Father mentioned at the letter's start would be the author of *De Libero Arbitrio*.

Descartes begins by declaring himself in perfect agreement with Pétau's doctrine.[23] Times have greatly changed. We once saw Descartes write Mersenne that he was in perfect agreement with Gibieuf on the problem of freedom. Descartes had expressed himself in such terms in the Fourth Meditation that Mersenne thought he ought to point out to him the similarity of his doctrine with that of *Augustinus*. Descartes' Thomism is now in full retreat. He concedes everything without being troubled about contradictions and finally falls into Pétau's position, which, by trying to grant both the conclusions of Thomism and Molinism on freedom, arrives at the verbal solution we have reported.

Descartes first recognizes that two things can be meant by *indifference*. In the first place one can mean the state of the will when no perception of the true or the good pulls it toward one side rather than another. It is in this sense that Descartes understands it when he wrote that the lowest degree of our freedom is that in which we determine ourselves to that to which we are indifferent. That applies to the first species of indifference acknowledged by Pétau.[24]

Moreover, Descartes does not hide the fact that, according to his preference, this is the proper sense of the term indifference. But perhaps others understand by indifference the positive power of determining oneself to one of two contraries, that is to say, to pursue or to flee, to affirm or deny one of them. Descartes does not deny that this power *ad utrumlibet* is found in the will. Furthermore, he thinks that this power is found there not only in regard to acts about which no evident reason pushes us to choose one side rather than another, but even in regard to all our voluntary acts. There is only one voluntary action about which it cannot be said that it was in our power to choose a different one. Even when a very evident reason pulls us toward one side, although morally speaking we could hardly choose the contrary part, still absolutely speaking we could do so. It is always in our power to halt in the pursuit of a clearly known good or in the affirmation of a very evident truth, provided only that we deem it good to show our will's freedom by doing so. That goes for the second indifference required by Pétau, an

23 Letter to Mesland, February 9, 1645; IV, p. 173: "Quantum ad arbitrii libertatem, plane assentior iis quae hic a Reverendo Patre scripta sunt."

24 Letter to Mesland, February 9, 1645; IV, p. 173: "Atque ut meam opinionem planius exponam, in iis notari velim indifferentiam mihi videri proprie significare statum illum in quo est voluntas, cum a nulla veri vel boni perceptione in unam magis quam in aliam partem impellitur; sicque a me sumptum esse, cum scripsi infimum esse gradum libertatis, quo nos ad ea ad quae sumus indifferentes, determinemus."

indifference essential to freedom, which cannot be lost and which the Fathers of the Council of Trent require in claiming for the will the power of consenting *ita ut possit dissentire si velit*. Except for the word *indifference*, which he continues not to accept to designate our positive power of determining ourselves, Descartes grants the Molinists the residue of indifference that is always required, according to them, for our freedom's integrity.

But Descartes does not concede this without some scruple. By doing so, he falls into open contradiction with his own doctrine; or rather he exposes the contradiction that is at the heart of Pétau's doctrine. This contradiction is no less real for only existing in tendencies rather than in words, and Descartes sees it clearly. The two antagonistic notions of human freedom between which the struggle is waged during the whole controversy *de auxiliis gratiae* meet here and are found mixed and confused.

One notion starts from the principle that, by essence, the will is the desire of good perceived by the understanding. Since will and freedom are just one thing, in the same measure in which the will is itself, it is also free. The more clearly the understanding reveals the good to the will, the more intense is the desire that the will feels, and it is the intensity of this movement by which the will is brought toward the good that measures its freedom. Therefore, everything that has the effect of attaching our will to the good more closely, whether it is grace or our natural light, only makes freedom grow and confirms it. Ultimately, perfect freedom can only consist of an irresistible pull and an unchangeable attachment to the good clearly perceived by the understanding. That is what is constant under the different forms that the Thomist notion of freedom may assume. The Molinist notion is totally different. No doubt it conceives will as being characterized by the appetite for good that the understanding reveals to it, but it also wants to maintain contingency at the heart of freedom at all cost. To achieve this result, Molinism represents the will as an undetermined power whose moves are essentially unforeseeable. Every cause of determination that can be assigned to the will is also a cause of liberty being diminished. Therefore, Molinism affirms with Thomism that in conformity with the principle posited by St. Thomas, the will can never be constrained, but if Molinists and Thomists agree on the terms of this principle, they differ profoundly as to the sense that it is appropriate to give it. While the Thomists understood thereby simply that the will cannot fail to be free, the Molinists understood that the will always has the power of opting indifferently between two sides. This fundamental opposition explains all the secondary oppositions that flow from it. Confident in the principle that everything voluntary is free, the Thomists are not afraid to submit the movement of our will to grace. By contrast, the Molinists want to limit the action of grace by detaining it at the point where it compromises the indifference in willing.

The divergence of the two points of view is expressed in the clearest way in regard to certain questions, so familiar to theologians of the period that, according to the answers they offer, they can immediately be classified in one or the other party. Are the blessed in heaven free? No, answer the Molinists. Yes, answer the Thomists. Is the power of sinning required for the integrity of our freedom? The Thomists answer *no*, and the Molinists *yes*. In both cases, the conclusions agree in spirit with the principles. Pétau and, following him, Descartes, want to maintain these two contradictory tendencies simultaneously. They agree that the will consists in the power of doing evil, even when the will is in the presence of the supreme good clearly perceived. Pétau sees no difficulty in that. Descartes, on the contrary, certainly sees a problem and to resolve it, he writes the last page of his response to Mesland. In order to be able to retain his two contradictory notions of freedom simultaneously, the one he formerly had and the one he has just adopted, he will appeal to a distinction that is the last recourse of many theologians on the issue of grace and that will also be Descartes' last word on the subject.

Descartes announces his solution by first proposing a distinction between freedom considered before the choice of the action and freedom considered during the choice of the action. This distinction is not new. Molinists and Thomists knew it, and each in their own way exploited it. Ockham and certain other nominalists maintained that at the moment when the will chooses its volition, it is not free not to choose or to choose a contrary action. It would only be free in the moment preceding the determination. It is only in the preceding moment that the will could freely decide the determination, indifferent to that at which it will detain itself in the following moment. At the present moment it is free to decree that at the next moment it will want or not want this or that object, but at the same moment at which it wills an action, the will is not free to want another, because what happens, while it happens, cannot fail to happen. Therefore, the will would be free before, but not during its determination.[25]

25 Molina, *Concordia*, question 14, article 13, disputation 24: "Guglielmus Ochamus in primo, d. XXXVIII, questione 1 quem sequuntur Gabriel ibidem, et quidam alii ex doctoribus nominalibus, asseverat voluntatem, in quo instanti elicit volitionem non esse liberam ad eam non eliciendam, aut ad eliciendum contrarium actum, et

This doctrine had not satisfied Molina, who judged it not only false but also even dangerous and irresponsible. To avoid the innumerable difficulties that it provokes, Molina appeals to a particular application of the *sensus compositus et divisus*, and substitutes a priority of nature for a priority of time that the previous conception supposes. Adopting a subtle distinction from Scotus, Molina admits that at whatever the point of time the will is considered, the will is prior to its act by a priority of nature, just as any other cause is naturally prior to its effect. By nature the will is found to exist in a certain moment of time before an act emanates from it in this same moment. The will is a free cause, it can want or not want indifferently this or that object, and can therefore decide itself freely at the beginning of this moment in which it is situated. Insofar as it is prior to its act by nature, it is in its power to choose this or that act or to abstain from it, and do so in the same moment of time. All difficulties are thereby resolved. First of all, we are not obliged to say that the will was free at the previous instant, but not at the instant in which it determines itself. It is free in that very instant, since by nature it is prior to its act. On the other hand, we are not obliged to affirm that what happens can fail to happen while it happens. Ockham's argument ought to be accepted or rejected according to whether it is considered in the composed or the divided sense. We may consider the argument in the divided sense, that is to say, by considering separately the will and the act that emanates from it in the same moment. In that case we will reject the affirmation that when the will wants something at a certain point in time, it cannot fail to want it or cannot want another thing at the same moment. If we consider it in the compound sense, that is to say considering the will and the act that emanates from it together at the same time, then we will grant that it is contradictory to say that the will wants something and that at the same time it does not want it.[26] By substituting a priority of nature for a

e converso, in quo instanti non vult, aut nolitionem elicit, liberam non esse ad volendum idem objectum: sed solum ante illud instans fuisse in ea libertatem, ut cum ad illud idem instans pervenerit, indifferenter vellet, aut non vellet, nolletve objectum... non vero esse liberam ut in illo eodem instanti indifferenter nam et eamdem rem velit at nolit.

"Probit hanc sententiam, quoniam nulla potentia fieri potest ut voluntas, in quo instanti vult non velit . . . Confirmatur rursus, quoniam id, quod est, quando est, non potest non esse."

26 Molina, *Concordia*, question 14, article 13, disputation 24: "Ad argumentum ergo Ochami, si antecedens sumatur in sensu composito, ita ut sit sensus, nulla potentia fieri posse, ut, si jam voluntas in instanti aliquo temporis elicuerit volitionem, non

priority of time through this dialectical device, Molina believes he avoids all difficulties.

It is hardly necessary to say that the Thomists were not satisfied by so little. For them, despite all the distinctions that can be conjured up, Molina's thesis is not distinguished from Ockham's. However Molinism is taken, it cannot avoid putting freedom before the choice of the action, since, for Molinism, freedom consists in the power the will would have to choose a different action. It is evident that once the action is chosen, all possibility of a contrary choice at the same moment is excluded, and arbitrarily the affirmation of some kind of priority of the will in relation to its act is imposed on the defenders of this doctrine. The Thomists make a completely different use of this distinction. They maintain that since at the same time the will chooses its action, it cannot fail to choose it, indifference in the choice of an action does not constitute freedom. Is it not absurd to maintain that the choice, the paradigmatic free act, finds itself stripped of all freedom at the moment in which it is exercised? Is it not equally absurd to admit that the will acts necessarily when it acts and that it would only be free in relation to future acts considered as such? The stratagem of the compound sense and the divided sense therefore has no value. We must be able to say in both senses that the will is free and that the one who acts, at the same time that he acts, acts freely *in sensu composito*, which perfectly agrees with the thesis that indifference in the choice of the action does not constitute our freedom.[27]

possit non velle idem objectum, concedendum est. Nec pugnat nobiscum, qui non in eo sensu dicimus voluntatem, in quo instanti aliquid vult, liberam esse ad illud non volendum, aut nolendum in eo instanti. Si vero sumatur in sensu diviso, ita ut sit sensus nulla potentia fieri posse ut voluntas quae in aliquo puncto temporis aliquid vult, non possit tunc non velle illud, vel vacando ab omni suo actu, vel per contrarium actum illud rejiciendo, si modo spectetur ut existit in eodem temporis puncto prior naturae ordine quam illud idem velit, negandum erit antecedens. Ad probationem vero dicendum est, implicare quidem contradictionem, voluntatem in sensu composito, in quo instanti aliquid vult, illud idem non velle: non vero in sensu diviso."

27 Gibieuf, *De Libertate*, I, 24, 3: "Secundum corollarium est de sensu composito et diviso. Vulgaris est doctrina eum qui agit quando agit (nimirum in sensu composito) necessario agere, istam tamen necessitatem non ideo obesse libertati, quia cum agens fuit in procinctu ad agendum, potuit non agere: quod est dicere libertatem nostram esse ad actus futuros, qua futuri sint. Quod revera dicere coguntur, qui quicumque ponunt libertatem in indifferentia absoluta ad actus: illa enim nulla est in eo qui actu agit, sed in eo tantum qui acturus est cum potestate non agendi. Nos autem, longe pro veritate et libertate fortiores, tuemur ex praejactis fundamentis, ideo necessitatem sensus compositi cum libertate optime cohaerere, quia qui agit, etiam cum agit, libere agit."

Therefore, the very nature of the present doctrines leads them to adopt contradictory positions on this question: is the will free before or during the choice of the action? The Molinists, who situate freedom in indifference, must also place it before the choice of the action. The Thomists, who situate freedom in the movement by which the will adheres to the good, must also place it during the choice of the act. This opposition of points of view suggests the solution to Descartes of the contradiction in which he is placed. To harmonize Thomism and Molinism, which he has approved in turn, he declares that one is true during the choice of the action and the other before the choice of the action. More exactly, since he will always retain a slight preference for Thomism, he holds that Thomism and Molinism are equally true before the choice of action, and that during the choice of action, Thomism alone remains true.

Let us consider freedom before the choice of the action, and let us recall the two indifferences that Pétau distinguished. The first species of indifference, the one that consists in the understanding's ignorance, cannot be situated there. On Pétau and Mesland's own admisison, this indifference constitues a defect and an infirmity of our freedom. Consequently, we cannot consider it as being part of that same freedom, either during or before the choice of the action. There remains the second species of indifference, which consists in the positive power that we possess of determining ourselves and is part of our freedom considered before the choice of the action. At this moment, therefore, two different species of freedom can be found: that of Gibieuf and that of Molina, and neither involves the first indifference, which was condemned by Descartes and by Pétau. Let us consider freedom as the Thomists understand it. It essentially consists of the ease of movement by which the will is determined. This ease increases by reason of the evidence with which our understanding reveals the good. The more clearly we see what is good to do, the more easily our will is resolved to it, and the orders our understanding gives to our will cannot be compared to orders that might be imposed on us by another person. It is quite certain that we are freer in our actions when we follow our own judgment than when we are constrained to conform to instructions that another imposes on us. But it cannot be said that when an action appears to us as being neither good or bad, or as containing as much evil as good, we are more free to do it than when it appears to contain much more good than evil, since freedom then consists precisely in the movement by which our will is brought to embrace the good that the understanding reveals to it.

On the other hand, let us consider the will as the Molinists understand it, that is to say, as a positive power of choosing between two contrary terms. Again we see that our freedom grows in the measure that our understanding's ignorance diminishes. If our freedom consists in the power of doing evil, even when we know the good, and of reversing the direction of our will's natural flow through a violent effort, the more intense the effort is, the greater our freedom will be. In regard to indifferent objects, ones that appear neither good nor bad to us, we have no effort of the kind to make. By contrast, when our will is faced with a clearly perceived good, an enormous effort is necessary to turn it away and choose evil. Therefore, freedom considered as power *ad utrumlibet* does not consist in simple ignorance of evil but in the power to choose evil against the clear awareness of good that our understanding may have. Even when we understand freedom in this sense, it remains true to say with Mesland that we do things that are commanded much less freely than those that we are not commanded to do. The judgment by which we believe that things are difficult to do is opposed to that by which we believe that it is good to do what we are commanded. Our will, caught between these two judgments, does not know upon which to settle and, consequently, does not have to make any considerable effort to struggle against the pull that would incline it to one of the two sides. Therefore, even in this case, the understanding's ignorance is not part of our authentic freedom, but it includes the power *ad utrumlibet* that always permits it to direct itself toward either one of two opposed actions.

It remains to be settled what freedom of the will is at the exact moment when the will chooses its action. At that moment it includes no kind of indifference in any sense. Molinism becomes false, and Thomism alone remains true. The reason for this is simple, and it is the same one Thomists invoke to condemn Molina's doctrine: what happens cannot fail to happen at the time it happens. Therefore, at the same moment when the will chooses an action, it cannot choose another, and its freedom could not consist in turning itself away from it. At this moment freedom can only consist in the ease with which the will determines itself. During the choice of the action, spontaneity and voluntariness are the same, and the more we incline ourselves willingly toward one of the two terms, the more we also choose it freely. Accordingly, neither our will's uncertainty nor the violence of this effort could constitute our freedom at this moment. The spontaneity or voluntariness, the specific movement by which the will inclines itself by itself toward what it desires and by which the will loves and embraces that, is confused with freedom, that is, with the power that the will retains of turning itself away, if it wanted to, from the act to which it consents.[28]

In this sense, in the Thomistic sense, Descartes writes in the Fourth Meditation that the more numerous the reasons that push us toward a certain side, the more freely we embrace it also, since our will then moves with more ease and impetuosity.[29]

By this completely Scholastic distinction, Descartes intends to harmonize the notion of free choice suggested by his reading of Gibieuf with the one to which he is led by external circumstances and the knowledge he gained from *De Libero Arbitrio*. He finally arrives at a certain theological eclecticism in which the two opposing doctrines that have long been at war

28 For the meaning of these terms in Pétau see *De Libero Arbitrio*, III, 2, 5: "Duo sunt, ut antea saepe dixi, in voluntate libera consideranda, alterum, τὸ ἑκούσιον, id est *spontaneum*; alterum, τὸ αὐτεξούσιον , quod est liberum, ac *sui juris*, et *potestatis*. Prius hoc confert, ut voluntas ex se et proprio nutu inclinet in id quod appetit, et hoc amet amplectaturque. Posterius vero, ut *ita consentiat* rei alicui, ut *si vellet, dissentire posset*; ut habet Tridentina formula. Multum autem inter se ambo ista discrepant. Etenim nunnulla faciunt homines ingrati et inviti, hoc est ἀκουσίως, quae tamen libere et cum potestate alterius faciunt. Veluti cum metu impedentis mali, vel praesentis dolere coguntur id eligere, quo alioque detestantur. Ita fit ut libertati, qua *spontanee* agendi principium est, contraria sit necessitas cogens, sive violentia; eidem vero, qua est αὐτεξούσιον, et utrumque habens in potestate, opposita sit necessitas simplex." Also, Pétau, *De Libero Arbitrio*, III, 2, 9: "Qui bene voluntatem opponet necessitati, hoc est τὸ ἑκούσιον, *spontaneum*, invito, et vi necessitatis expresso. Itaque necessitas hujusmodi libertatem non perimit, sive προαίρεσιν, electionem liberam: sed *spontaneo* duntaxat repugnat, quod et *voluntarium* nonnunquam dicitur Graece autem ἑκούσιον." Lastly, let us note that Pétau constantly mixes Latin and Greek. Pétau's procedure leaves a trace in the text of Descartes, where we meet the Greek word ἀδιάφορα, very frequently employed by Pétau and notably in *De Libero Arbitrio*, III, 11, 2.

29 Letter to Mesland, February 9, 1645; IV, pp. 173–175: "Notandum etiam libertatem considerari posse in actionibus voluntatis, vel antequam eliciantur, vel dum eliciuntur. Et quidem spectata in iis, antequam eliciantur, involvit indifferentiam secundo modo sumptam, non autem primo modo... Major enim libertas consistit vel in majori facilitate se determinandi, vel in majori uso positivae illius potestatis quam habemus, sequendi deteriora, quamvis meliora videamus... Libertas autem spectata in actionibus voluntatis, eo ipso tempore quo iliciuntur, nullam indifferentiam, nec primo nec secundo modo sumptam, involvit; quis quod fit, non potest manere infectum, quandoquidem fit. Sed consistit in sola operandi facilitate; itaque tunc liberum, et spontaneum, et volutarium plane idem sunt. Quo sensu scripsi me eo liberius ad aliquid ferri quo a pluribus rationibus impellor; quia certum est voluntatem nostram majori tunc cum facilitate atqui impetu se movere."

in the controversy *de auxiliis* are accepted and legitimated. Perhaps he exhibits a slight sentimental preference for Thomism and an irreducible perseverance in the affirmation that the understanding's ignorance cannot be an integral part of our genuine freedom. Beyond the fundamental point that Pétau himself concedes, Descartes does not persist in any notion of free choice. He does not take the analysis further than proving that ultimately his philosophy is acceptable to all parties and does not rest upon any metaphysical foundation that could make any of them reject it. This late conciliatoriness, which looks very much like an expedient to put a stop to an inopportune controversy, is also Descartes' last word about the problem of freedom.

Conclusion

The Cartesian doctrine of freedom seems closely allied in structure and development to theological controversies on the problem of grace, which are carried on throughout the first half of the seventeenth century. On the other hand, we know that his education at La Flèche and the philosophy of St. Thomas greatly influenced Descartes' thinking on the topics of error, judgment, and the relations between understanding and will. Our task is to discover whether Cartesian philosophy has an essentially theological inspiration or whether the theological elements it contains are an accidental and external accretion, without genuine connection to the system's deep sense. After having uncovered so much theology in Descartes' thinking, it remains to determine what exact place theology occupies in it, and whether it plays the role of protagonist or supporting actor.

When we consider the peculiar trappings in which Cartesian thought is clothed, it is tempting to believe that it is theological in essence. Seeing Descartes take up St. Thomas's teaching on election, enlisting in the Thomist camp against Molinism, trying to harmonize his thinking with Fr. Petau's, or simply reading the subtitle of the *Meditations* — *De Existentia Dei et Animae Immortalitate* — we have the impression of being confronted by a defender of the Christian faith who proposes primarily to justify the Church's traditional teaching by renewing it though a new method. Therefore, the heart of Cartesian thought would be neither metaphysics nor physics; it would be religion.

In fact, this is the thesis that Victor Albert Espinas wanted to establish in the remarkable articles he devoted to Descartes with such penetrating analyses.[1] Like all moral and political theories, Descartes' conceptions would be the more or less faithful expression of collective wills and would derive from a national movement that in 1614 carried France "toward a kingdom of order and the establishment of an authority that could discipline

1 Cf. Bibliography.

minds and rally hearts."[2] In the first half of the seventeenth century, French society saw as its essential task the completion of the war against Protestants and the triumph of the monarchy against the powers that limited it. Above all, it had "the will to remain orthodox in Catholicism and to protect the absolute monarchy." In 1627 after the capture of La Rochelle, the Protestantism was very close to being conquered. But the radical negation of the libertines replaced the Protestant schism and "lay thinkers came to the aid of theology and to enter into the combat with new weapons against the first threats of this new peril." Descartes was the most illustrious of the lay thinkers who wished to give their support to the Christian religion. Espinas devotes himself to explaining how Descartes' education at La Flèche prepared him to undertake this role of gentleman defender of the rights of God. Descartes was indelibly stamped by the education he received from the Jesuits. He left school with a very great interest in method, a concern that the school at La Flèche imbued in its students through its practical, thoughtful spirit. His will was trained by the pedagogical formation in which the Society of Jesus excelled. He retained "a foundation of piety of unshakable solidity," the dread of infidelity to dogma, "not on account of the social risks that were its consequence during the period, but in itself and as a sin." Lastly, he held the rooted belief "that philosophy merits praise only insofar as it is harmony with dogma, and that its normal role is to sustain religion."[3] We may add that the Descartes' Jesuit education the encouraged his spontaneous tendency to view a Christian gentleman as essentially a man of action. We should remember that the bull creating the Society of Jesus described it as "principally instituted to work for the progress of souls in Christian life and doctrine" and that, in the eyes of the Jesuits, action takes precedence over knowledge, With all this, it will be understood that when Descartes left La Flèche, he was completely ready to enter the lists against the libertines. He only needed an opportunity to move him to action. His sojourn in Paris and his relationship with Cardinal de Bérulle, whom he chose as his spiritual director, provided it. Descartes was told that it was his duty to put his philosophical ideas at the service of religion. He did not hesitate. He had been formed for the task, and he became the defender of the existence of God

2 Victor Albert Espinas, *Revue Blue*, first semester 1906, p. 257. [Translator: Espinas published a series of Articles in *Revue Blue* in the first semester of 1906: "Le point de départ de Descartes," March 3, "Le point de départ de Descartes," continuation, March 10; "Descartes de seize à vingt-neuf ans," March 23; "Descartes de seize à vingt-neuf ans," continuation, March 30.]

3 Espinas, *Revue Blue*, first semester 1906, p. 295.

and the immortality of the soul against the libertines. This would be the main standpoint from which to perceive the real meaning of Cartesian metaphysics.

It would be beyond the scope of this book to embark on a global discussion of this point that could have a place only in a comprehensive study of Descartes, but it is not inappropriate to ask whether Espinas' claim has been confirmed within the limits of our study. It is important to find out whether the Scholastic theological approach to which Cartesian thought adjusts is an accidental, external veneer, which gives no indication of the work's deep sense, or whether it really constitutes the matter and the very substance of Cartesian philosophy. Is Descartes a physicist who builds his science on the materials furnished by the philosophy and theology of his time? Is he, on the contrary, a lay champion of the Christian religion who wants to rebuild the wobbly edifice of Scholasticism through the mathematical method? That is what must be decided if we want to give its exact value and proper meaning to what Cartesian metaphysics receives from Scholasticism and theology.

Let us first note that there can be no question here of denying the reality and sincerity of Descartes' religious convictions. Everything Espinas has demonstrated about the deep impact his teachers at La Flèche made upon the philosopher, about the kind of lifelong veneration he professed for the clergy, about the unshakable confidence he retained as to the truth of the Catholic faith, all that remains beyond doubt and definitively established. Still, can we say that Descartes considered himself and really was the lay defender of the Church against the libertines? Can we admit that this preoccupation was the center of his work and the key to its meaning? To answer this question it will be enough to gather the scattered results that we have collected during this study.

If Descartes' great preoccupation, the mission he believed had been entrusted to him, was the defense of religion, it would be quite extraordinary that we should find no trace of this in his work or in his correspondence. Not only did our philosopher not have to dissemble it, but also he could do nothing better for his success and personal security than to broadcast it and to boast about it. There is no indisputable sign of this preoccupation, no text that irrefutably proves its existence, none that lets us consider it as the expression of the very basis of Descartes' thought. No doubt, in the dedication of the Meditations, the theological concerns are in the foreground, or more exactly, we see only them. Descartes wants to prove the existence of God and the immortality of the soul. These two truths are the chief among those that the philosopher commits himself to demonstrating. We might believe we are listening to a Scholastic. We have quotations from the book of Wisdom and from St. Paul. The authority of the Lateran Council is invoked. Descartes ends by daring to commend "the cause of God and of religion." to the Doctors of the Sorbonne in recommending his *Meditations* to them. This language at the beginning of this kind of work would be decisive evidence if it were not so evidently self-serving. We know in what circumstances and with what goal Descartes tried to obtain the approbation of the Sorbonne. He needed to achieve a solid position in his war against the Jesuits, and in these conditions there is nothing surprising in his presenting himself to his judges as the defender of the cause of God and religion. But at the same time that he made this useful display, Descartes was confidentially unveiling his true goal to Mersenne: to get his metaphysics accepted was to get his physics accepted. Once the first was officially approved, he judged that the second, which was explicitly grounded in the first, had to be accepted and approved.[4] Is not the confession that he made to his most intimate confidant more significant than a public attitude that the worst enemies of religion were adopting during the same period?

For the rest, Descartes, whose character is so complex, rarely appears to pursue disinterested goals. Just one time, on an impulse that will not be repeated, he proposes to reduce to silence those fools at whom he is furious for attacking God. But, beside this single chivalrous impulse, there is much personal worry, many precautions, ruses, strategies, to assure the rapid success and early spread of his philosophy. We have seen deep pride at work and an ambition that never abated until the ultimate failure of the *Principles of Philosophy*. If his education at La Flèche had an influence on Descartes' mind, was it that he dreamed his whole life of returning as a teacher to the philosophy class where he was a pupil, secretly envying that Aristotle who ruled from on high over minds in logic, physics, metaphysics, ethics, and even in classes on medicine? There lies the real preoccupation of this anxious recluse and voluntary exile. To defeat Aristotle, he disposes of only one weapon: the force, the irresistible evidence of truth. It is because he places all his hope in his philosophy's evidence that we see him so extraordinarily irritable and touchy each time his philosophy is misunderstood or he thinks it is attacked. Every criticism causes him personal pain. Every new adversary pushes back into the distance the success that his philosophy deserves immediately. This is why Descartes watches in all directions. He wants to

4 Letter to Mersenne, January 28, 1641; III, pp. 297–298.

identify all his adversaries. He wants to keep abreast of every attack, in order to respond to it as it deserves. He fears the unknown, hidden enemy above all, because against the latter, the invincible method is left impotent. Finally, if the success of his philosophy is his deepest and most constant care, rebuilding his relations with the Jesuits is its surest guaranty. On this point, Descartes always hopes for a dramatic twist. We see him surveying philosophy classes and particularly physics courses to follow the progress or failures of his ideas. We see him strive to win and keep as many friends as possible within the Society of Jesus. The success of true philosophy had its price, and his correspondence proves that he is continually haunted by worry about assuring it. As for the Church, Descartes respects and, above all, fears it deeply. Much less worried about defending it than about defending himself from it, he tries everything to get along with it.

This seems to be the authentic Descartes. Less chivalrous and doubtless also less likeable than the previous one, he still moves us by the sincerity of his constant worries and the deep suffering of this soul in which everything leaves open wounds and which is unceasingly haunted by a burning, insatiable desire for peace. But he never devotes himself to anything but his own cause. It is true that he always identifies that cause with the cause of philosophy, and precisely this gives certain grandeur to his attitude: the total, constant, and definitive certainty of being in possession of the truth without any restriction.

So, from our standpoint, concern for religious apologetics appears to play only a secondary, modest role in Cartesian thinking. Since truth is one, Descartes was always convinced that the true philosophy would definitively establish the certainty of true religion. But we cannot say that the profound intention of his metaphysic was to inaugurate this defense of the good cause against the attacks of the libertines.

Descartes did not set himself an essentially theological end. Nonetheless, he mined a considerable amount of materials from contemporary theology. Furthermore, he did not develop them in depth. His elaboration dealt less with the content of the theological elements utilized than with the order and disposition it suited him to give them. That is palpable in the proofs of the existence of God and the doctrine of innate ideas, and even more in the doctrine of freedom. But the place theology occupies in the Cartesian system cannot be fixed in an overall formula. In what concerns just the problem of freedom, the answer to be given is not simple and varies according to whether we consider the doctrine of divine freedom or that of human freedom. Plausibly, his notion of divine freedom was elaborated very early, and we have good reason to believe that along with the radical distinction of body and soul, it is the most personal and novel product of Descartes' metaphysical reflection. It is not, however, without debt to its intellectual environment. However original this notion of freedom may be, it nonetheless has multiple roots in contemporary theology, but Descartes was not mistaken in the impression that he was an innovator on this subject. In its moment, we have tried to signal what he added to his predecessors' doctrine and to show his elaboration of the Neo-Platonic notion of the One in order to draw from it the negation of final causes and the creation of eternal truths.

The same cannot be said in regard to human freedom. The materials Descartes utilizes are scarcely or not elaborated, and overall this doctrine constitutes a kind of accretion without a deep connection to the rest of the system. The whole Fourth Meditation is a fabric of loans from the theologies of St. Thomas and the Oratory. It is not exaggerated to say it contains nothing original, unless it is the order in which these materials are arranged. On this point, Descartes' thought lives off his reading and recollections. His notion of evil comes to him from St. Augustine through Gibieuf and de Bérulle. From St. Thomas he takes the arguments that justify his cosmological optimism, the conception of the relations of understanding and will, and the doctrine of judgment. From Gibieuf he takes his notion of freedom. But all that is so poorly integrated into the rest of the system, that, according to the circumstances, Descartes will abandon certain of his early positions or will raise problems that he leaves unsolved. Sometimes, the apparent contradictions of Descartes are resolved in the philosophy of St. Thomas, but he retains antithetical theses that Scholasticism contrasted, by suppressing the solution that reconciled them, without finding a new one. This is the case in the relationship of understanding and will. Other times, Descartes inserts a complete theological doctrine at the risk of having to extricate himself from the situation however he can if the insertion raises difficulties. On those occasions, what might be taken as deepening his thinking only expresses the awkwardness he experiences in getting out of a misstep. This is the case of his critique of indifference and of his concept of human freedom. On all these points, Cartesian thought marks much less an advance than an impoverishment in regard to the sources from which it derives.The fact is that the authentic goal pursued by Descartes falls outside metaphysics. He only transforms traditional notions when he finds himself forced to do so, that is to say, when the requirements of his physics are incompatible with the theology commonly taught. Then Descartes appears to us as an original metaphysician capable not only of arranging old materials according to rules of a new method, but also of replenishing the resources upon which metaphysical thought lives and providing it with new ones. Still, whenever it is possible, he dispenses with that effort, and he always reduces it to a minimum. In general, everything transpires as if Descartes proposed to adapt the theses of traditional theology to the requirement of the new physics by making them undergo a minimum of deformation. In the last analysis that is precisely what seems to justify what we remarked at the beginning of this study: the historian must put Descartes back into the theological environment in which his thought was constituted. Only the comparison of the texts allows us to determine what each one of Descartes' doctrines proposed that was new and in what measure it was only a reflection of the past.

Bibliography

Adam, Charles, *Vie et oeuvres de Descartes. Étude historique*, Paris: Cerf, 1910, pp. 1–661 in Descartes. *Oeuvres*, vol. XII, ed. Adam Tannery.

Álvarez, Diego, de *Auxiliis Divinae Gratiae et Humani Arbitriis Viribus, et Libertate, ac Legitima Eius cum Efficatia Eorumdem Concordia, libri duodecim*, Lyon: Horatius Cardon, 1611.

Annat, François, S.J., *Eugenii Philadelphi Romani, Exercitatio Scholastica Tripartita, contra Novam Rationem Tuendi Physicas Praemotiones Liberorum Agentium, Eorumque Libertatem Exponendi Quam Auctor Operis De Libertate Dei et Creaturae Nuper Invexit.* Cum appendice ad Guilelmum Carmerarium Scotum, Cadurci: Jean d'Alvy, 1632.

Anselm, St., *De Conceptione Virginis*, [Translator: *Sermo de Conceptione Mariae Virginis*, *Patrologia Latina*, vol. CLIX, columns 319–324 A, rather than *Liber de Conceptu Virginali et Originali Peccato*, *Patrologia Latina*, vol. CLVIII, columns. 431 B–462].

Aquinas, St. Thomas, *Opera Omnia*, Leonine Edition 12 volumes 1882–1906; and Paris: Vivès, 1871–1880 [editions cited by Gilson in *Index Scolastico-Cartésien*].

— *Compendium Theologiae*, pp. 9–138 in *Opuscula Theologica*, volume I, Turin-Rome: Marietti, 1954.

— *De Aeternitate Mundi contra Murmurantes* [pp. 52–61 in *Opuscula Philosophica*, vol. I of *Opuscula Omnia,* edited by Joannes Perrier, O.P., Paris: P. Lethielleux, 1949].

— *Quaestiones Disputatae*, 4 vols., Paris: Bloud et Barral, 1883.

De Malo (Questions 1–5, vol. I; 6–11, vol. II).

De Potentia (vol. I).

De Veritate (Questions 1–20, vol. III; 21–29, vol. IV).

— *Summa Contra Gentes* (*Summa contra Gentiles*, 2 vols., bilingual edition, edited by Laureano Robles Carcelo, O.P., and Adolfo Robles Sierra,

O.P., introduction by José María de Garganta, O.P, Madrid: Biblioteca de Autores Cristianos, 1967, 1968. Latin text reproduces the Leonine edition).

— *Summa Theologiae* (Madrid: Biblioteca de Autores Cristianos, Prima pars, 1961; Prima Secundae, 1962. Reproduces the Leonine edition).

Augustine, St., *Confessions*, *Patrologia Latina*, vol. XXXII.

— *Contra Academicos*, *Patrologia Latina*, vol. XXXII.

— *Contra Julianum*, *Patrologia Latina*, vol. XLIV.

— *De Civitate Dei*, *Patrologia Latina*, vol. XLI.

— *De Genesi contra Manichaeos*, *Patrologia Latina*, vol. XXXIV.

— *De Genesi ad Litteram Imperfectus*, *Patrologia Latina*, vol. XXXIV.

— *De Vera Religione*, *Patrologia Latina*, vol. XXXIV.

— *Enchiridion*, *Patrologia Latina*, vol. XL.

Backer, S.J., Augustin de, Editor and author *Bibliothèque des écrivains de la Compagnie de Jésus*, first edition, Liège: Grandmont-Donders, 1853–1861; co-editor and co-author second edition Liège and Paris: 1869–1876, and publisher at Liège.

Baillet, Adrien, *Vie de M. Descartes*, Paris: Daniel Horthermels, 1691 (reprinted New York: Garland, 1987).

Batterel, Louis, *Mémoires domestiques pour servir à l'histoire de l'Oratoire: les pères de l'Oratoire recomendables par la pieté ou par les lettres*, edited and published for the first time by Augustin Marie Pierre Ingold, starting in 1902.

Bernard, St. *De Gratia et Libero Arbitrio*, *Patrologia Latina*, vol. CLXXXII, columns 999–1030 A.

— *Meditationes Piissimae de Cognitione Humanae Conditionis*. *Patrologia Latina*, vol. CLXXXIV, columns 485–508 B.

— Sermon 80 in *Sermones in Cantica Canticorum*, *Patrologia Latina*, 183, cols. 785–1198.

Bérulle, Cardinal Pierre de, *Discours de l'État et des Grandeurs de Jésus*, Paris: Antoine, Etienne, 1623, two vols. (In volume III of *Oeuvres Complètes*, Paris: J.-P. Migne, 1856; Alexandria, VA, Alexandria Street Press, 2007).

— *Lettre à Richelieu contre les Jésuites*, in *Oeuvres Complètes*, Migne, col. 1596.

Bible:

Deuteronomy.

Genesis.

St. Paul, I Corinthians.

St. Paul Hebrews.

Psalm 8.

Biographies de différents pères de la Congrégation, Archives nationales, manuscript 220.

Bonaventure, St., *Commentaria in Quatuor Libros Sententiarum Magistri Petri Lombardi*, Ad Claras Aquas: Typographia Collegii Sancti Bonaventurae, 1934–1941 (available on line Turnhout: Brepols, 2011–2013).

Borel, Pierre. *Vitae Renati Cartesii, Summi Philosophi, Compendium*, Paris: Billaine, 1656.

Boutroux, Émile, *De Veritatibus Aerternis apud Cartesium*, Paris: G. Baillière, 1874, reproduced by Kessenger Publications.

Cajetan, Cardinal Thomas de Vio, *Commentaria Summae Theologiae, Angelici Doctoris Sancti Thomae Aquinatis*, Lier, Belgium: Joseph Van In, 1892.

Chalmers, William, *Guillelmi Camerarii Scoti Congregationis Oratorii Domini Jesus Presbyteri, Selectae Disputationes Philosophicae, in Tres Partes Distributae. Pars Prima, Praecipuas Disputationes Logicae et Moralis Philosophiae Complectens*, Paris: Charles Chapelain, 1630.

Cloyseault, Charles Edme, *Recueil des vies de quelques prêtres de la congrégation de l'Oratoire*, Paris: Poussielque, 1882, edited by Augustin Marie Pierre Ingold.

Conimbricenses, collective name of authors of *Commentaria Collegii Conimbricensis Societatis Iesu.* Originally printed at Coimbra and Lisbon, during Descartes' lifetime the series was reprinted in whole or part at Venice, Cologne, and Mainz.

— Commentarium Collegii Conimbricensis Societatis Jesu in octo libros *Physicorum* Aristotelis Stagyritae (Coimbra; A. Mariz, 1592; Lyon: 1594; reproduced Hildesheim: Olms, 1984).

— Commentarium Collegii Conimbricensis Societatis Iesu in quatuor libros *De Coelo* Aristotelis Stagiritae (Coimbra: 1592; Lisboa: S. Lopes, 1593).

— Commentarium Collegii Conimbricensis S. I. in libros *Metereororum* Aristotelis Stagiritae (Coimbra: 1592; Lisboa: S. Lopes, 1593).

— Commentarium Collegii Conimbricensis S. I. in libros Aristotelis qui *Parva Naturalia* appellantur (Lisboa: S. Lopes, 1593).

— In libros *Ethicorum* Aristotelis *ad Nicomachum* aliquot Conimbricensis Cursus disputationes, in quibus praecipua quaedam Ethicae disciplinae capita continentur (Lisboa: S. Lopes, 1593; Coimbra: 1594).

— Commentarium Collegii Conimbricensis S. I. in duos libros de *Generatione et Corruptione* Aristotelis Stagiritae (Coimbra: A. Mariz, 1597).

— Commentarium Collegii Conimbricensis S. I. in tres libros *De Anima* Aristotelis Stagiritae (Coimbra: A. Mariz, 1598).

— Commentarium Collegii Conimbricensis S. I. in universam *Dialecticam* Aristotelis (Coimbra: D. G. Loureiro, 1606; reproduced by Hildesheim: Olms, 1976, 1984).

Coste, Brother Hilarion de, *Recueil*, Bibliothèque nationale Manuscript section, the Collection formed of the original letters sent to Fr. Marin Mersenne (Fonds français, nouvelles acquisitions, 3 vols. numbers 6204–6206).

Cusa, Nicholas de, *De Docta Ignorantia* [*Nicholas of Cusa On Learned Ignorance: A translation and Appraisal of* De Docta Ignorantia, by Jasper Hospers, Minneapolis: Banning Press, 1981, second edition 1985; *De Docta Ignorantia*, Bari: Laterza, 1913, ed. Paolo Rotta].

Descartes *Oeuvres*, edited by Charles Adam and Paul Tannery, 13 volumes, Paris: L. Cerf, 1897–1910. [*The Philosophical Writings of Descartes*, Cambridge: Cambridge University Press, volume I, 1985; volume II, 1984; volume III, 1981. Volumes I and II are translated by John Cottingham, Robert Stoothoff, and Dugald Murdoch. Volume III the Correspondence is translated by John Cottingham, Robert Stoothoff, Dugald Murdoch, and Anthony Kenny. In some cases letters are abridged. Pages from CSMK are indicated below in square brackets.]

— Conversation with Burman, April 16,1648; V, pp. 146–179. [332–354].

— *Discourse on Method*, VI, pp. 1–78.

— *Geometry*, VI, pp. 367–515.

— Letter to Arnauld, July 29, 1648; V, pp. 219–224. [356–359].

— Letter to Bourdin, September 7, 1642; III, pp. 575–577. [Not in CSMK].

— Letter to Bourdin, October 1644; IV, pp. 143–147. [Not in CSMK].

— Letter to Bourdin, February 9, 1645; IV, pp. 160–161. [Not in CSMK].

— Letter to Carcavi, June 11, 1649; V, pp. 365–3569. [379].

— Letter to Chanut, June 6, 1647; V, pp. 50–58. [319–323].

— Letter to Charlet, October 1644; IV, pp. 139–141. [238–239].

— Letter to Charlet, February 9, 1645; IV, pp. 156–158 [240–241].

— Letter to Clerselier, April 23, 1649; V, pp. 352–357. [376–378].

— Letter to De Launay, July 22, 1641; III, pp. 419–421. [188].

— Letter of Elizabeth to Descartes, October 28, 1645; IV, pp. 320–324. [Not in CSMK].

— Letter from Elizabeth to Descartes, November 30, 1645; IV, p. 335–337. [Not in CSMK].

— Letter to Dinet, October 1644; IV, p. 142. [Not in CSMK].

— Letter to Dinet, February 9, 1645; IV, pp. 158–160. [Not in CSMK].

— Letter to Dinet;, VII, pp. 563–603. [II, 384–397].

— Letter to Du Puy, January 5, 1645; IV, pp. 130–152. [Not in CSMK].

— Letter to Elizabeth, September 15, 1645; IV, pp. 290–296. [265–267].

— Letter from Elizabeth, September 30, 1645; IV, pp. 301–304. [Not in CSMK].

— Letter to Elizabeth, October 6, 1645; IV, pp. 304–317. [268–273].

— Letter from Elizabeth, October 28, 1645; IV, pp. 320–324. [276–278].

— Letter to Elizabeth, November 30, 1645; IV, pp. 335–338. [Not in CSMK].

— Letter to Elizabeth, January 1646; IV, pp. 351–357. [281–283].

— Letter to Ferrier, October 8, 1629; I, pp. 32–38. [Not in CSMK].

— Letter to Gibieuf, January 19, 1642; III, pp. 472–480. [201–204].

— Letter to Grandamy, May 2, 1644; IV, pp. 121–123. [236–237].

— Letter to Huygens, January 31, 1641; III, p. 520–525. [Not in CSMK].

— Letter to Hypersaspistes, August 1641; III, pp. 422–435, [188–197].

— Letter to Mersenne April 15, 1630; I, pp. 135–147. [20–23].

— Letter to Mersenne, December 23, 1630; I, pp. 192–196. [29].

— Letter to Mersenne, May 6, 1630; I, pp. 147–150. [24–25].

— Letter to Mersenne, Amsterdam, May 27, 1630 (?); I, pp. 151–154. [25–26].

— Letter to Mersenne, November 4, 1630; I, pp. 171–176. [Not in CSMK].

— Letter to Mersenne, October 1631; I, pp. 219–226. [33–34].

— Letter to Mersenne, March 31, 1638; II, pp. 81–103. [Not in CSMK].

— Letter to Mersenne, May 27, 1638; vol. II, pp. 134–153. [102–105].

— Letter to Mersenne, July 27, 1638; II, pp. 253–280. [118–119].

— Letter to Mersenne, December 25, 1639; II, pp. 626–630. [141–142].

— Letter to Mersenne, July 30, 1640; III, pp. 120–127. [148–150].

— Letter to Mersenne, September 30, 1640; III, pp. 183–192. [153–154].

— Letter to Mersenne, November 11, 1640; III, pp. 230–240. [156–157].

— Letter to Mersenne, December 3, 1640; III, pp. 248–252. [160].

— Letter to Mersenne, December 1640; III, pp. 253–261. [160–161].

— Letter to Mersenne, January 21, 1641; III, pp. 281–286. [168–169].

— Letter to Mersenne, January 28, 1641; III, pp. 292–300. [171–173].

— Letter to Mersenne, March 4, 1641; III, pp. 318–332. [173–175].

— Letter to Mersenne, March 18, 1641; VII, pp. 334–340. [175–177].

— Letter to Mersenne April 21, 1641; III, pp. 359–362. [179–181].

— Letter to Mersenne, June 23, 1641; III, pp. 384–389. [184].

— Letter to Mersenne, July 22, 1641; III, pp. 415–418, [187].

— Letter to Mersenne, September 1641; III, pp. 436–437. [198].

— Letter to Mersenne, December 22, 1641; III, p. 465–470. [Not in CSMK].

— Letter to Mersenne, January 19, 1642; III, p. 480–485. [204–205].

— Letter to Mersenne, March 1642; III, pp. 542–549. [210–212].

— Letter to Mersenne, November 11, 1642; III, pp. 581–584. [Not in CSMK].

— Letter to Mersenne, January 4, 1643; III, pp. 607–611. [Not in CSMK].

— Letter to Mersenne, March 23, 1643; III, pp. 637–646. [Not in CSMK].

— Letter to Mesland, May 2, 1644; IV, pp. 110–120. [Not in CSMK].

— Letter to Mesland, February 9, 1645; IV, pp. 172–175. [244–246].

— Letter to Morus [More], February 5, 1649; V, pp. 267–279. [360–367].

— Letter to Père ..., 1643; IV, pp. 65–67 [Not in CSMK].

— Letter to Picot, April 1, 1644; IV, pp. 103–106. [Not in CSMK].

— Letter to Plempius, February 15, 1638; I, pp. 521–536. [79–85].

— Letter to Pollot, October 6, 1642; III, pp. 577–578. [214–215].

— Letter to Regius, December 1641; III, pp. 454–456. [199].

— Letter to Schooten, September 1639; II pp. 574–578. [Not in CSMK].

— Letter to Vatier, November 17, 1641; III, pp. 594–797. [Not in CSMK].

— Letter to ..., September 12, 1638; II, pp. 377–379. [123–124].

— Letter to ..., 1645 or 1646,; IV, pp. 348–350. [279–281].

— *Méditations Métaphysiques*, IX, pp. 1–244. [This translation by the Duke of Luynes with responses and objections translated by Clerselier appeared in 1647, i.e., during Descartes' lifetime, and was reedited in 1661 and 1673. Adam and Tannery. It is placed at the beginning of volume IX, with page numbers beginning again for the translation of *Principia Philosophiae*.].

— *Meditations on First Philosophy* [*Meditationes de Prima Philosophiae. Meditations on First* Philosophy, bilingual edition, introduction, edited, and translated by George Heffernan, Notre Dame, Indiana: University of Notre Dame Press, 1990. Volume II of Cottingham, Stoothoff, and Murdoch contains a translation of the *Meditations*, complete objections and responses, and the letter to Father Dinet.].

— *Notae in Programma Quoddam, Belgium*, 1647; VIII, pp. 335–369. [This is a response to Regius.].

— *Passions of the Soul*, XI, pp. 293–497 [Contained in volume I of Cottingham, Stoothoff, and Murdoch.].

— *Principia Philosophiae* [Adam Tannery, vol. VIII, pp. 1–348; pagination then starts over. Kessinger Press has reproduced, Renati Des-Cartes, *Principia Philosophiae*, Amsterdam: Daniel Elizavirius, 1672. Volume II of Cottingham, Stoothoff, and Murdoch contains an abridged translation.].

Dionysius Areopagite: see Pseudo-Dionysius.

Endres, Josef-Anton, *Petrus Damiani und die weltliche Wissenschaft* (*Beiträge zur Geschichte der Philosophie des Mittelalters*, volume VIII, tome 3), Münster: Aschendorff, 1910.

Espinas, Alfred, "Pour l'histoire du Cartésianisme," *Revue de métaphysique et de morale*, May 1906.

Eustachius a Sancto Paulo, *Summa Philosophiae, Quadripartita, de Rebus Dialectiics, Moralibus, Physicis et Metaphysicis*, 2 volumes, Paris: Charles Chastellain, 1609.

Féret, Pierre, *Un curé de Charenton aux dix-septième siècle*, Paris: J. Gervais, 1881.

Fonsegrive, "Duns Scot," in *Grande Encyclopédie*, vol. XV (31 volumes, 1886–1902).

Fouillée, Alfred, *Descartes*, Paris: Hachette, 1893, 1919.

Georget, A. [Stanislas Henry?], *Une découverte qui n'est pas une*, Tours Ladevèze, 1870.

Gerberon, Gabriel, *Histoire générale du Jansenisme, contenant ce qui s'est passé en France, en Espagne, en Italie, dans les Païs-Bas, etc.*, Amsterdam: J. Louis de Lorme, 1700.

Géry, I. M. [Translator: believed to be pseudonym of Pasquier Quesnel.] *Apologie historique des deux censures de Louvain et de Douay,* Cologne: Nicholas Schouten, 1678].

Ghent, Henry of / Henricus Gandavus, *Summa Quaestionum Ordinarium Theologiae*, in folio Paris: Badius, 1520.

— *Quodlibeta Magistri Henrici Goethals a Gandavo*, in folio, Paris: Badius, 1519.

Gibieuf, Guillaume (Guillelmus), *De Libertate Dei et Creaturae*, libri duo, Paris: apud Josephum Cottereau, 1630.

— *Mémoire pour servir à une nouvelle édition des oeuvres de notre B. Père*, Archives Nationales, manuscript 223.

— "Sentiment du Père Gibieuf de l'Oratoire touchant le jansenisme," in *Recueil sur le Jansenisme* Arsenal Library manuscript 2009 (55 T. F.).

Gilson, Étienne, *Index scolastico-cartésien*, Paris: F. Alcan, 1912 and Paris: J. Vrin, second edition, 1979.

Grandgeorge, L., *Saint Augustin et le néo-platonisme*, Paris: Ernest Leroux, 1896, Bibliothéque de l'École des hautes etudes. Sciences religieuses, (reproduced Frankfurt a.M.: Minerva Gmbh, 1967).

Groll, Joannes, *Theses Theologicae de Gratia, Libero Arbitrio, Praedestinatione, etc.*, in quibus doctrina theologorum Societatis Jesu contra Cornelii Jansenii *Augustinum* defenditur; in VI capita divisae: Praeside Reverendo Patre Joanne de Jonghe, S.J. Sacrae Theologiae Professore.

Defendet Joannes Groll ejusdem Societatis. Louvanii in Collegio Societatis Jesu 1641.

Habert, Germain, *La Vie du cardinal de Bérulle*, Paris: Camvsat et le Petit, 1646.

Hamelin, Octave, *Le système de Descartes*, edited by L. Robin, preface by Émile Durkheim, Paris: F. Alcan, 1911, second revised edition, 1921; reprinted New York: Garland, 1987.

Hermant, Godefroi, *Mémoires de Godefroi Hermant sur l'histoire ecclésiastique du XVIIe siècle (1630–1663),* edited and introduction by A. Gazier, Paris: Plon-Nourit, 1905.

Hertling, George Freiherr von, "Descartes' Bezeihung zur Scholastik," in *Königliche Bayrisch Akademie de Wissenschaften*, Munich, 1897.

Houssaye, Michel. *Le Cardinal de Bérulle et le cardinal de Richelieu,* 1625–1629, Paris: Plon, 1875.

Jansen/Jansenius Cornelius, Episcopi Iprensis, *Augustinus*, Louvain: 1640, three tomes in one volume, in folio.

Kahl, Wilhelm, *Die Lehre vom primat des Wille bei Augustinus Duns Scotus und Descartes*, Strassburg: K. J. Trübner, 1886.

Lasswitz, Kurt, *Geschichte de Atomistik von Mittelalter bis Newton*, Hamburg & Leipzig: L. Voss, 1890, vol. II, pp. 58–59 (Hildesheim: G. Olms, 1963).

Lettres de M. Cornelius Jansénius *à M. Jean du Verger de Hauranne*, with comments by François du Vizier (Gerberon), 1702.

Levy, Louis-Germain, *Maïmonde*, Paris: F. Alcan, 1911 (second edition, Pairs: Alcan, 1932).

Mausbach, Joseph, *Die Ethik des heiligen Augustinus*, Freiburg im Breisgau: Herder, 1909 and 1929.

Maumus, Élisée-Vincent, *Saint Thomas d'Aquin et la philosophie cartésienne*, Paris: Lecoffre, 1890.

Mersenne, Marin, *l'Impiété des Déistes*, Paris: Billaine, 1624 (facsimile reproduction Stuttgart-Bad Canstatt: Frommann, 1975; available on line Chicago: ARTFL Project, 1996).

Mersenne, Marin, *Quaestiones Celeberrimae in Genesim*, Paris: Sebastianus Cramoisy, 1623.

Minges, Parthenius, *Ist Duns Scotus indeterminist?* Münster: Aschendorff, 1905.

Molina, Luis de S.J., *Corcordia liberi arbitrii cum gratiae donis: divina praescientia, providentia, praedestinatione*, Lisbon, Apud Antonium Riberium, 1588 (electronic resource, Alexandria, VA: Alexandria St. Press, 2007).

Patrologia Latina = *Patrologiae Cursus Completus. Series Latina*, first edition, Paris: Jacques-Paul Migne, 1844–1655 and 1862–1865; available on disk Alexandria, VA: Chadwick-Healey, 1995.

Pétau, Denis, S.J. / Dionysii Petavii, S.J., *De Libero Arbitrio*, libri tres, in folio, Paris: Cramoisy, 1643.

Picavet, François, *Esquisse d'une histoire générale et comparée des philosophes médiévales*, Paris: F. Alcan, second and revised edition, 1907.

— *Roscelin, philosophe et théologien, d'après la légende et d'après l'histoire, sa place dans l'histoire générale et comparée des philosophes médiévale*s, Paris: F. Alcan, 1911, pp. 30 ff.

Pleix, Scipion du, *Corps de Philosophie*, vol. I, *Physique*, 1627 edition.

Préville, Sieur de / Pierre Bulteau, *La Naissance du jansénisme découverte a M. le chancelier*, Louvain, Vve. J. Gnavius, 1654.

Pseudo-Dionysius, [*De Divinis Nominibus*, cols. 586–996 in] *Patrologia Graeca*, vol. 3.

Radwin, Émile Claude Armand Pluzanski de, *Essai sur la philosophie de Duns Scot*, Paris, E. Thorin, 1888.

Rapin, René, S.J., *Mémoires du P. René Rapin de la Compagnie de Jésus sur l'église, la societé et la cour*, edited from the autograph manuscript by Léon Aubineau, Paris: Gaume Frères et J. Dupey, 1865 (reprinted Farnborough: Gregg, 1972).

Raynaud, Théophile, S. J. *Calvinismus Bestiarum Religio, et Appelatio pro Domiico Banne Calvinismo Damnato, per Reverendum Patrem A. Rivière, Doctorem Parisensem. Ordinis Sancti Augustini*, Paris: 1630. *Editio Altera Parisiensi Nitidior: Benedicite Omnes Bestiae et Pecora Domino (Daniel, 3),* Lyon Claude Landry, 1630. Reprinted in Théophile Raynaud, *Opera*, volume XV (Lyon: Horatius Boissat et Georgius Remeus, 1665–1669. Reproduction also available as *Calvinismus Bestiarum Religio*, Kessinger, 2009, 194 pp.

Raynaud, Théophile, S. J., *Non Causa ut Causa, Subjuncta Vera Causa. Elenchus Sophismatis Gulielmi Camerarii Scoti*, Fastemburg: Petrus Baretius et Joannes Altemius, 1635. Published under the name of Fr.

du Pasquier, doctor in theology, former student of Raynaud. Reprinted with Raynaud's name, *Opera*, volume XVII, pp. 135–152.

— *Nova Libertatis Explicatio ad Lucem Obscurissimis Quibusque Theologicis Difficultatibus affundendam Nuper Adinventa et Duobis Libris proposita, Hac Antistropha Tratactione Discussa a Theophilo Raynaud, Societis Jesus Theologo*. Accessit examen novae theologiae, negantis concursum Dei nobiscum ad actos liberos. Paris: Sebastien Chappelet, 1632.

Règnon, Théodore de, S. J., *Banes et Molina, histoire, doctrines, critique métaphysique*, Paris: H. Oudin, 1883.

Rivière, Antoine: see Raynaud, Théophile, S.J.

Rochemonteix, Camille de, S.J., *Le Collège Henri IV de La Flèche*, 4 vols., Le Mans: Leguicheux, 1889.

Sainte-Beuve, Charles-Augustin, *Port-Royal*, Paris: Rendeuel, 1840–1859.

Scotus, John Duns, *Opera Omnia*, Wadding, Lyon: 1639 [Paris: Vivès, 1891–1895].

— *De Rerum Principio*, Wadding, volume III [Paris: Vivès, 1891., volume IV., pp. 265–717].

— *Opus Oxoniense: Ordinatio In Libos Sententiarum*, Wadding, volumes V–VIII [Vivès volumes VIII-XXI].

—*Meteorologia*, Vivès volume IV [Vivès, volume IV, pp. 1–263].

— *Reportata Parisisensia*, Wadding volume XI [Vivès volumes XXII-XXIV].

Secrétan, Charles, *Philosophie de la liberté*, Paris: L. Hachette, 1849, 3rd. ed., vol. 1.

Silhon, Jean, de, *De l'immortalité de l'âme*, Paris: P. Billaine, 1634.

Sommervogel, Carlos, S. J., "Véron" in Carlos Sommervogel co-author and co-editor, *Bibliothèque des écrivains de la Compagnie de Jésus*, second edition, Paris and Liége: 1869–1876, publisher in Paris, Carlos Sommervogel; thereafter, *Bibliothèque de la Compagnie de Jésus*, editor Carlos Sommervogel.

Strowski, Fortunat, *Pascal et son temps.* , 3 vols., Paris: Plon-Nourrit, 1907–1908 (re-edited 1921–1922).

Suárez, Francisco *Disputationes Metaphysicae*, Salamanca: 1597, 2 folio vols. Also in vols. 25 and 26 of the 28- volume *Opera Omnia*, several editors, Paris: Louis Vivès, 1856–1878 (reproduced Hildesheim: G. Olms, 1975).

Toletus, *Commentarium in tres libros De Anima*, Lyon: Veyrat, 1602.

— *Physica* = *Commentaria una cum Quaestionibus in octo libros de Physica auscultatione*, Venice: 1573.

Veron, François, *Methodus Veroniana qua nimirum ex quibusvis Bibliis cuivis haeretico ministro silentium imponitur*,. Rome.

— *Règle générale de la foi catholique*, edited by Jean Labouderie, Paris-Besançon: 1825.

Index